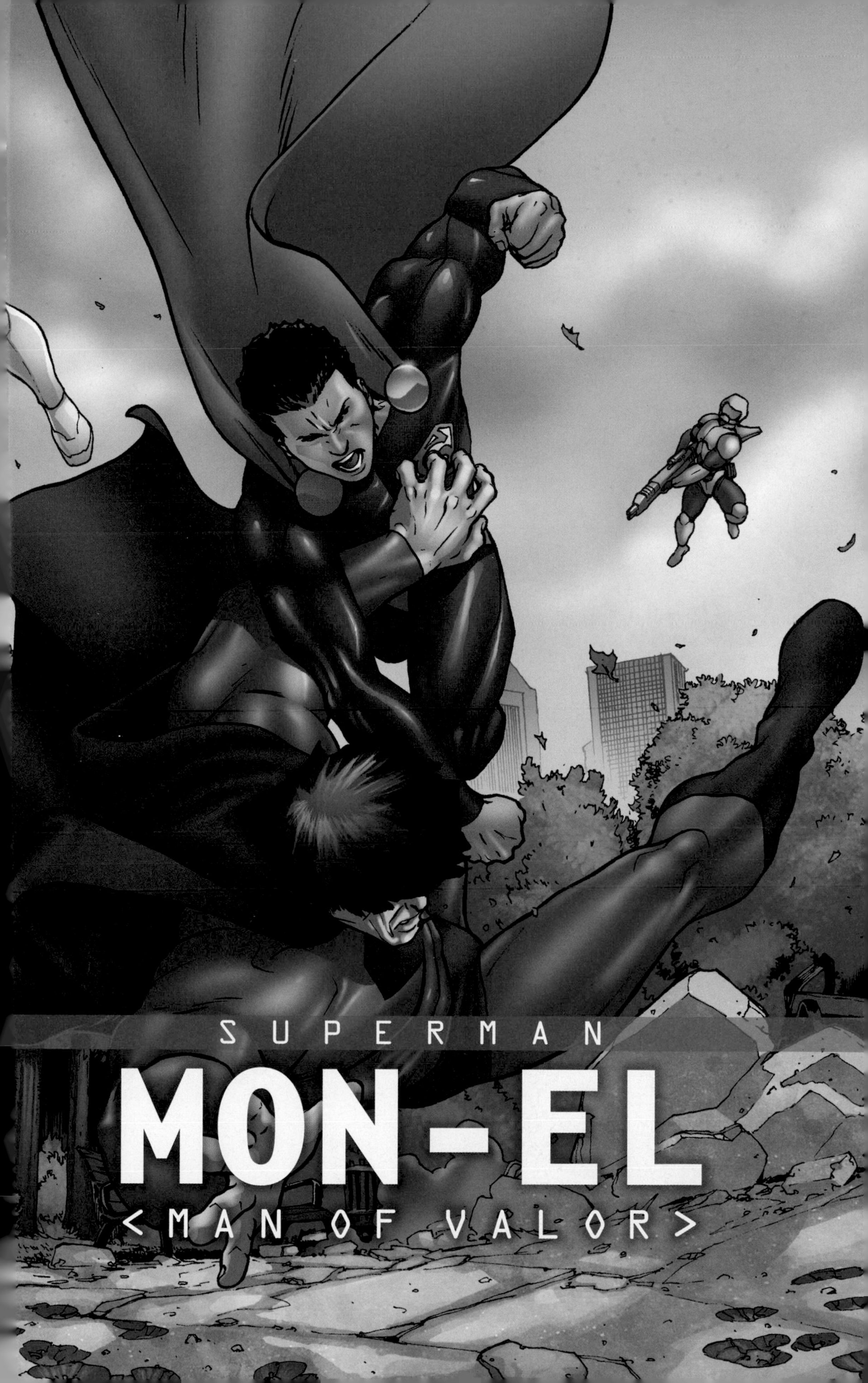
SUPERMAN
MON-EL
<MAN OF VALOR>

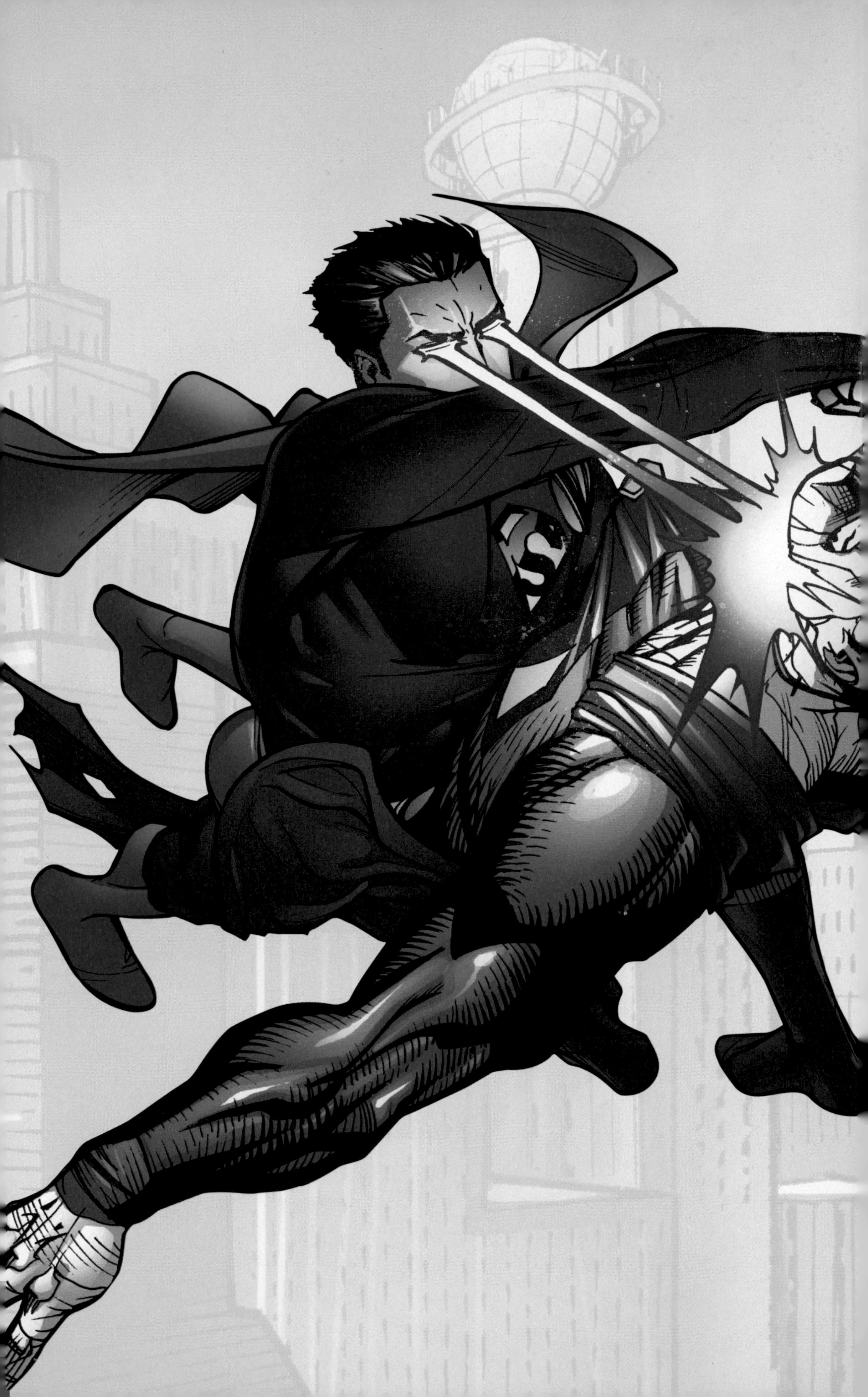

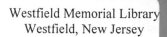

SUPERMAN
MON-EL
\<MAN OF VALOR\>

JAMES ROBINSON
\<WRITER\>

JAVIER PINA
FERNANDO DAGNINO & RAÚL FERNANDEZ
BERNARD CHANG
MATT CAMP
\<ARTISTS\>

BLOND
HI-FI
DAVID CURIEL
\<COLORISTS\>

JOHN J. HILL
TRAVIS LANHAM
SAL CIPRIANO
\<LETTERERS\>

RENATO GUEDES
\<COLLECTION COVER ARTIST\>

\<SUPERMAN\>
CREATED BY JERRY SIEGEL AND JOE SHUSTER

MATT IDELSON <EDITOR-ORIGINAL SERIES>
WIL MOSS <ASSISTANT EDITOR-ORIGINAL SERIES>
BOB HARRAS <GROUP EDITOR-COLLECTED EDITIONS>
SEAN MACKIEWICZ <EDITOR>
ROBBIN BROSTERMAN <DESIGN DIRECTOR-BOOKS>

DC COMICS
DIANE NELSON <PRESIDENT>
DAN DIDIO AND JIM LEE <CO-PUBLISHERS>
GEOFF JOHNS <CHIEF CREATIVE OFFICER>
PATRICK CALDON <EVP-FINANCE AND ADMINISTRATION>
JOHN ROOD <EVP-SALES, MARKETING AND BUSINESS DEVELOPMENT>
AMY GENKINS <SVP-BUSINESS AND LEGAL AFFAIRS>
STEVE ROTTERDAM <SVP-SALES AND MARKETING>
JOHN CUNNINGHAM <VP-MARKETING>
TERRI CUNNINGHAM <VP-MANAGING EDITOR>
ALISON GILL <VP-MANUFACTURING>
DAVID HYDE <VP-PUBLICITY>
SUE POHJA <VP-BOOK TRADE SALES>
ALYSSE SOLL <VP-ADVERTISING AND CUSTOM PUBLISHING>
BOB WAYNE <VP-SALES>
MARK CHIARELLO <ART DIRECTOR>

SUPERMAN: MON-EL — MAN OF VALOR
PUBLISHED BY DC COMICS. COVER, TEXT AND COMPILATION
COPYRIGHT © 2010 DC COMICS. ALL RIGHTS RESERVED.

DC COMICS, 1700 BROADWAY, NEW YORK, NY 10019.
A WARNER BROS. ENTERTAINMENT COMPANY.
PRINTED BY QUAD/GRAPHICS, VERSAILLES, KY, USA.
8/18/10. FIRST PRINTING.
HC ISBN:978-1-4012-2937-5
SC ISBN:978-1-4012-2938-2

COVER BY **RENATO GUEDES**

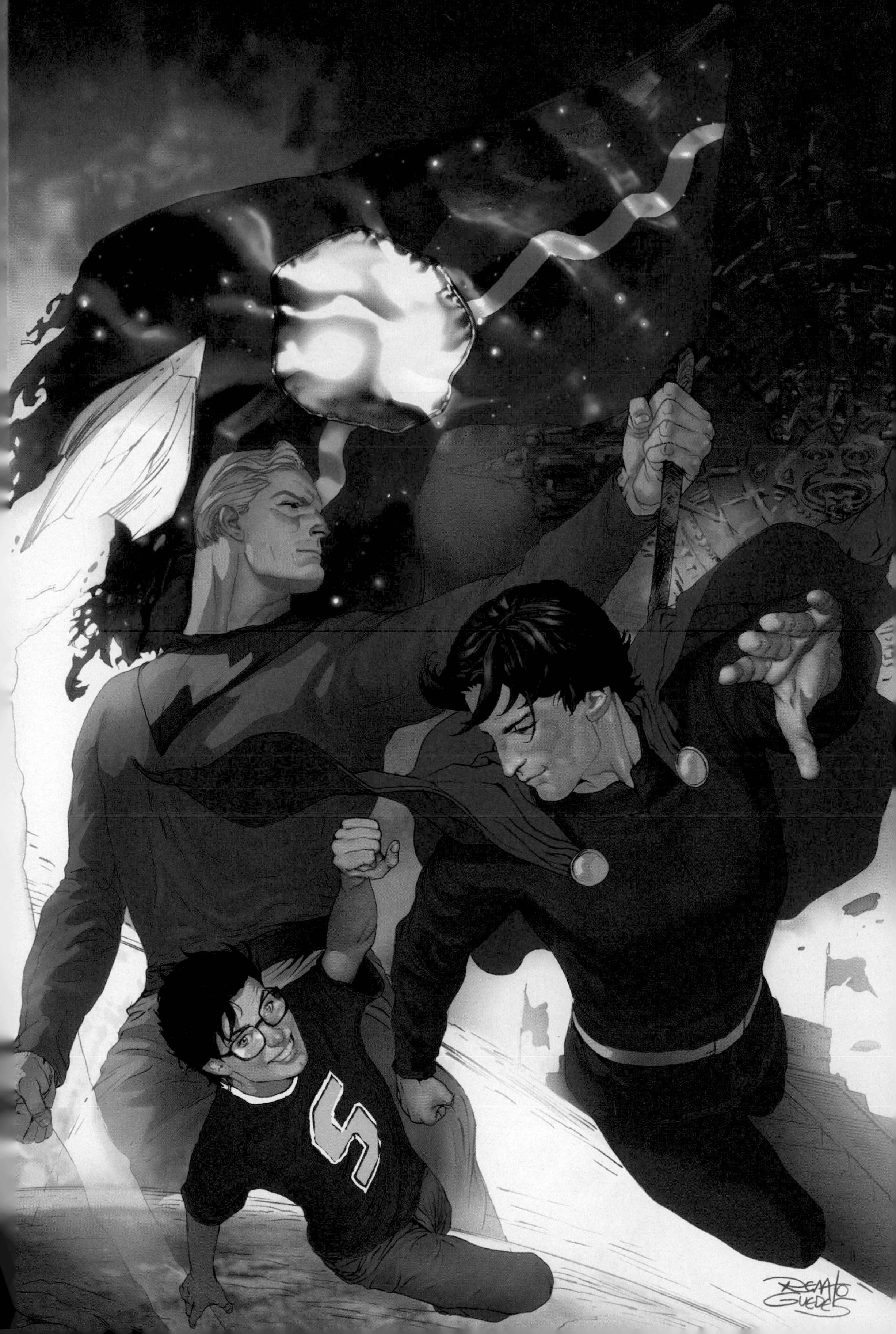
RENATO GUEDES

THE HISTORY LESSON
JAVIER PINA <ARTIST>

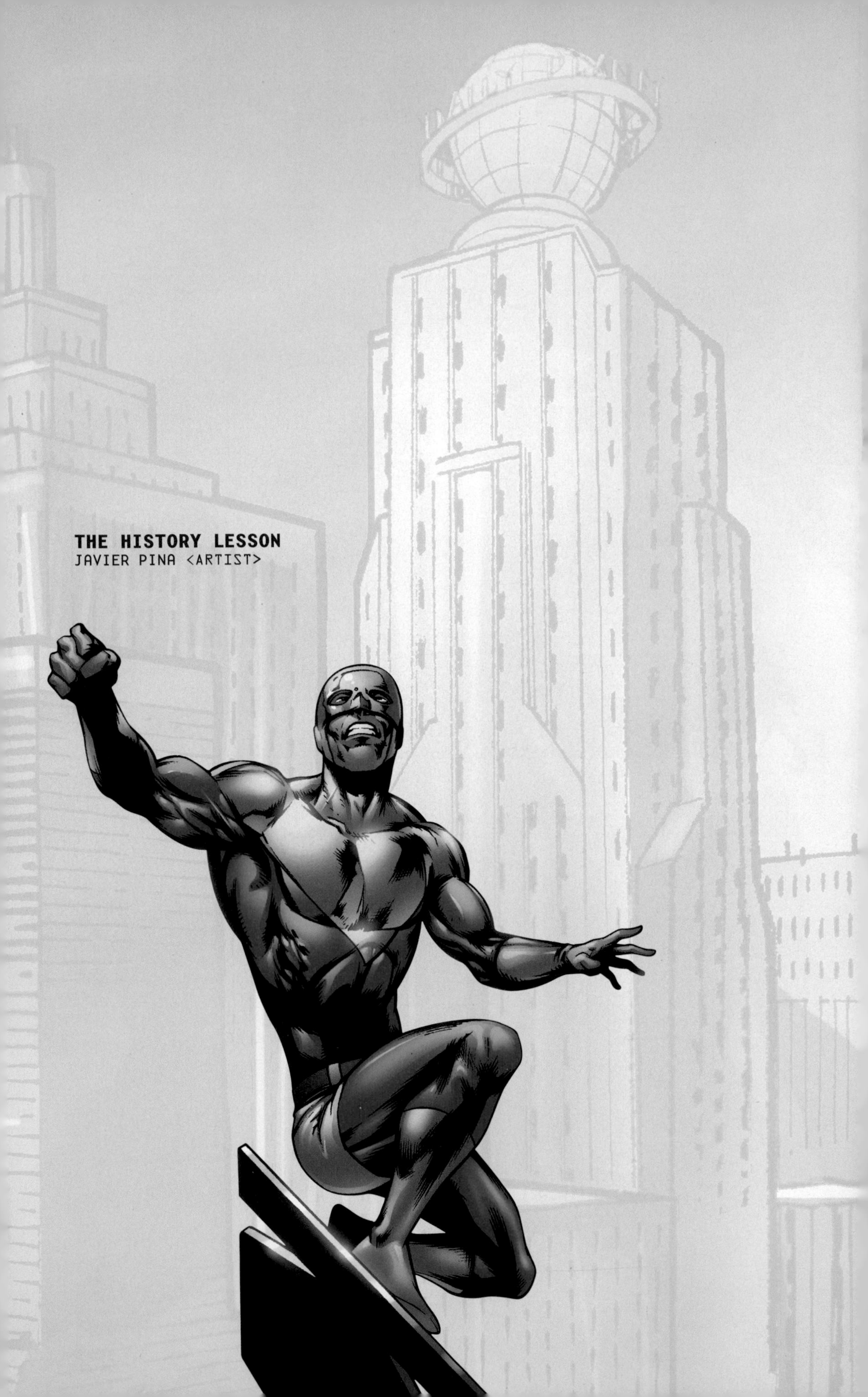

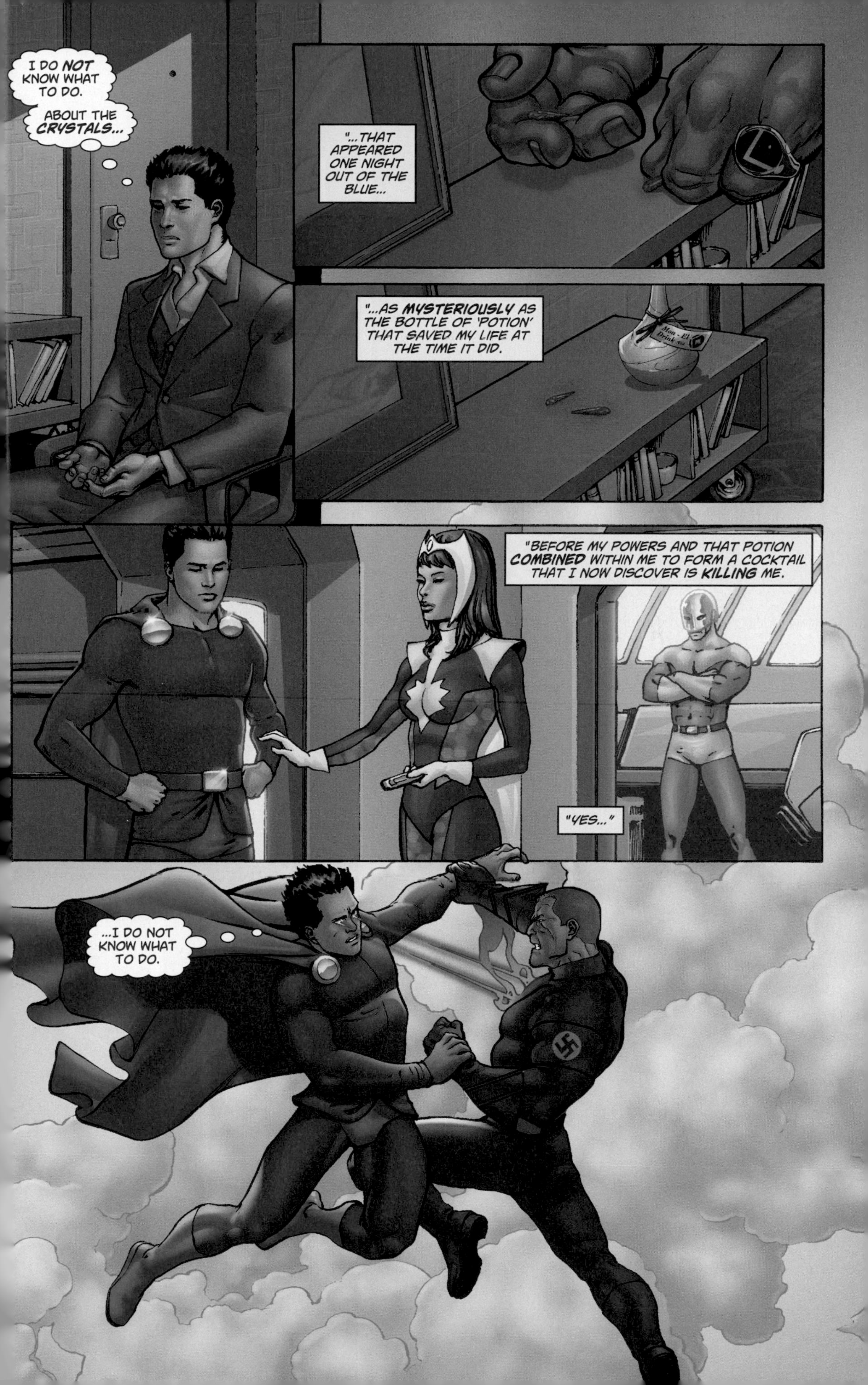
I DO NOT KNOW WHAT TO DO.
ABOUT THE CRYSTALS...
"...THAT APPEARED ONE NIGHT OUT OF THE BLUE...
"...AS MYSTERIOUSLY AS THE BOTTLE OF 'POTION' THAT SAVED MY LIFE AT THE TIME IT DID.
Mon-El Drink me
"BEFORE MY POWERS AND THAT POTION COMBINED WITHIN ME TO FORM A COCKTAIL THAT I NOW DISCOVER IS KILLING ME.
"YES..."
...I DO NOT KNOW WHAT TO DO.

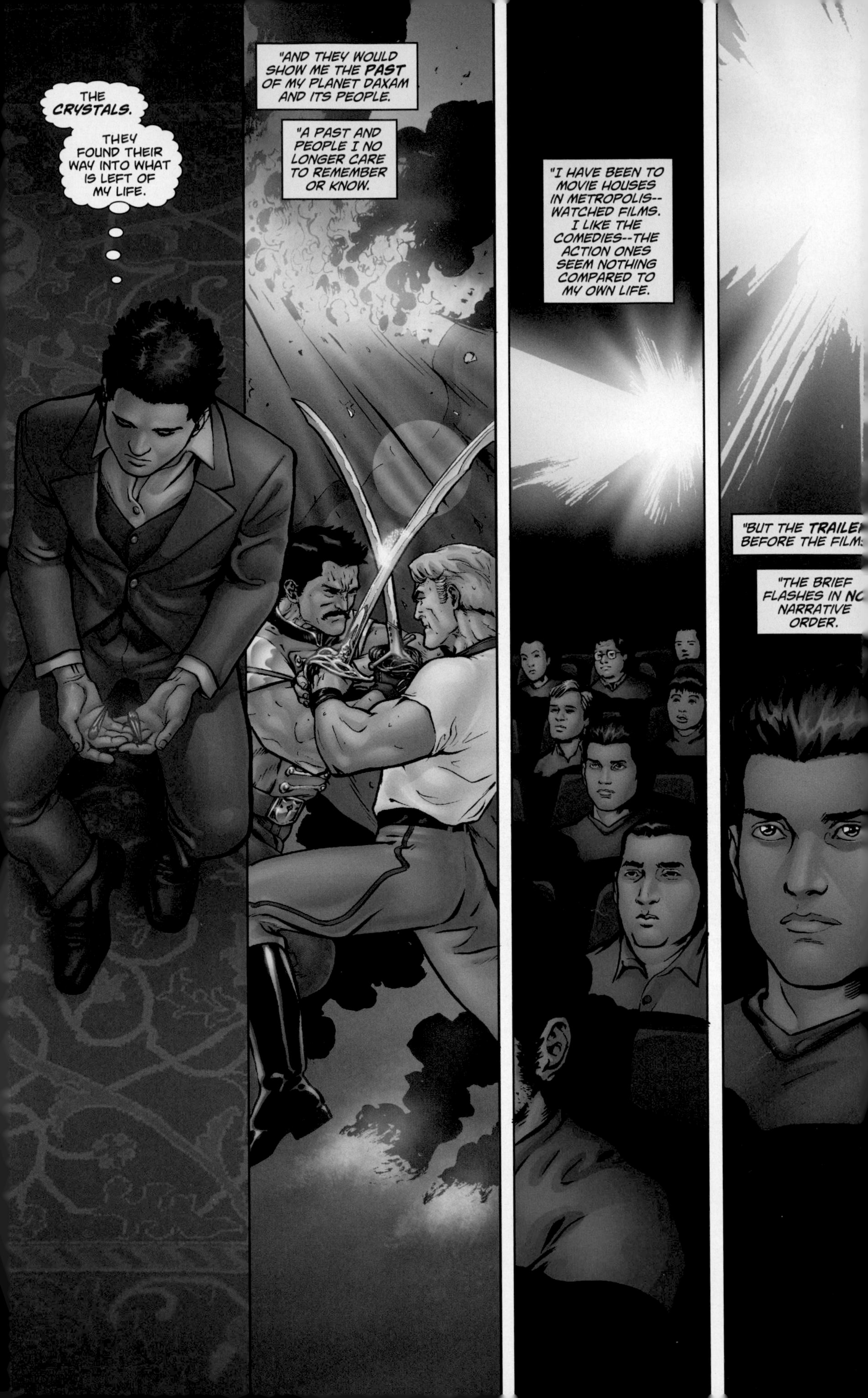
THE CRYSTALS.
THEY FOUND THEIR WAY INTO WHAT IS LEFT OF MY LIFE.
"AND THEY WOULD SHOW ME THE PAST OF MY PLANET DAXAM AND ITS PEOPLE.
"A PAST AND PEOPLE I NO LONGER CARE TO REMEMBER OR KNOW.
"I HAVE BEEN TO MOVIE HOUSES IN METROPOLIS--WATCHED FILMS. I LIKE THE COMEDIES--THE ACTION ONES SEEM NOTHING COMPARED TO MY OWN LIFE.
"BUT THE TRAILE BEFORE THE FILMS
"THE BRIEF FLASHES IN NO NARRATIVE ORDER.

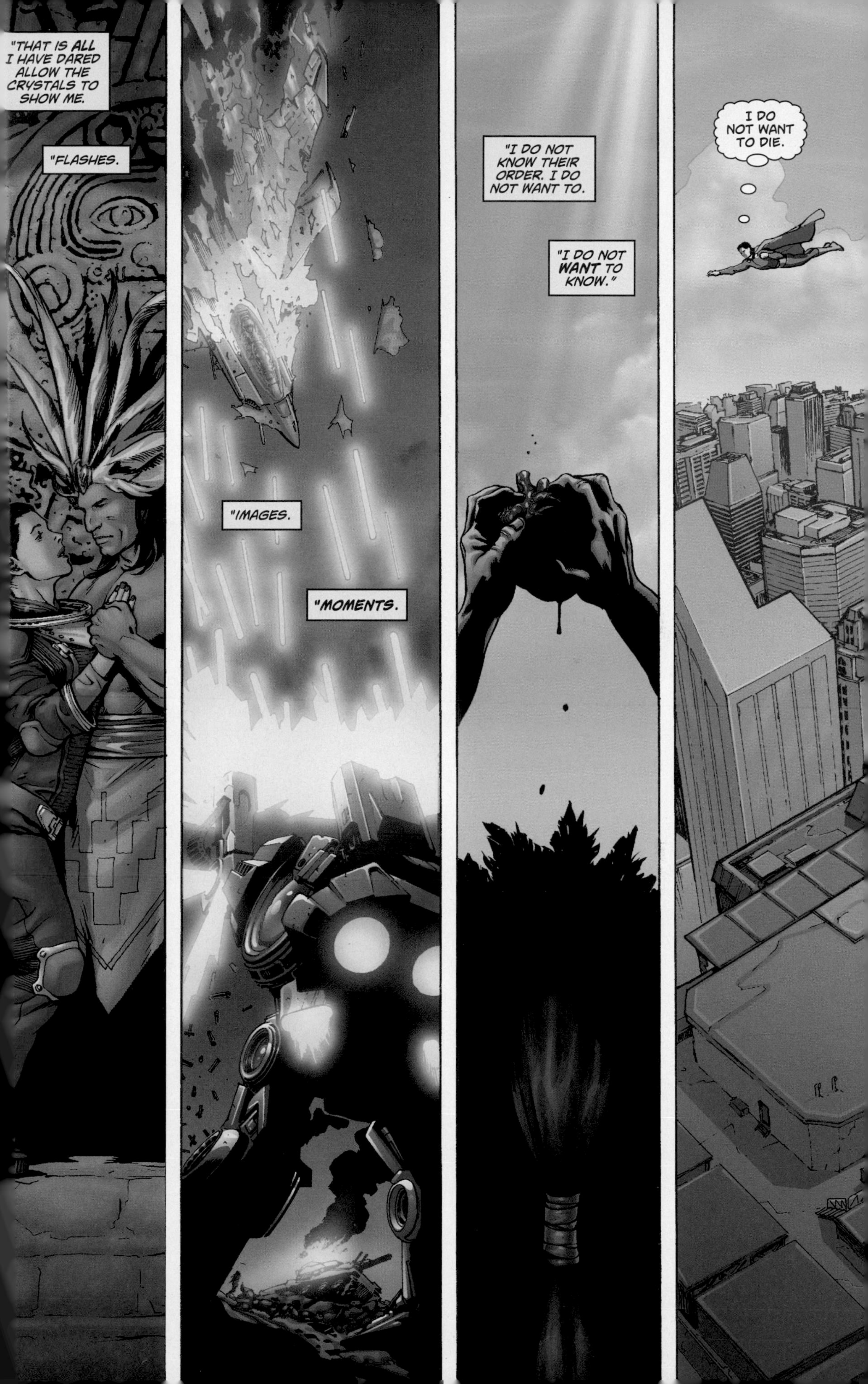
"THAT IS ALL I HAVE DARED ALLOW THE CRYSTALS TO SHOW ME.
"FLASHES.
"IMAGES.
"MOMENTS.
"I DO NOT KNOW THEIR ORDER. I DO NOT WANT TO.
"I DO NOT WANT TO KNOW."
I DO NOT WANT TO DIE.

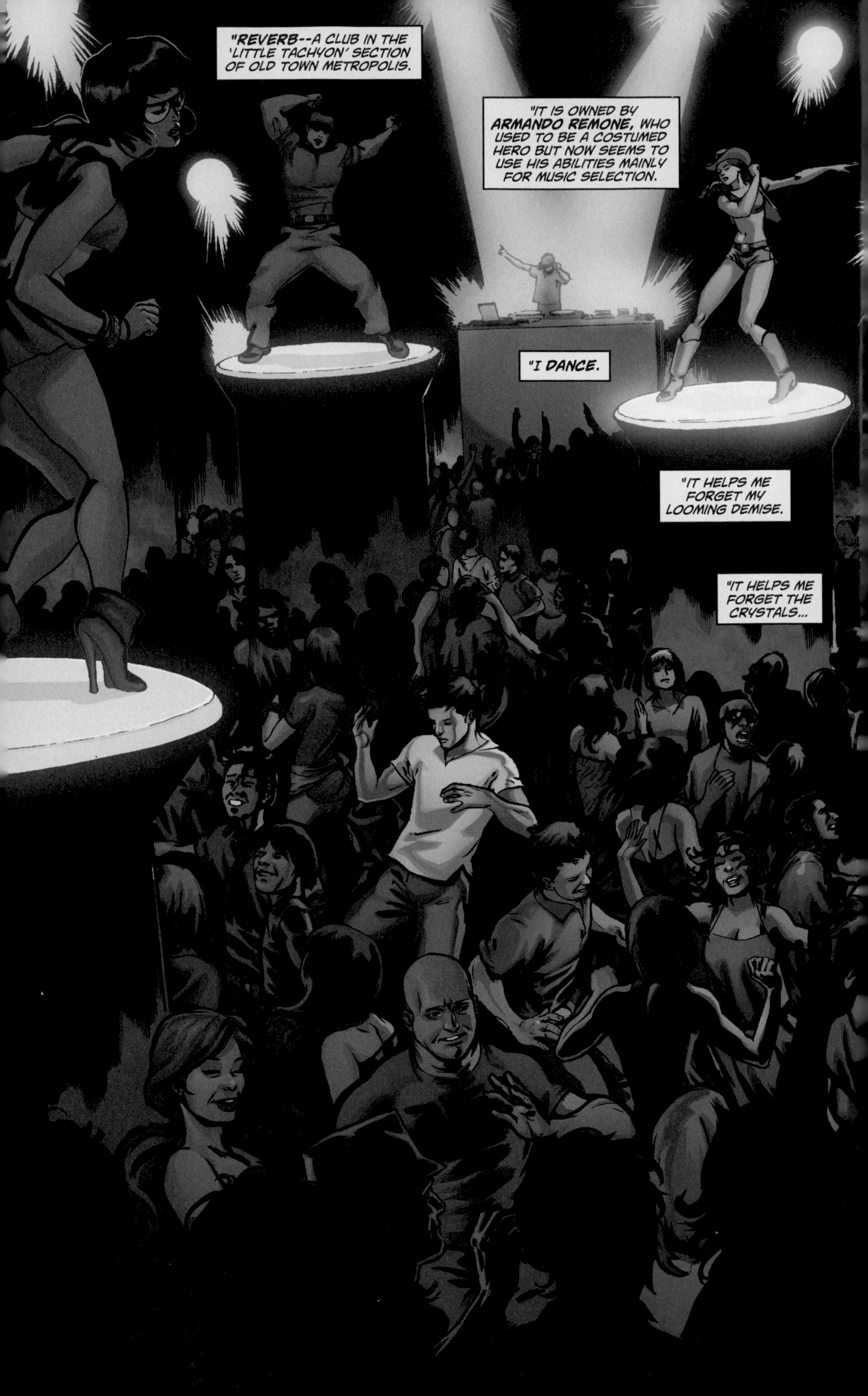
"REVERB--A CLUB IN THE 'LITTLE TACHYON' SECTION OF OLD TOWN METROPOLIS.
"IT IS OWNED BY ARMANDO REMONE, WHO USED TO BE A COSTUMED HERO BUT NOW SEEMS TO USE HIS ABILITIES MAINLY FOR MUSIC SELECTION.
"I DANCE.
"IT HELPS ME FORGET MY LOOMING DEMISE.
"IT HELPS ME FORGET THE CRYSTALS...

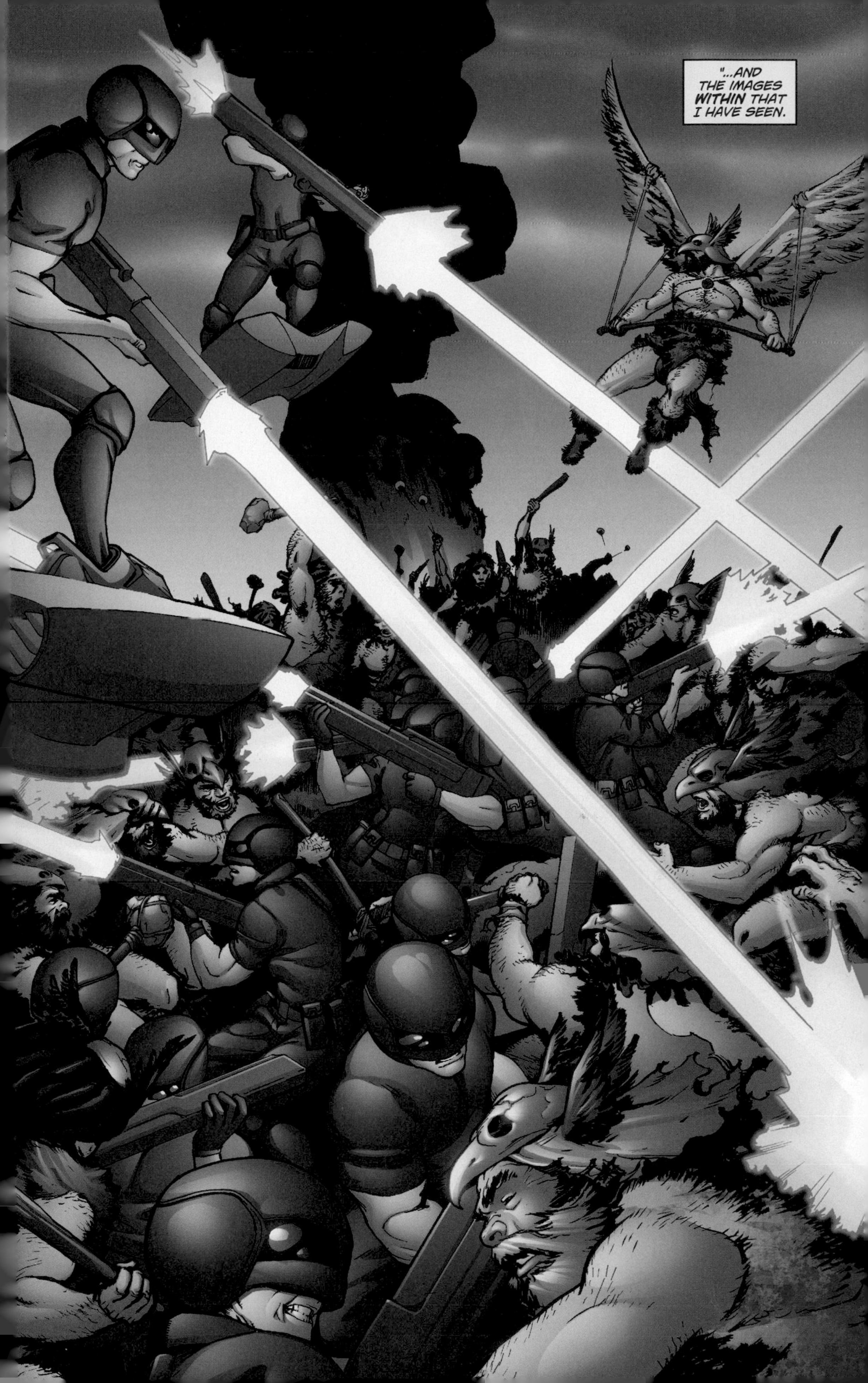
"...AND THE IMAGES WITHIN THAT I HAVE SEEN.

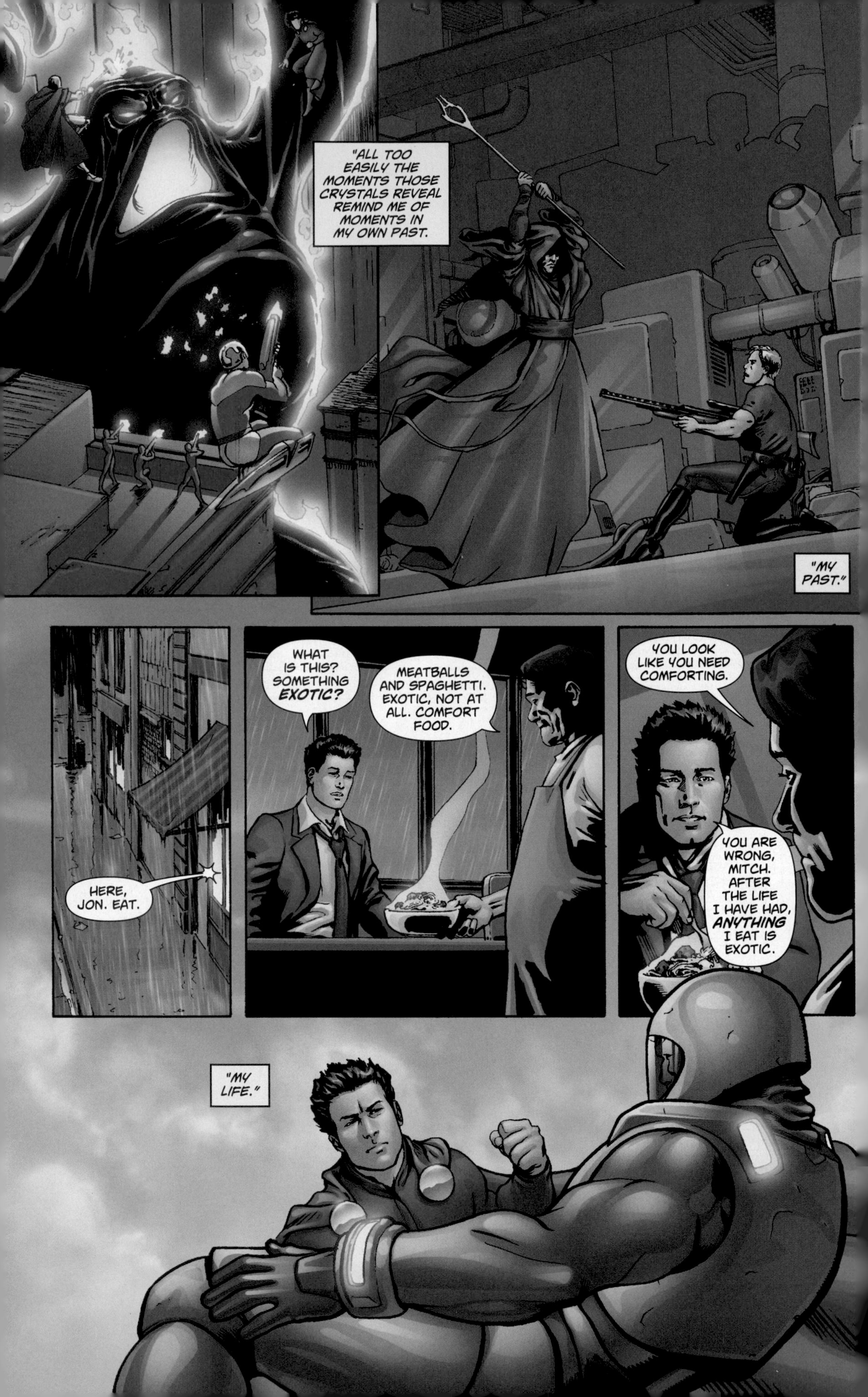
"ALL TOO EASILY THE MOMENTS THOSE CRYSTALS REVEAL REMIND ME OF MOMENTS IN MY OWN PAST.
"MY PAST."
HERE, JON. EAT.
WHAT IS THIS? SOMETHING EXOTIC?
MEATBALLS AND SPAGHETTI. EXOTIC, NOT AT ALL. COMFORT FOOD.
YOU LOOK LIKE YOU NEED COMFORTING.
YOU ARE WRONG, MITCH. AFTER THE LIFE I HAVE HAD, ANYTHING I EAT IS EXOTIC.
"MY LIFE."

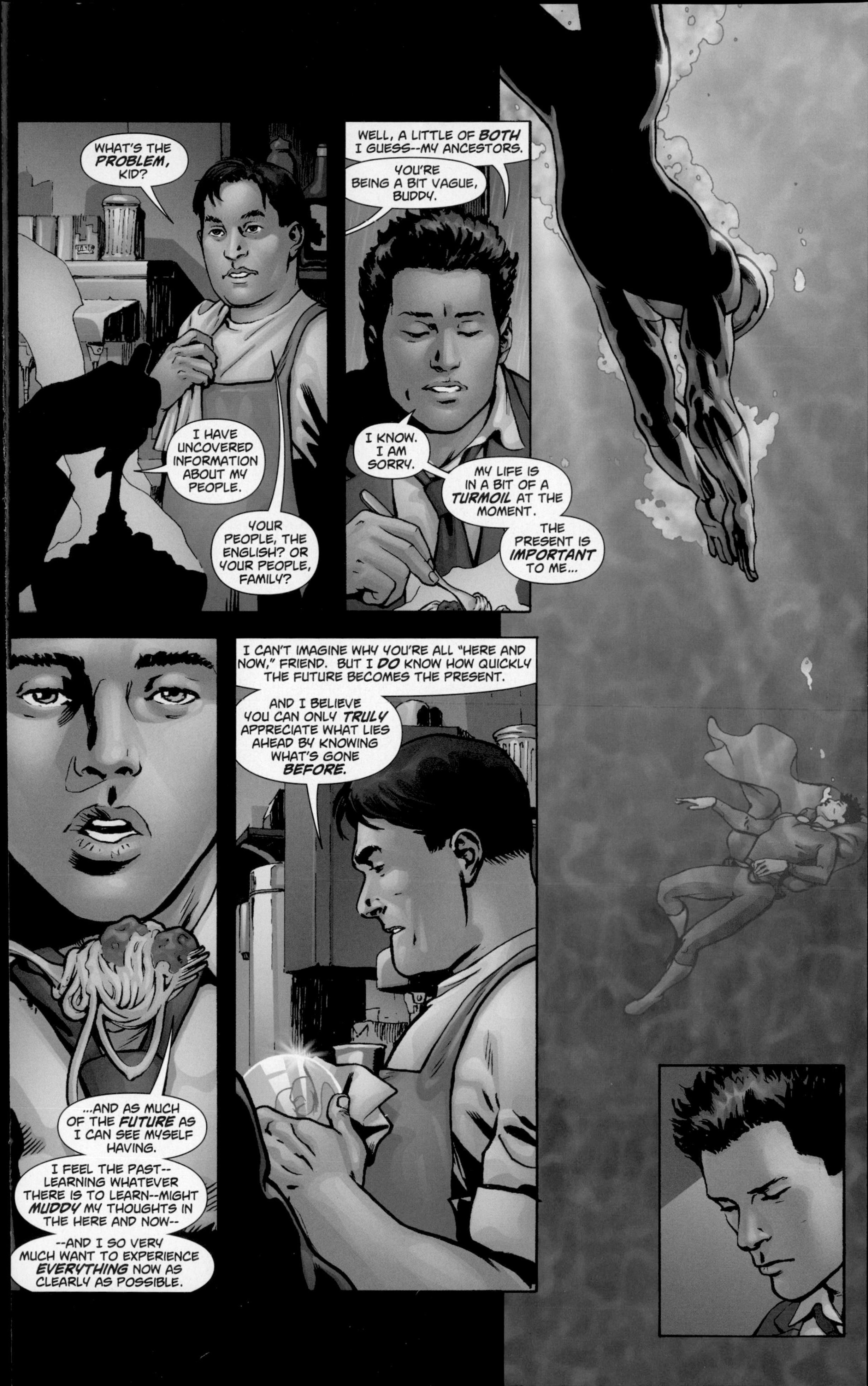
WHAT'S THE PROBLEM, KID?
I HAVE UNCOVERED INFORMATION ABOUT MY PEOPLE.
YOUR PEOPLE, THE ENGLISH? OR YOUR PEOPLE, FAMILY?
WELL, A LITTLE OF BOTH I GUESS--MY ANCESTORS.
YOU'RE BEING A BIT VAGUE, BUDDY.
I KNOW. I AM SORRY.
MY LIFE IS IN A BIT OF A TURMOIL AT THE MOMENT.
THE PRESENT IS IMPORTANT TO ME...
...AND AS MUCH OF THE FUTURE AS I CAN SEE MYSELF HAVING.
I FEEL THE PAST--LEARNING WHATEVER THERE IS TO LEARN--MIGHT MUDDY MY THOUGHTS IN THE HERE AND NOW--
--AND I SO VERY MUCH WANT TO EXPERIENCE EVERYTHING NOW AS CLEARLY AS POSSIBLE.
I CAN'T IMAGINE WHY YOU'RE ALL "HERE AND NOW," FRIEND. BUT I DO KNOW HOW QUICKLY THE FUTURE BECOMES THE PRESENT.
AND I BELIEVE YOU CAN ONLY TRULY APPRECIATE WHAT LIES AHEAD BY KNOWING WHAT'S GONE BEFORE.

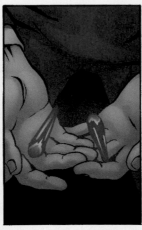

LAR GAND, CHILD OF **DAXAM**. KNOW YOU THIS.

THE HISTORY OF OUR **OUR** PLANET BEGINS NOT WITH OUR PLANET AT ALL, BUT WITH **ANOTHER**-- A GALAXY AWAY.

ITS NAME WAS **KRYPTON**.

ITS PEOPLE DRAGGED THEMSELVES FROM THE MUD AS ALL PEOPLE DO.

IT TOOK THEM MILLENNIA.

UNTIL THEIR LIVES WERE PERFECT.

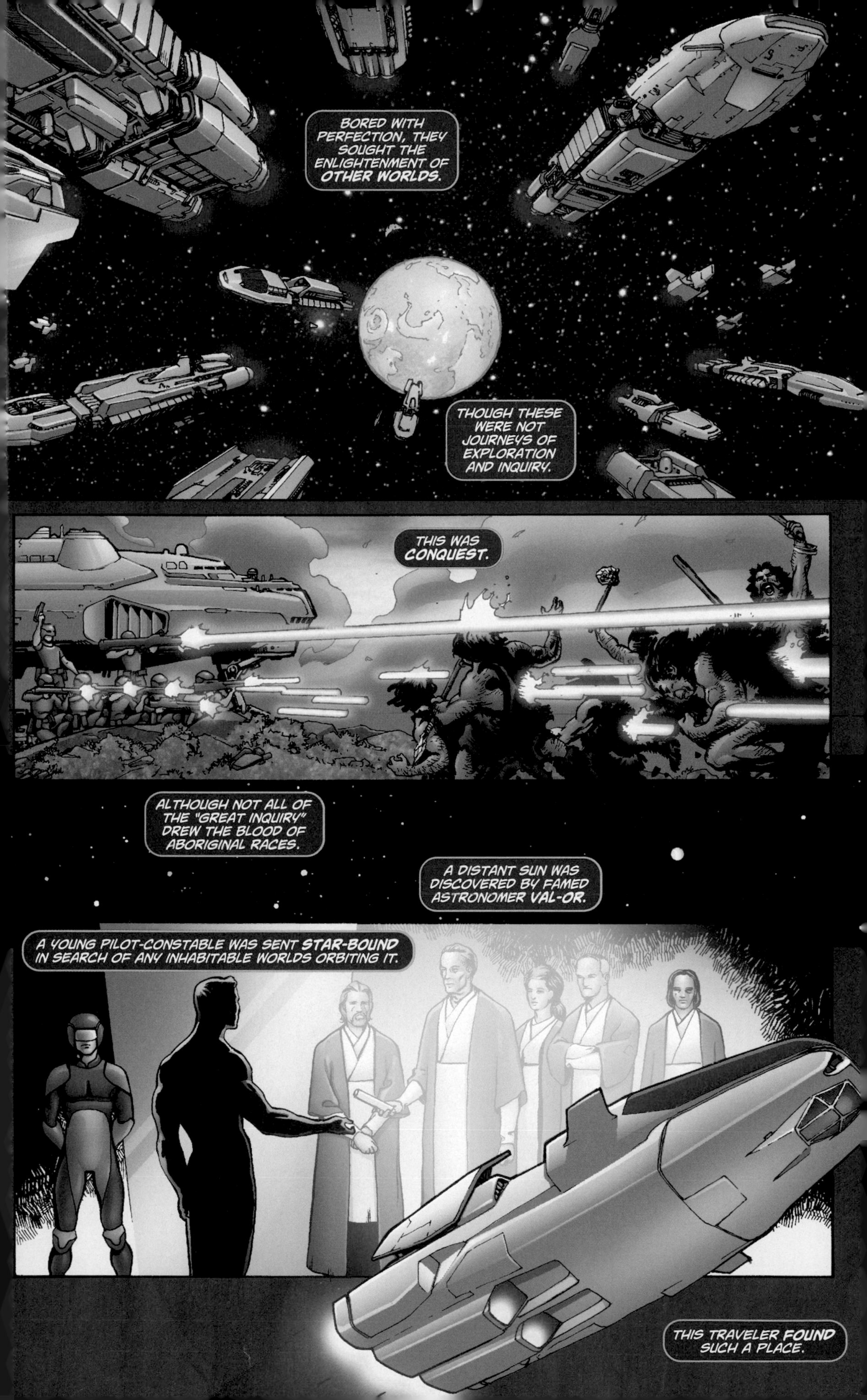
BORED WITH PERFECTION, THEY SOUGHT THE ENLIGHTENMENT OF OTHER WORLDS.
THOUGH THESE WERE NOT JOURNEYS OF EXPLORATION AND INQUIRY.
THIS WAS CONQUEST.
ALTHOUGH NOT ALL OF THE "GREAT INQUIRY" DREW THE BLOOD OF ABORIGINAL RACES.
A DISTANT SUN WAS DISCOVERED BY FAMED ASTRONOMER VAL-OR.
A YOUNG PILOT-CONSTABLE WAS SENT STAR-BOUND IN SEARCH OF ANY INHABITABLE WORLDS ORBITING IT.
THIS TRAVELER FOUND SUCH A PLACE.

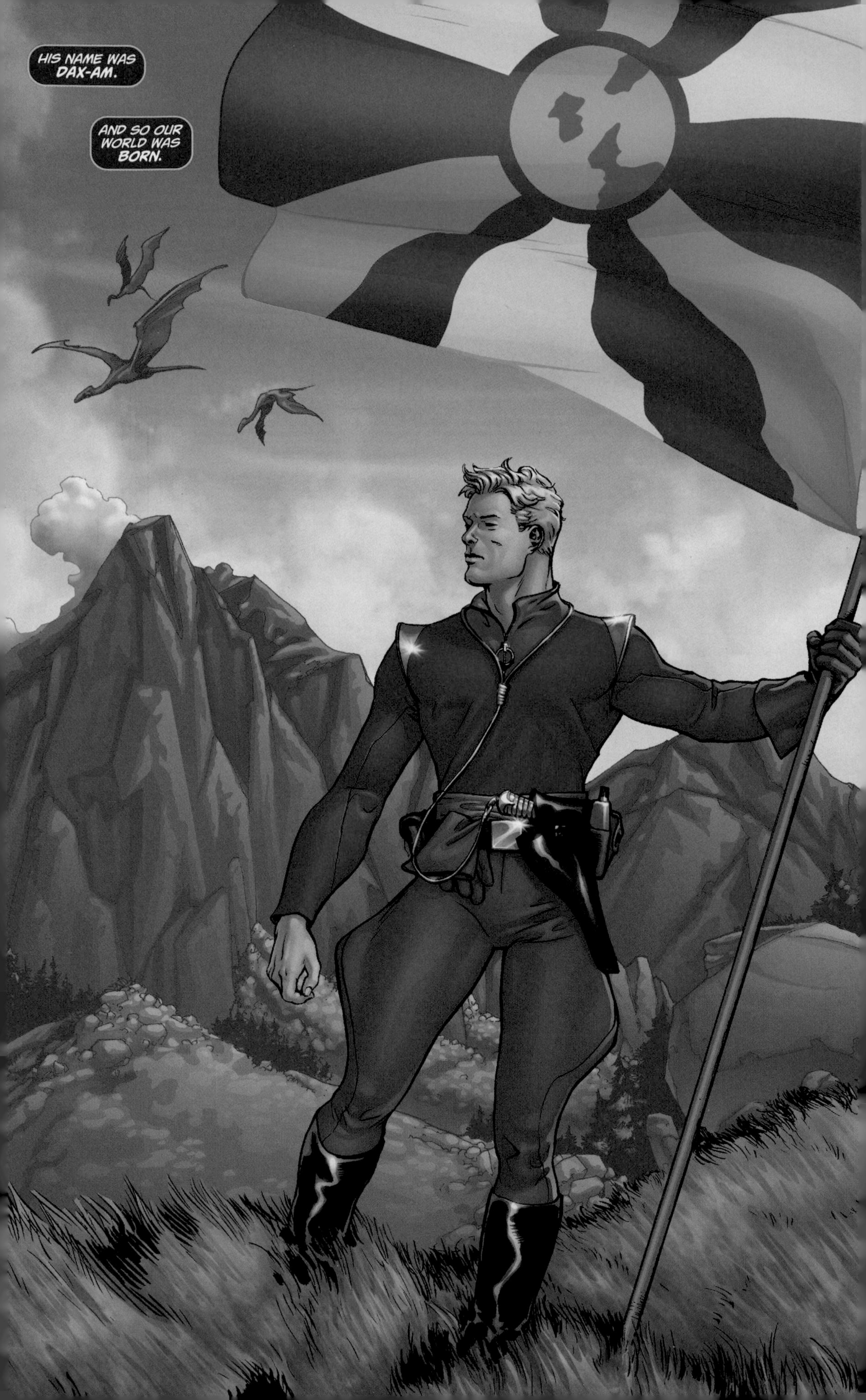
HIS NAME WAS DAX-AM.
AND SO OUR WORLD WAS BORN.

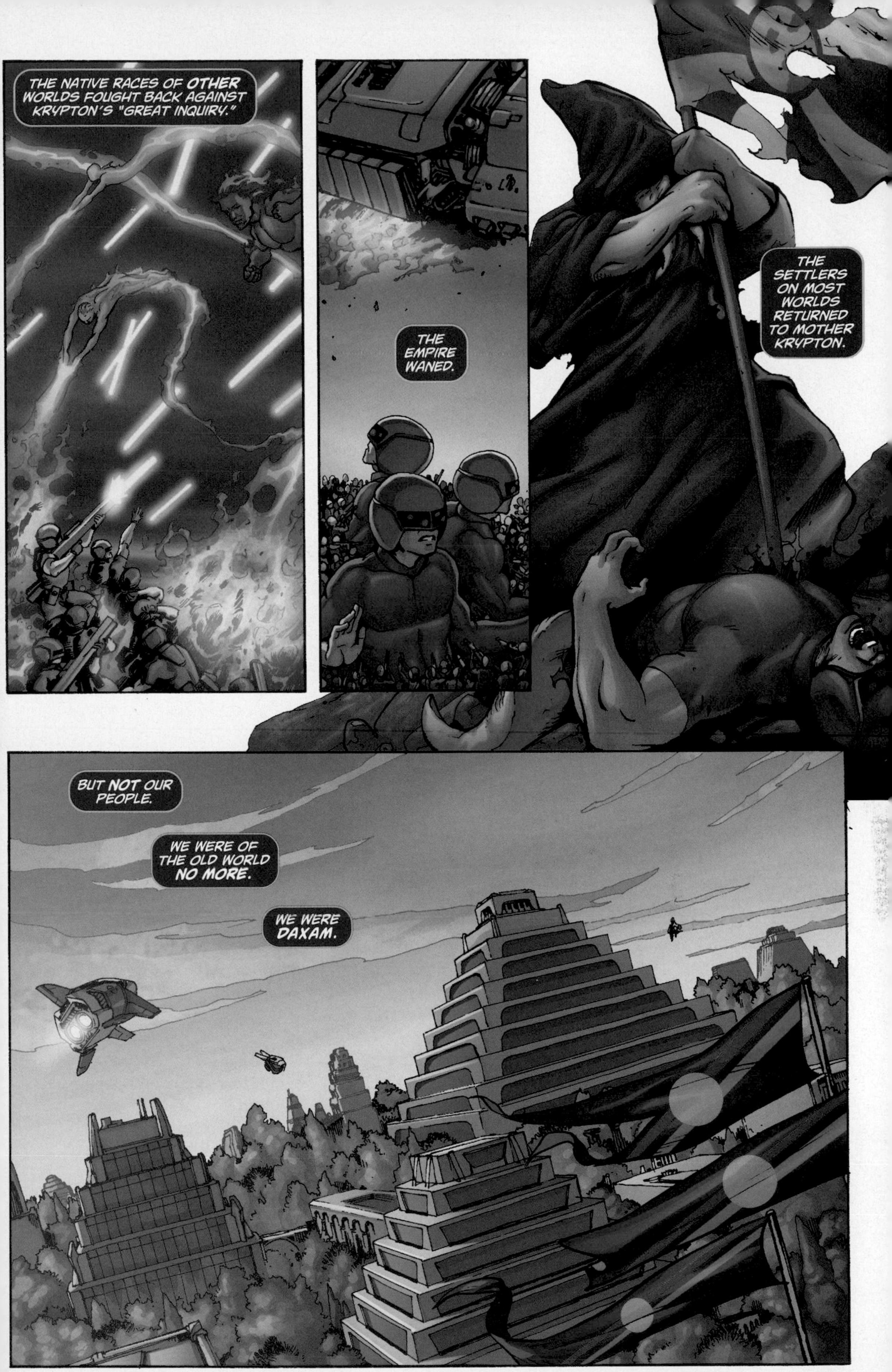
THE NATIVE RACES OF OTHER WORLDS FOUGHT BACK AGAINST KRYPTON'S "GREAT INQUIRY."
THE EMPIRE WANED.
THE SETTLERS ON MOST WORLDS RETURNED TO MOTHER KRYPTON.
BUT NOT OUR PEOPLE.
WE WERE OF THE OLD WORLD NO MORE.
WE WERE DAXAM.

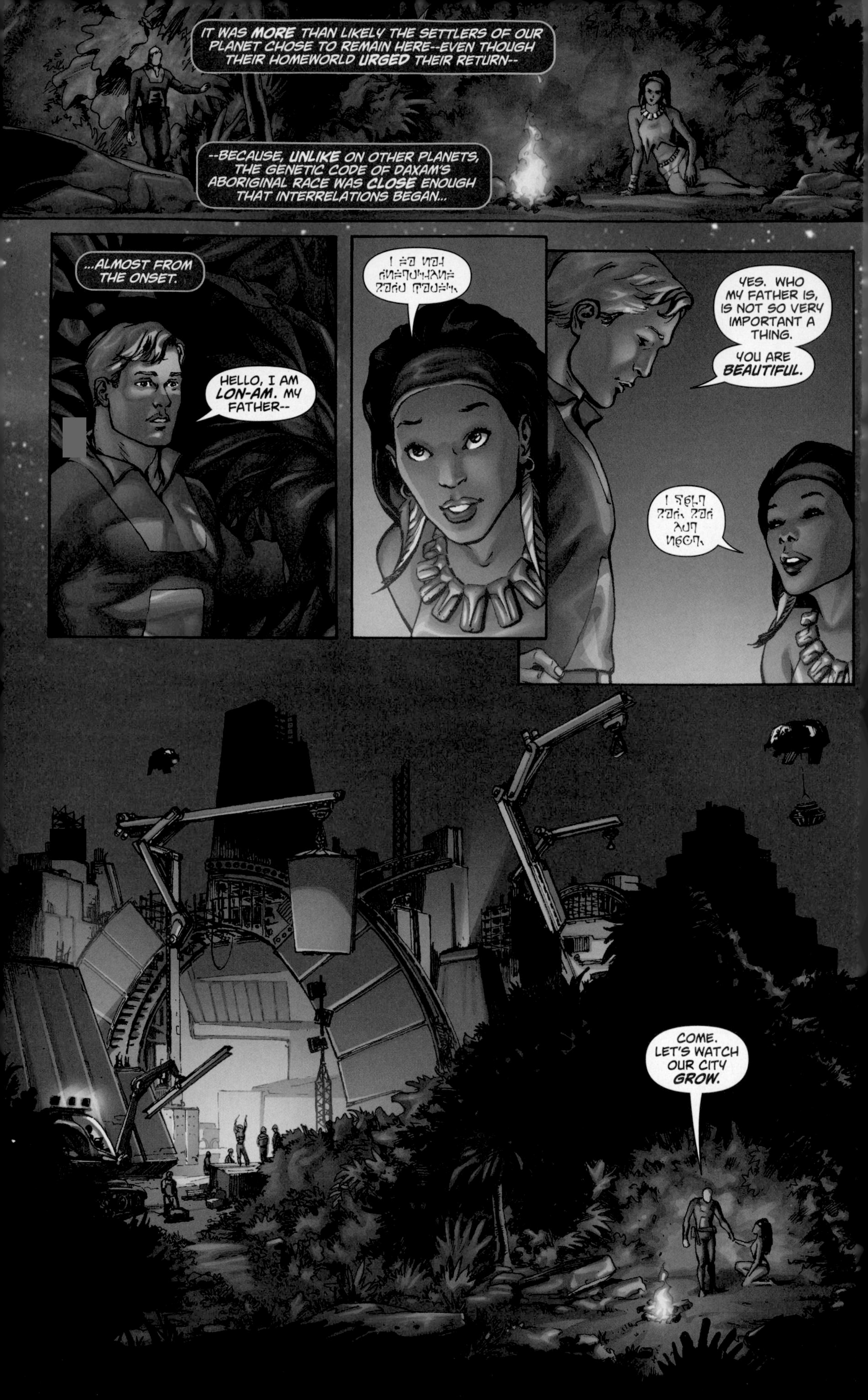
IT WAS MORE THAN LIKELY THE SETTLERS OF OUR PLANET CHOSE TO REMAIN HERE--EVEN THOUGH THEIR HOMEWORLD URGED THEIR RETURN--
--BECAUSE, UNLIKE ON OTHER PLANETS, THE GENETIC CODE OF DAXAM'S ABORIGINAL RACE WAS CLOSE ENOUGH THAT INTERRELATIONS BEGAN...
...ALMOST FROM THE ONSET.
HELLO, I AM LON-AM. MY FATHER--
YES. WHO MY FATHER IS, IS NOT SO VERY IMPORTANT A THING.
YOU ARE BEAUTIFUL.
COME. LET'S WATCH OUR CITY GROW.

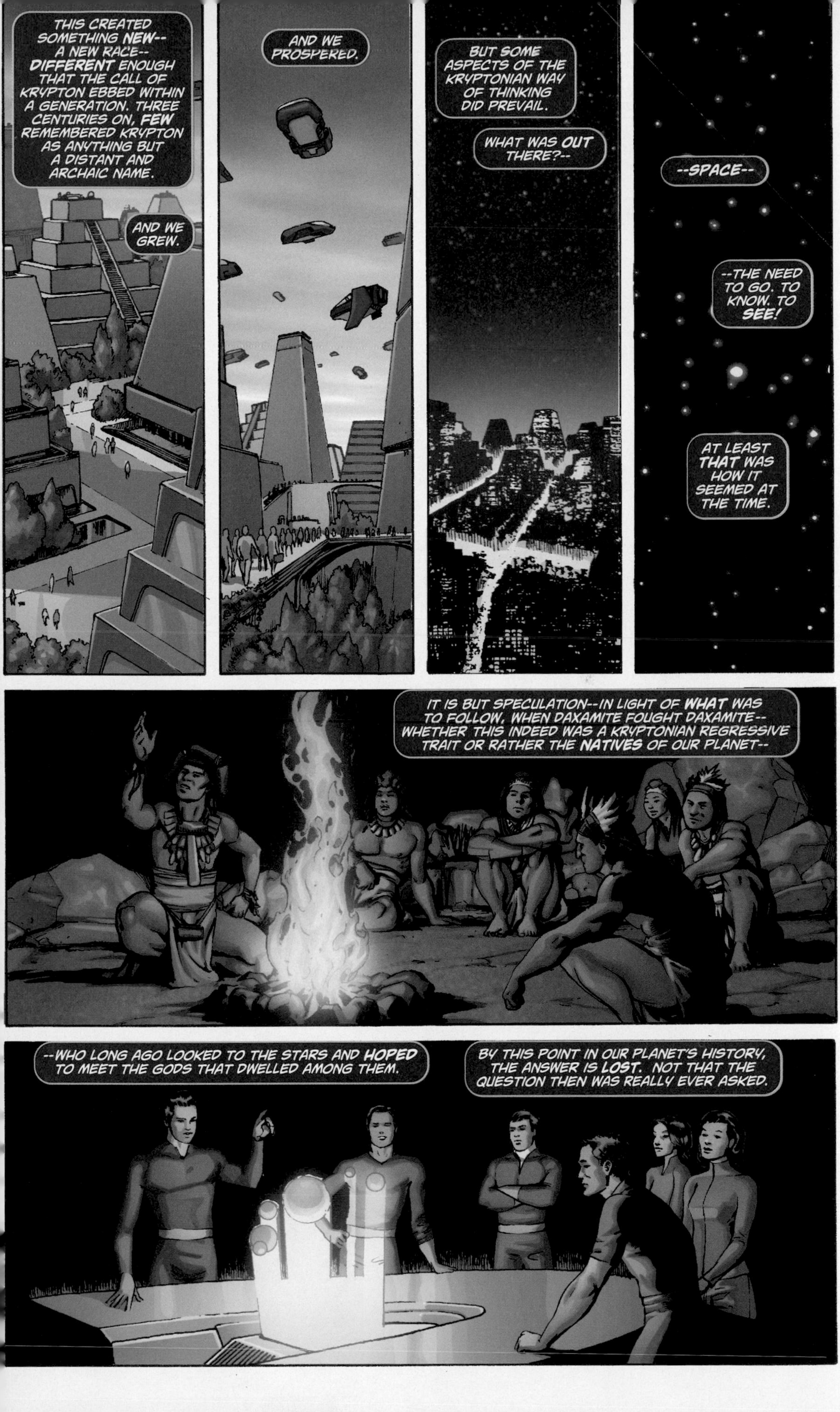
THIS CREATED SOMETHING NEW-- A NEW RACE-- DIFFERENT ENOUGH THAT THE CALL OF KRYPTON EBBED WITHIN A GENERATION. THREE CENTURIES ON, FEW REMEMBERED KRYPTON AS ANYTHING BUT A DISTANT AND ARCHAIC NAME.
AND WE GREW.
AND WE PROSPERED.
BUT SOME ASPECTS OF THE KRYPTONIAN WAY OF THINKING DID PREVAIL.
WHAT WAS OUT THERE?--
--SPACE--
--THE NEED TO GO. TO KNOW. TO SEE!
AT LEAST THAT WAS HOW IT SEEMED AT THE TIME.
IT IS BUT SPECULATION--IN LIGHT OF WHAT WAS TO FOLLOW, WHEN DAXAMITE FOUGHT DAXAMITE-- WHETHER THIS INDEED WAS A KRYPTONIAN REGRESSIVE TRAIT OR RATHER THE NATIVES OF OUR PLANET--
--WHO LONG AGO LOOKED TO THE STARS AND HOPED TO MEET THE GODS THAT DWELLED AMONG THEM.
BY THIS POINT IN OUR PLANET'S HISTORY, THE ANSWER IS LOST. NOT THAT THE QUESTION THEN WAS REALLY EVER ASKED.

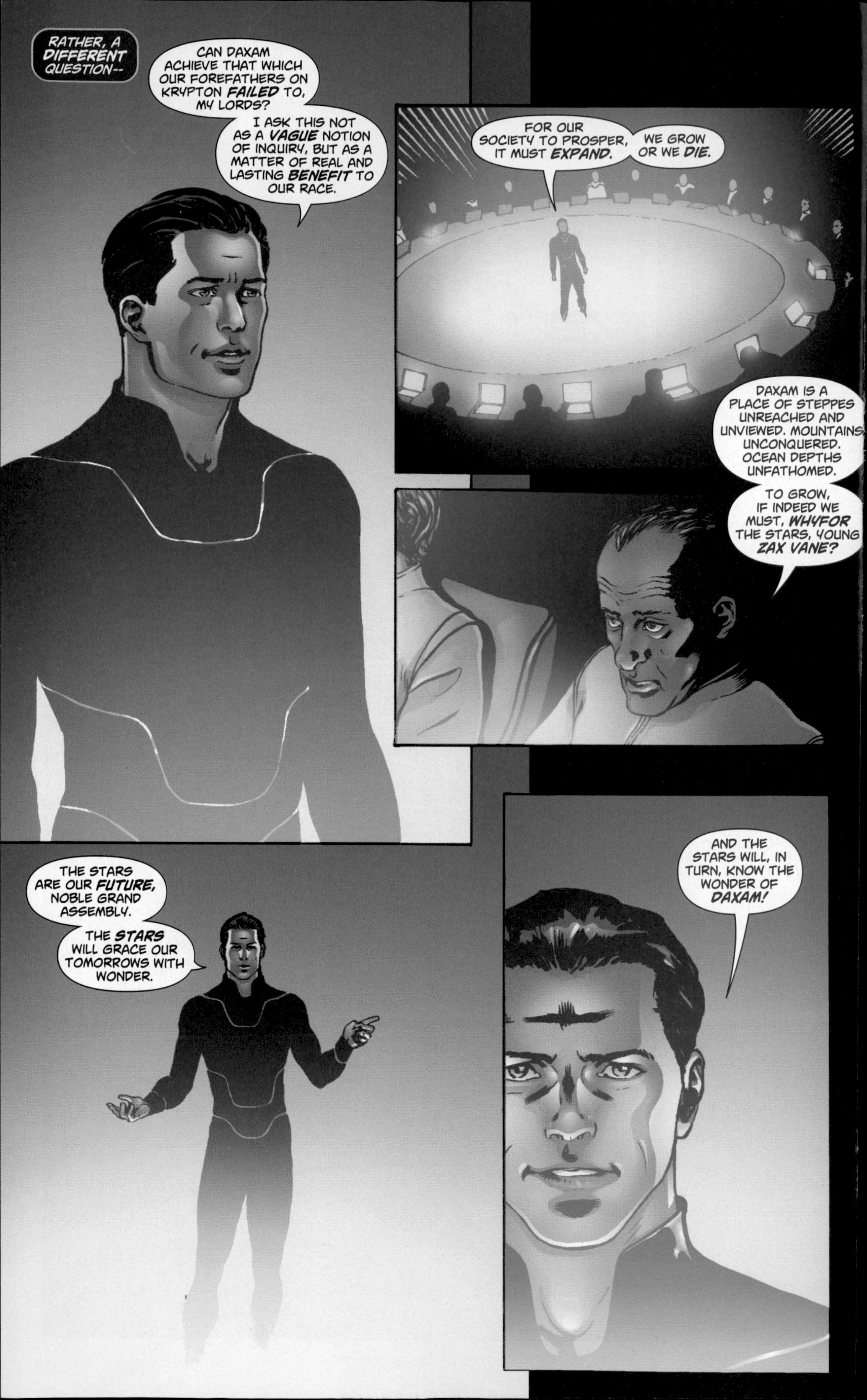

RATHER, A DIFFERENT QUESTION--
CAN DAXAM ACHIEVE THAT WHICH OUR FOREFATHERS ON KRYPTON FAILED TO, MY LORDS?
I ASK THIS NOT AS A VAGUE NOTION OF INQUIRY, BUT AS A MATTER OF REAL AND LASTING BENEFIT TO OUR RACE.
FOR OUR SOCIETY TO PROSPER, IT MUST EXPAND.
WE GROW OR WE DIE.
DAXAM IS A PLACE OF STEPPES UNREACHED AND UNVIEWED. MOUNTAINS UNCONQUERED. OCEAN DEPTHS UNFATHOMED.
TO GROW, IF INDEED WE MUST, WHYFOR THE STARS, YOUNG ZAX VANE?
THE STARS ARE OUR FUTURE, NOBLE GRAND ASSEMBLY.
THE STARS WILL GRACE OUR TOMORROWS WITH WONDER.
AND THE STARS WILL, IN TURN, KNOW THE WONDER OF DAXAM!

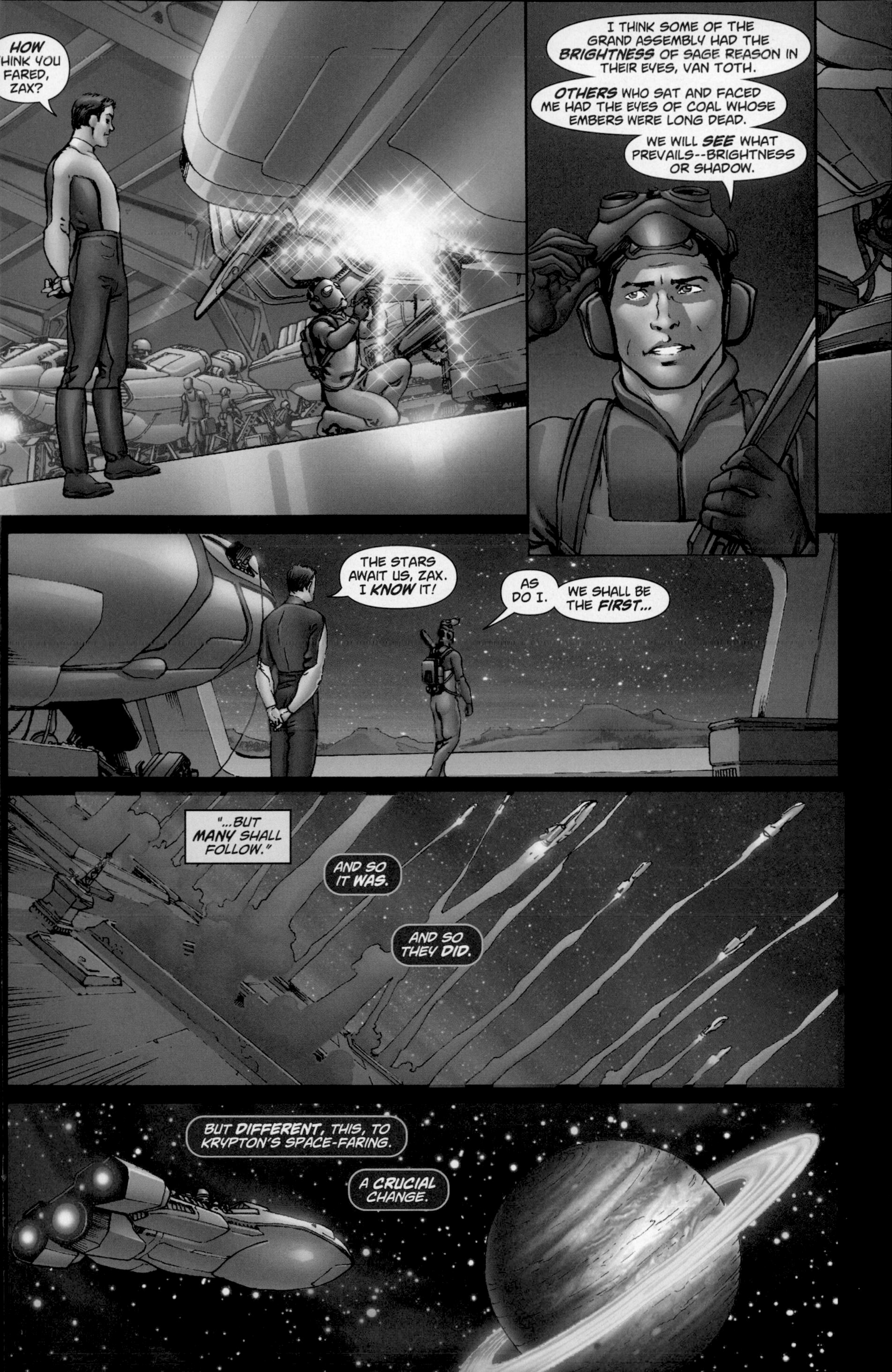
HOW THINK YOU FARED, ZAX?
I THINK SOME OF THE GRAND ASSEMBLY HAD THE BRIGHTNESS OF SAGE REASON IN THEIR EYES, VAN TOTH.
OTHERS WHO SAT AND FACED ME HAD THE EYES OF COAL WHOSE EMBERS WERE LONG DEAD.
WE WILL SEE WHAT PREVAILS--BRIGHTNESS OR SHADOW.
THE STARS AWAIT US, ZAX. I KNOW IT!
AS DO I.
WE SHALL BE THE FIRST...
"...BUT MANY SHALL FOLLOW."
AND SO IT WAS.
AND SO THEY DID.
BUT DIFFERENT, THIS, TO KRYPTON'S SPACE-FARING.
A CRUCIAL CHANGE.

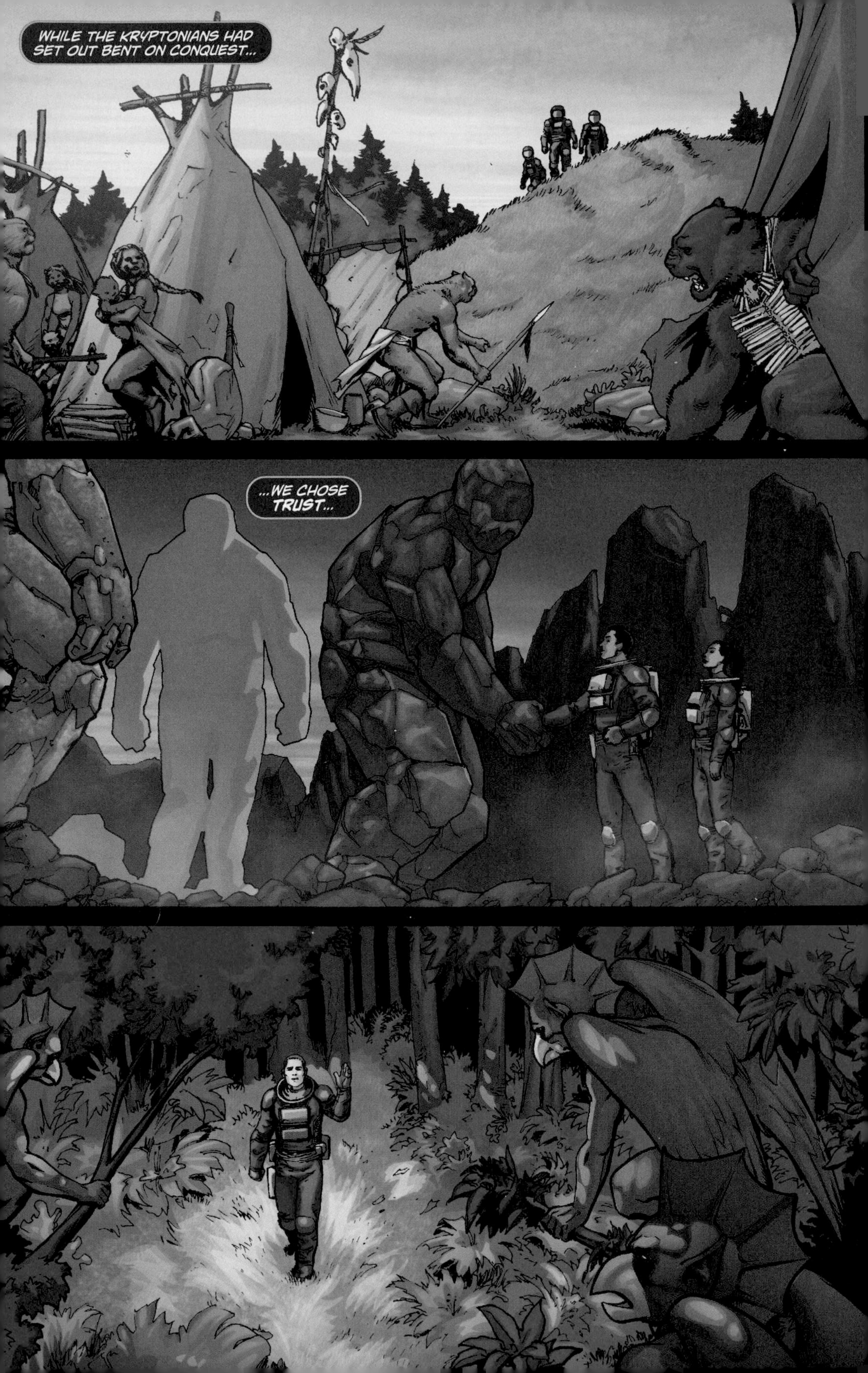
WHILE THE KRYPTONIANS HAD SET OUT BENT ON CONQUEST...
...WE CHOSE TRUST...

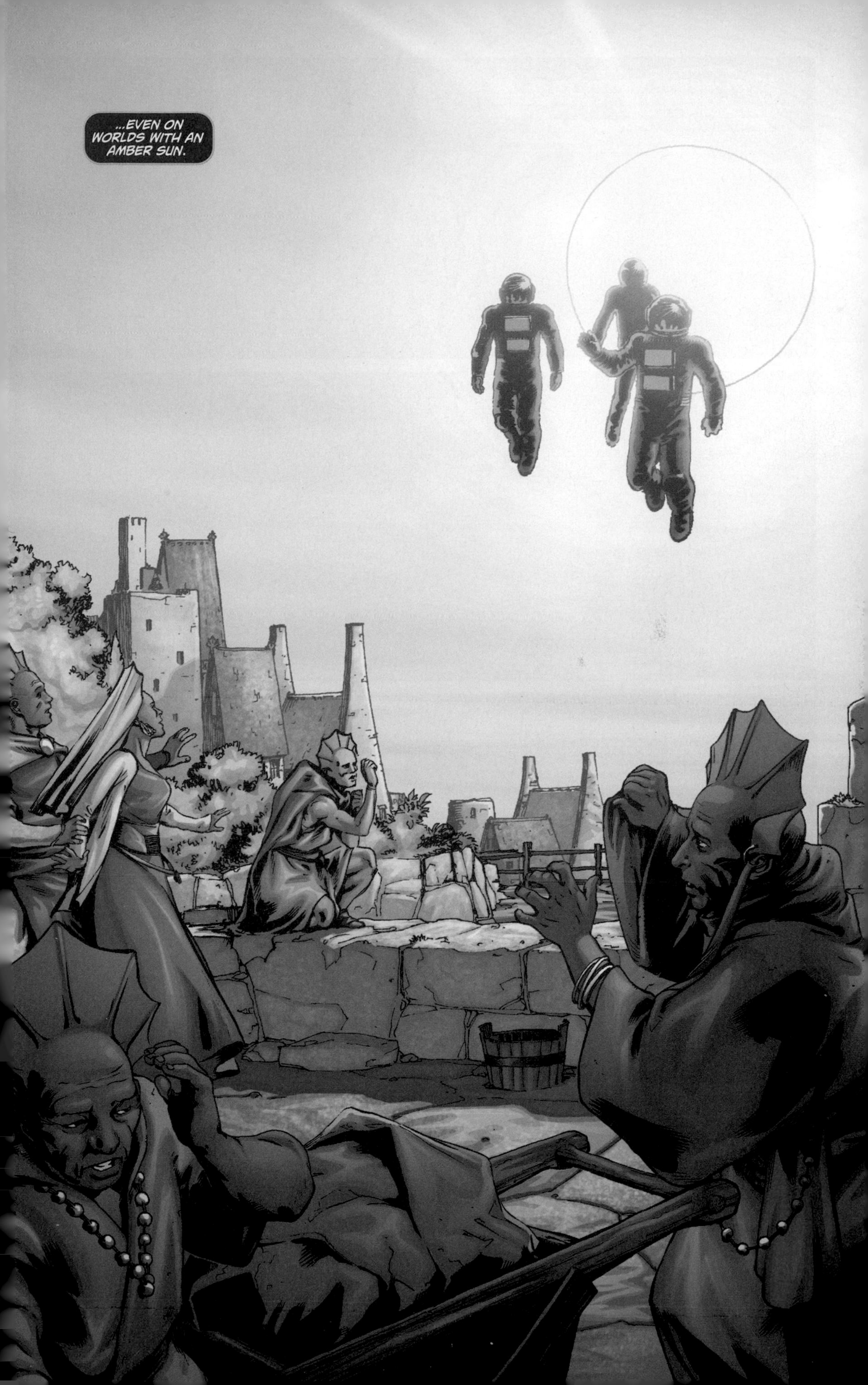
...EVEN ON WORLDS WITH AN AMBER SUN.

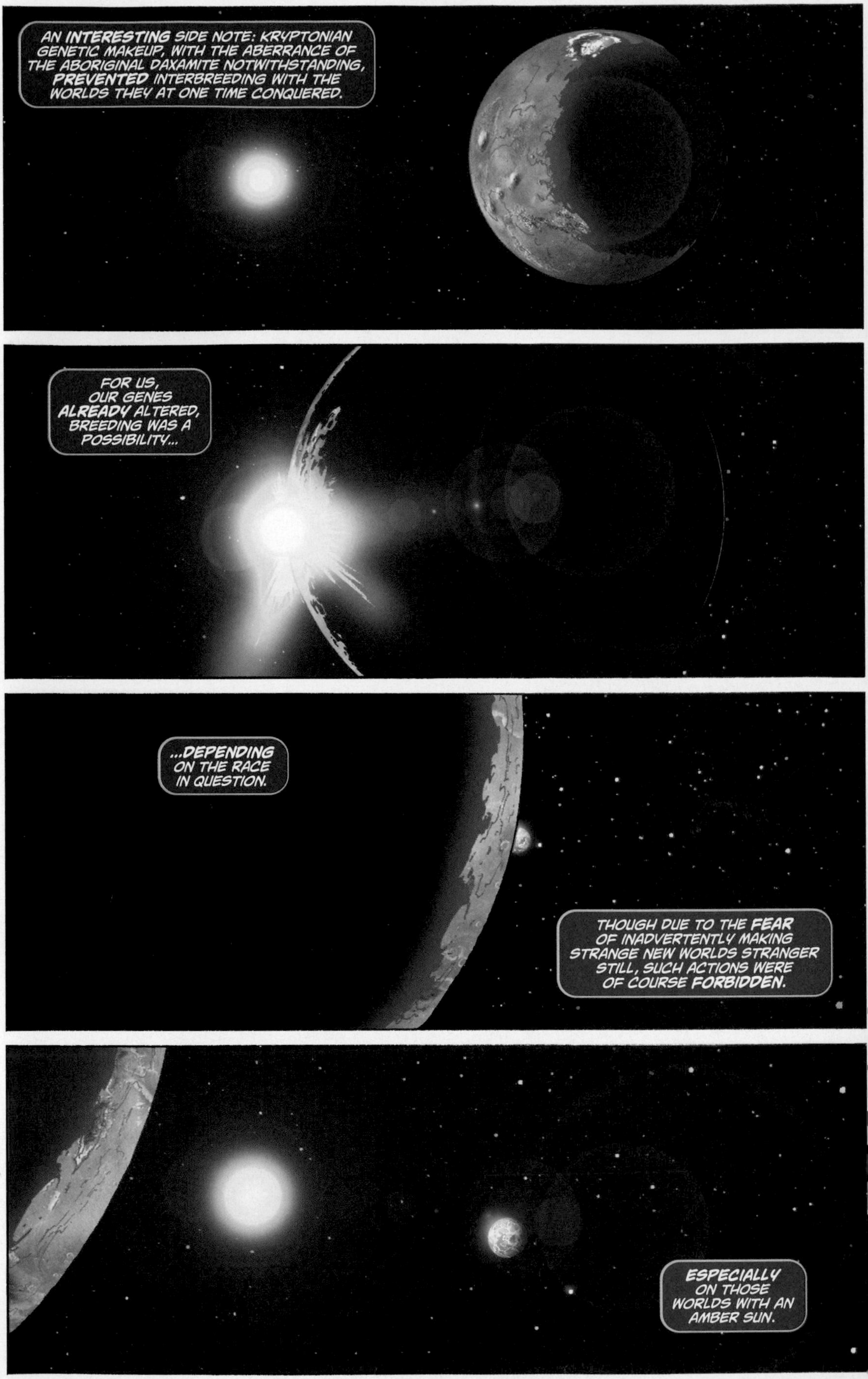
AN INTERESTING SIDE NOTE: KRYPTONIAN GENETIC MAKEUP, WITH THE ABERRANCE OF THE ABORIGINAL DAXAMITE NOTWITHSTANDING, PREVENTED INTERBREEDING WITH THE WORLDS THEY AT ONE TIME CONQUERED.
FOR US, OUR GENES ALREADY ALTERED, BREEDING WAS A POSSIBILITY...
...DEPENDING ON THE RACE IN QUESTION.
THOUGH DUE TO THE FEAR OF INADVERTENTLY MAKING STRANGE NEW WORLDS STRANGER STILL, SUCH ACTIONS WERE OF COURSE FORBIDDEN.
ESPECIALLY ON THOSE WORLDS WITH AN AMBER SUN.

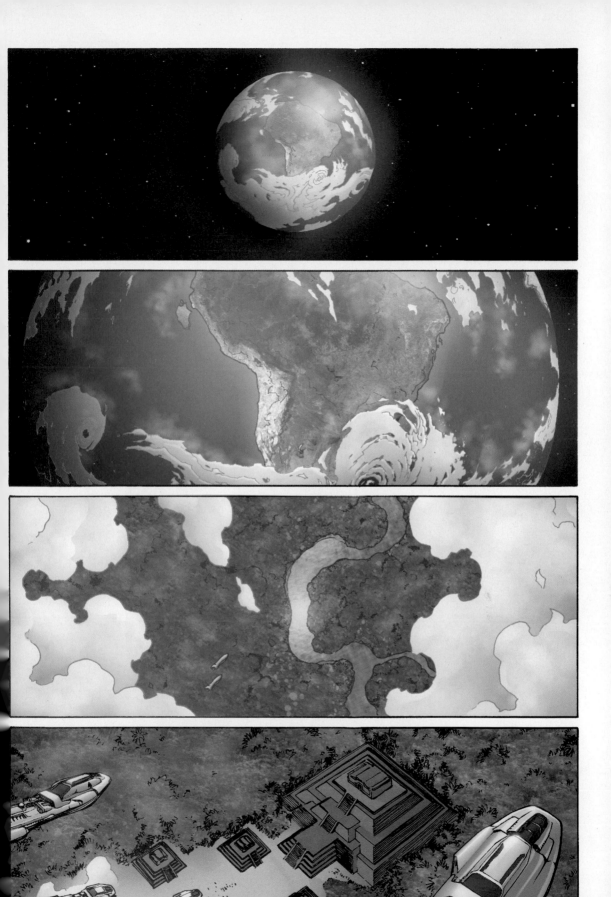

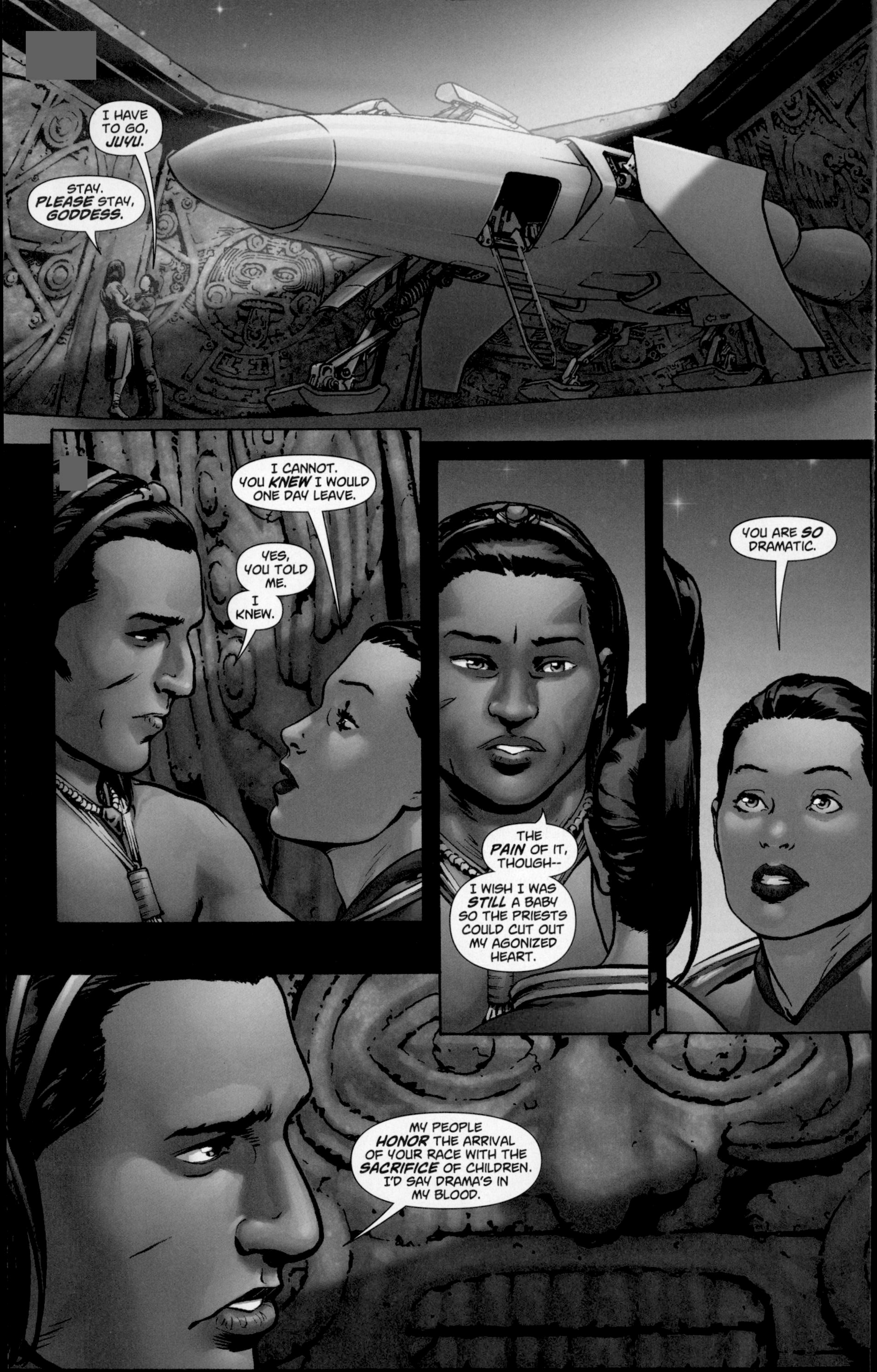
I HAVE TO GO, JUYU.
STAY. PLEASE STAY, GODDESS.
I CANNOT. YOU KNEW I WOULD ONE DAY LEAVE.
YES, YOU TOLD ME.
I KNEW.
THE PAIN OF IT, THOUGH--
I WISH I WAS STILL A BABY SO THE PRIESTS COULD CUT OUT MY AGONIZED HEART.
YOU ARE SO DRAMATIC.
MY PEOPLE HONOR THE ARRIVAL OF YOUR RACE WITH THE SACRIFICE OF CHILDREN. I'D SAY DRAMA'S IN MY BLOOD.

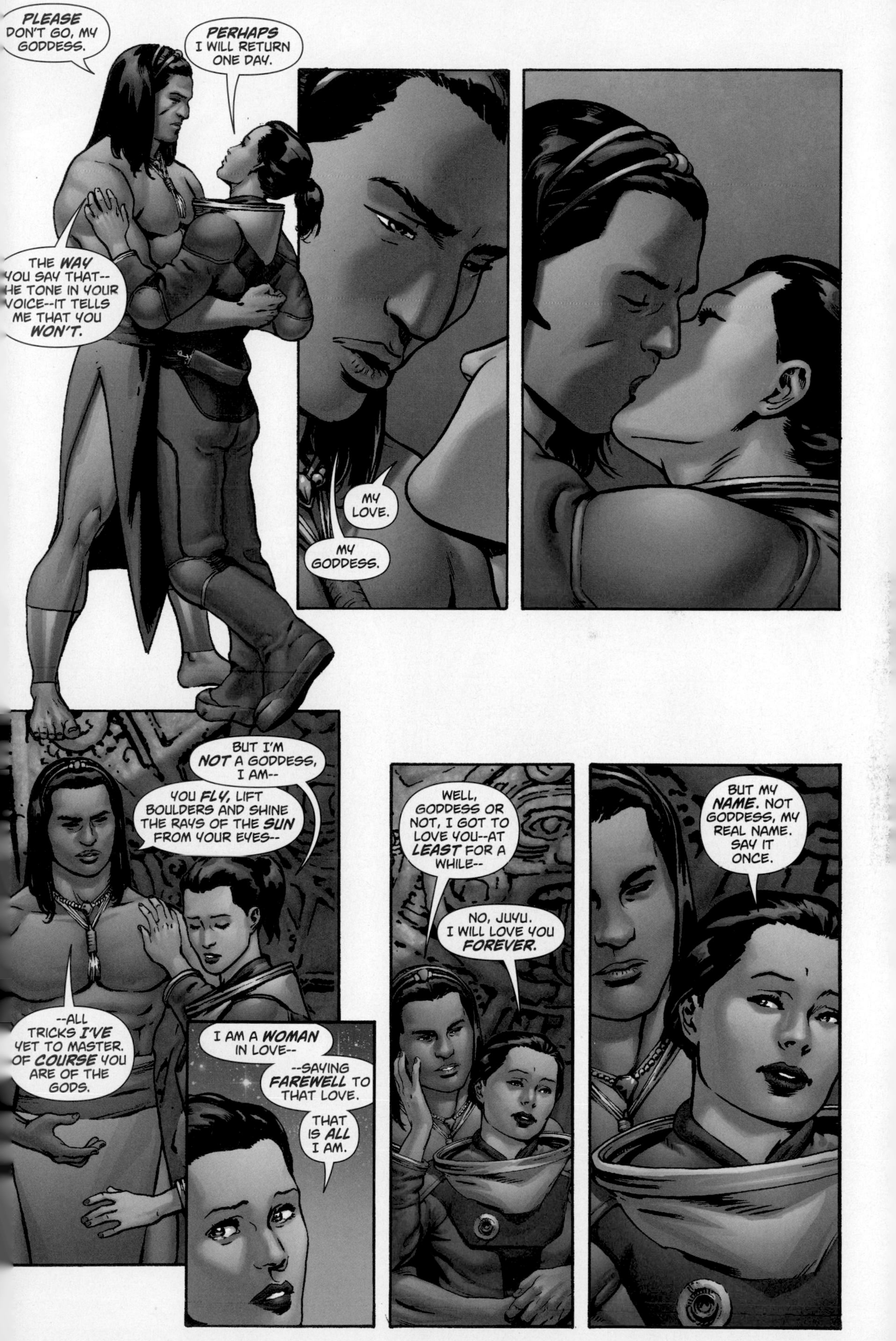
PLEASE DON'T GO, MY GODDESS.
PERHAPS I WILL RETURN ONE DAY.
THE WAY YOU SAY THAT--HE TONE IN YOUR VOICE--IT TELLS ME THAT YOU WON'T.
MY LOVE.
MY GODDESS.
BUT I'M NOT A GODDESS, I AM--
YOU FLY, LIFT BOULDERS AND SHINE THE RAYS OF THE SUN FROM YOUR EYES--
--ALL TRICKS I'VE YET TO MASTER. OF COURSE YOU ARE OF THE GODS.
I AM A WOMAN IN LOVE--
--SAYING FAREWELL TO THAT LOVE.
THAT IS ALL I AM.
WELL, GODDESS OR NOT, I GOT TO LOVE YOU--AT LEAST FOR A WHILE--
NO, JUYU. I WILL LOVE YOU FOREVER.
BUT MY NAME. NOT GODDESS, MY REAL NAME. SAY IT ONCE.

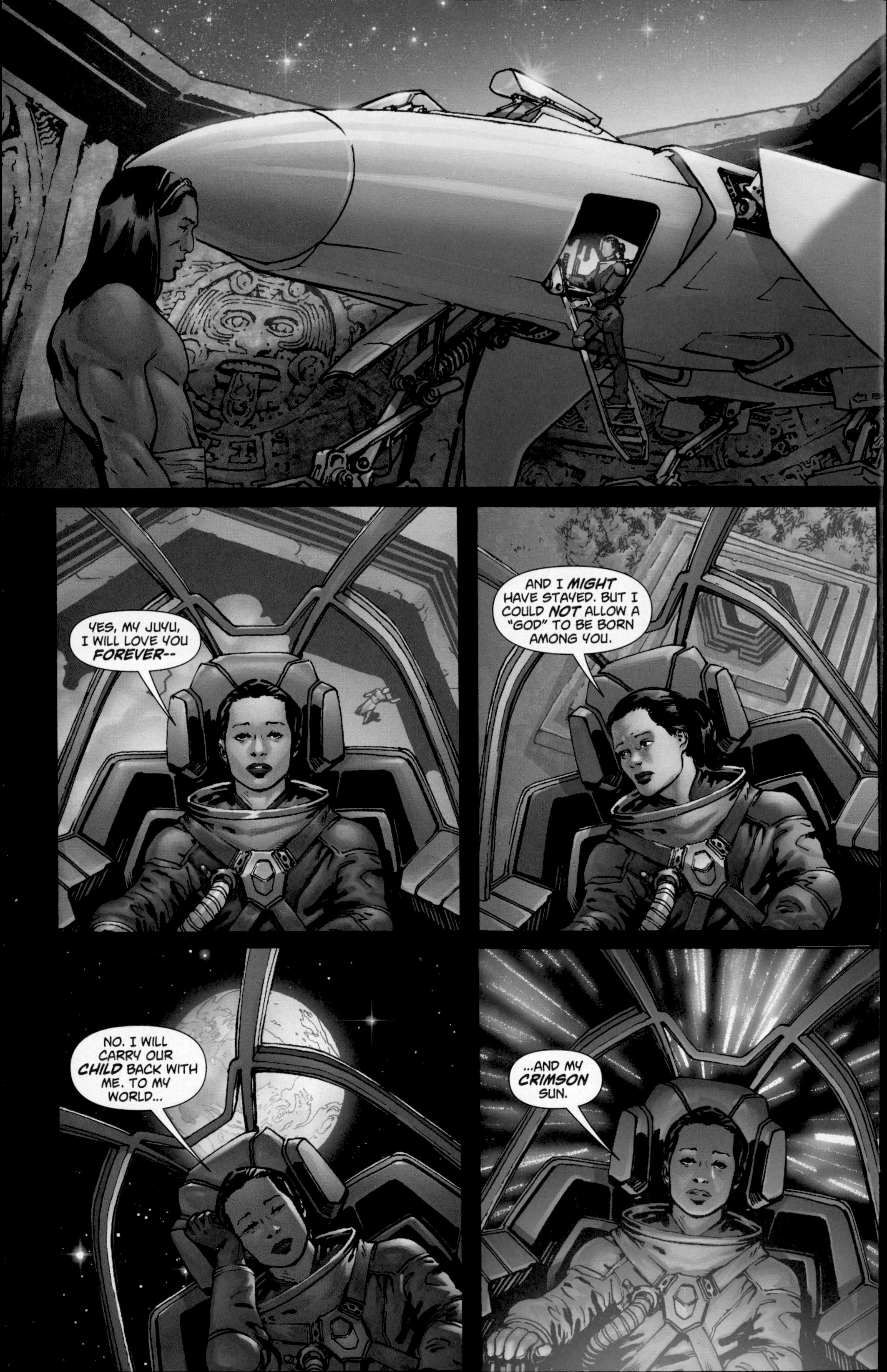
YES, MY JUYU, I WILL LOVE YOU FOREVER--
AND I MIGHT HAVE STAYED. BUT I COULD NOT ALLOW A "GOD" TO BE BORN AMONG YOU.
NO. I WILL CARRY OUR CHILD BACK WITH ME. TO MY WORLD...
...AND MY CRIMSON SUN.

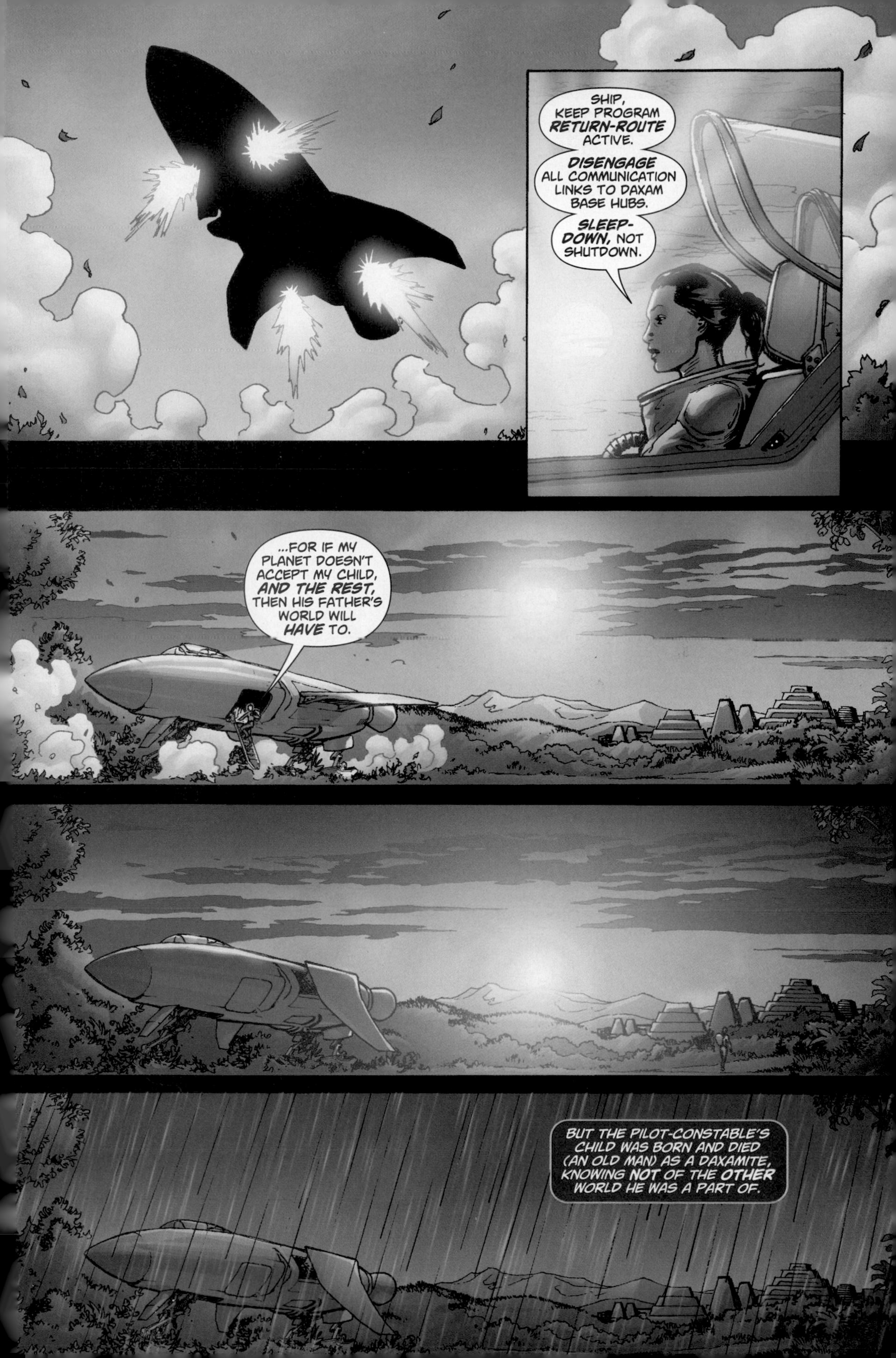
SHIP, KEEP PROGRAM RETURN-ROUTE ACTIVE.
DISENGAGE ALL COMMUNICATION LINKS TO DAXAM BASE HUBS.
SLEEP-DOWN, NOT SHUTDOWN.
...FOR IF MY PLANET DOESN'T ACCEPT MY CHILD, AND THE REST, THEN HIS FATHER'S WORLD WILL HAVE TO.
BUT THE PILOT-CONSTABLE'S CHILD WAS BORN AND DIED (AN OLD MAN) AS A DAXAMITE, KNOWING NOT OF THE OTHER WORLD HE WAS A PART OF.

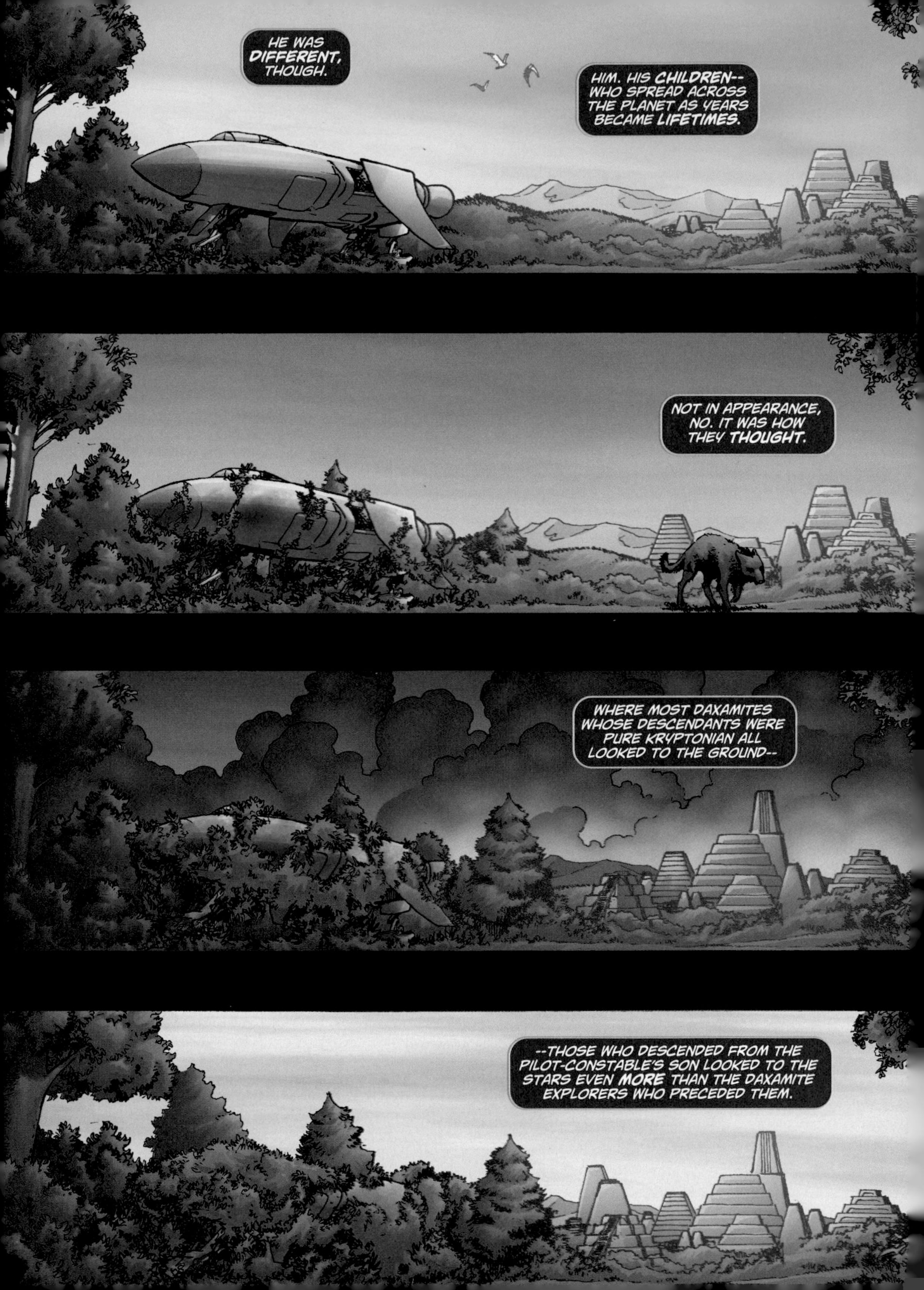
HE WAS DIFFERENT, THOUGH.
HIM. HIS CHILDREN-- WHO SPREAD ACROSS THE PLANET AS YEARS BECAME LIFETIMES.
NOT IN APPEARANCE, NO. IT WAS HOW THEY THOUGHT.
WHERE MOST DAXAMITES WHOSE DESCENDANTS WERE PURE KRYPTONIAN ALL LOOKED TO THE GROUND--
--THOSE WHO DESCENDED FROM THE PILOT-CONSTABLE'S SON LOOKED TO THE STARS EVEN MORE THAN THE DAXAMITE EXPLORERS WHO PRECEDED THEM.

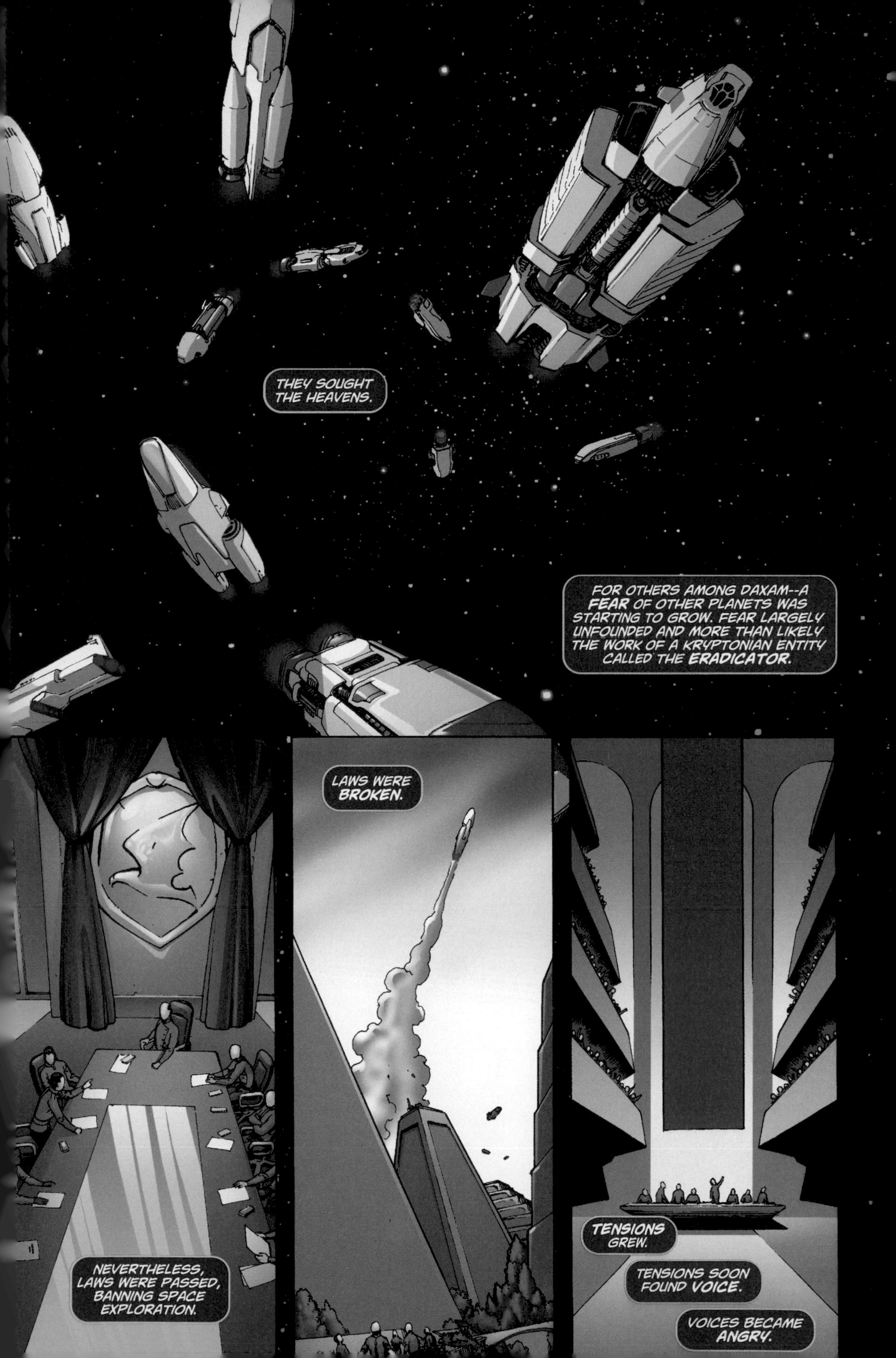
THEY SOUGHT THE HEAVENS.
FOR OTHERS AMONG DAXAM--A FEAR OF OTHER PLANETS WAS STARTING TO GROW. FEAR LARGELY UNFOUNDED AND MORE THAN LIKELY THE WORK OF A KRYPTONIAN ENTITY CALLED THE ERADICATOR.
NEVERTHELESS, LAWS WERE PASSED, BANNING SPACE EXPLORATION.
LAWS WERE BROKEN.
TENSIONS GREW.
TENSIONS SOON FOUND VOICE.
VOICES BECAME ANGRY.

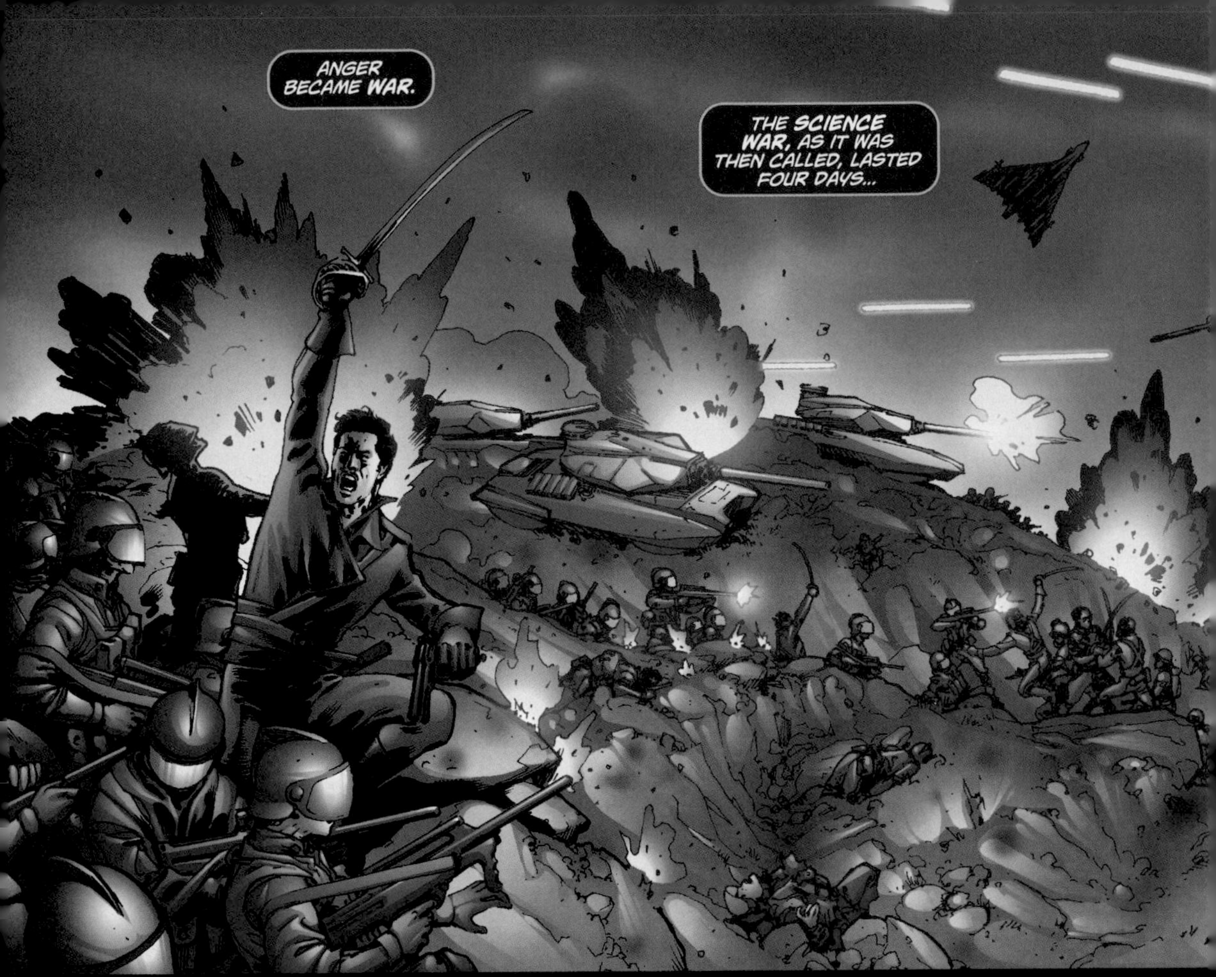
ANGER BECAME WAR.
THE SCIENCE WAR, AS IT WAS THEN CALLED, LASTED FOUR DAYS...

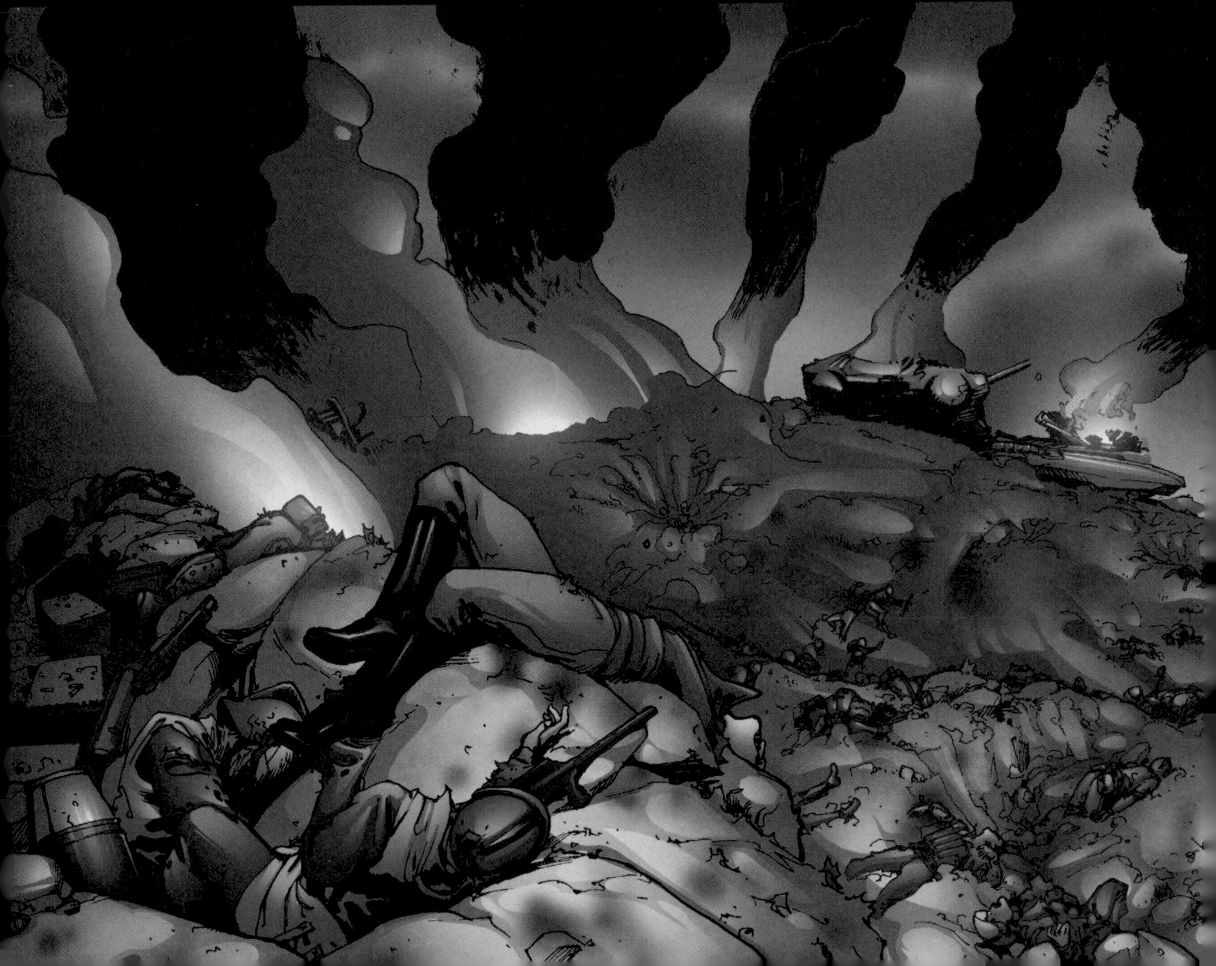

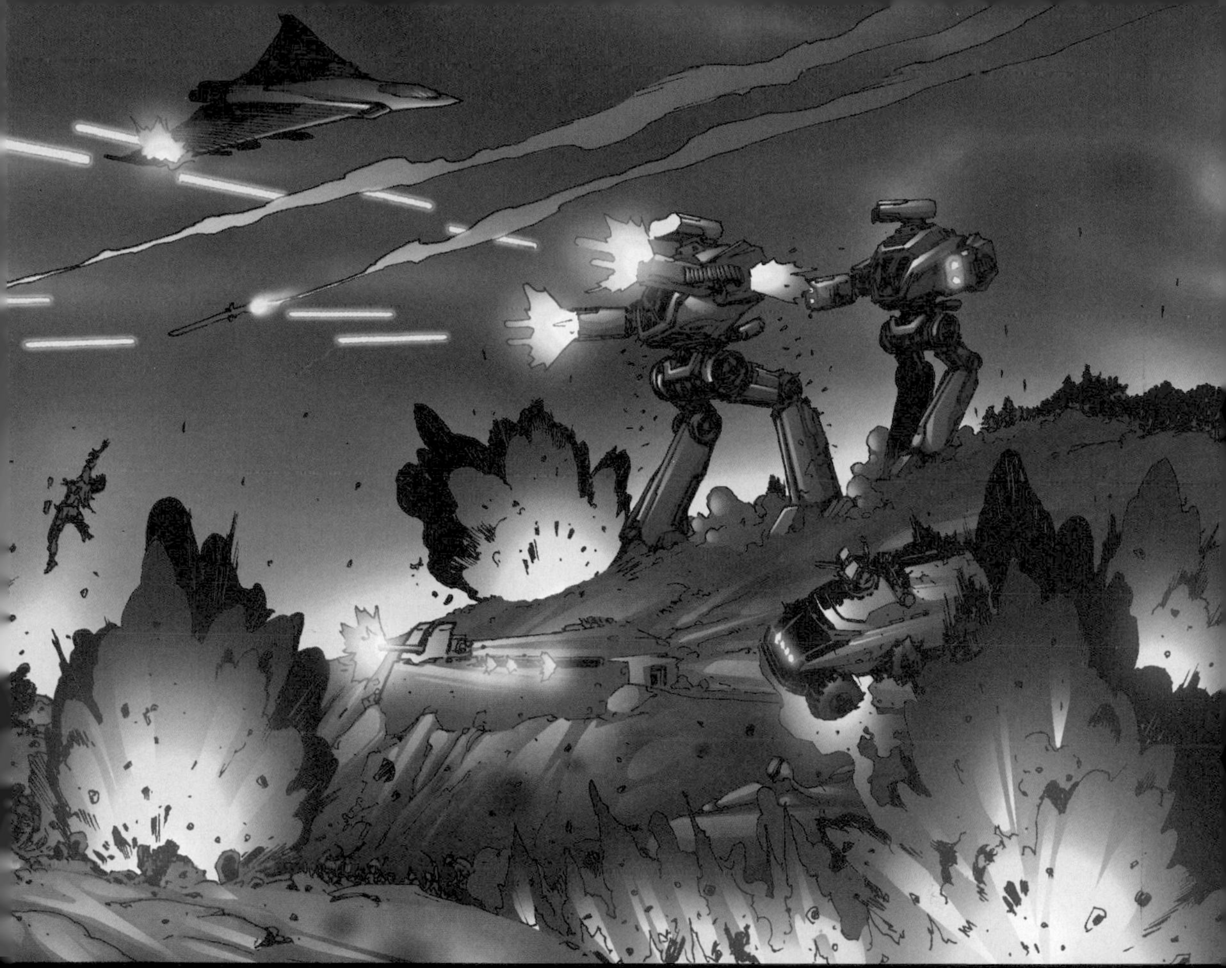

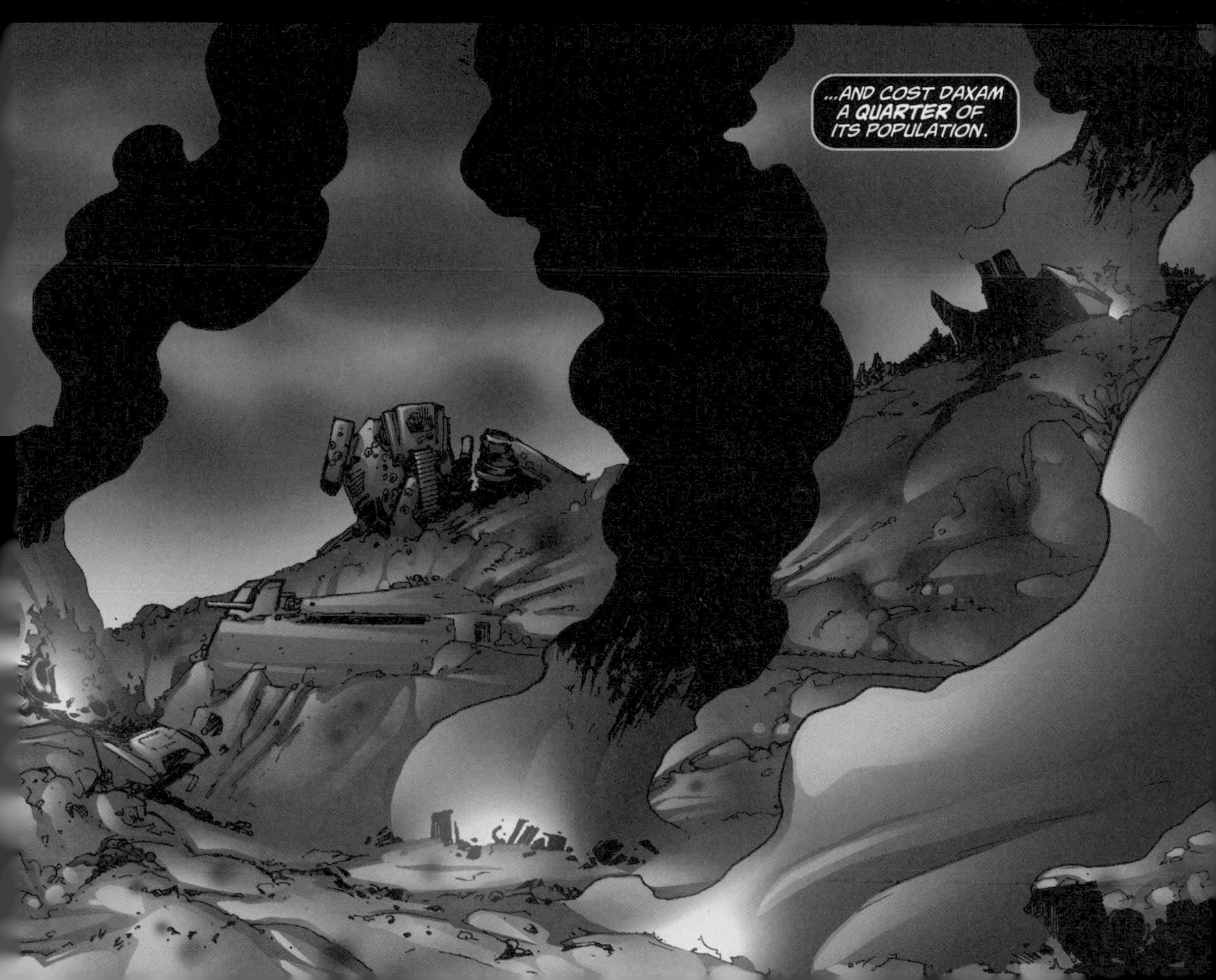
...AND COST DAXAM A QUARTER OF ITS POPULATION.

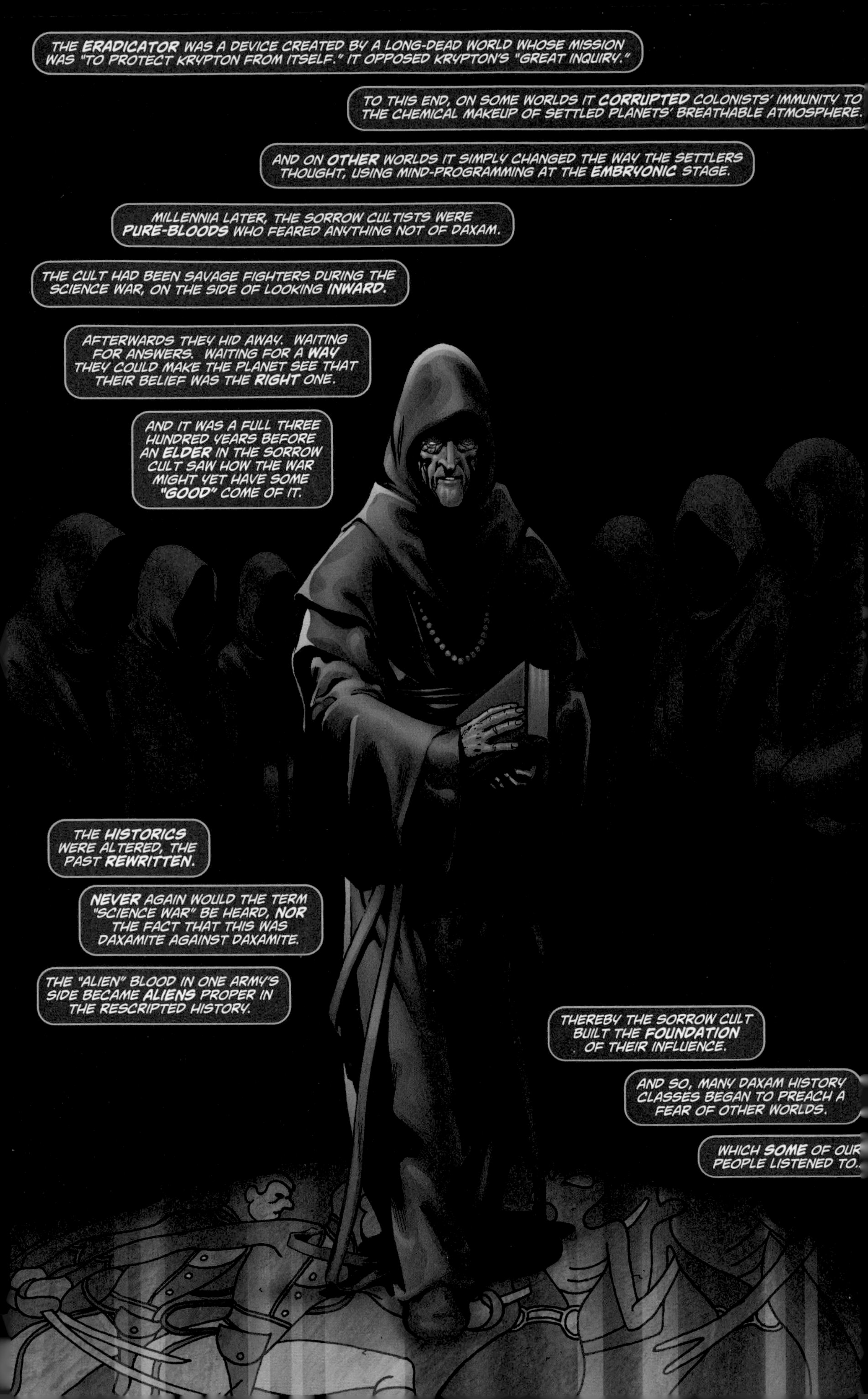
THE ERADICATOR WAS A DEVICE CREATED BY A LONG-DEAD WORLD WHOSE MISSION WAS "TO PROTECT KRYPTON FROM ITSELF." IT OPPOSED KRYPTON'S "GREAT INQUIRY."
TO THIS END, ON SOME WORLDS IT CORRUPTED COLONISTS' IMMUNITY TO THE CHEMICAL MAKEUP OF SETTLED PLANETS' BREATHABLE ATMOSPHERE.
AND ON OTHER WORLDS IT SIMPLY CHANGED THE WAY THE SETTLERS THOUGHT, USING MIND-PROGRAMMING AT THE EMBRYONIC STAGE.
MILLENNIA LATER, THE SORROW CULTISTS WERE PURE-BLOODS WHO FEARED ANYTHING NOT OF DAXAM.
THE CULT HAD BEEN SAVAGE FIGHTERS DURING THE SCIENCE WAR, ON THE SIDE OF LOOKING INWARD.
AFTERWARDS THEY HID AWAY. WAITING FOR ANSWERS. WAITING FOR A WAY THEY COULD MAKE THE PLANET SEE THAT THEIR BELIEF WAS THE RIGHT ONE.
AND IT WAS A FULL THREE HUNDRED YEARS BEFORE AN ELDER IN THE SORROW CULT SAW HOW THE WAR MIGHT YET HAVE SOME "GOOD" COME OF IT.
THE HISTORICS WERE ALTERED, THE PAST REWRITTEN.
NEVER AGAIN WOULD THE TERM "SCIENCE WAR" BE HEARD, NOR THE FACT THAT THIS WAS DAXAMITE AGAINST DAXAMITE.
THE "ALIEN" BLOOD IN ONE ARMY'S SIDE BECAME ALIENS PROPER IN THE RESCRIPTED HISTORY.
THEREBY THE SORROW CULT BUILT THE FOUNDATION OF THEIR INFLUENCE.
AND SO, MANY DAXAM HISTORY CLASSES BEGAN TO PREACH A FEAR OF OTHER WORLDS.
WHICH SOME OF OUR PEOPLE LISTENED TO.

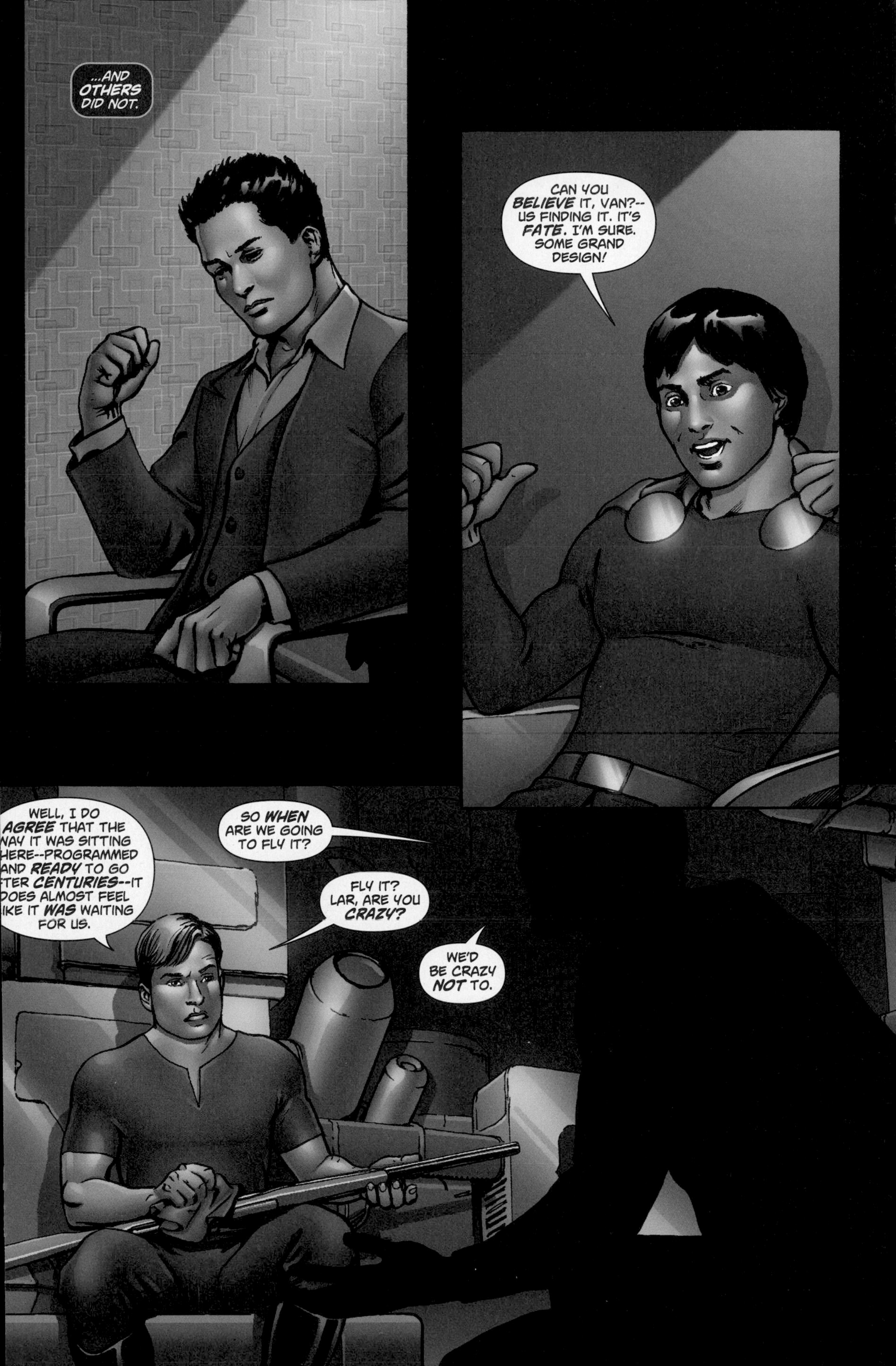
...AND OTHERS DID NOT.
CAN YOU BELIEVE IT, VAN?-- US FINDING IT. IT'S FATE. I'M SURE. SOME GRAND DESIGN!
WELL, I DO AGREE THAT THE WAY IT WAS SITTING THERE--PROGRAMMED AND READY TO GO AFTER CENTURIES--IT DOES ALMOST FEEL LIKE IT WAS WAITING FOR US.
SO WHEN ARE WE GOING TO FLY IT?
FLY IT? LAR, ARE YOU CRAZY?
WE'D BE CRAZY NOT TO.

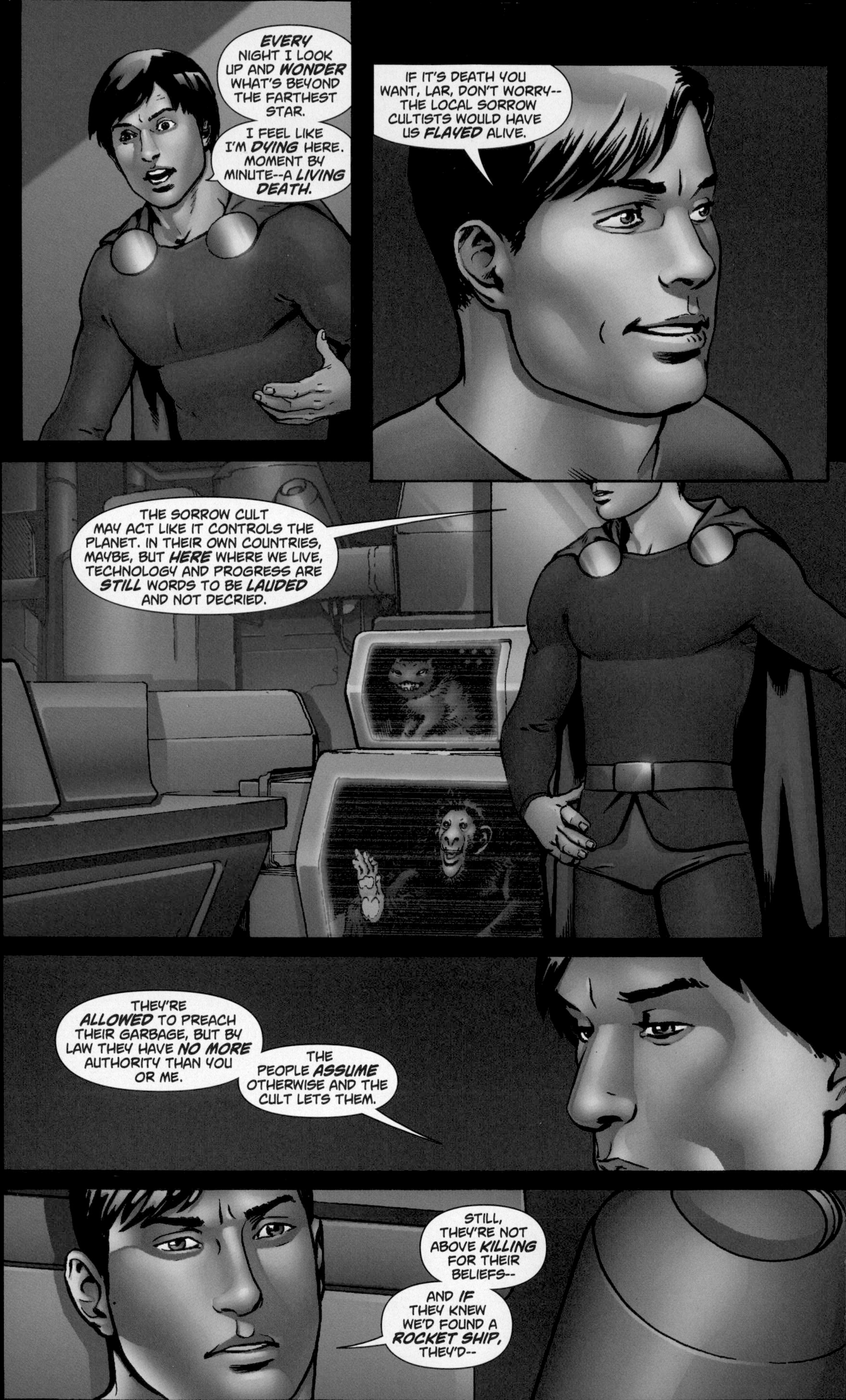
EVERY NIGHT I LOOK UP AND WONDER WHAT'S BEYOND THE FARTHEST STAR.
I FEEL LIKE I'M DYING HERE. MOMENT BY MINUTE--A LIVING DEATH.
IF IT'S DEATH YOU WANT, LAR, DON'T WORRY-- THE LOCAL SORROW CULTISTS WOULD HAVE US FLAYED ALIVE.
THE SORROW CULT MAY ACT LIKE IT CONTROLS THE PLANET. IN THEIR OWN COUNTRIES, MAYBE, BUT HERE WHERE WE LIVE, TECHNOLOGY AND PROGRESS ARE STILL WORDS TO BE LAUDED AND NOT DECRIED.
THEY'RE ALLOWED TO PREACH THEIR GARBAGE, BUT BY LAW THEY HAVE NO MORE AUTHORITY THAN YOU OR ME.
THE PEOPLE ASSUME OTHERWISE AND THE CULT LETS THEM.
STILL, THEY'RE NOT ABOVE KILLING FOR THEIR BELIEFS--
AND IF THEY KNEW WE'D FOUND A ROCKET SHIP, THEY'D--

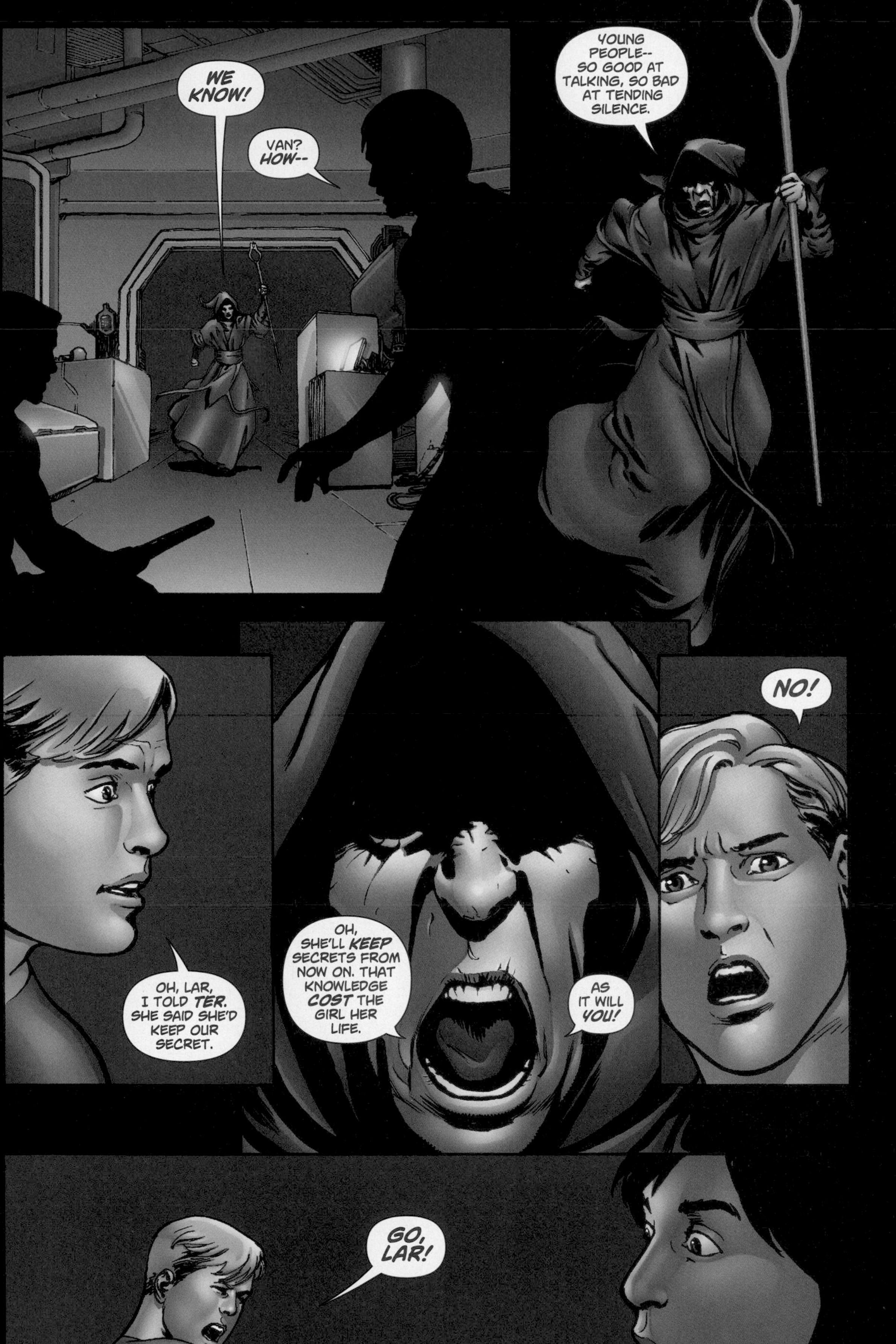
WE KNOW!
VAN? HOW--
YOUNG PEOPLE-- SO GOOD AT TALKING, SO BAD AT TENDING SILENCE.
OH, LAR, I TOLD TER. SHE SAID SHE'D KEEP OUR SECRET.
OH, SHE'LL KEEP SECRETS FROM NOW ON. THAT KNOWLEDGE COST THE GIRL HER LIFE.
AS IT WILL YOU!
NO!
GO, LAR!

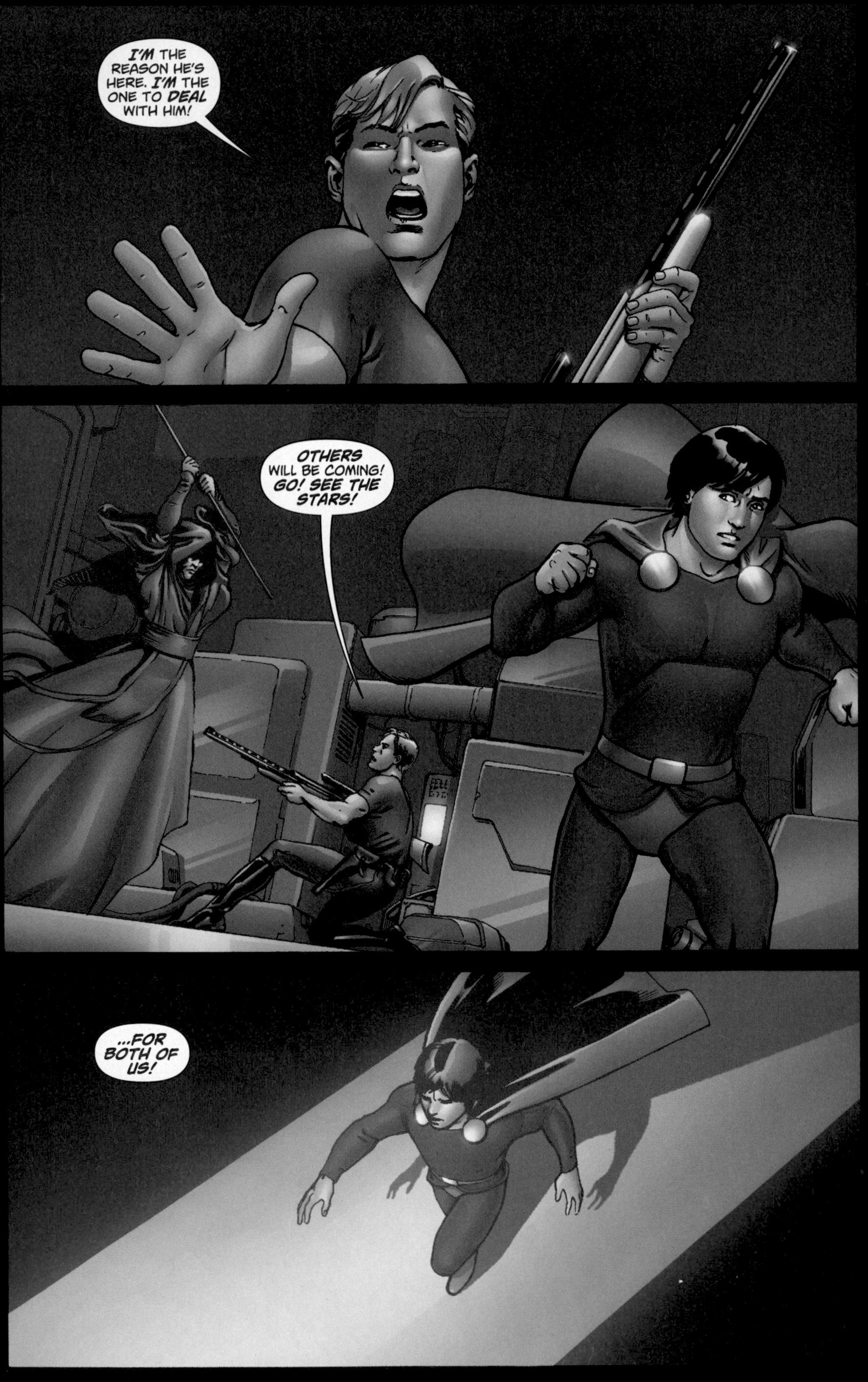
I'M THE REASON HE'S HERE. I'M THE ONE TO DEAL WITH HIM!
OTHERS WILL BE COMING! GO! SEE THE STARS!
...FOR BOTH OF US!

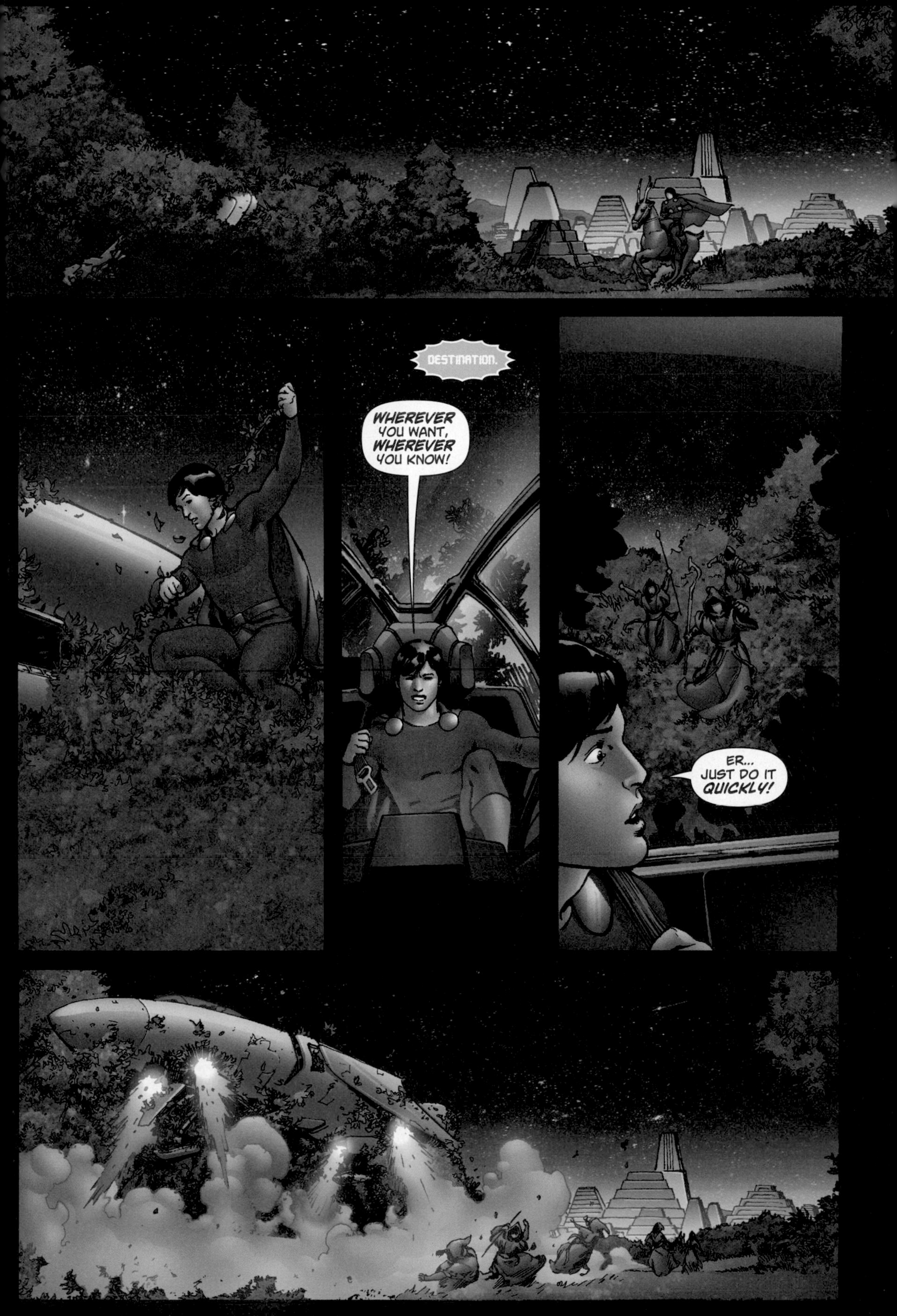
DESTINATION.
WHEREVER YOU WANT, WHEREVER YOU KNOW!
ER... JUST DO IT QUICKLY!

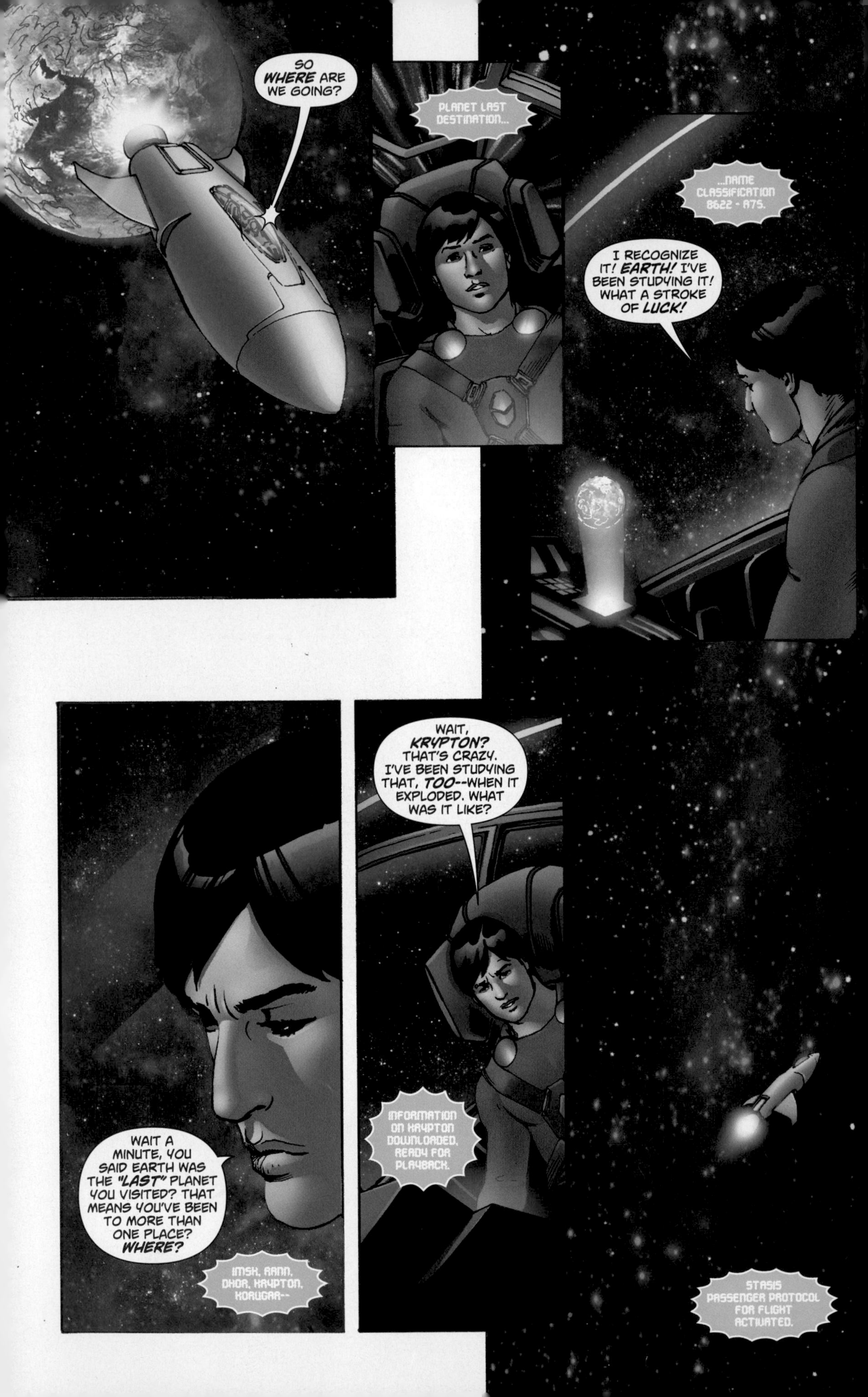
SO WHERE ARE WE GOING?
PLANET LAST DESTINATION...
...NAME CLASSIFICATION 8622 - A75.
I RECOGNIZE IT! EARTH! I'VE BEEN STUDYING IT! WHAT A STROKE OF LUCK!
WAIT A MINUTE, YOU SAID EARTH WAS THE "LAST" PLANET YOU VISITED? THAT MEANS YOU'VE BEEN TO MORE THAN ONE PLACE? WHERE?
IMSK, RANN, DHOR, KRYPTON, KORUGAR--
WAIT, KRYPTON? THAT'S CRAZY. I'VE BEEN STUDYING THAT, TOO--WHEN IT EXPLODED. WHAT WAS IT LIKE?
INFORMATION ON KRYPTON DOWNLOADED, READY FOR PLAYBACK.
STASIS PASSENGER PROTOCOL FOR FLIGHT ACTIVATED.

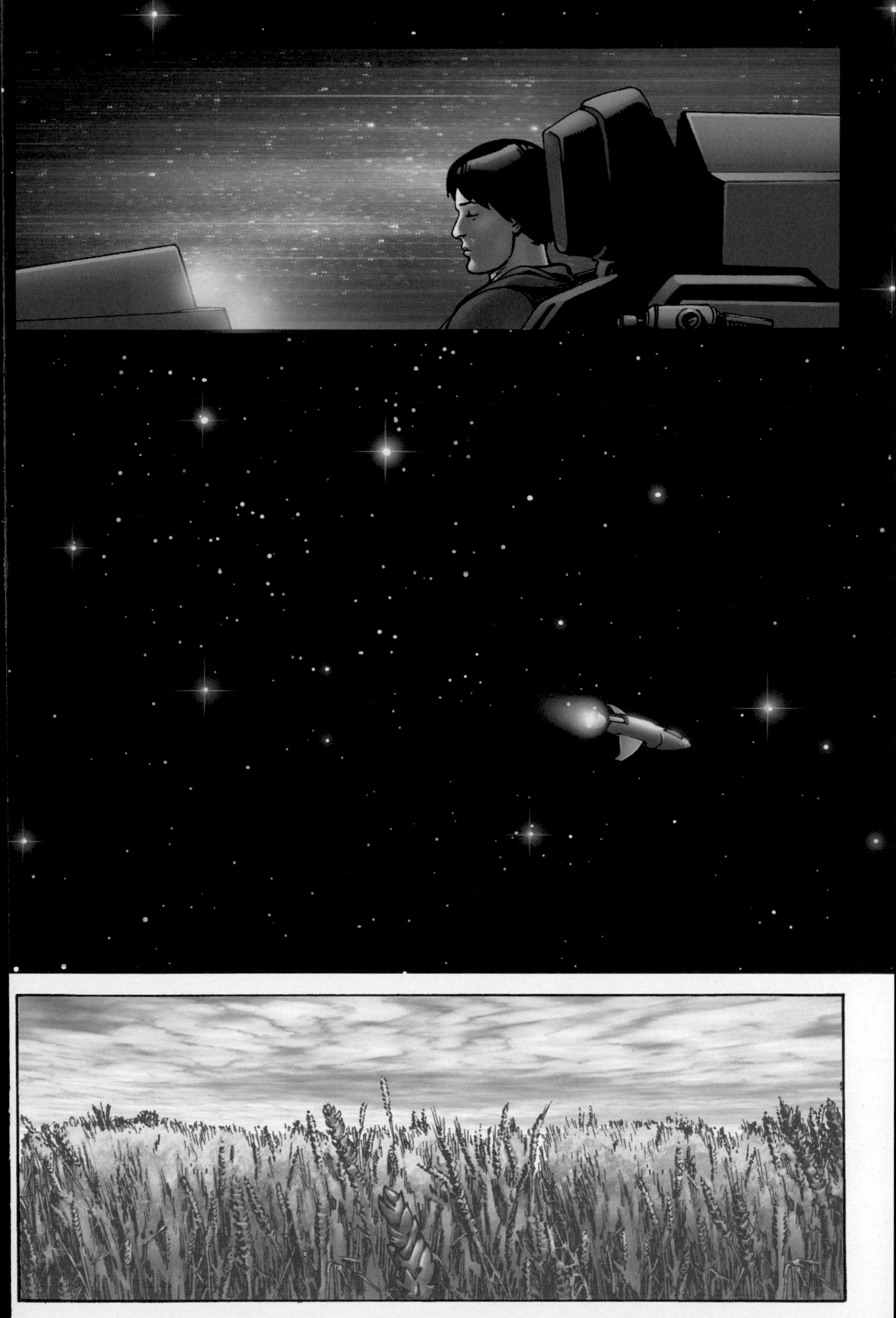

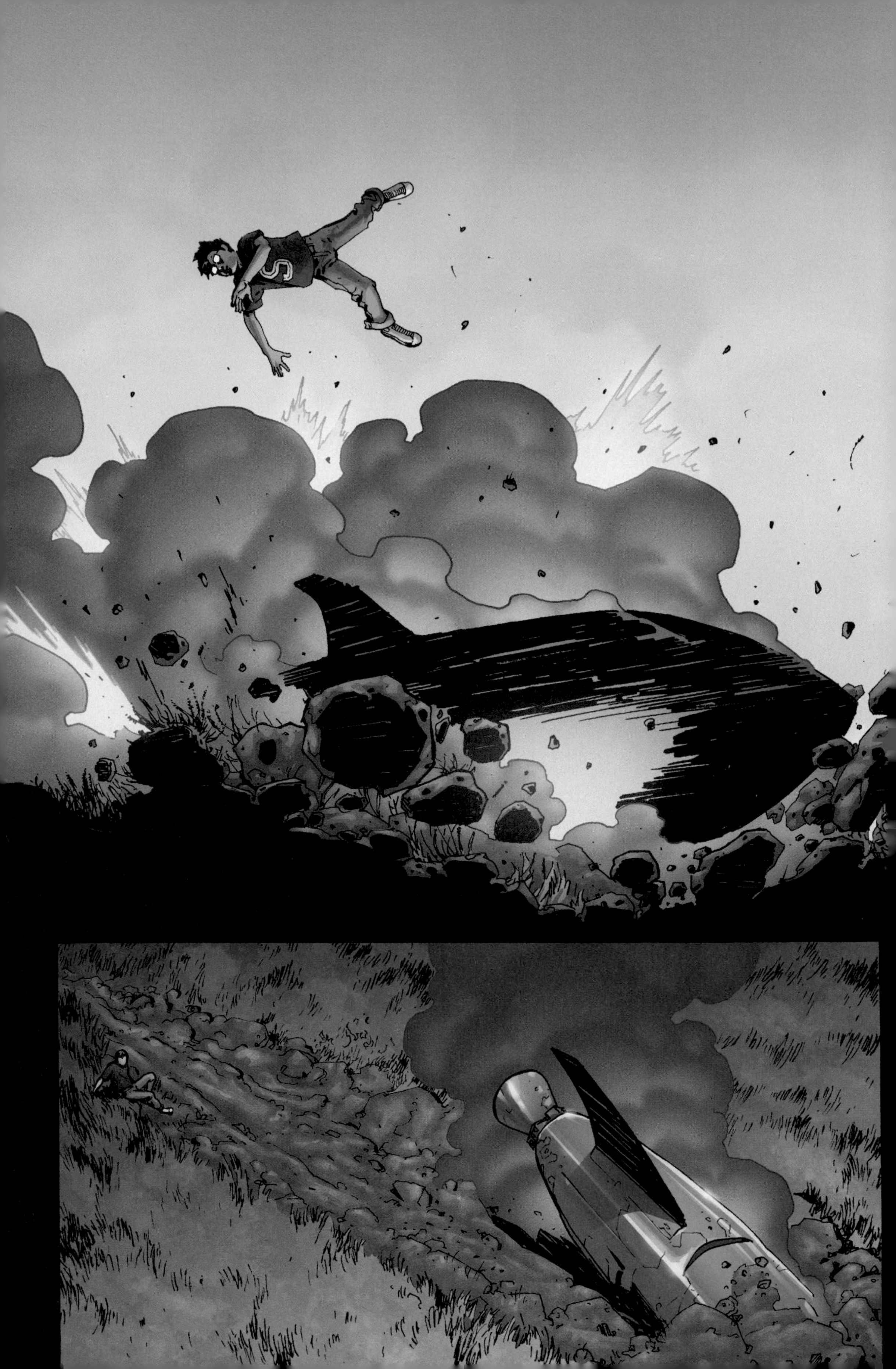

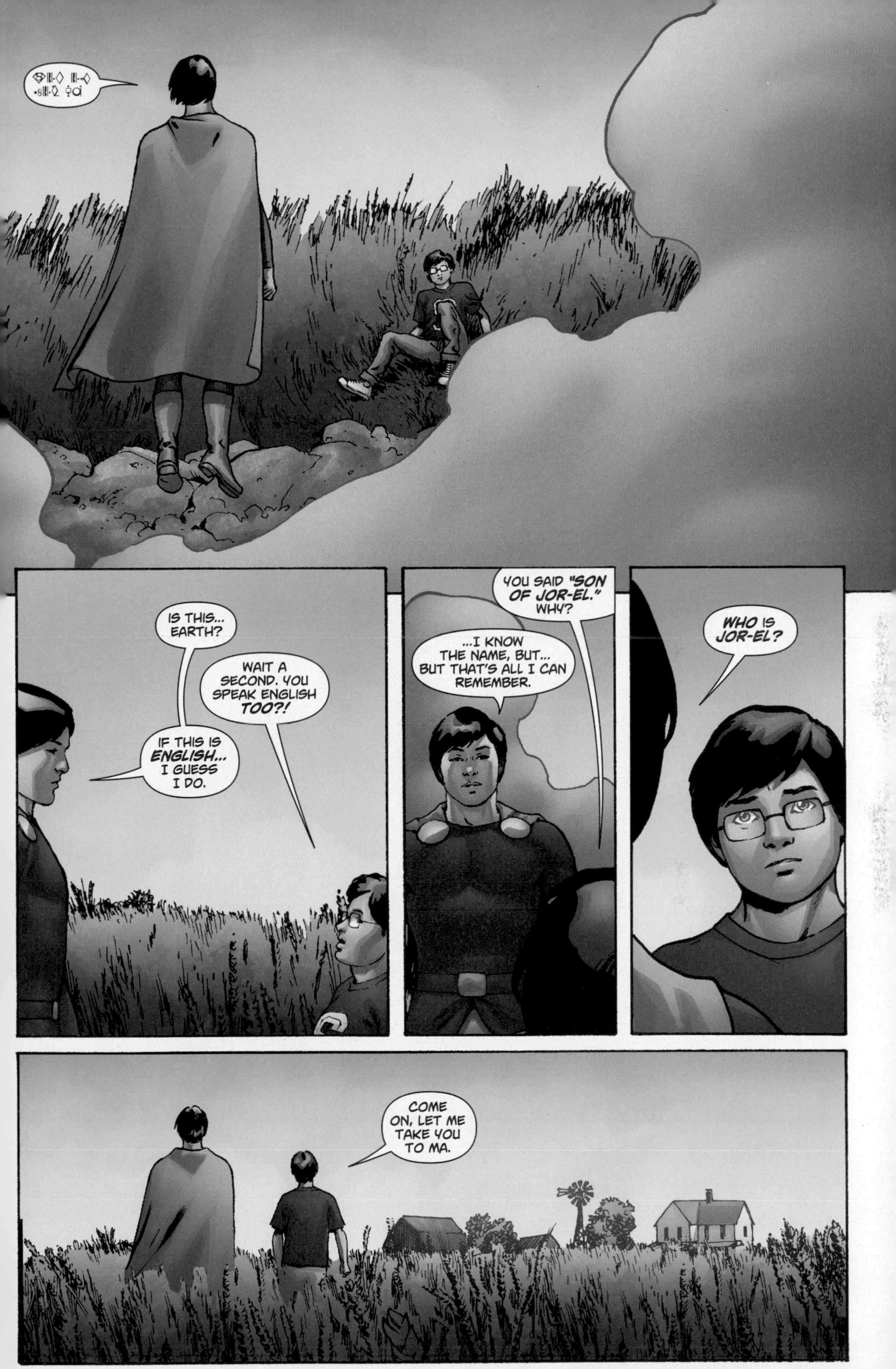
IS THIS... EARTH?
WAIT A SECOND. YOU SPEAK ENGLISH *TOO?!*
IF THIS IS *ENGLISH*... I GUESS I DO.
YOU SAID *"SON OF JOR-EL."* WHY?
...I KNOW THE NAME, BUT... BUT THAT'S ALL I CAN REMEMBER.
WHO IS *JOR-EL?*
COME ON, LET ME TAKE YOU TO MA.

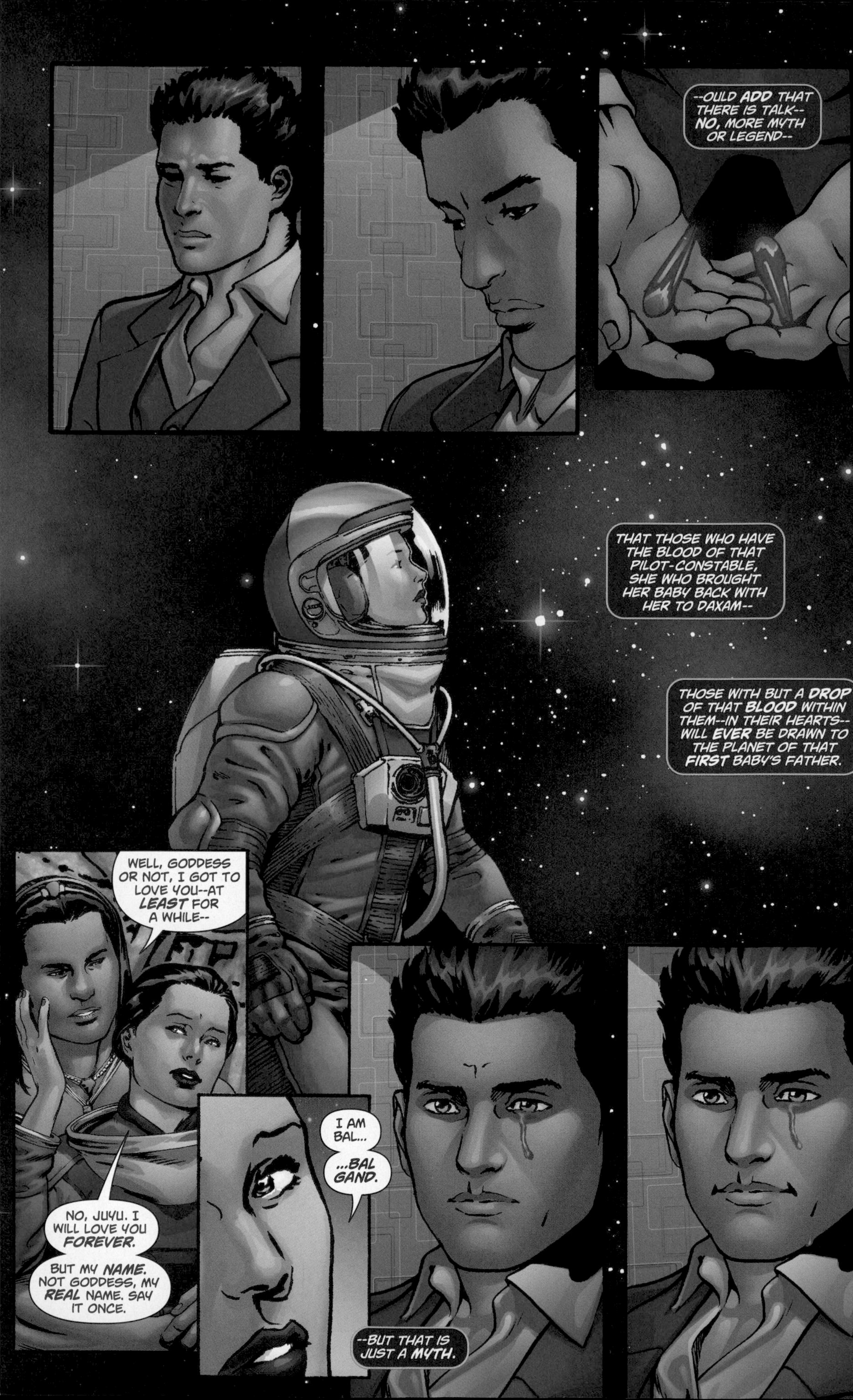

--OULD ADD THAT THERE IS TALK-- NO, MORE MYTH OR LEGEND--
THAT THOSE WHO HAVE THE BLOOD OF THAT PILOT-CONSTABLE, SHE WHO BROUGHT HER BABY BACK WITH HER TO DAXAM--
THOSE WITH BUT A DROP OF THAT BLOOD WITHIN THEM--IN THEIR HEARTS-- WILL EVER BE DRAWN TO THE PLANET OF THAT FIRST BABY'S FATHER.
WELL, GODDESS OR NOT, I GOT TO LOVE YOU--AT LEAST FOR A WHILE--
NO, JUYU. I WILL LOVE YOU FOREVER.
BUT MY NAME. NOT GODDESS, MY REAL NAME. SAY IT ONCE.
I AM BAL...
...BAL GAND.
--BUT THAT IS JUST A MYTH.

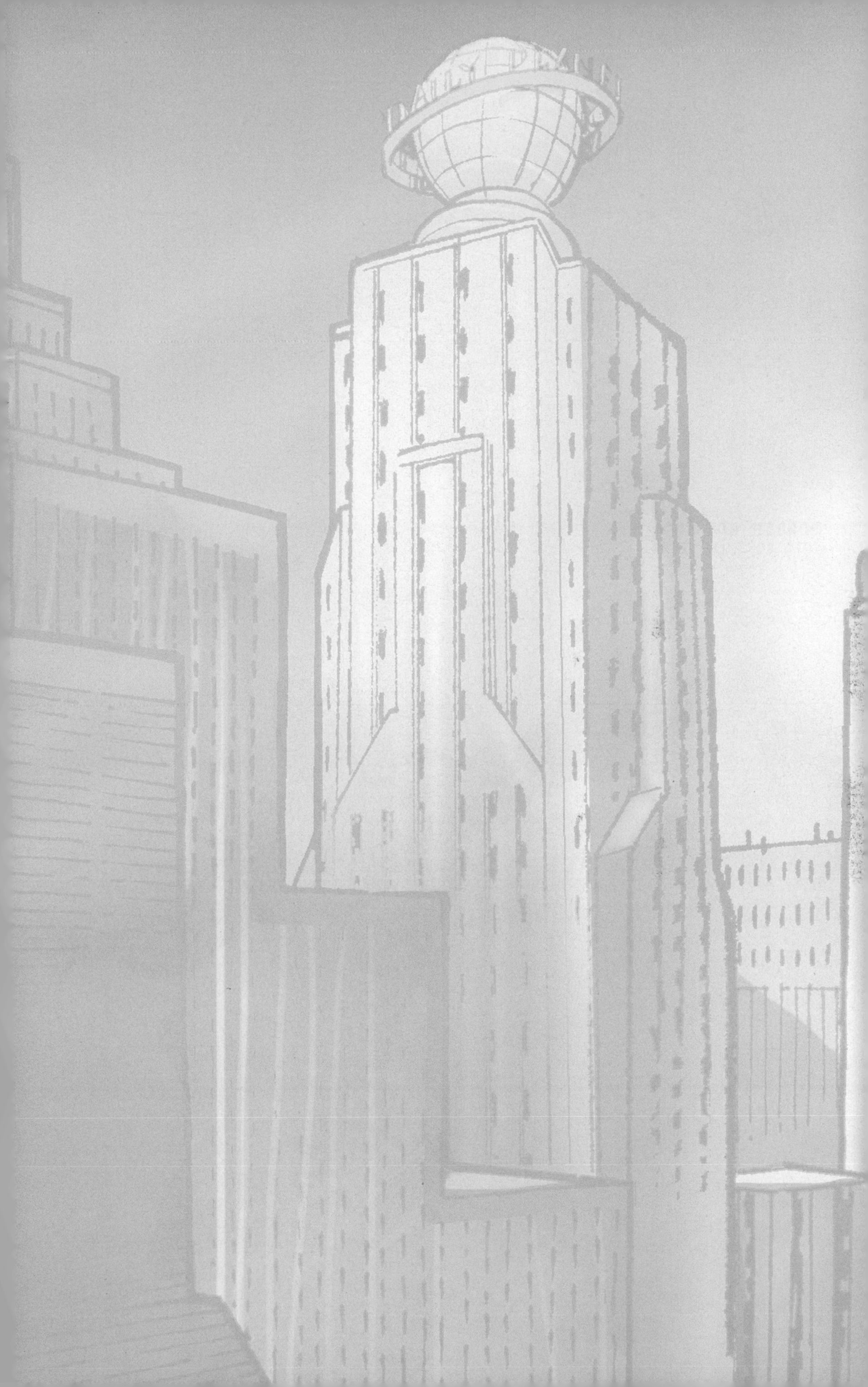

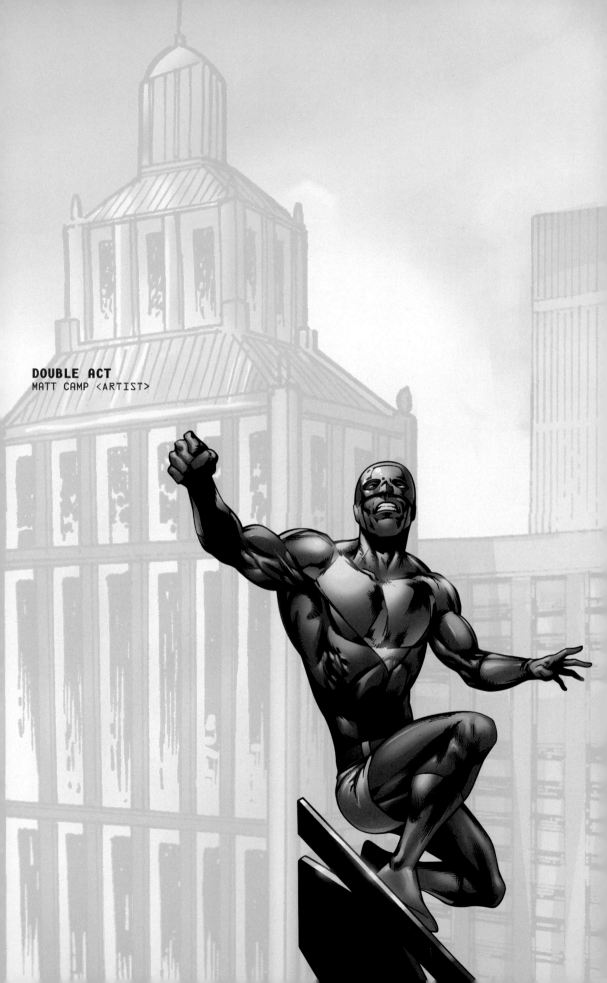

DOUBLE ACT
MATT CAMP <ARTIST>

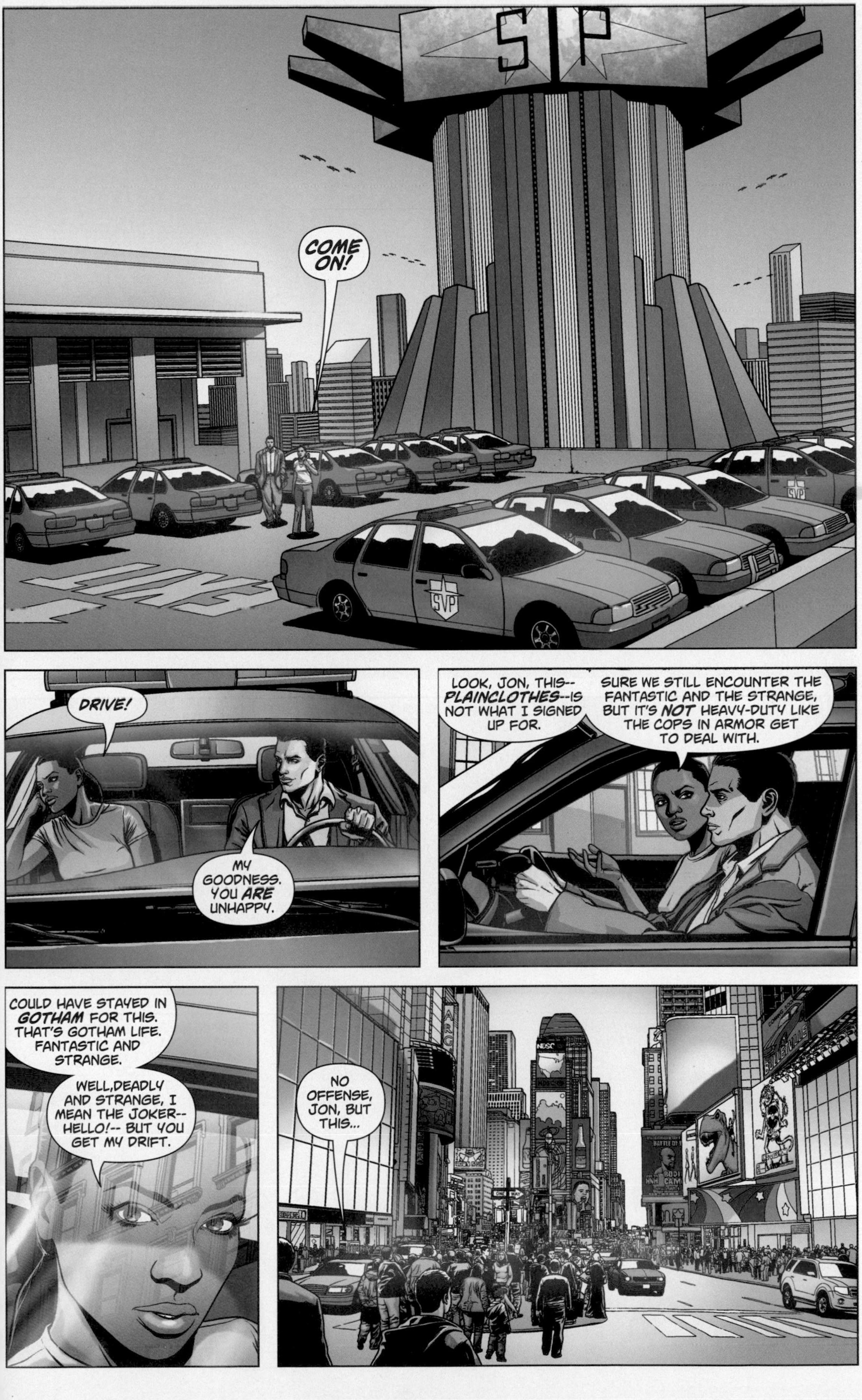
SVP
COME ON!
DRIVE!
MY GOODNESS. YOU *ARE* UNHAPPY.
LOOK, JON, THIS-- *PLAINCLOTHES*--IS NOT WHAT I SIGNED UP FOR.
SURE WE STILL ENCOUNTER THE FANTASTIC AND THE STRANGE, BUT IT'S *NOT* HEAVY-DUTY LIKE THE COPS IN ARMOR GET TO DEAL WITH.
COULD HAVE STAYED IN *GOTHAM* FOR THIS. THAT'S GOTHAM LIFE. FANTASTIC AND STRANGE.
WELL, DEADLY AND STRANGE, I MEAN THE JOKER-- HELLO!-- BUT YOU GET MY DRIFT.
NO OFFENSE, JON, BUT THIS...

"...THIS IS GOING TO *BORE* ME TO TEARS."

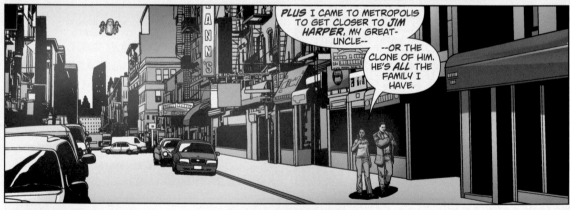

PLUS I CAME TO METROPOLIS TO GET CLOSER TO *JIM HARPER*, MY GREAT-UNCLE--

--OR THE CLONE OF HIM. HE'S *ALL* THE FAMILY I HAVE.

DO YOU *KNOW* WHAT IT'S LIKE TO BE COMPLETELY ALONE, JON?

I'M *SORRY*, JON. I DIDN'T THINK WHEN I SAID THAT. I MEAN--I DON'T KNOW ANYTHING ABOUT YOU.

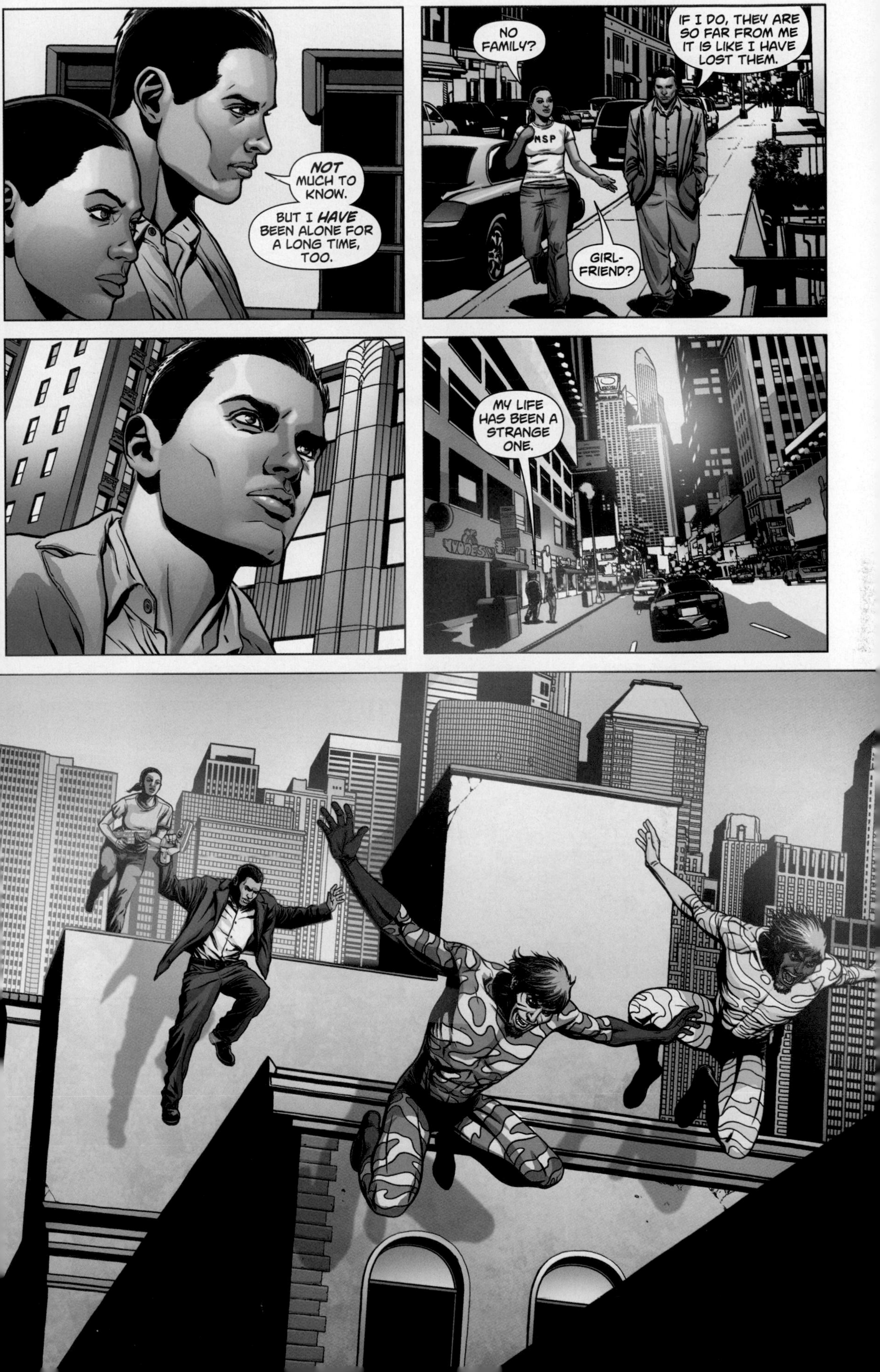
NOT MUCH TO KNOW.
BUT I HAVE BEEN ALONE FOR A LONG TIME, TOO.
NO FAMILY?
IF I DO, THEY ARE SO FAR FROM ME IT IS LIKE I HAVE LOST THEM.
GIRL-FRIEND?
MY LIFE HAS BEEN A STRANGE ONE.
MSP

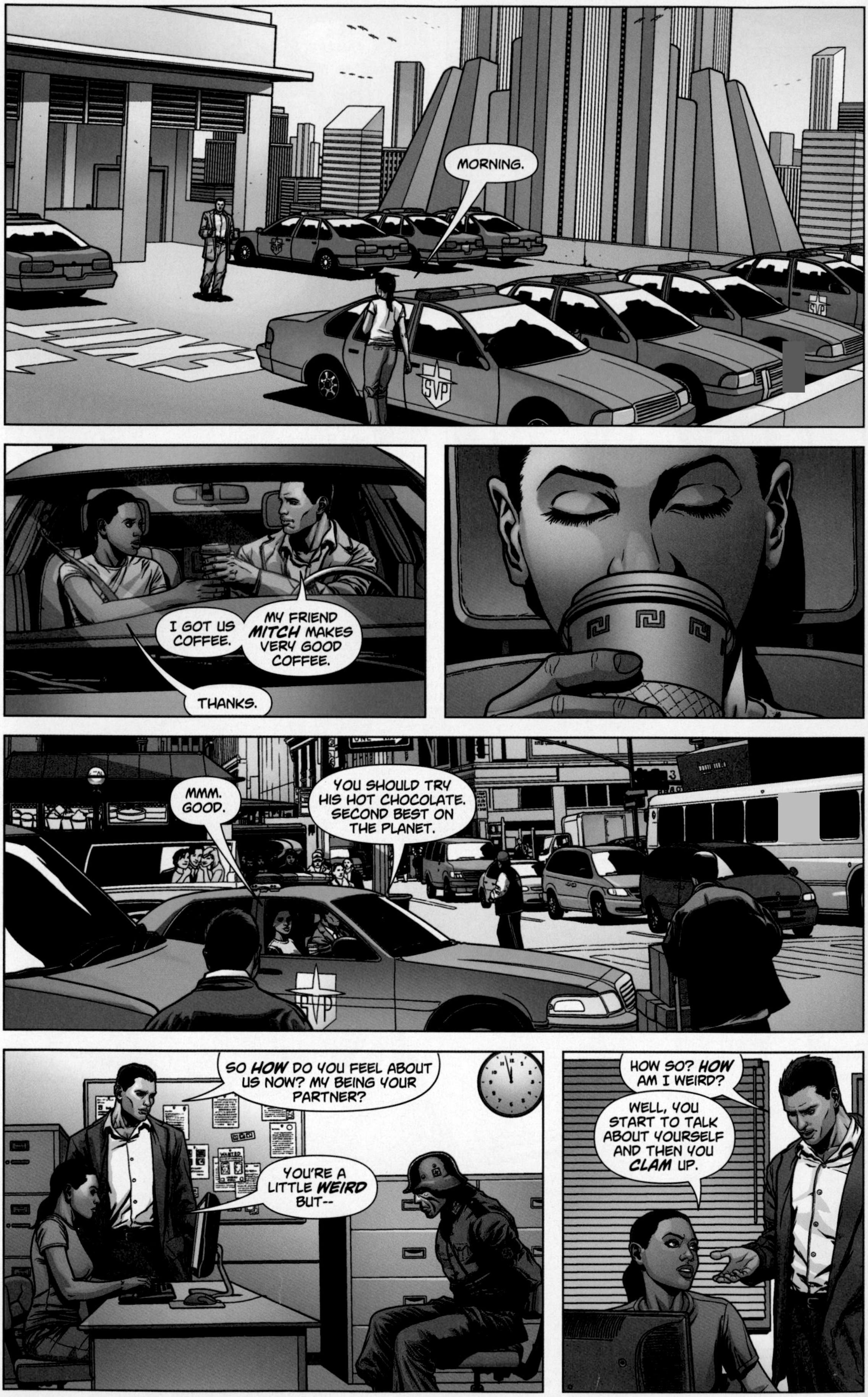
MORNING.
I GOT US COFFEE.
MY FRIEND MITCH MAKES VERY GOOD COFFEE.
THANKS.
MMM. GOOD.
YOU SHOULD TRY HIS HOT CHOCOLATE. SECOND BEST ON THE PLANET.
SO HOW DO YOU FEEL ABOUT US NOW? MY BEING YOUR PARTNER?
YOU'RE A LITTLE WEIRD BUT--
HOW SO? HOW AM I WEIRD?
WELL, YOU START TO TALK ABOUT YOURSELF AND THEN YOU CLAM UP.

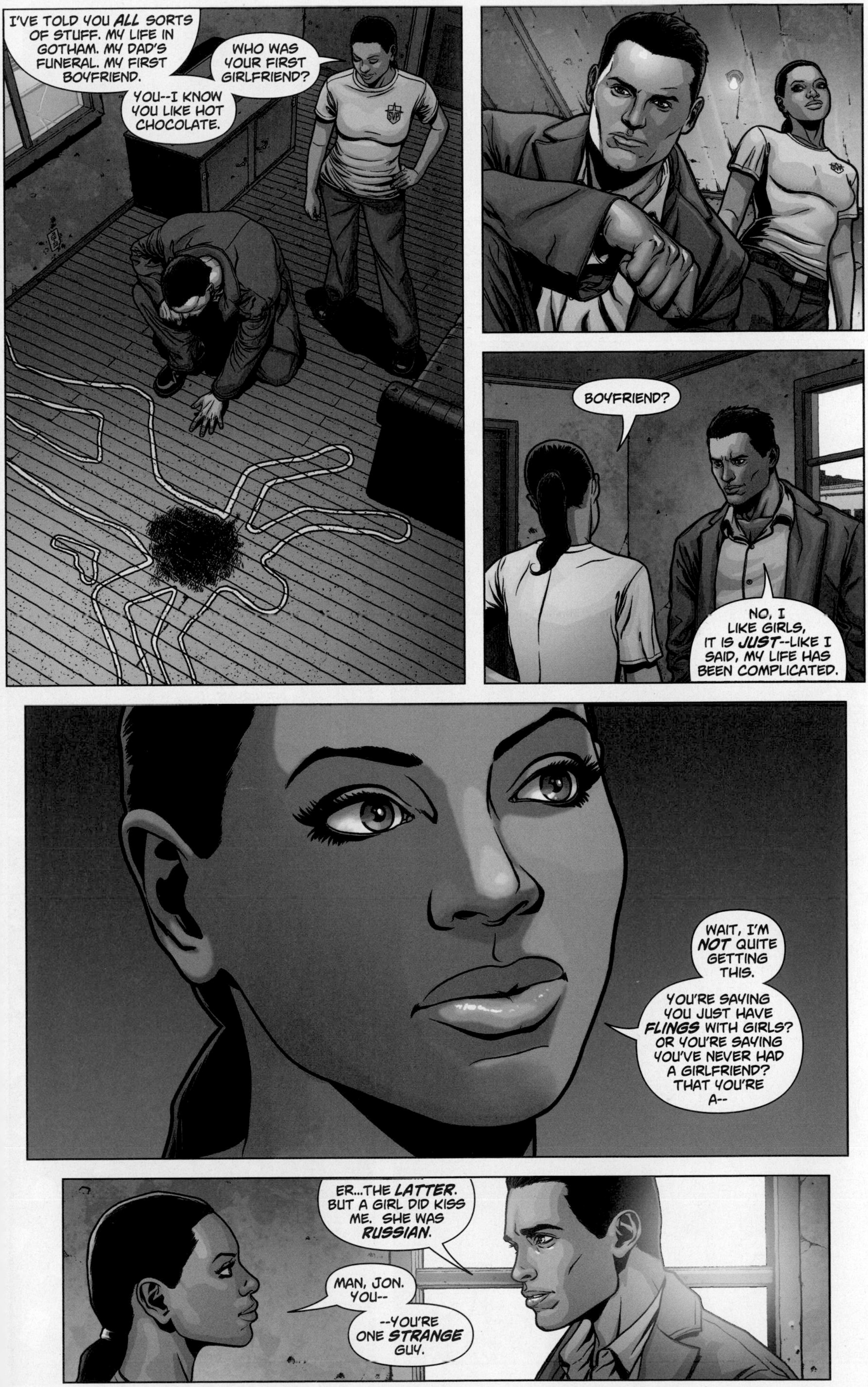
I'VE TOLD YOU ALL SORTS OF STUFF. MY LIFE IN GOTHAM. MY DAD'S FUNERAL. MY FIRST BOYFRIEND.
YOU--I KNOW YOU LIKE HOT CHOCOLATE.
WHO WAS YOUR FIRST GIRLFRIEND?
BOYFRIEND?
NO, I LIKE GIRLS, IT IS JUST--LIKE I SAID, MY LIFE HAS BEEN COMPLICATED.
WAIT, I'M NOT QUITE GETTING THIS.
YOU'RE SAYING YOU JUST HAVE FLINGS WITH GIRLS? OR YOU'RE SAYING YOU'VE NEVER HAD A GIRLFRIEND? THAT YOU'RE A--
ER...THE LATTER. BUT A GIRL DID KISS ME. SHE WAS RUSSIAN.
MAN, JON. YOU--
--YOU'RE ONE STRANGE GUY.

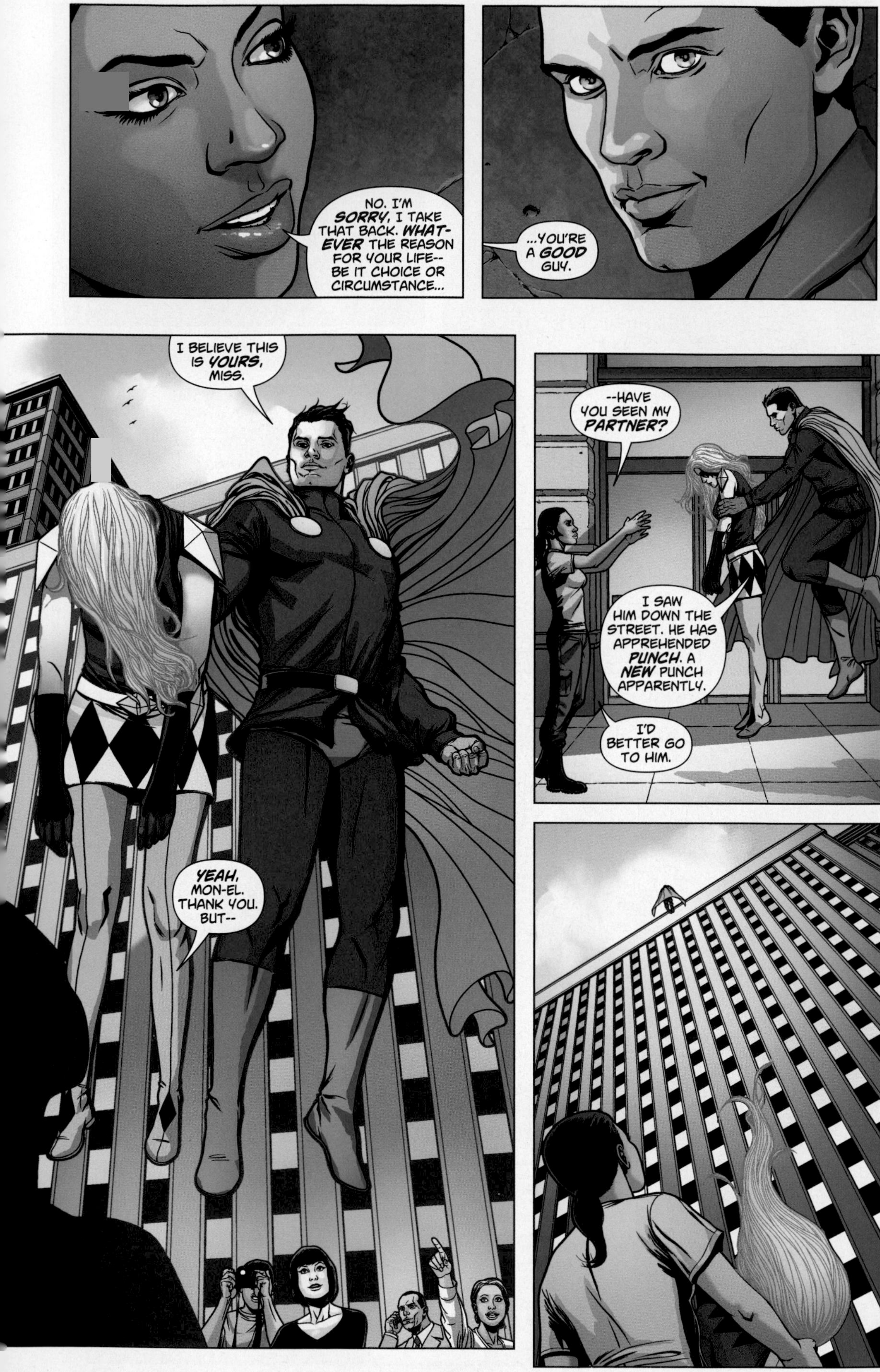
NO. I'M SORRY, I TAKE THAT BACK. WHATEVER THE REASON FOR YOUR LIFE-- BE IT CHOICE OR CIRCUMSTANCE...
...YOU'RE A GOOD GUY.
I BELIEVE THIS IS YOURS, MISS.
YEAH, MON-EL. THANK YOU. BUT--
--HAVE YOU SEEN MY PARTNER?
I SAW HIM DOWN THE STREET. HE HAS APPREHENDED PUNCH. A NEW PUNCH APPARENTLY.
I'D BETTER GO TO HIM.

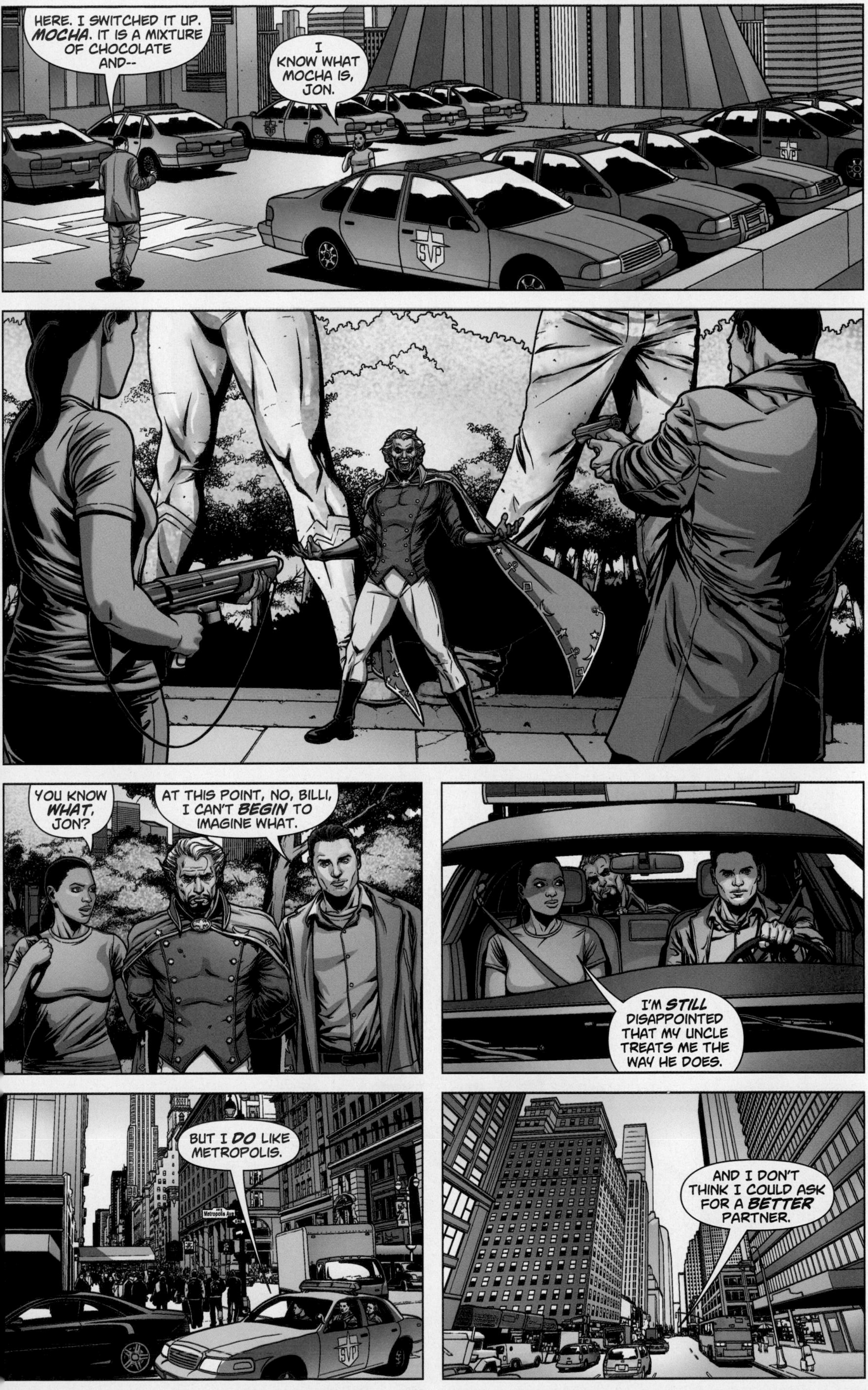

HERE. I SWITCHED IT UP. MOCHA. IT IS A MIXTURE OF CHOCOLATE AND--
I KNOW WHAT MOCHA IS, JON.
SVP
YOU KNOW WHAT, JON?
AT THIS POINT, NO, BILLI, I CAN'T BEGIN TO IMAGINE WHAT.
I'M STILL DISAPPOINTED THAT MY UNCLE TREATS ME THE WAY HE DOES.
BUT I DO LIKE METROPOLIS.
Metropolis Ave
AND I DON'T THINK I COULD ASK FOR A BETTER PARTNER.

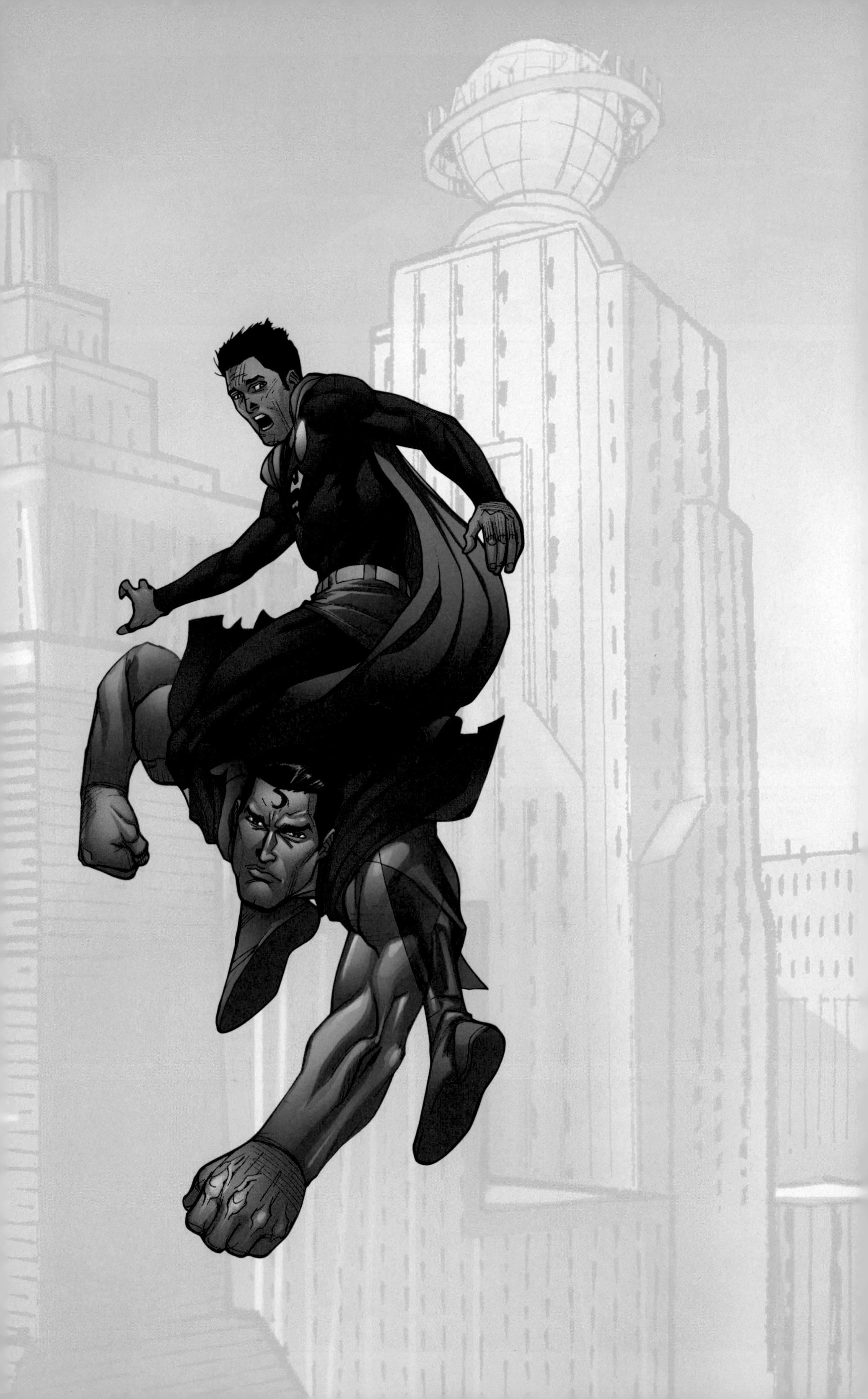

COVER BY CAFU WITH SANTIAGO ARCAS

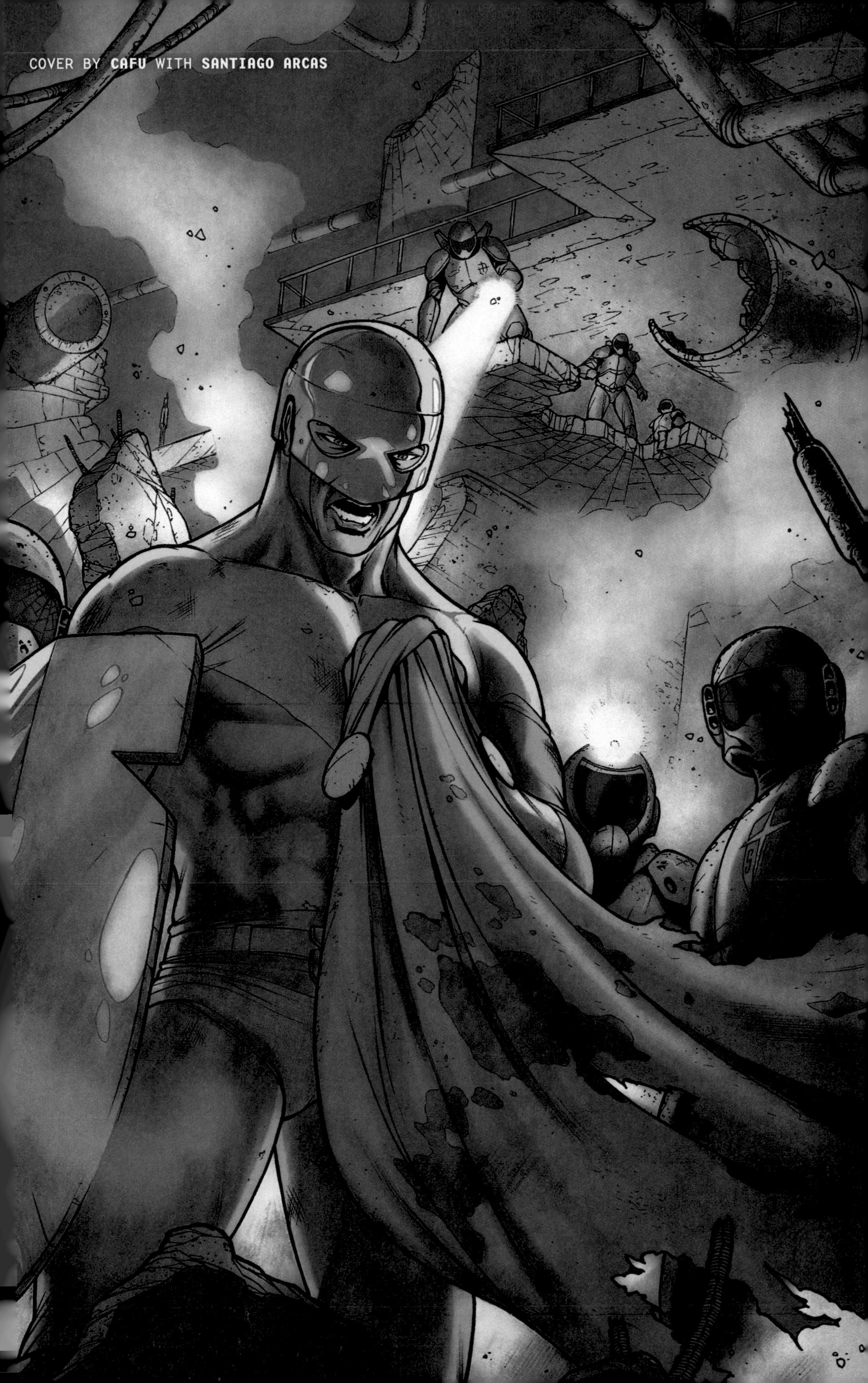

‹PREVIOUSLY IN›
SUPERMAN:CODENAME: PATRIOT

In an effort to discredit Kryptonians in the eyes of the people of Earth, General Sam Lane, Lois Lane's father, staged a fight in the sewers of Metropolis so that it looked like the heroes Supergirl, Nightwing and Flamebird murdered Mon-El. In reality, Mon-El was fighting the villains Metallo, Reactron and Mirabai, who used her magic powers to make them appear to be the heroes. During the conflict, the trio detonated a bomb, destroying the sewers.

Meanwhile, General Lane stopped a rogue Kryptonian from killing the President of the United States in front of the world's media. What the public doesn't know is that Lane orchestrated the Kryptonian's attack. Now Lane is seen as the hero of Earth, and Kryptonians look like a bigger threat than ever.

As for Mon-El, his true fate remains a mystery...

DOWN TIME
FERNANDO DAGNINO ‹PENCILLER›

RAÚL FERNANDEZ ‹INKER›

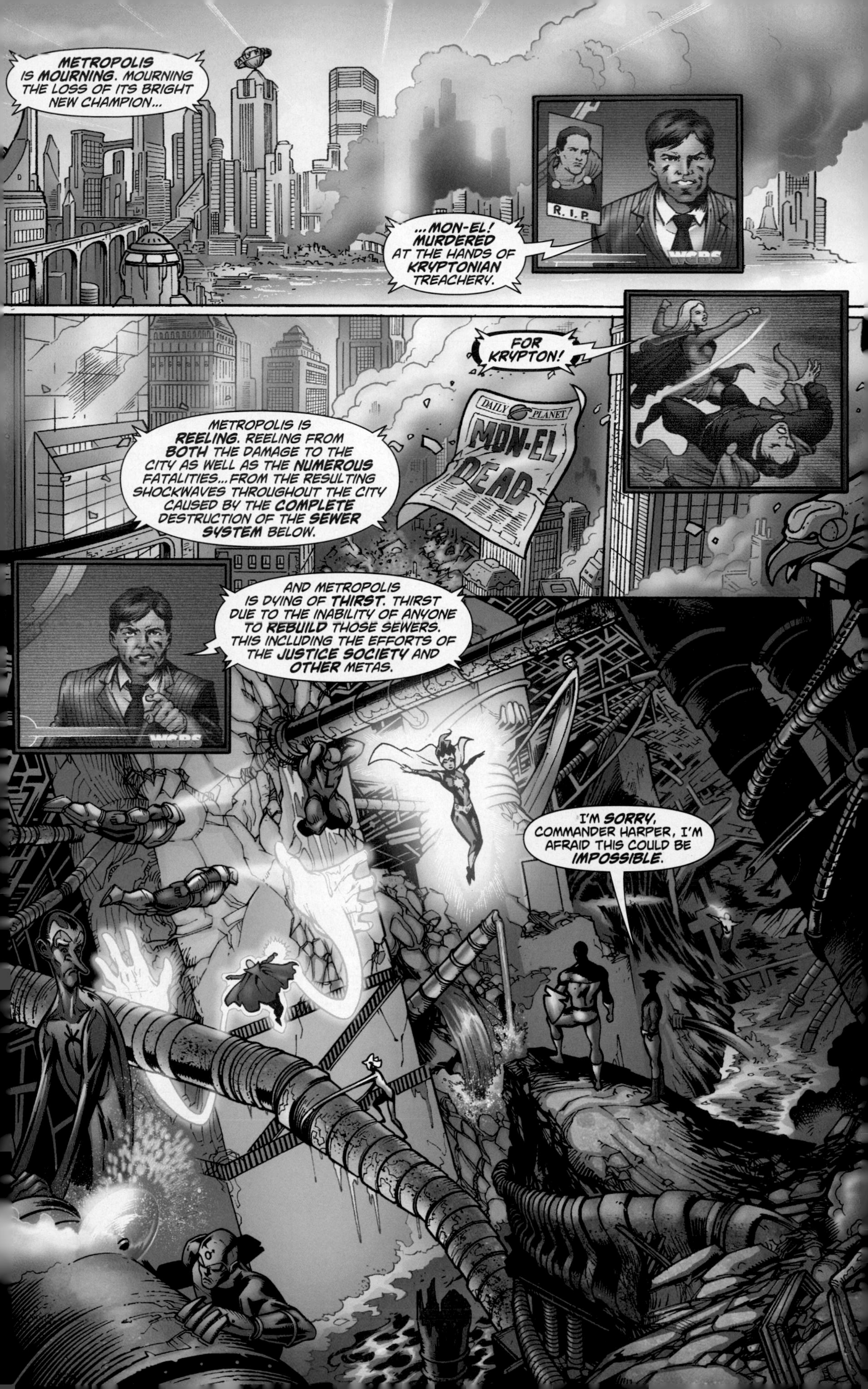
METROPOLIS IS MOURNING. MOURNING THE LOSS OF ITS BRIGHT NEW CHAMPION...
...MON-EL! MURDERED AT THE HANDS OF KRYPTONIAN TREACHERY.
R.I.P.
WCBS
FOR KRYPTON!
DAILY PLANET
MON-EL DEAD
METROPOLIS IS REELING. REELING FROM BOTH THE DAMAGE TO THE CITY AS WELL AS THE NUMEROUS FATALITIES...FROM THE RESULTING SHOCKWAVES THROUGHOUT THE CITY CAUSED BY THE COMPLETE DESTRUCTION OF THE SEWER SYSTEM BELOW.
AND METROPOLIS IS DYING OF THIRST. THIRST DUE TO THE INABILITY OF ANYONE TO REBUILD THOSE SEWERS. THIS INCLUDING THE EFFORTS OF THE JUSTICE SOCIETY AND OTHER METAS.
WCBS
I'M SORRY, COMMANDER HARPER, I'M AFRAID THIS COULD BE IMPOSSIBLE.

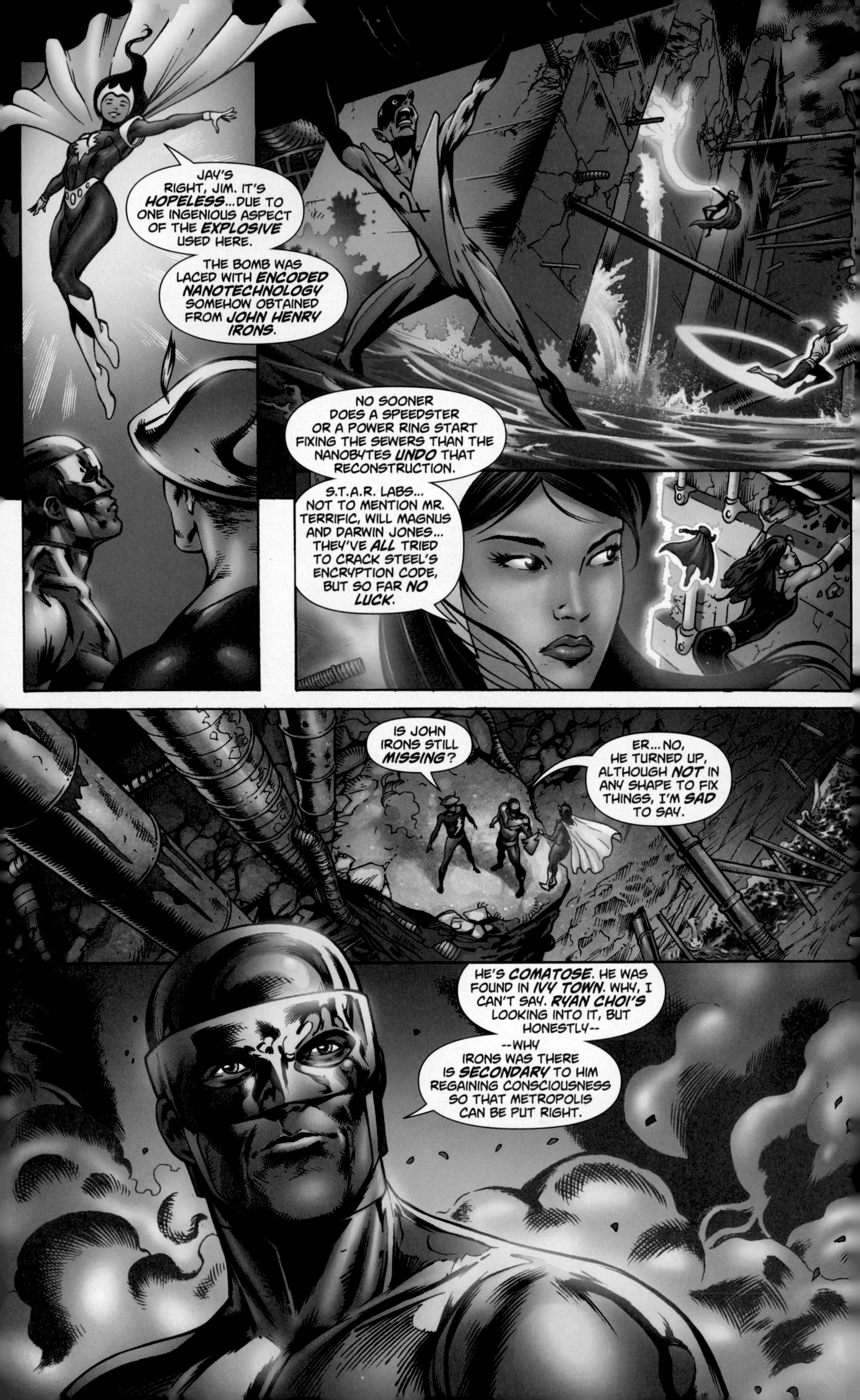

JAY'S RIGHT, JIM. IT'S HOPELESS...DUE TO ONE INGENIOUS ASPECT OF THE EXPLOSIVE USED HERE.
THE BOMB WAS LACED WITH ENCODED NANOTECHNOLOGY SOMEHOW OBTAINED FROM JOHN HENRY IRONS.
NO SOONER DOES A SPEEDSTER OR A POWER RING START FIXING THE SEWERS THAN THE NANOBYTES UNDO THAT RECONSTRUCTION.
S.T.A.R. LABS... NOT TO MENTION MR. TERRIFIC, WILL MAGNUS AND DARWIN JONES... THEY'VE ALL TRIED TO CRACK STEEL'S ENCRYPTION CODE, BUT SO FAR NO LUCK.
IS JOHN IRONS STILL MISSING?
ER...NO, HE TURNED UP, ALTHOUGH NOT IN ANY SHAPE TO FIX THINGS, I'M SAD TO SAY.
HE'S COMATOSE. HE WAS FOUND IN IVY TOWN. WHY, I CAN'T SAY. RYAN CHOI'S LOOKING INTO IT, BUT HONESTLY--
--WHY IRONS WAS THERE IS SECONDARY TO HIM REGAINING CONSCIOUSNESS SO THAT METROPOLIS CAN BE PUT RIGHT.

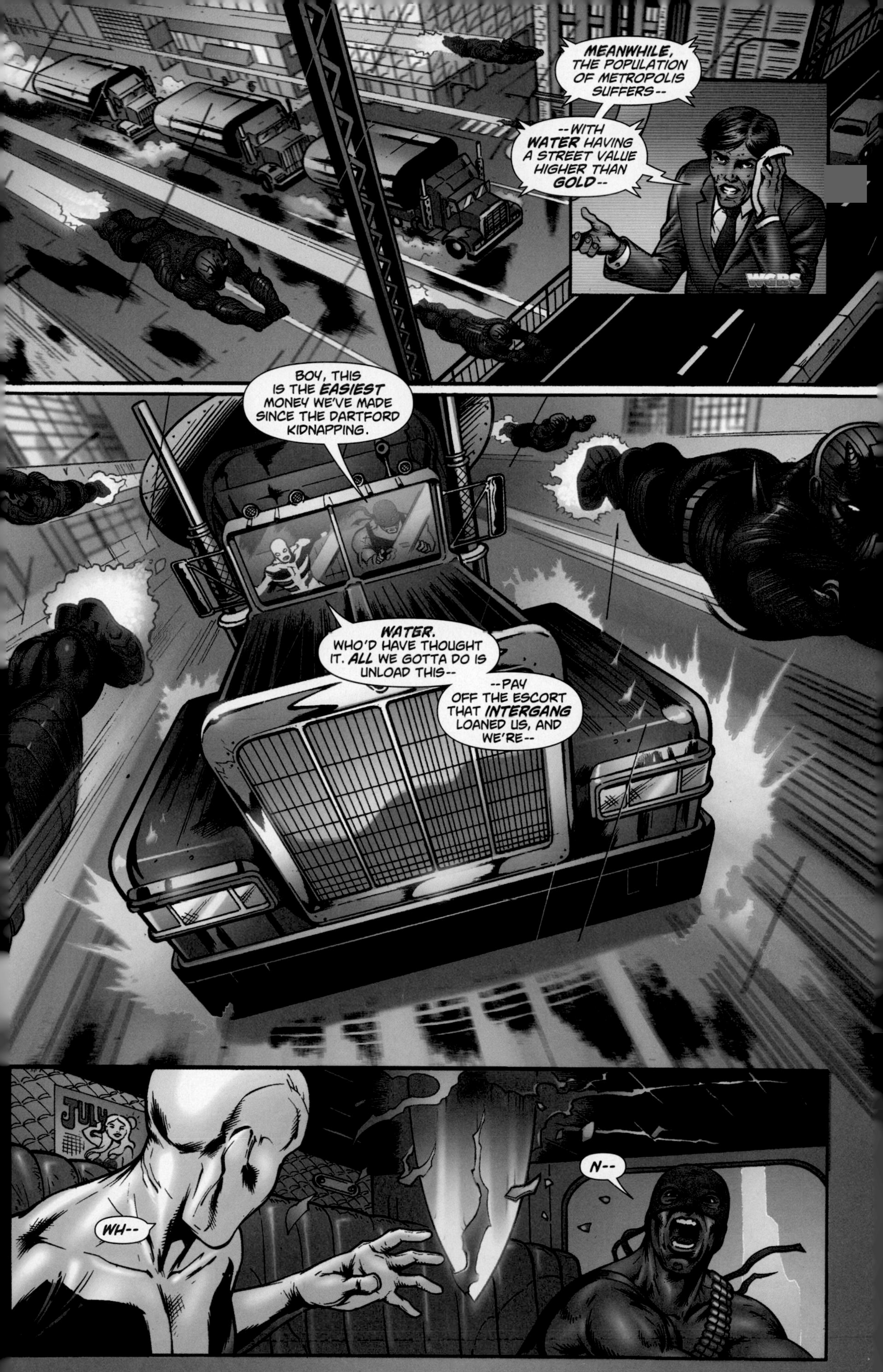
MEANWHILE, THE POPULATION OF METROPOLIS SUFFERS--
--WITH WATER HAVING A STREET VALUE HIGHER THAN GOLD--
WGBS
BOY, THIS IS THE EASIEST MONEY WE'VE MADE SINCE THE DARTFORD KIDNAPPING.
WATER. WHO'D HAVE THOUGHT IT. ALL WE GOTTA DO IS UNLOAD THIS--
--PAY OFF THE ESCORT THAT INTERGANG LOANED US, AND WE'RE--
JULY
WH--
N--

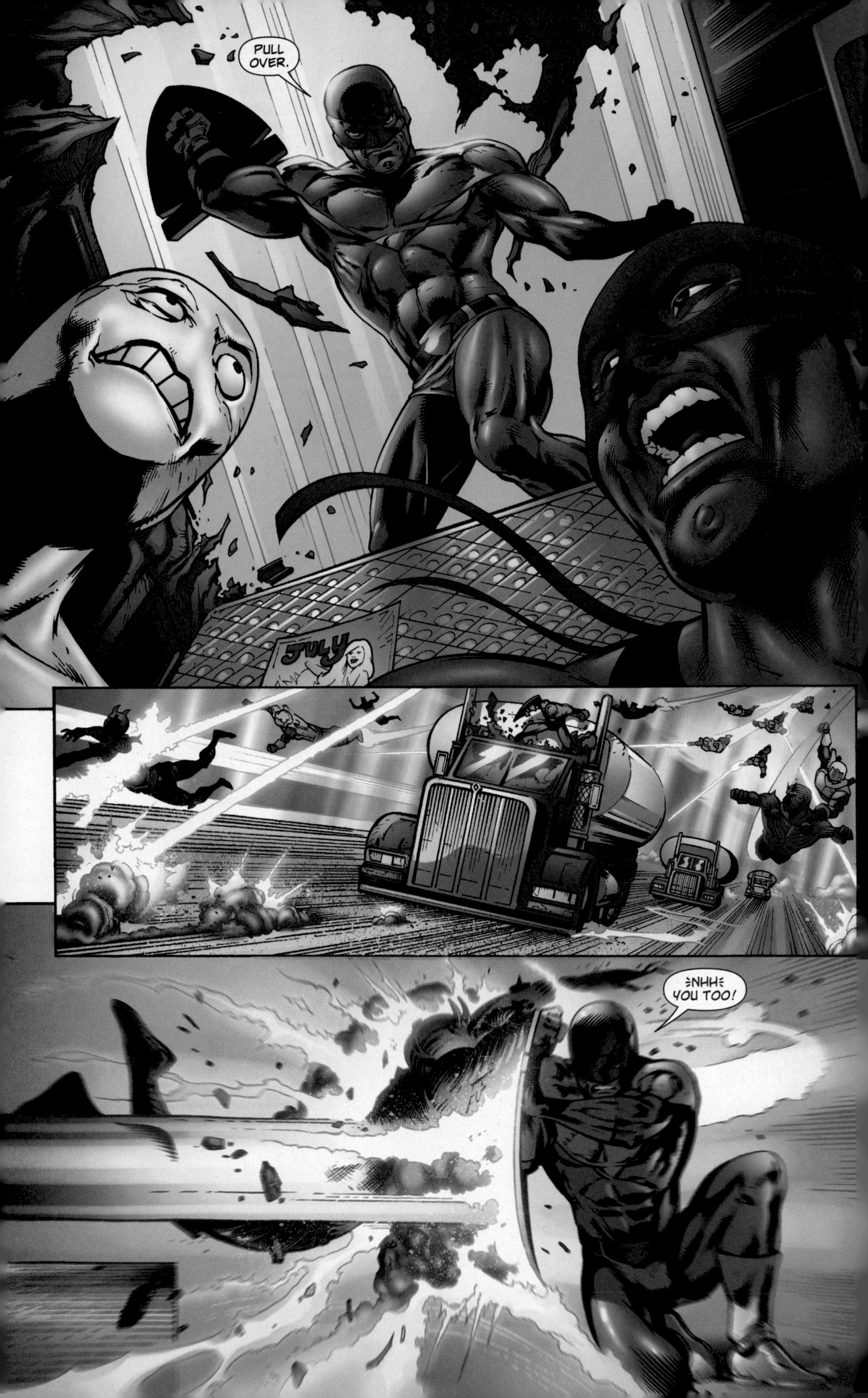
PULL OVER.
JULY
NHH YOU TOO!

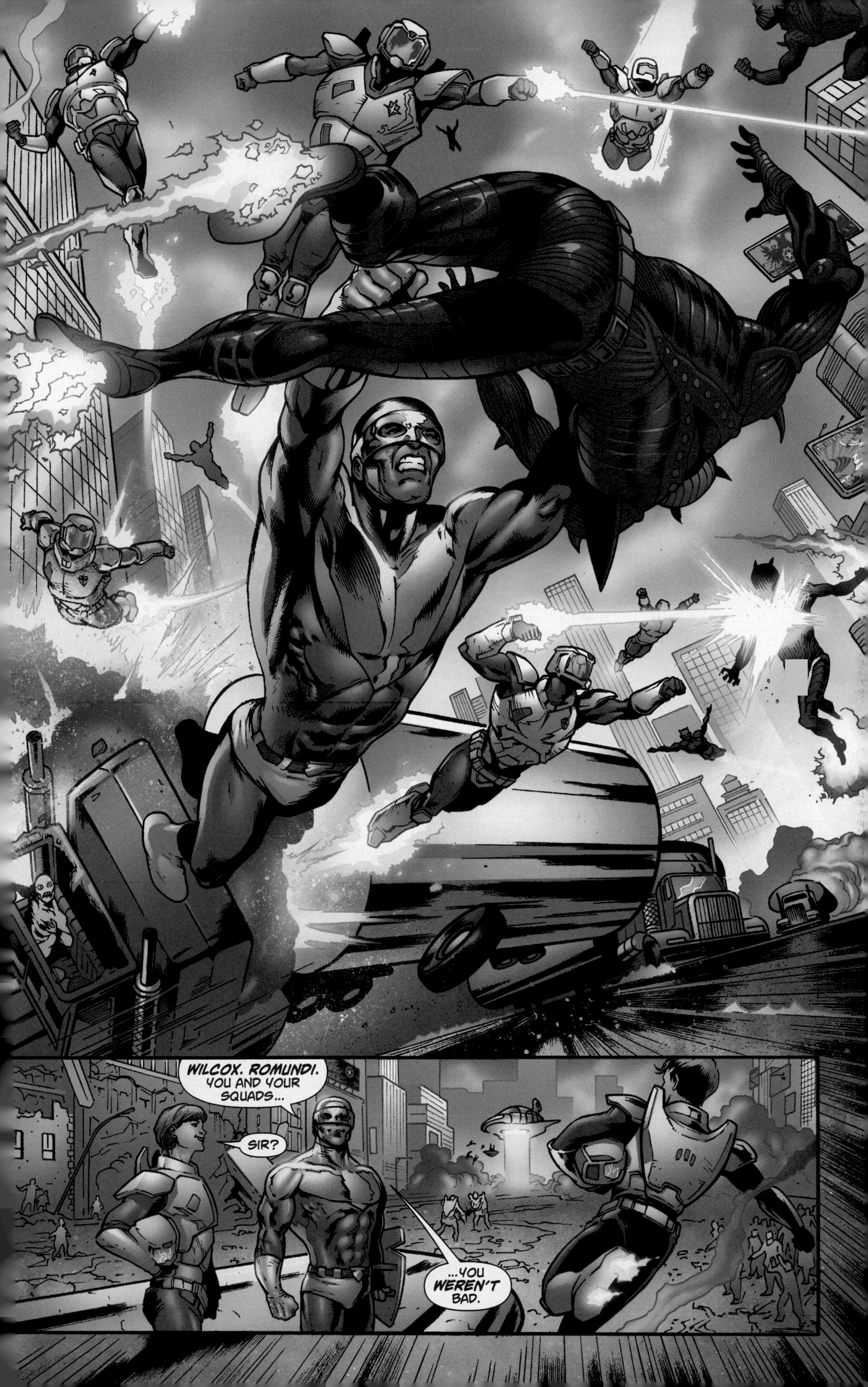
WILCOX. ROMUNDI. YOU AND YOUR SQUADS...
SIR?
...YOU WEREN'T BAD.

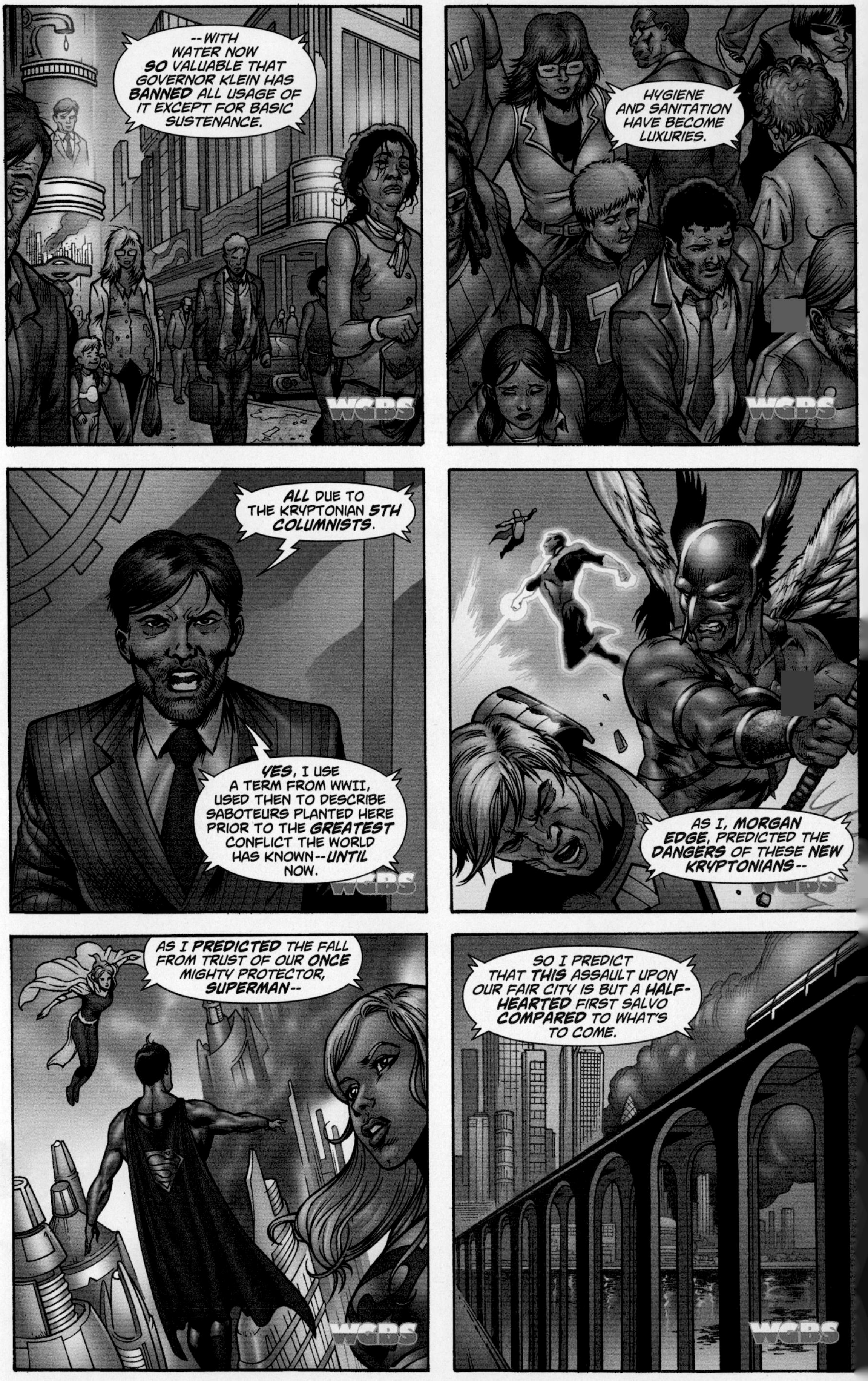
--WITH WATER NOW SO VALUABLE THAT GOVERNOR KLEIN HAS BANNED ALL USAGE OF IT EXCEPT FOR BASIC SUSTENANCE.
HYGIENE AND SANITATION HAVE BECOME LUXURIES.
ALL DUE TO THE KRYPTONIAN 5TH COLUMNISTS.
YES, I USE A TERM FROM WWII, USED THEN TO DESCRIBE SABOTEURS PLANTED HERE PRIOR TO THE GREATEST CONFLICT THE WORLD HAS KNOWN--UNTIL NOW.
AS I, MORGAN EDGE, PREDICTED THE DANGERS OF THESE NEW KRYPTONIANS--
AS I PREDICTED THE FALL FROM TRUST OF OUR ONCE MIGHTY PROTECTOR, SUPERMAN--
SO I PREDICT THAT THIS ASSAULT UPON OUR FAIR CITY IS BUT A HALF-HEARTED FIRST SALVO COMPARED TO WHAT'S TO COME.

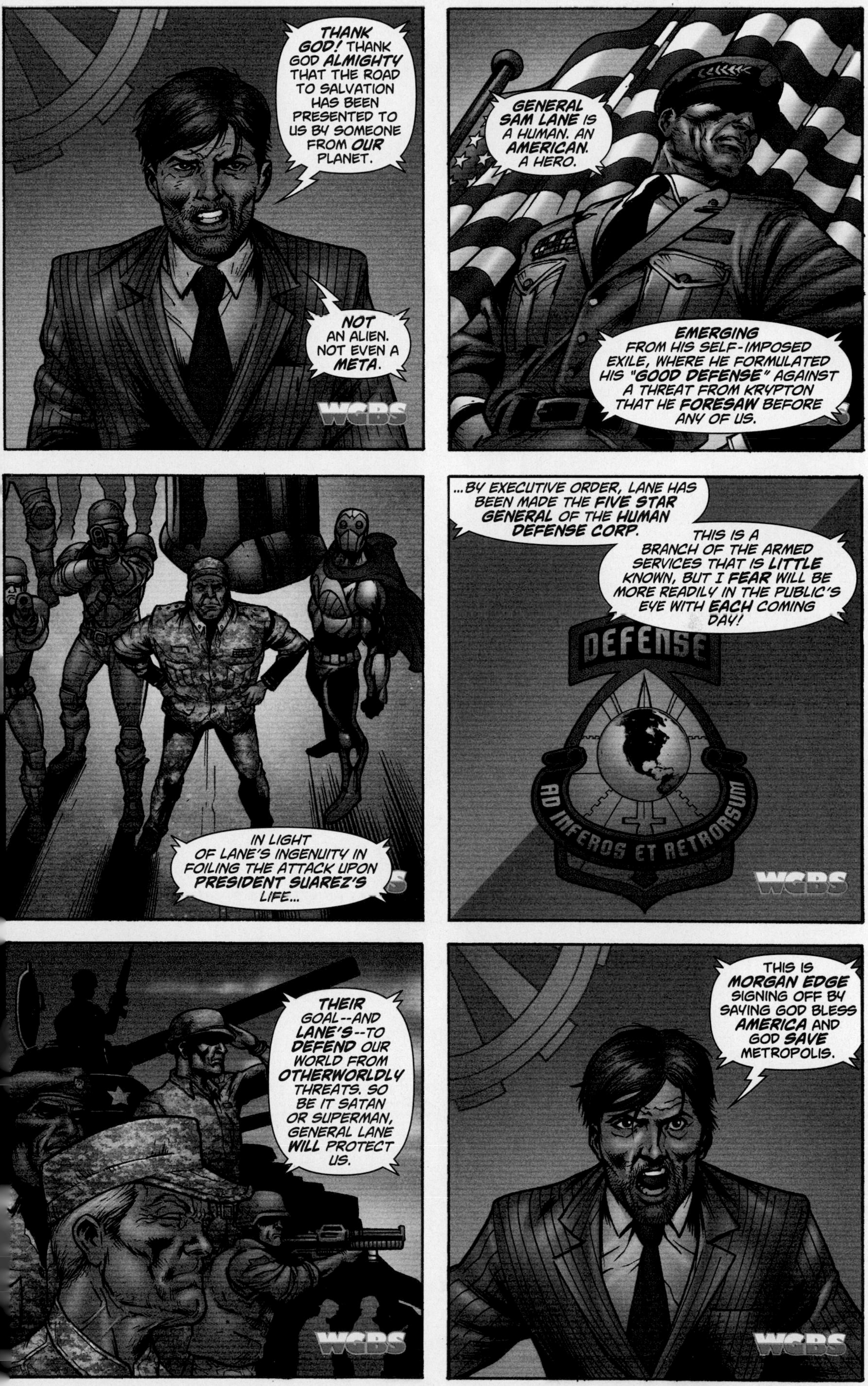
THANK GOD! THANK GOD ALMIGHTY THAT THE ROAD TO SALVATION HAS BEEN PRESENTED TO US BY SOMEONE FROM OUR PLANET.
NOT AN ALIEN. NOT EVEN A META.
WGBS
GENERAL SAM LANE IS A HUMAN. AN AMERICAN. A HERO.
EMERGING FROM HIS SELF-IMPOSED EXILE, WHERE HE FORMULATED HIS "GOOD DEFENSE" AGAINST A THREAT FROM KRYPTON THAT HE FORESAW BEFORE ANY OF US.
IN LIGHT OF LANE'S INGENUITY IN FOILING THE ATTACK UPON PRESIDENT SUAREZ'S LIFE...
...BY EXECUTIVE ORDER, LANE HAS BEEN MADE THE FIVE STAR GENERAL OF THE HUMAN DEFENSE CORP.
THIS IS A BRANCH OF THE ARMED SERVICES THAT IS LITTLE KNOWN, BUT I FEAR WILL BE MORE READILY IN THE PUBLIC'S EYE WITH EACH COMING DAY!
DEFENSE
AD INFEROS ET RETRORSUM
WGBS
THEIR GOAL--AND LANE'S--TO DEFEND OUR WORLD FROM OTHERWORLDLY THREATS. SO BE IT SATAN OR SUPERMAN, GENERAL LANE WILL PROTECT US.
WGBS
THIS IS MORGAN EDGE SIGNING OFF BY SAYING GOD BLESS AMERICA AND GOD SAVE METROPOLIS.
WGBS

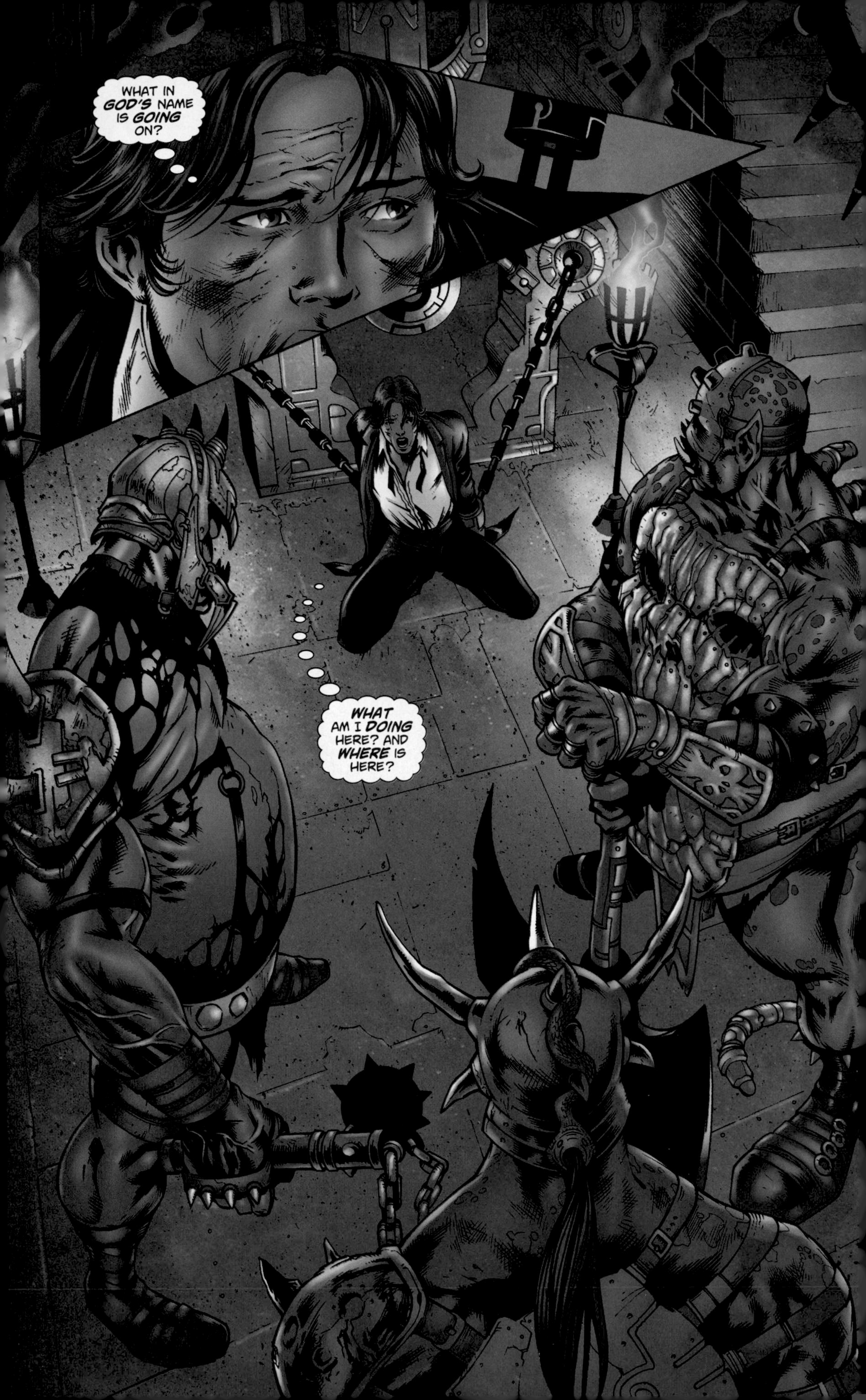
WHAT IN GOD'S NAME IS GOING ON?
WHAT AM I DOING HERE? AND WHERE IS HERE?

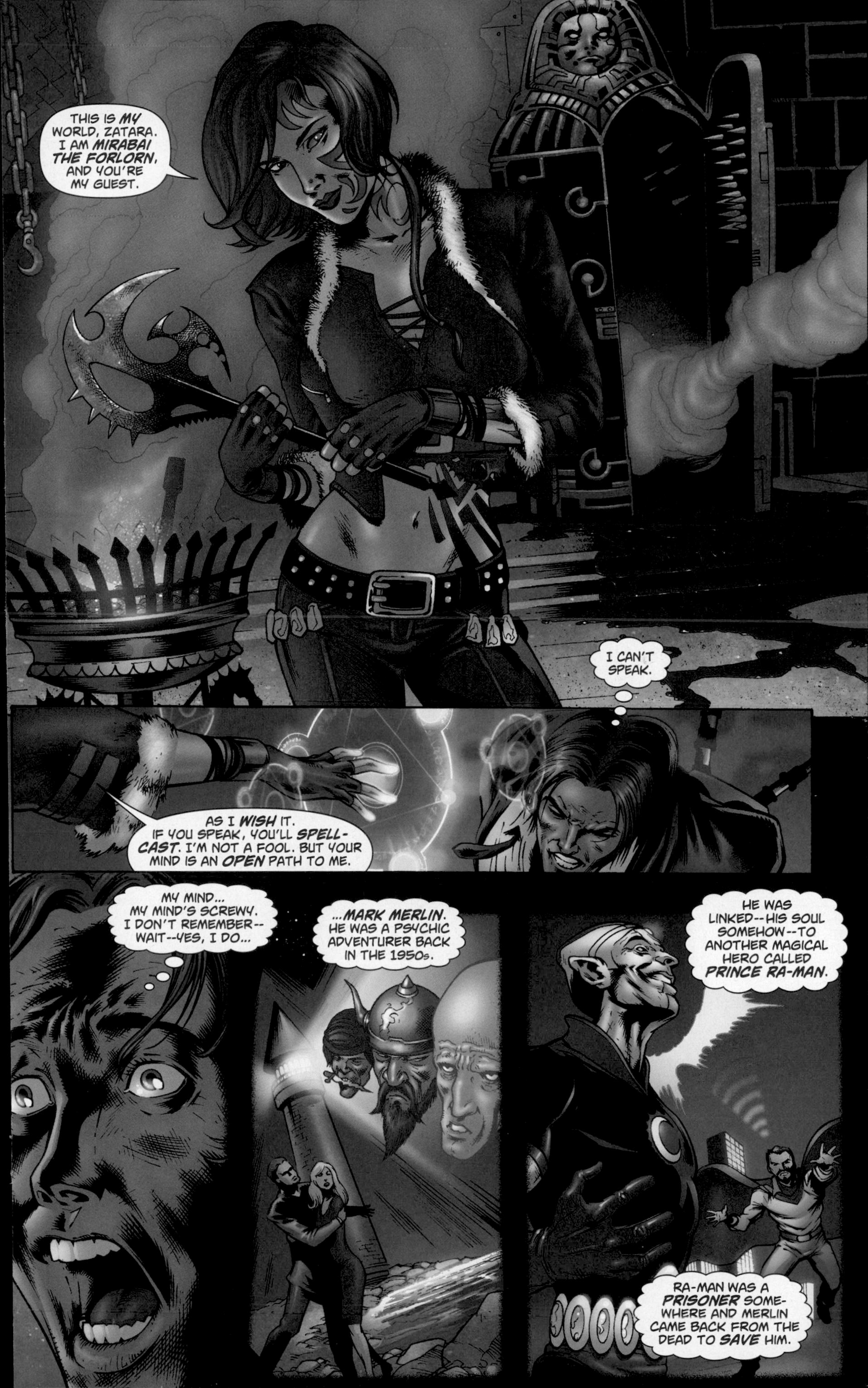
THIS IS MY WORLD, ZATARA. I AM MIRABAI THE FORLORN, AND YOU'RE MY GUEST.
I CAN'T SPEAK.
AS I WISH IT. IF YOU SPEAK, YOU'LL SPELL-CAST. I'M NOT A FOOL. BUT YOUR MIND IS AN OPEN PATH TO ME.
MY MIND... MY MIND'S SCREWY. I DON'T REMEMBER-- WAIT--YES, I DO...
...MARK MERLIN. HE WAS A PSYCHIC ADVENTURER BACK IN THE 1950s.
HE WAS LINKED--HIS SOUL SOMEHOW--TO ANOTHER MAGICAL HERO CALLED PRINCE RA-MAN.
RA-MAN WAS A PRISONER SOME-WHERE AND MERLIN CAME BACK FROM THE DEAD TO SAVE HIM.

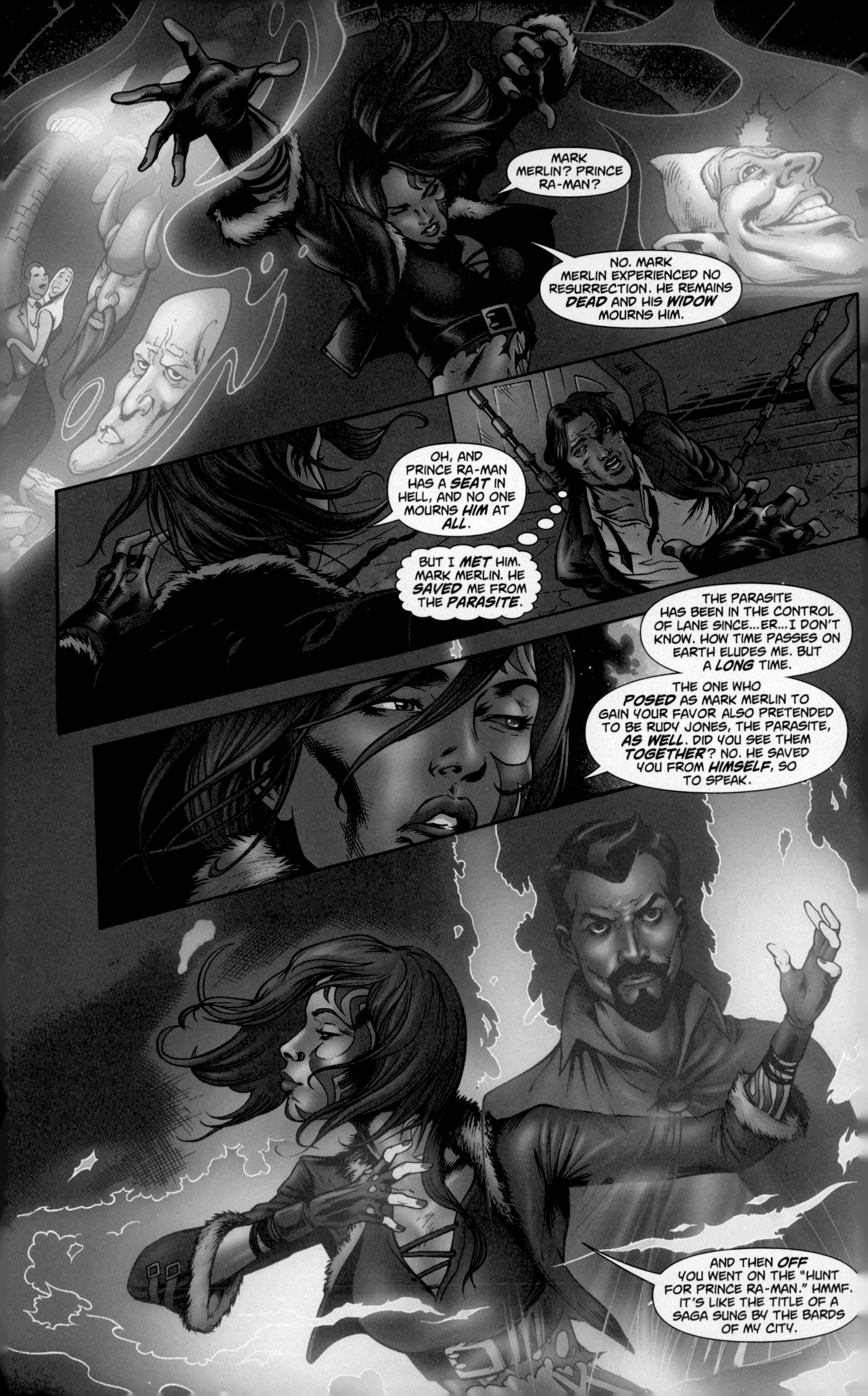
MARK MERLIN? PRINCE RA-MAN?
NO. MARK MERLIN EXPERIENCED NO RESURRECTION. HE REMAINS *DEAD* AND HIS *WIDOW* MOURNS HIM.
OH, AND PRINCE RA-MAN HAS A *SEAT* IN HELL, AND NO ONE MOURNS *HIM* AT *ALL*.
BUT I *MET* HIM. MARK MERLIN. HE *SAVED* ME FROM THE *PARASITE*.
THE PARASITE HAS BEEN IN THE CONTROL OF LANE SINCE...ER...I DON'T KNOW. HOW TIME PASSES ON EARTH ELUDES ME. BUT A *LONG* TIME.
THE ONE WHO *POSED* AS MARK MERLIN TO GAIN YOUR FAVOR ALSO PRETENDED TO BE RUDY JONES, THE PARASITE, *AS WELL*. DID YOU SEE THEM *TOGETHER*? NO. HE SAVED YOU FROM *HIMSELF*, SO TO SPEAK.
AND THEN *OFF* YOU WENT ON THE "HUNT FOR PRINCE RA-MAN." HMMF. IT'S LIKE THE TITLE OF A SAGA SUNG BY THE BARDS OF MY CITY.

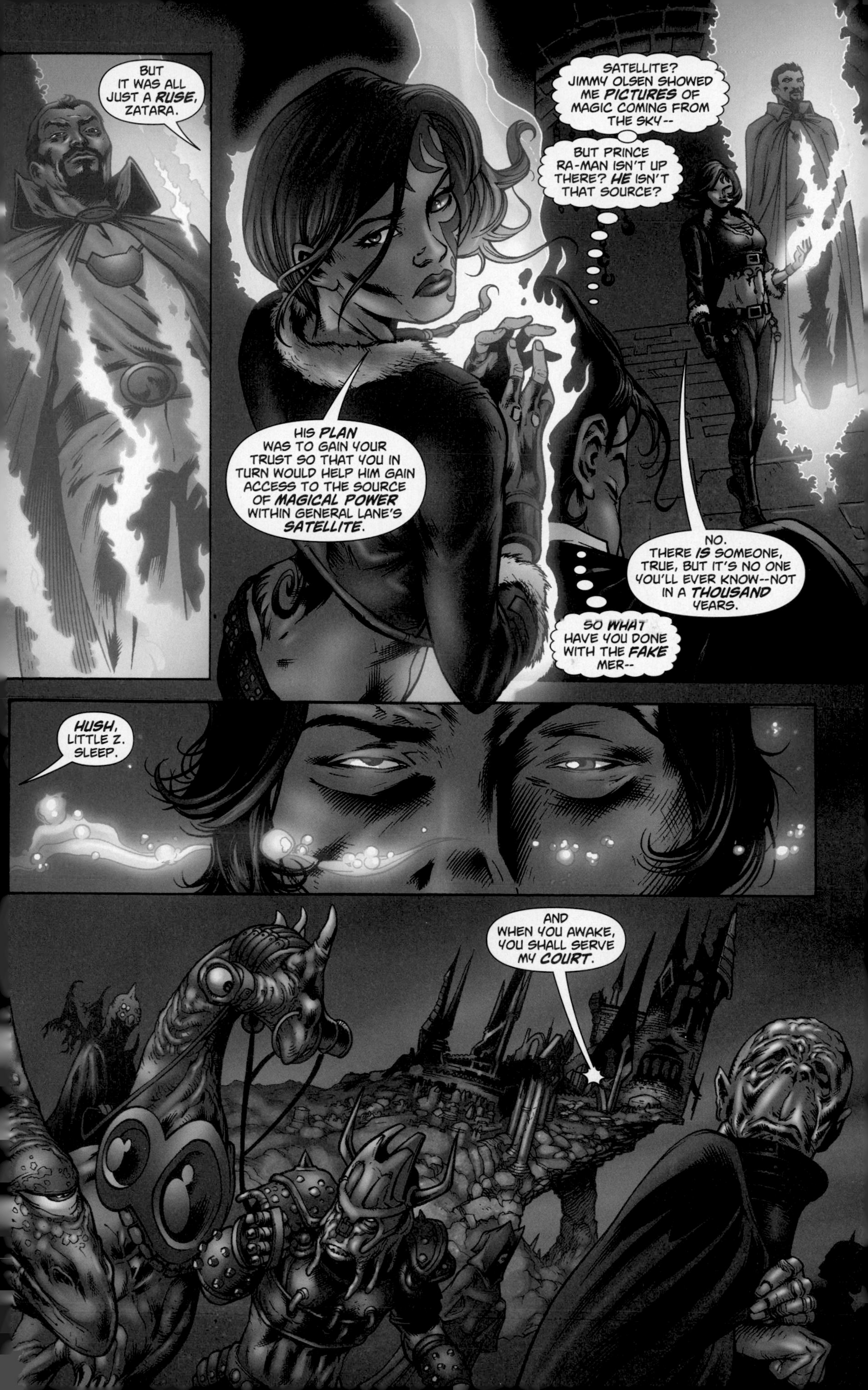
BUT IT WAS ALL JUST A RUSE, ZATARA.
SATELLITE? JIMMY OLSEN SHOWED ME PICTURES OF MAGIC COMING FROM THE SKY--
BUT PRINCE RA-MAN ISN'T UP THERE? HE ISN'T THAT SOURCE?
HIS PLAN WAS TO GAIN YOUR TRUST SO THAT YOU IN TURN WOULD HELP HIM GAIN ACCESS TO THE SOURCE OF MAGICAL POWER WITHIN GENERAL LANE'S SATELLITE.
NO. THERE IS SOMEONE, TRUE, BUT IT'S NO ONE YOU'LL EVER KNOW--NOT IN A THOUSAND YEARS.
SO WHAT HAVE YOU DONE WITH THE FAKE MER--
HUSH, LITTLE Z. SLEEP.
AND WHEN YOU AWAKE, YOU SHALL SERVE MY COURT.

SO THE *REASON* I BROUGHT YOU HERE--

--I MEAN, THIS IS A *COPS'* BAR, SO MOST OF YOU WOULD BE HERE *ANYWAY*--

IT'S BEEN *ROUGH* FOR US--

--WHAT WITH *MON-EL* BUYING IT. THE SEWERS. WATER, OR THE *LACK* OF IT.

BUT IT GETS *WORSE*, I'M AFRAID. I'M HERE TO REVEAL WE LOST ONE OF OUR OWN-- A COP--

--*WHEN* MON-EL DIED.

JONATHAN KENT WASN'T WHO YOU THOUGHT HE WAS.

HE *WASN'T* INTERPOL. HE *CERTAINLY* WAS ENGLISH.

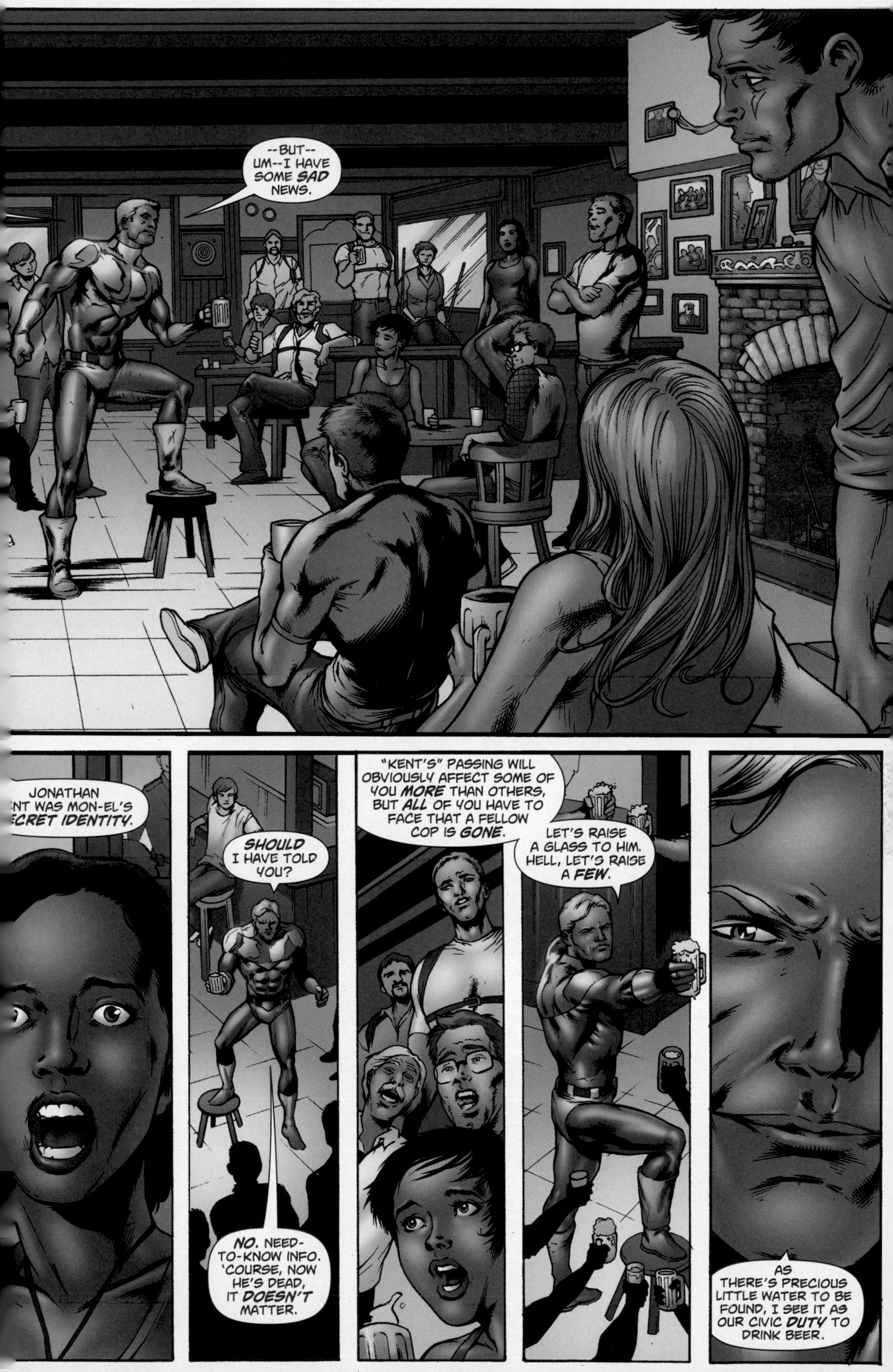
--BUT--
UM--I HAVE
SOME SAD
NEWS.
JONATHAN
ENT WAS MON-EL'S
ECRET IDENTITY.
SHOULD
I HAVE TOLD
YOU?
NO. NEED-TO-KNOW INFO. 'COURSE, NOW HE'S DEAD, IT DOESN'T MATTER.
"KENT'S" PASSING WILL OBVIOUSLY AFFECT SOME OF YOU MORE THAN OTHERS, BUT ALL OF YOU HAVE TO FACE THAT A FELLOW COP IS GONE.
LET'S RAISE A GLASS TO HIM. HELL, LET'S RAISE A FEW.
AS THERE'S PRECIOUS LITTLE WATER TO BE FOUND, I SEE IT AS OUR CIVIC DUTY TO DRINK BEER.

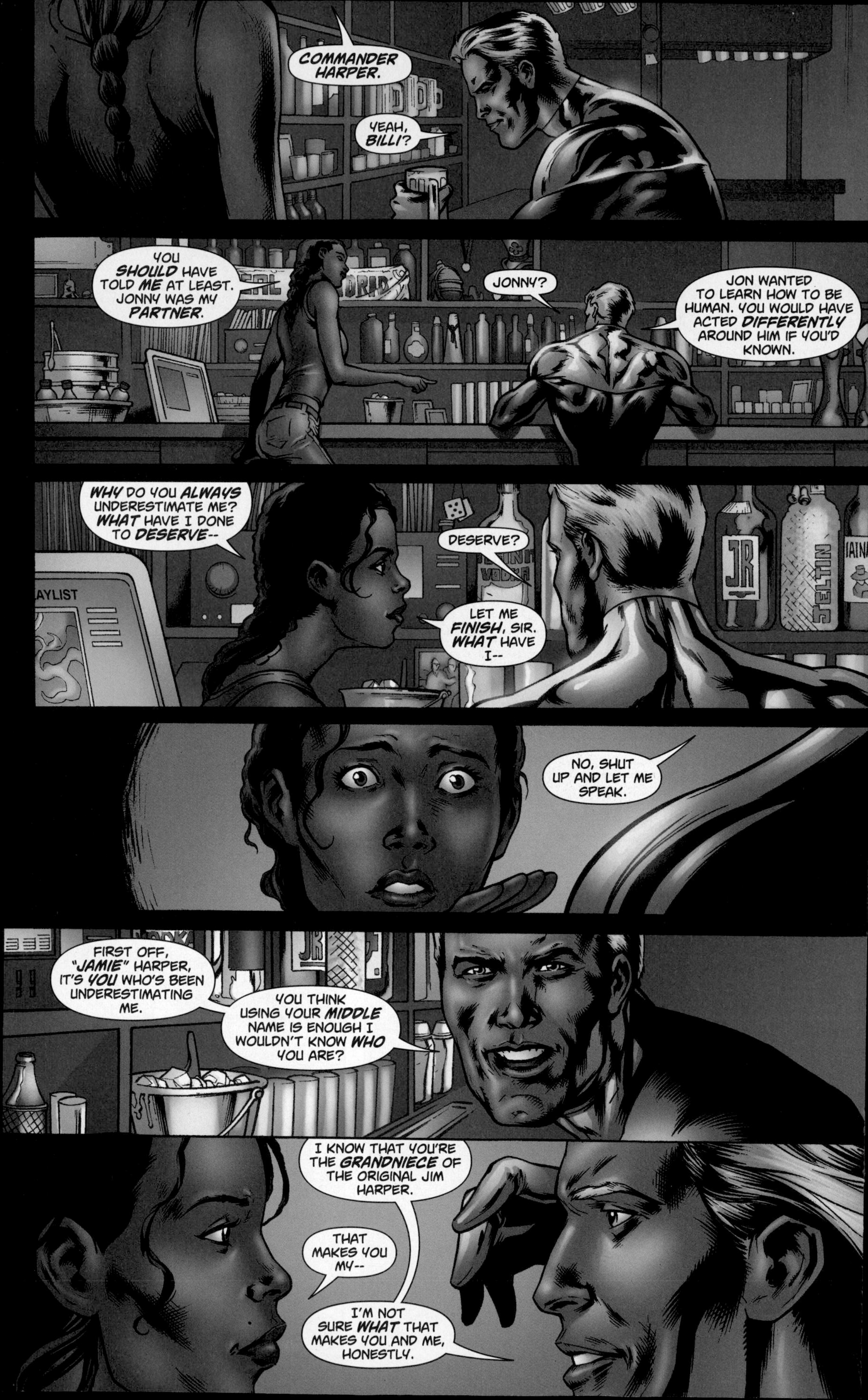
COMMANDER HARPER.
YEAH, BILLI?
YOU SHOULD HAVE TOLD ME AT LEAST. JONNY WAS MY PARTNER.
JONNY?
JON WANTED TO LEARN HOW TO BE HUMAN. YOU WOULD HAVE ACTED DIFFERENTLY AROUND HIM IF YOU'D KNOWN.
WHY DO YOU ALWAYS UNDERESTIMATE ME? WHAT HAVE I DONE TO DESERVE--
DESERVE?
LET ME FINISH, SIR. WHAT HAVE I--
NO, SHUT UP AND LET ME SPEAK.
FIRST OFF, "JAMIE" HARPER, IT'S YOU WHO'S BEEN UNDERESTIMATING ME.
YOU THINK USING YOUR MIDDLE NAME IS ENOUGH I WOULDN'T KNOW WHO YOU ARE?
I KNOW THAT YOU'RE THE GRANDNIECE OF THE ORIGINAL JIM HARPER.
THAT MAKES YOU MY--
I'M NOT SURE WHAT THAT MAKES YOU AND ME, HONESTLY.

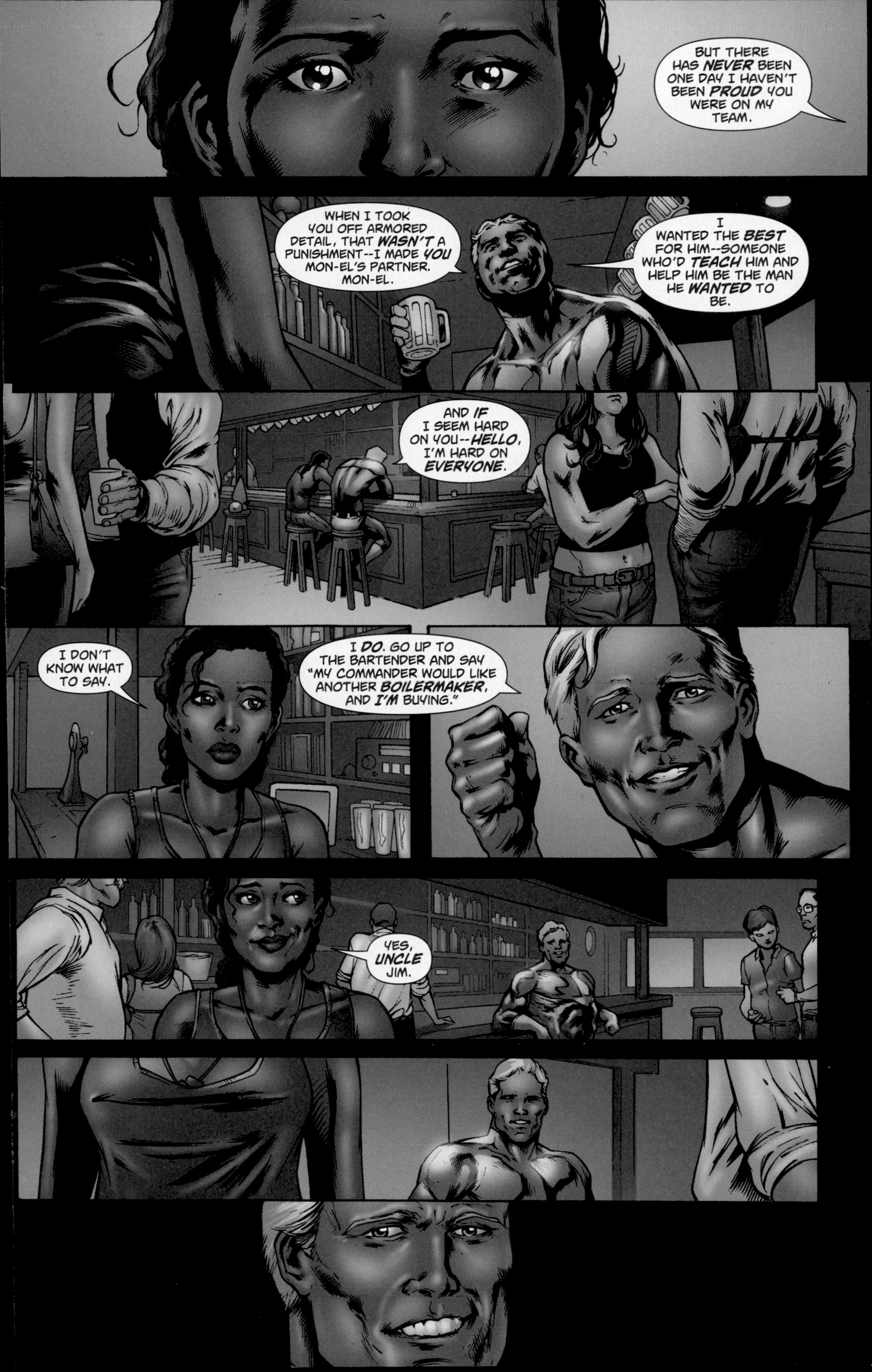
BUT THERE HAS NEVER BEEN ONE DAY I HAVEN'T BEEN PROUD YOU WERE ON MY TEAM.
WHEN I TOOK YOU OFF ARMORED DETAIL, THAT WASN'T A PUNISHMENT--I MADE YOU MON-EL'S PARTNER. MON-EL.
I WANTED THE BEST FOR HIM--SOMEONE WHO'D TEACH HIM AND HELP HIM BE THE MAN HE WANTED TO BE.
AND IF I SEEM HARD ON YOU--HELLO, I'M HARD ON EVERYONE.
I DON'T KNOW WHAT TO SAY.
I DO. GO UP TO THE BARTENDER AND SAY "MY COMMANDER WOULD LIKE ANOTHER BOILERMAKER, AND I'M BUYING."
YES, UNCLE JIM.

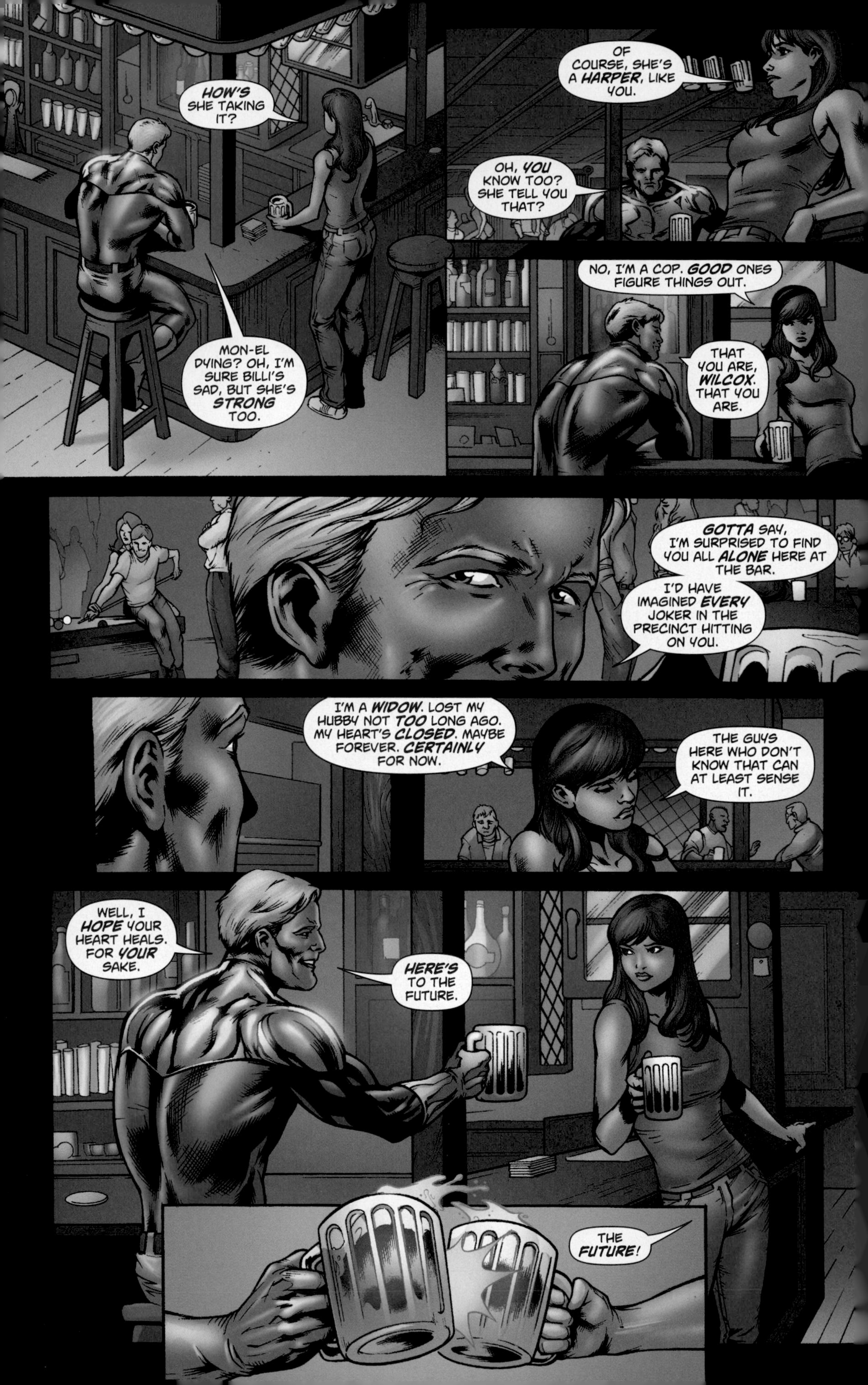

HOW'S SHE TAKING IT?
MON-EL DYING? OH, I'M SURE BILLI'S SAD, BUT SHE'S STRONG TOO.
OF COURSE, SHE'S A HARPER, LIKE YOU.
OH, YOU KNOW TOO? SHE TELL YOU THAT?
NO, I'M A COP. GOOD ONES FIGURE THINGS OUT.
THAT YOU ARE, WILCOX. THAT YOU ARE.
GOTTA SAY, I'M SURPRISED TO FIND YOU ALL ALONE HERE AT THE BAR.
I'D HAVE IMAGINED EVERY JOKER IN THE PRECINCT HITTING ON YOU.
I'M A WIDOW. LOST MY HUBBY NOT TOO LONG AGO. MY HEART'S CLOSED. MAYBE FOREVER. CERTAINLY FOR NOW.
THE GUYS HERE WHO DON'T KNOW THAT CAN AT LEAST SENSE IT.
WELL, I HOPE YOUR HEART HEALS. FOR YOUR SAKE.
HERE'S TO THE FUTURE.
THE FUTURE!

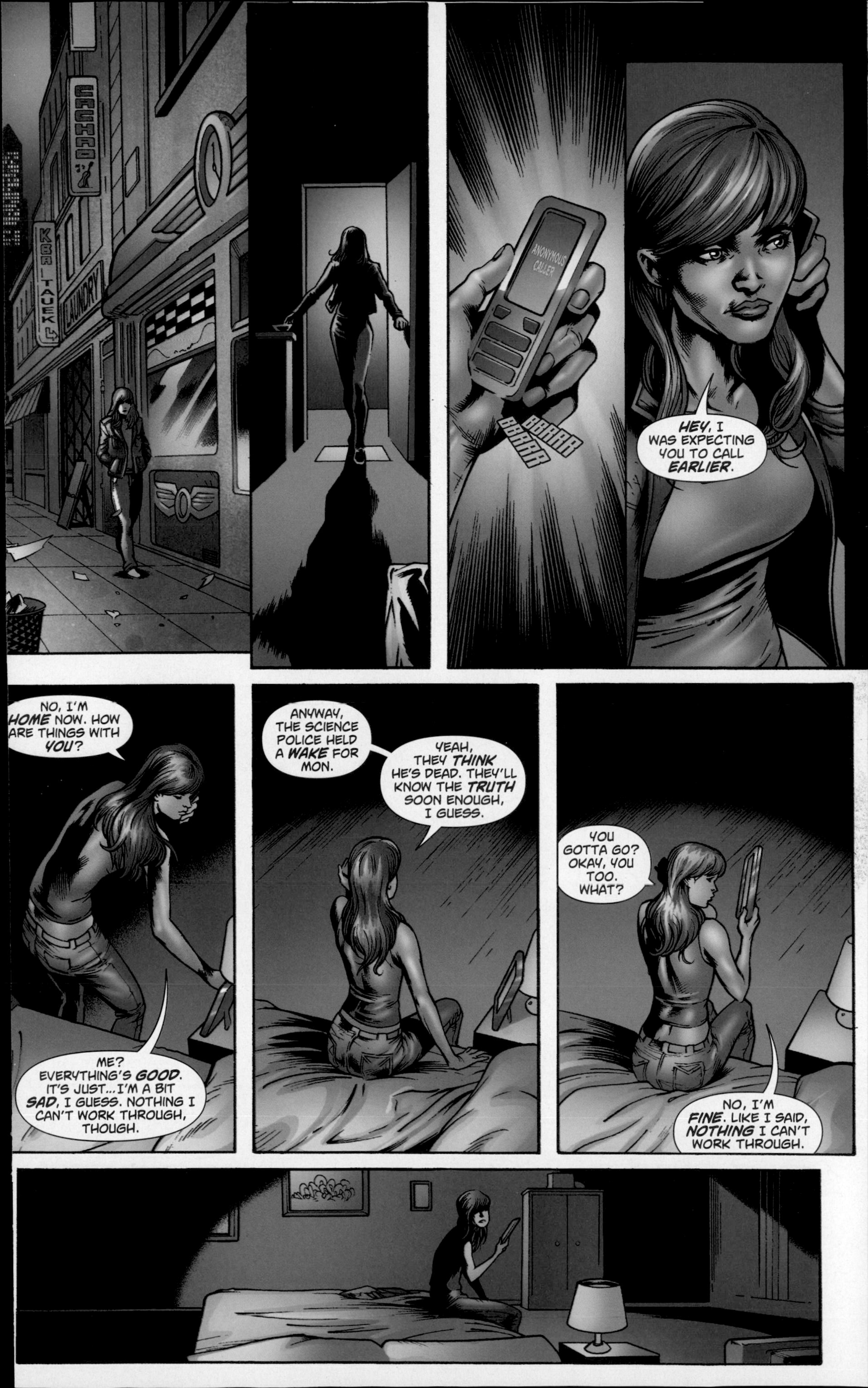
CACHAO
LAUNDRY
ANONYMOUS CALLER
BBRRRR
BBRRRR
HEY, I WAS EXPECTING YOU TO CALL EARLIER.
NO, I'M HOME NOW. HOW ARE THINGS WITH YOU?
ME? EVERYTHING'S GOOD. IT'S JUST...I'M A BIT SAD, I GUESS. NOTHING I CAN'T WORK THROUGH, THOUGH.
ANYWAY, THE SCIENCE POLICE HELD A WAKE FOR MON.
YEAH, THEY THINK HE'S DEAD. THEY'LL KNOW THE TRUTH SOON ENOUGH, I GUESS.
YOU GOTTA GO? OKAY, YOU TOO. WHAT?
NO, I'M FINE. LIKE I SAID, NOTHING I CAN'T WORK THROUGH.

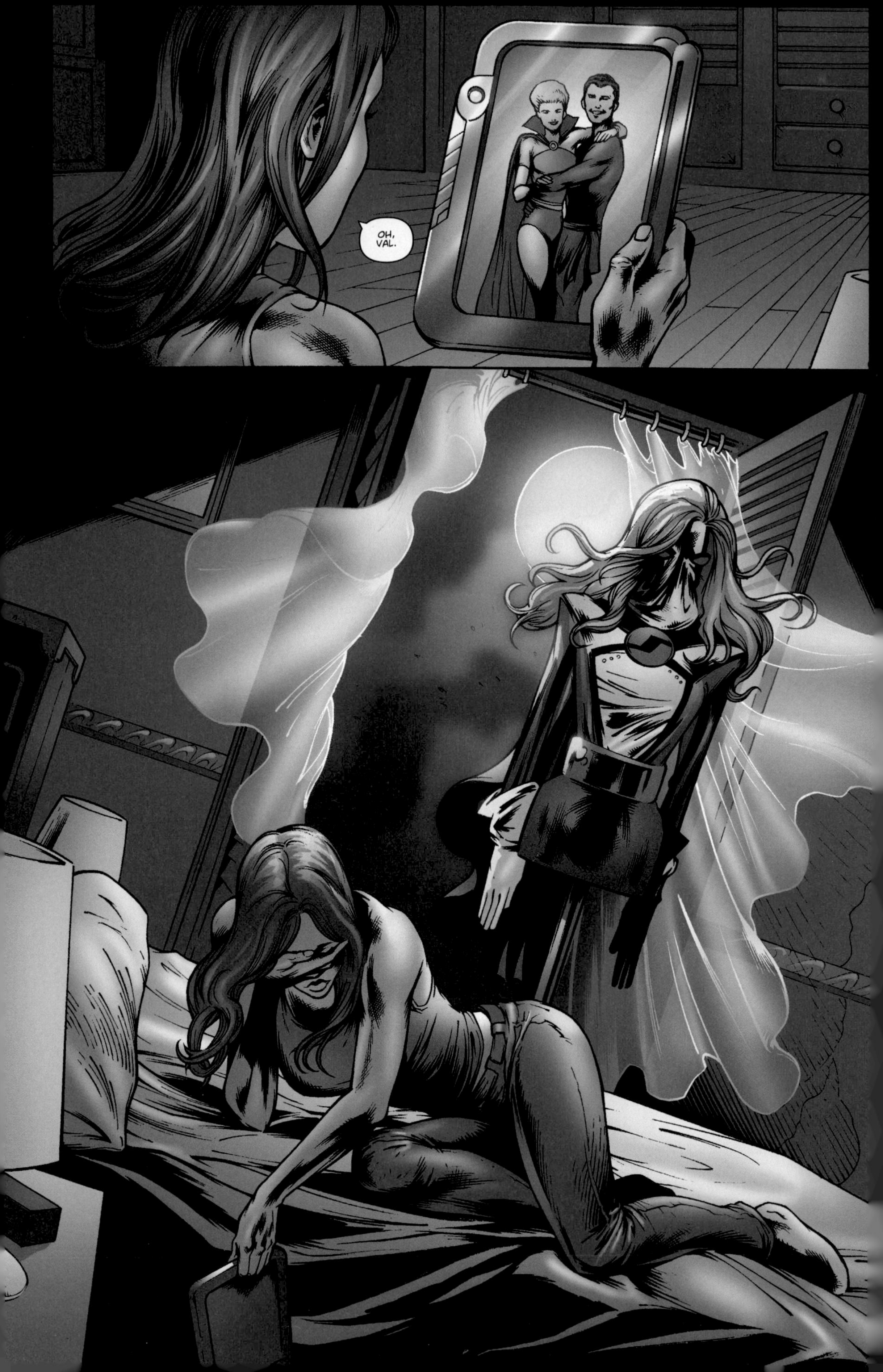
OH, VAL.

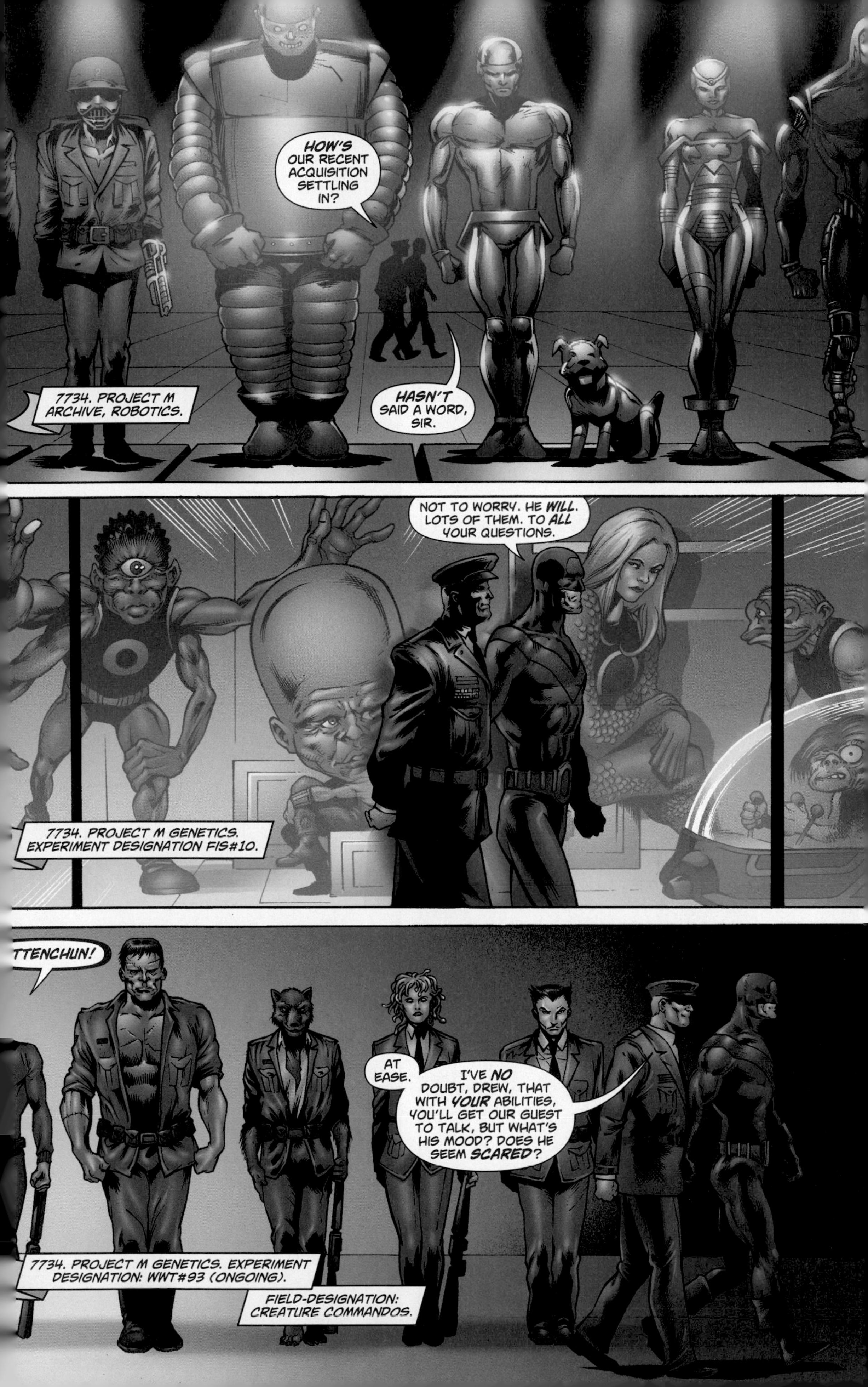
7734. PROJECT M ARCHIVE, ROBOTICS.
HOW'S OUR RECENT ACQUISITION SETTLING IN?
HASN'T SAID A WORD, SIR.
7734. PROJECT M GENETICS. EXPERIMENT DESIGNATION FIS#10.
NOT TO WORRY. HE WILL. LOTS OF THEM. TO ALL YOUR QUESTIONS.
TTENCHUN!
AT EASE.
I'VE NO DOUBT, DREW, THAT WITH YOUR ABILITIES, YOU'LL GET OUR GUEST TO TALK, BUT WHAT'S HIS MOOD? DOES HE SEEM SCARED?
7734. PROJECT M GENETICS. EXPERIMENT DESIGNATION: WWT#93 (ONGOING).
FIELD-DESIGNATION: CREATURE COMMANDOS.

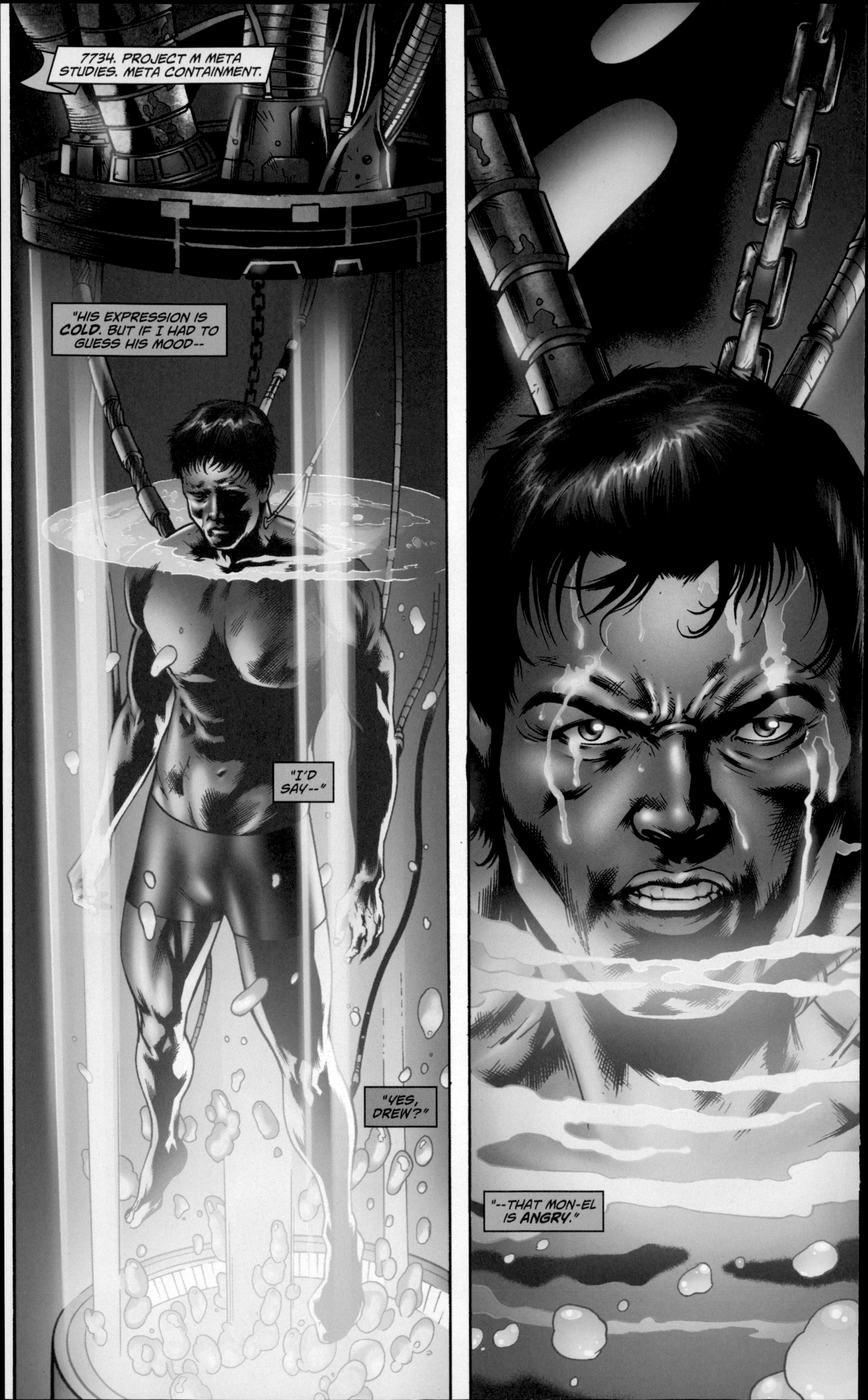
7734. PROJECT M META STUDIES. META CONTAINMENT.
"HIS EXPRESSION IS COLD. BUT IF I HAD TO GUESS HIS MOOD--
"I'D SAY--"
"YES, DREW?"
"--THAT MON-EL IS ANGRY."

COVER BY **CAFU** WITH **SANTIAGO ARCAS**

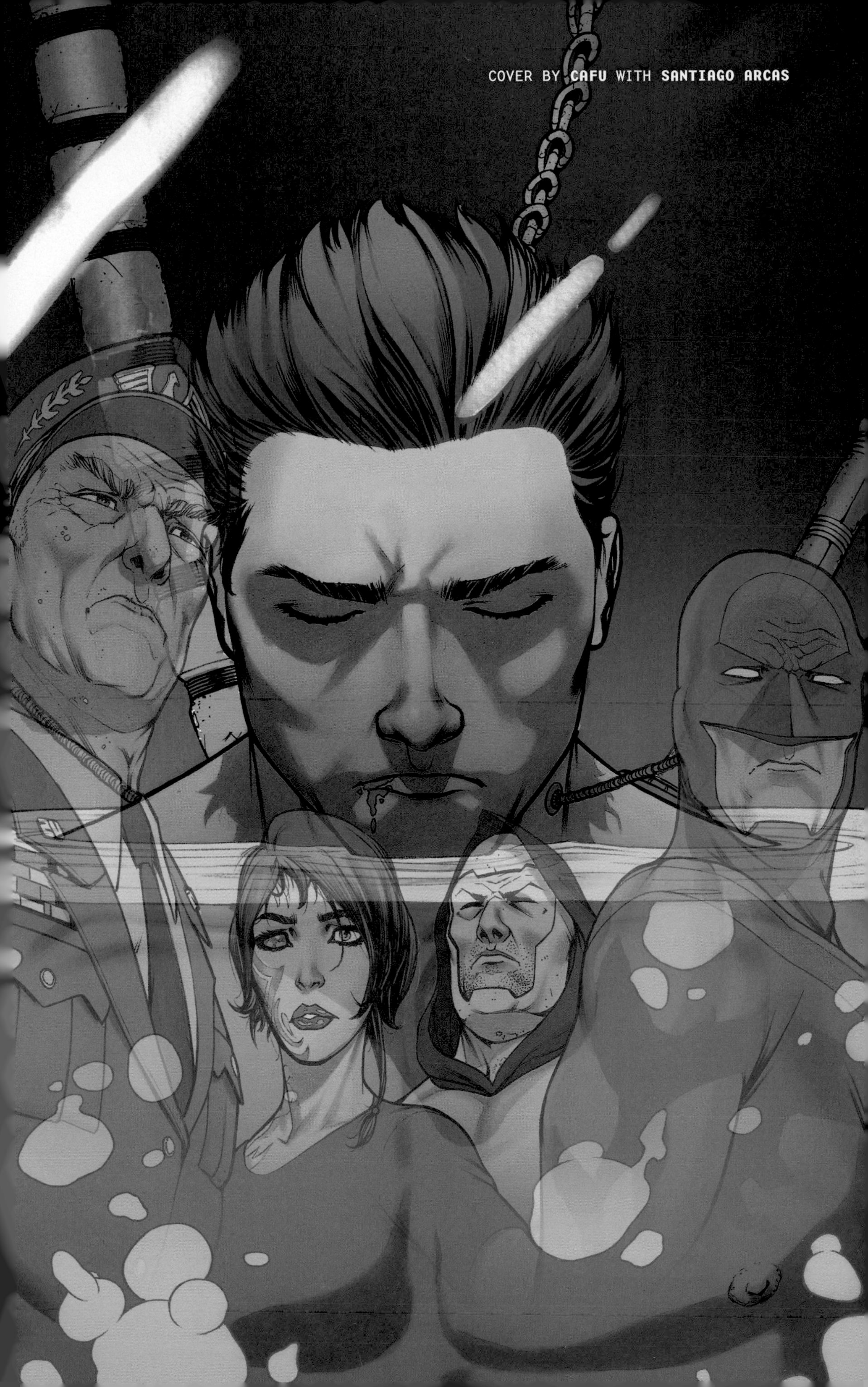

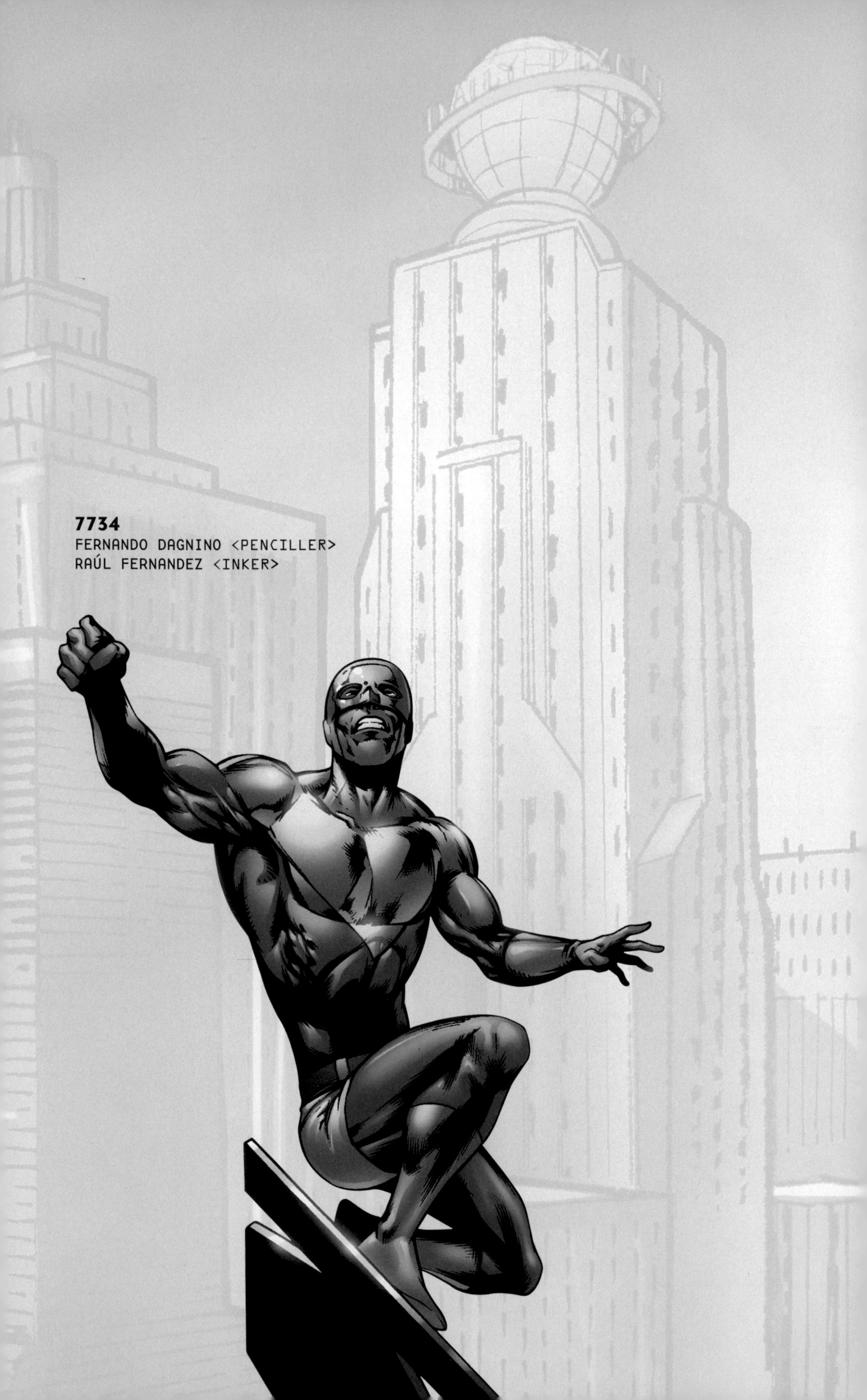

7734
FERNANDO DAGNINO <PENCILLER>
RAÚL FERNANDEZ <INKER>

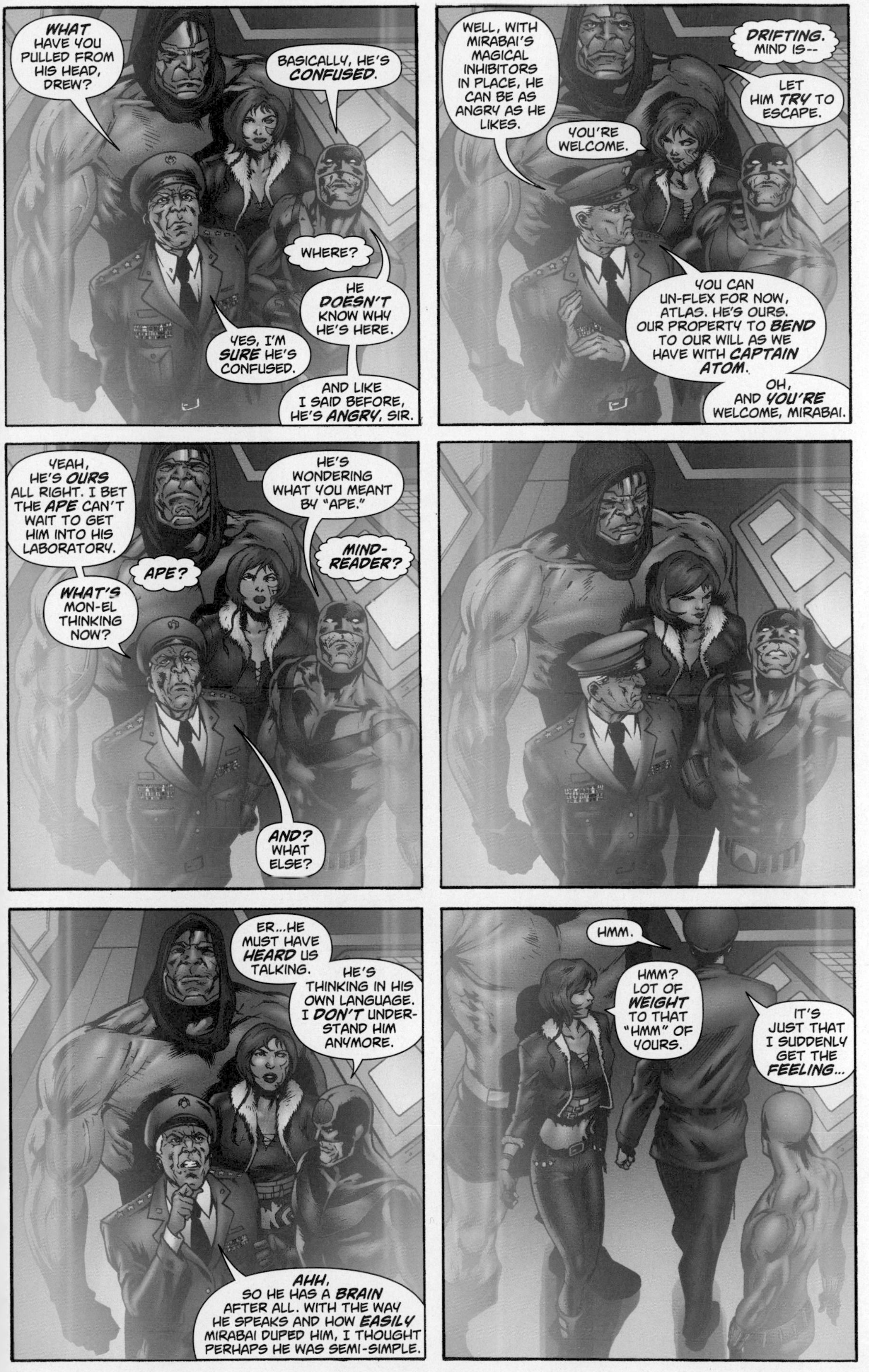
WHAT HAVE YOU PULLED FROM HIS HEAD, DREW?
BASICALLY, HE'S CONFUSED.
WHERE?
HE DOESN'T KNOW WHY HE'S HERE.
YES, I'M SURE HE'S CONFUSED.
AND LIKE I SAID BEFORE, HE'S ANGRY, SIR.
WELL, WITH MIRABAI'S MAGICAL INHIBITORS IN PLACE, HE CAN BE AS ANGRY AS HE LIKES.
DRIFTING. MIND IS--
LET HIM TRY TO ESCAPE.
YOU'RE WELCOME.
YOU CAN UN-FLEX FOR NOW, ATLAS. HE'S OURS. OUR PROPERTY TO BEND TO OUR WILL AS WE HAVE WITH CAPTAIN ATOM.
OH, AND YOU'RE WELCOME, MIRABAI.
YEAH, HE'S OURS ALL RIGHT. I BET THE APE CAN'T WAIT TO GET HIM INTO HIS LABORATORY.
HE'S WONDERING WHAT YOU MEANT BY "APE."
APE?
MIND-READER?
WHAT'S MON-EL THINKING NOW?
AND? WHAT ELSE?
ER...HE MUST HAVE HEARD US TALKING.
HE'S THINKING IN HIS OWN LANGUAGE. I DON'T UNDER-STAND HIM ANYMORE.
AHH, SO HE HAS A BRAIN AFTER ALL. WITH THE WAY HE SPEAKS AND HOW EASILY MIRABAI DUPED HIM, I THOUGHT PERHAPS HE WAS SEMI-SIMPLE.
HMM.
HMM? LOT OF WEIGHT TO THAT "HMM" OF YOURS.
IT'S JUST THAT I SUDDENLY GET THE FEELING...

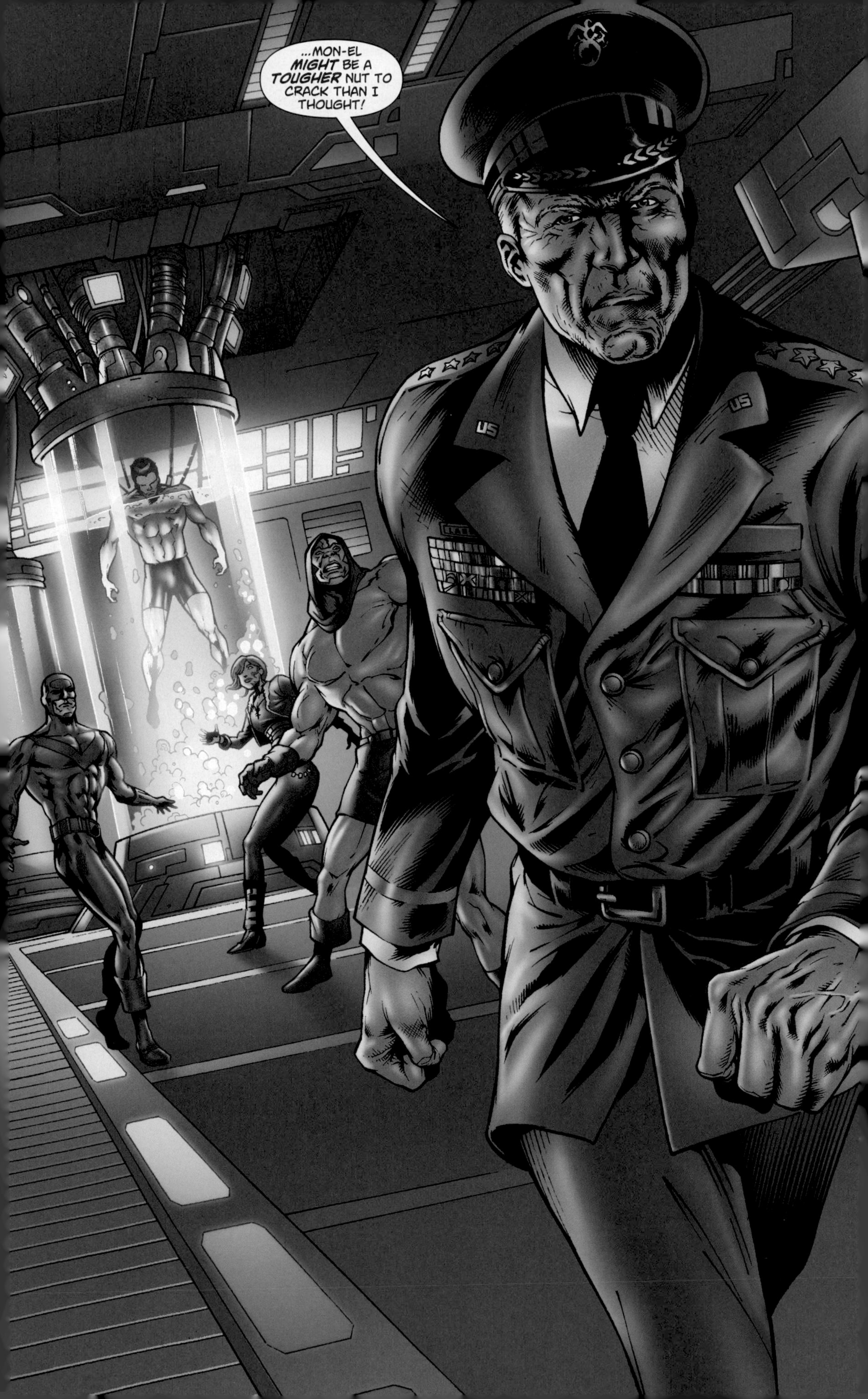
...MON-EL MIGHT BE A TOUGHER NUT TO CRACK THAN I THOUGHT!

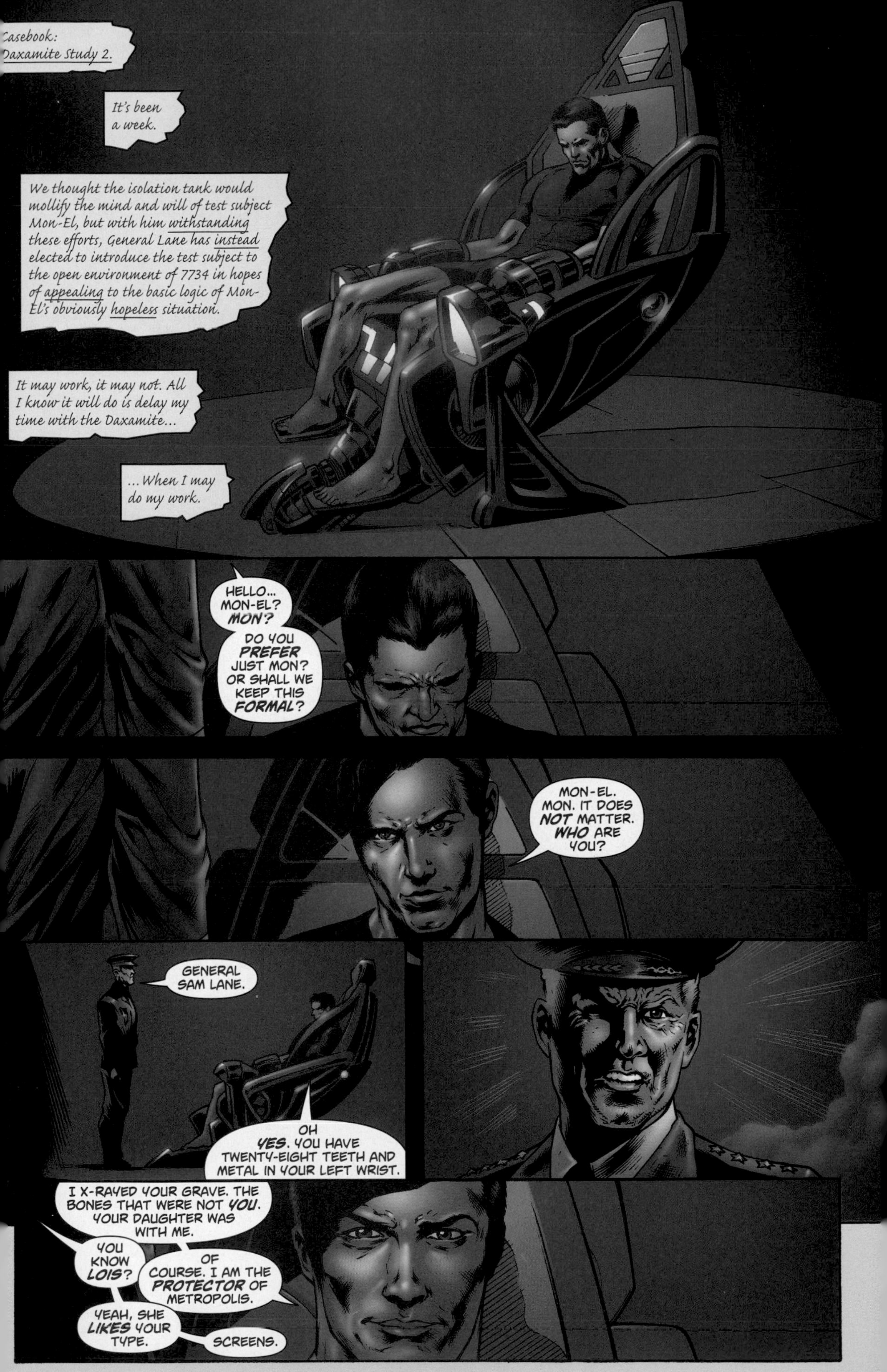
Casebook:
Daxamite Study 2.
It's been a week.
We thought the isolation tank would mollify the mind and will of test subject Mon-El, but with him withstanding these efforts, General Lane has instead elected to introduce the test subject to the open environment of 7734 in hopes of appealing to the basic logic of Mon-El's obviously hopeless situation.
It may work, it may not. All I know it will do is delay my time with the Daxamite...
...When I may do my work.
HELLO... MON-EL? MON?
DO YOU PREFER JUST MON? OR SHALL WE KEEP THIS FORMAL?
MON-EL. MON. IT DOES NOT MATTER. WHO ARE YOU?
GENERAL SAM LANE.
OH YES. YOU HAVE TWENTY-EIGHT TEETH AND METAL IN YOUR LEFT WRIST.
I X-RAYED YOUR GRAVE. THE BONES THAT WERE NOT YOU. YOUR DAUGHTER WAS WITH ME.
YOU KNOW LOIS?
OF COURSE. I AM THE PROTECTOR OF METROPOLIS.
YEAH, SHE LIKES YOUR TYPE.
SCREENS.

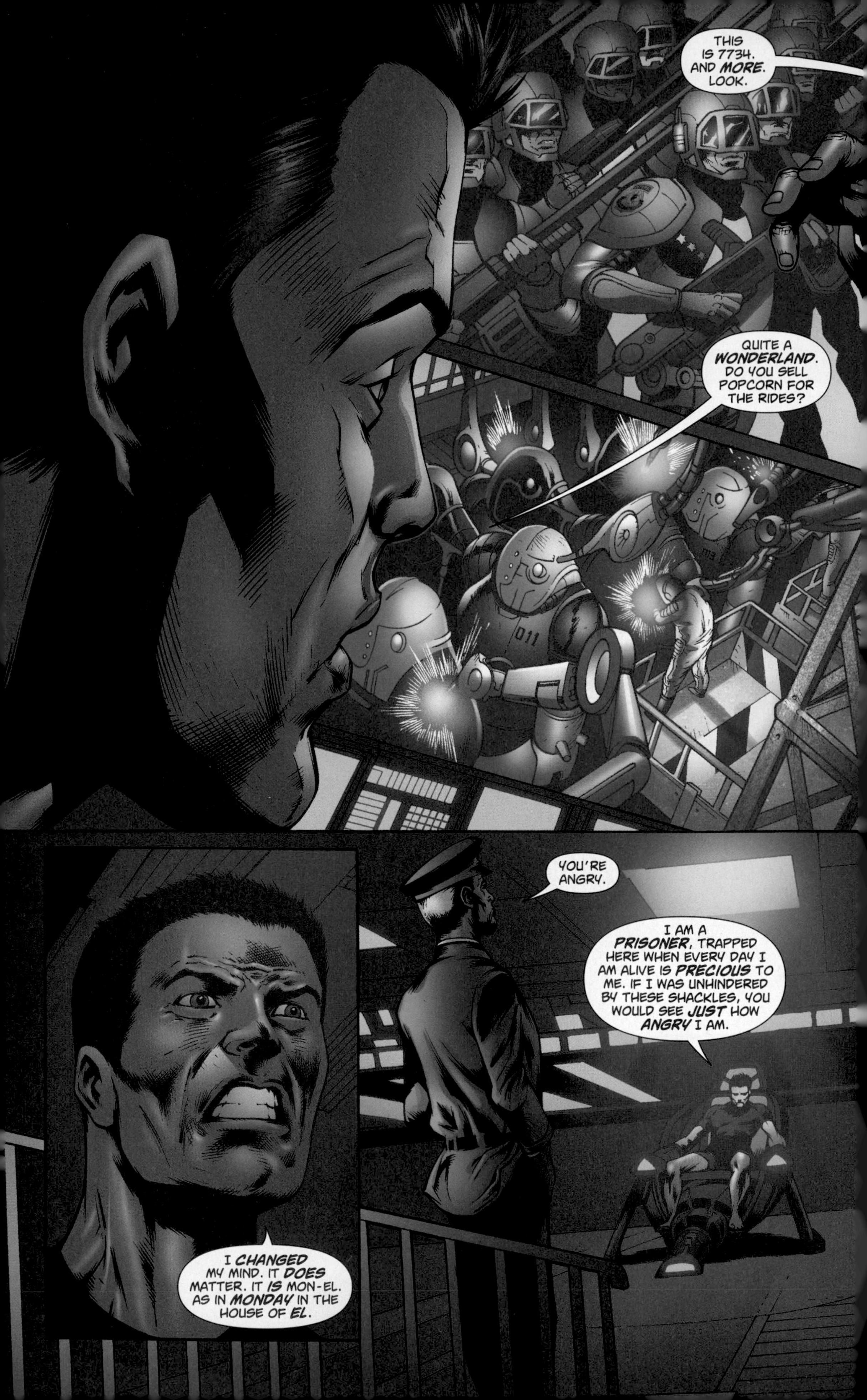
THIS IS 7734. AND MORE. LOOK.
QUITE A WONDERLAND. DO YOU SELL POPCORN FOR THE RIDES?
YOU'RE ANGRY.
I AM A PRISONER, TRAPPED HERE WHEN EVERY DAY I AM ALIVE IS PRECIOUS TO ME. IF I WAS UNHINDERED BY THESE SHACKLES, YOU WOULD SEE JUST HOW ANGRY I AM.
I CHANGED MY MIND. IT DOES MATTER. IT IS MON-EL. AS IN MONDAY IN THE HOUSE OF EL.

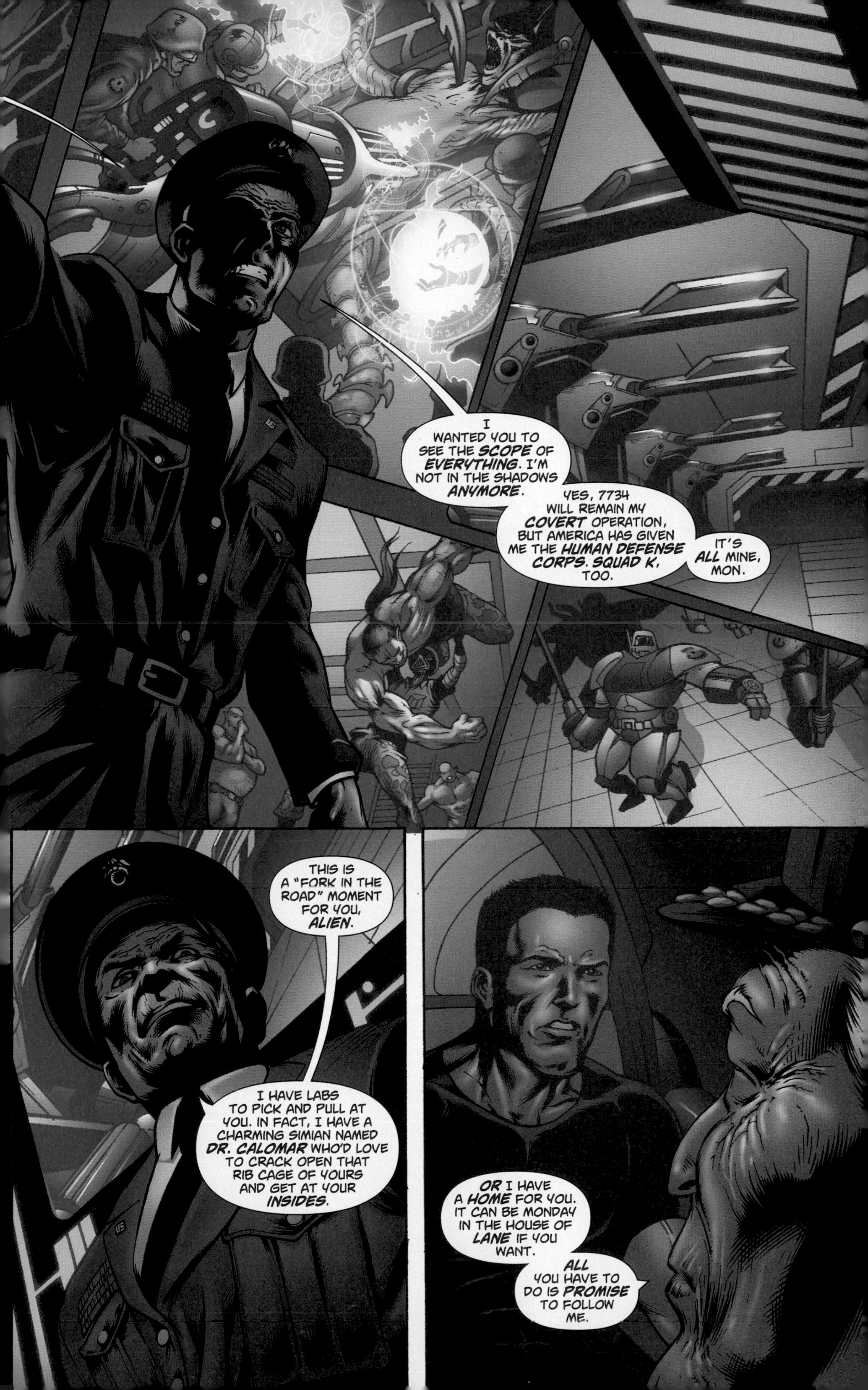
I WANTED YOU TO SEE THE SCOPE OF EVERYTHING. I'M NOT IN THE SHADOWS ANYMORE.
YES, 7734 WILL REMAIN MY COVERT OPERATION, BUT AMERICA HAS GIVEN ME THE HUMAN DEFENSE CORPS. SQUAD K, TOO.
IT'S ALL MINE, MON.
THIS IS A "FORK IN THE ROAD" MOMENT FOR YOU, ALIEN.
I HAVE LABS TO PICK AND PULL AT YOU. IN FACT, I HAVE A CHARMING SIMIAN NAMED DR. CALOMAR WHO'D LOVE TO CRACK OPEN THAT RIB CAGE OF YOURS AND GET AT YOUR INSIDES.
OR I HAVE A HOME FOR YOU. IT CAN BE MONDAY IN THE HOUSE OF LANE IF YOU WANT.
ALL YOU HAVE TO DO IS PROMISE TO FOLLOW ME.

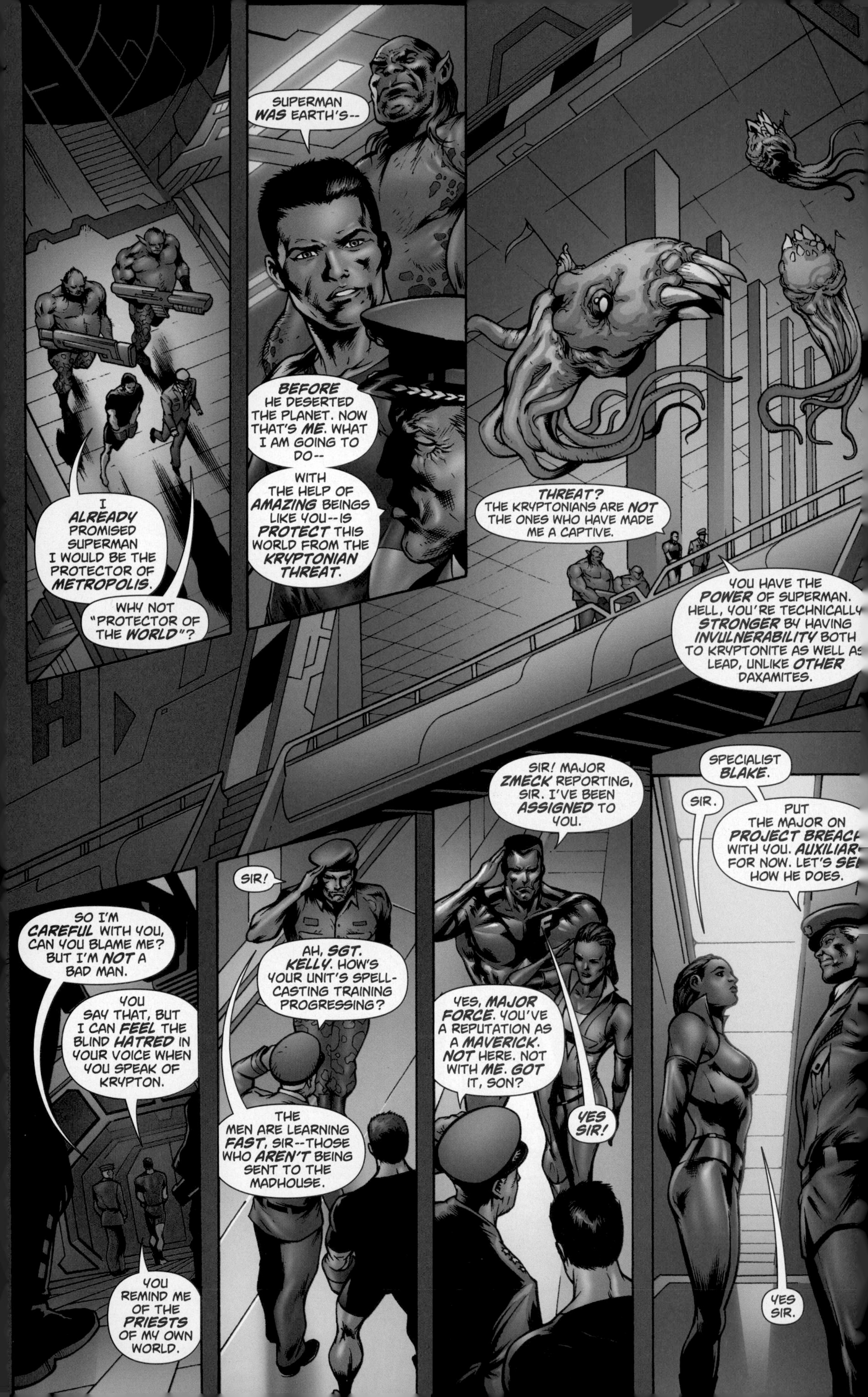

SUPERMAN WAS EARTH'S--
BEFORE HE DESERTED THE PLANET. NOW THAT'S ME. WHAT I AM GOING TO DO--
WITH THE HELP OF AMAZING BEINGS LIKE YOU--IS PROTECT THIS WORLD FROM THE KRYPTONIAN THREAT.
I ALREADY PROMISED SUPERMAN I WOULD BE THE PROTECTOR OF METROPOLIS.
WHY NOT "PROTECTOR OF THE WORLD"?
THREAT? THE KRYPTONIANS ARE NOT THE ONES WHO HAVE MADE ME A CAPTIVE.
YOU HAVE THE POWER OF SUPERMAN. HELL, YOU'RE TECHNICALLY STRONGER BY HAVING INVULNERABILITY BOTH TO KRYPTONITE AS WELL AS LEAD, UNLIKE OTHER DAXAMITES.
SO I'M CAREFUL WITH YOU, CAN YOU BLAME ME? BUT I'M NOT A BAD MAN.
YOU SAY THAT, BUT I CAN FEEL THE BLIND HATRED IN YOUR VOICE WHEN YOU SPEAK OF KRYPTON.
YOU REMIND ME OF THE PRIESTS OF MY OWN WORLD.
SIR!
AH, SGT. KELLY. HOW'S YOUR UNIT'S SPELL-CASTING TRAINING PROGRESSING?
THE MEN ARE LEARNING FAST, SIR--THOSE WHO AREN'T BEING SENT TO THE MADHOUSE.
SIR! MAJOR ZMECK REPORTING, SIR. I'VE BEEN ASSIGNED TO YOU.
YES, MAJOR FORCE. YOU'VE A REPUTATION AS A MAVERICK. NOT HERE. NOT WITH ME. GOT IT, SON?
YES SIR!
SPECIALIST BLAKE.
SIR.
PUT THE MAJOR ON PROJECT BREACH WITH YOU. AUXILIARY FOR NOW. LET'S SEE HOW HE DOES.
YES SIR.

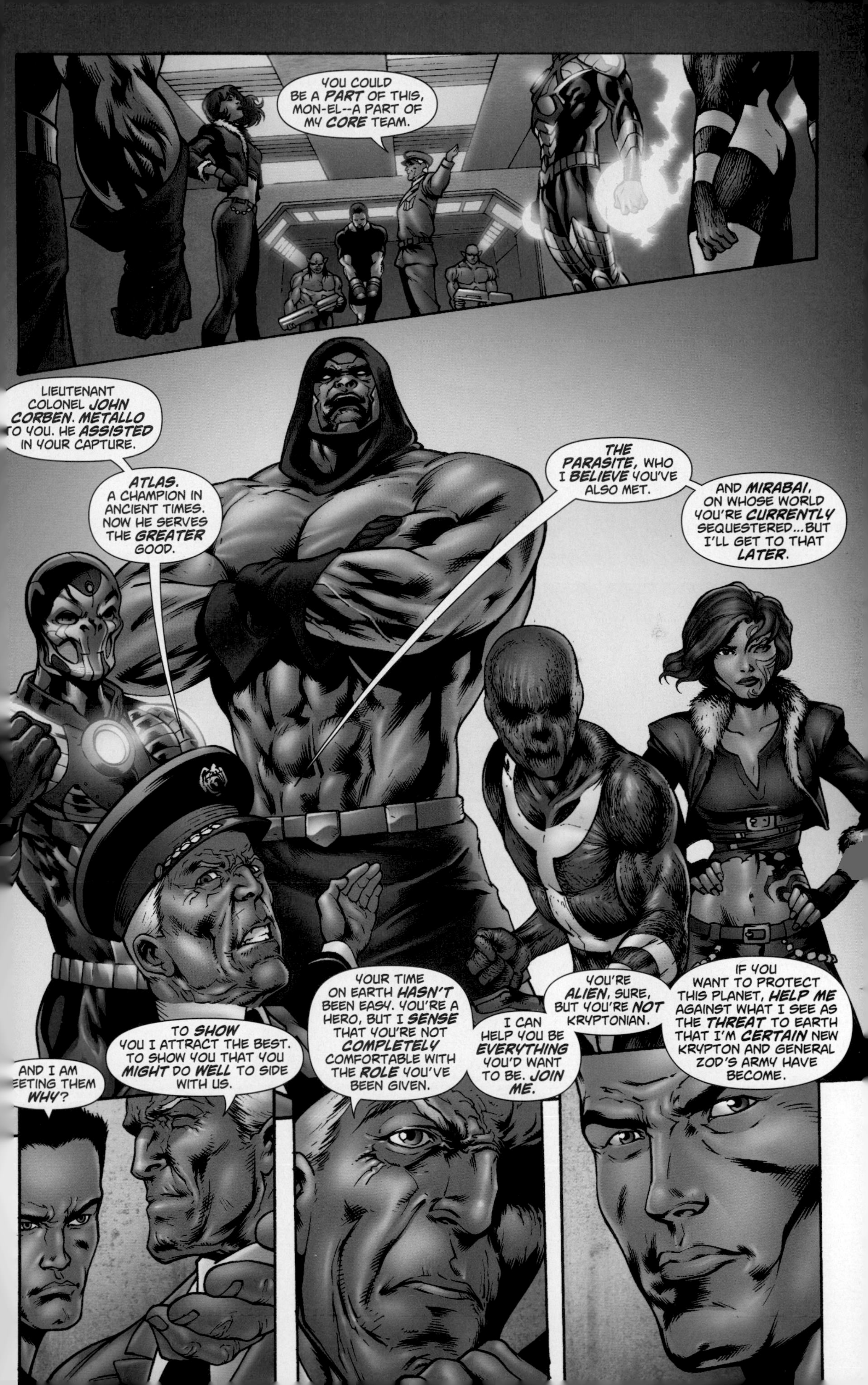
YOU COULD BE A PART OF THIS, MON-EL--A PART OF MY CORE TEAM.
LIEUTENANT COLONEL JOHN CORBEN. METALLO TO YOU. HE ASSISTED IN YOUR CAPTURE.
ATLAS. A CHAMPION IN ANCIENT TIMES. NOW HE SERVES THE GREATER GOOD.
THE PARASITE, WHO I BELIEVE YOU'VE ALSO MET.
AND MIRABAI, ON WHOSE WORLD YOU'RE CURRENTLY SEQUESTERED... BUT I'LL GET TO THAT LATER.
AND I AM EETING THEM WHY?
TO SHOW YOU I ATTRACT THE BEST. TO SHOW YOU THAT YOU MIGHT DO WELL TO SIDE WITH US.
YOUR TIME ON EARTH HASN'T BEEN EASY. YOU'RE A HERO, BUT I SENSE THAT YOU'RE NOT COMPLETELY COMFORTABLE WITH THE ROLE YOU'VE BEEN GIVEN.
I CAN HELP YOU BE EVERYTHING YOU'D WANT TO BE. JOIN ME.
YOU'RE ALIEN, SURE, BUT YOU'RE NOT KRYPTONIAN.
IF YOU WANT TO PROTECT THIS PLANET, HELP ME AGAINST WHAT I SEE AS THE THREAT TO EARTH THAT I'M CERTAIN NEW KRYPTON AND GENERAL ZOD'S ARMY HAVE BECOME.

THIS IS A *CHANCE* FOR YOU TO BE PART OF SOMETHING *GOOD*. NO, SOMETHING *GREAT!*

YOU PROMISED SUPERMAN YOU'D PROTECT EARTH, AND BELIEVE ME, YOU *WILL*.

OR IT'S THE LABORATORY OF DR. CALOMAR FOR YOU.

AND THE WORLD THINKS YOU'RE *DEAD*, SO *DON'T* EXPECT ANYONE TO COME LOOKING.

HOW DID YOU MAKE THEM BELIEVE I WAS DEAD?

YOUR *COSTUME*...SHREDDED BITS OF IT LACED WITH TRACE ELEMENTS OF DAXAMITE *TISSUE*--

--WE LEFT THAT TO BE FOUND IN THE WRECKAGE OF THE METROPOLIS SEWERS.

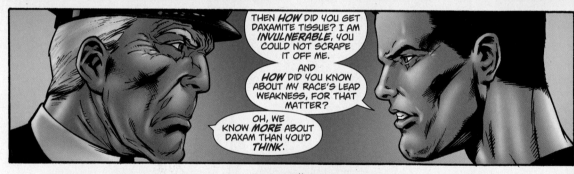

THEN *HOW* DID YOU GET DAXAMITE TISSUE? I AM *INVULNERABLE*, YOU COULD NOT SCRAPE IT OFF ME.

AND *HOW* DID YOU KNOW ABOUT MY RACE'S LEAD WEAKNESS, FOR THAT MATTER?

OH, WE KNOW *MORE* ABOUT DAXAM THAN YOU'D *THINK*.

NOW *ENOUGH* TALK, ALIEN. *CHOOSE*.

I MADE AN *OATH* TO SUPERMAN.

SUPERMAN IS KRYPTONIAN.

AND HE IS GOOD AND HE IS A *HERO*, WHICH IS MOR[E] THAN I CAN SAY FOR T[HE] ENTICING DISPLAY OF *GARBAGE* YOU HAVE COLLECTED.

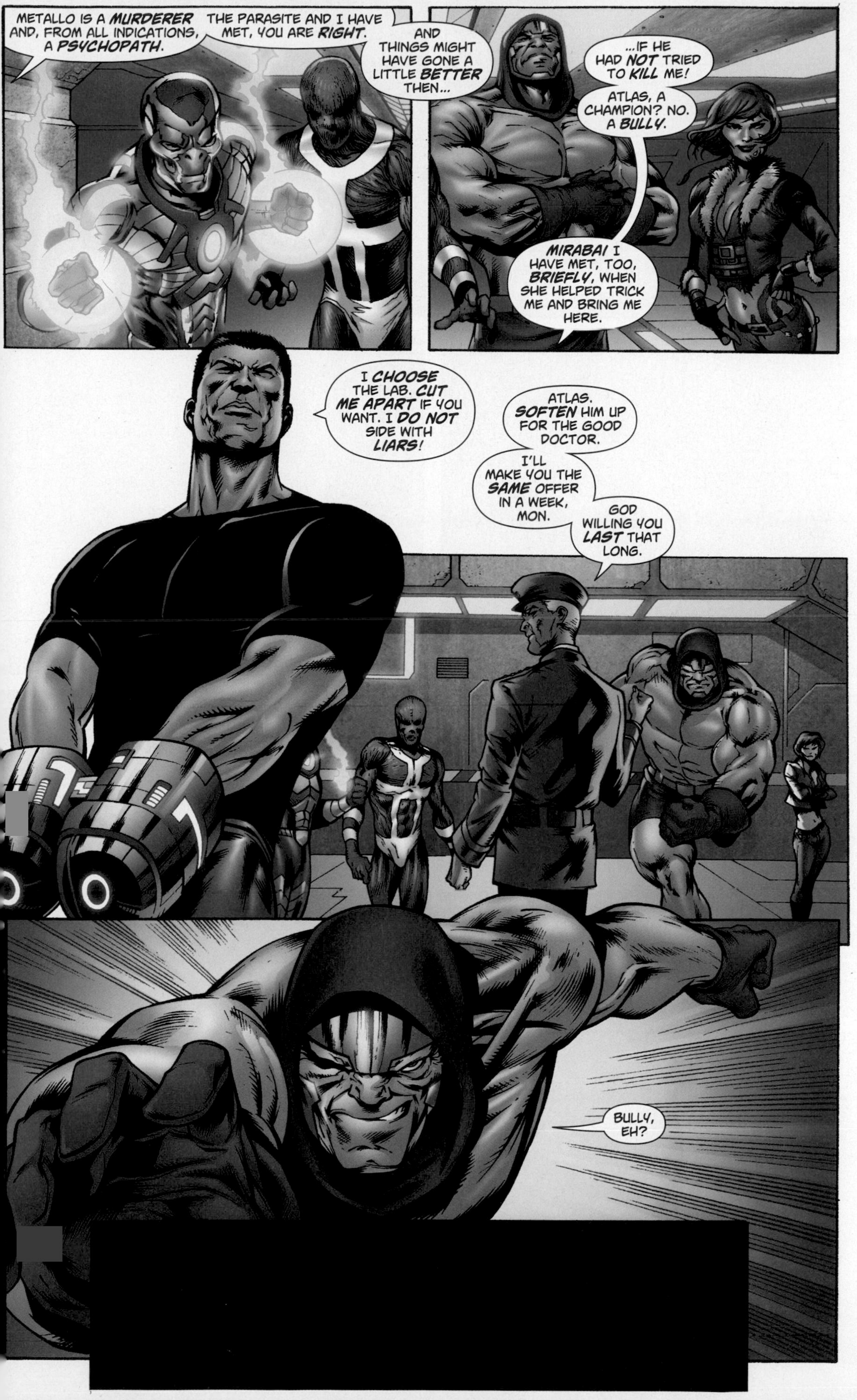
METALLO IS A MURDERER AND, FROM ALL INDICATIONS, A PSYCHOPATH.
THE PARASITE AND I HAVE MET, YOU ARE RIGHT.
AND THINGS MIGHT HAVE GONE A LITTLE BETTER THEN...
...IF HE HAD NOT TRIED TO KILL ME!
ATLAS, A CHAMPION? NO. A BULLY.
MIRABAI I HAVE MET, TOO, BRIEFLY, WHEN SHE HELPED TRICK ME AND BRING ME HERE.
I CHOOSE THE LAB. CUT ME APART IF YOU WANT. I DO NOT SIDE WITH LIARS!
ATLAS. SOFTEN HIM UP FOR THE GOOD DOCTOR.
I'LL MAKE YOU THE SAME OFFER IN A WEEK, MON.
GOD WILLING YOU LAST THAT LONG.
BULLY, EH?
[redacted]

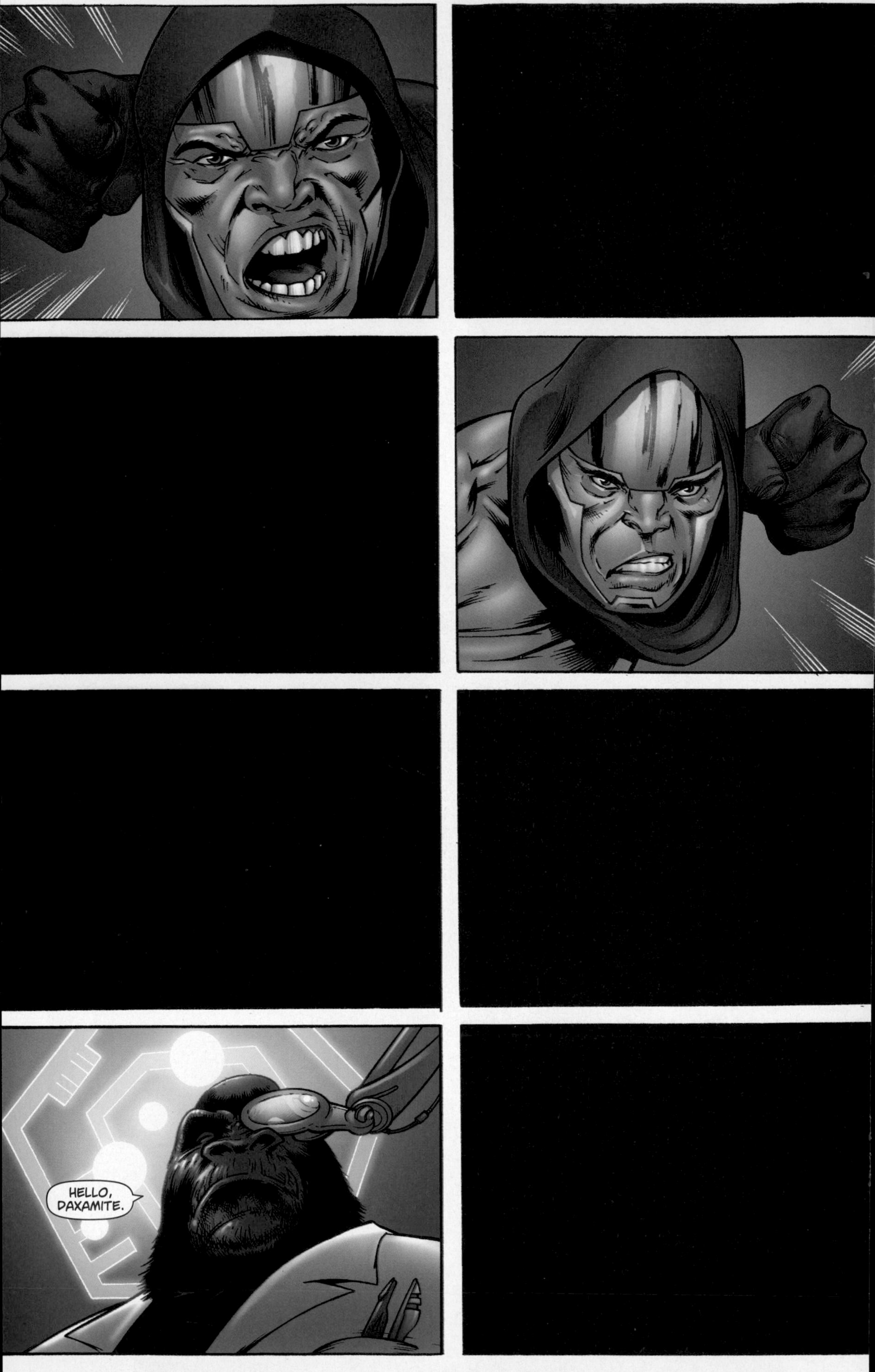
HELLO, DAXAMITE.

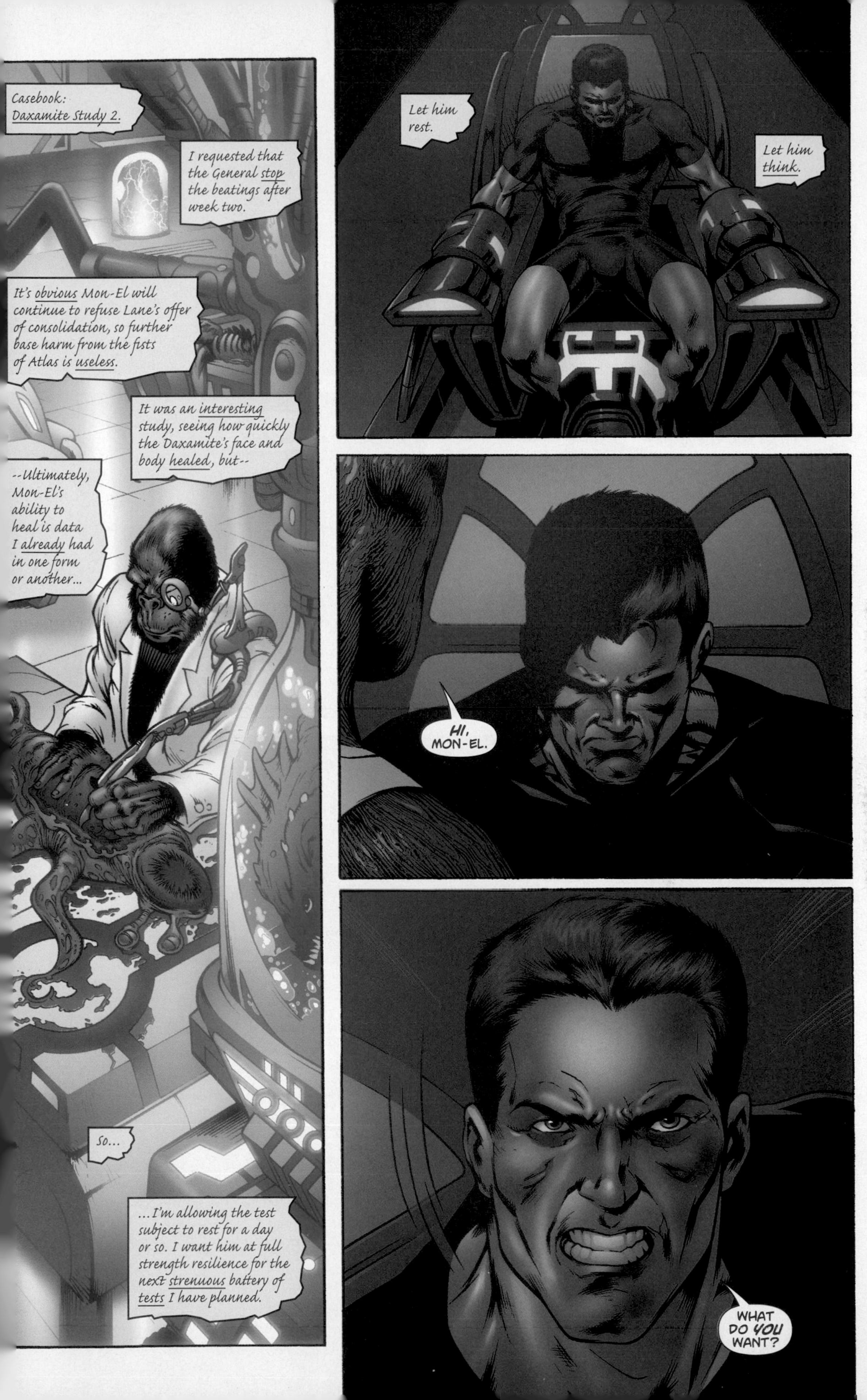
Casebook: Daxamite Study 2.
I requested that the General stop the beatings after week two.
It's obvious Mon-El will continue to refuse Lane's offer of consolidation, so further base harm from the fists of Atlas is useless.
It was an interesting study, seeing how quickly the Daxamite's face and body healed, but--
--Ultimately, Mon-El's ability to heal is data I already had in one form or another...
So...
...I'm allowing the test subject to rest for a day or so. I want him at full strength resilience for the next strenuous battery of tests I have planned.
Let him rest.
Let him think.
HI, MON-EL.
WHAT DO YOU WANT?

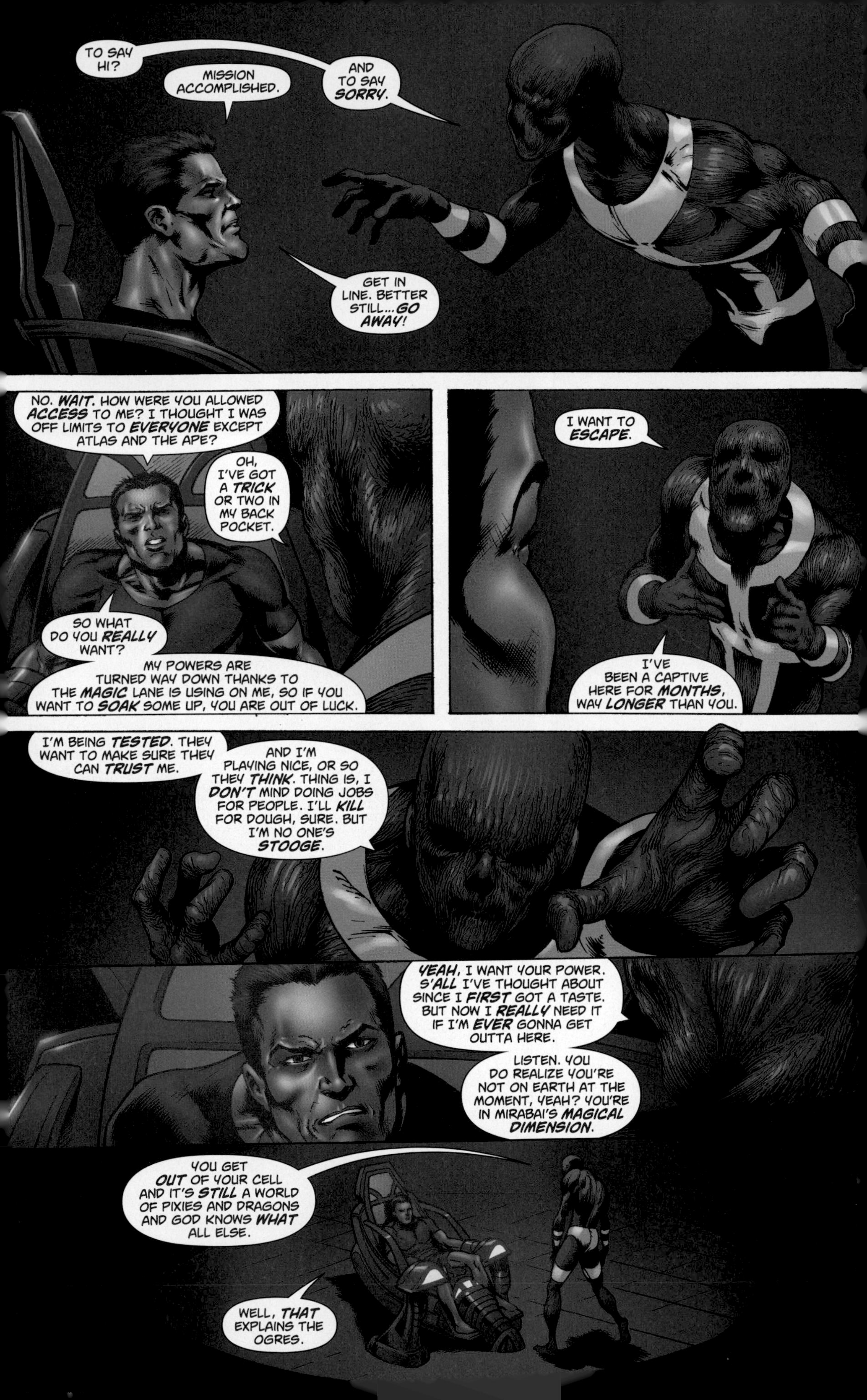
TO SAY HI?
MISSION ACCOMPLISHED.
AND TO SAY SORRY.
GET IN LINE. BETTER STILL...GO AWAY!
NO. WAIT. HOW WERE YOU ALLOWED ACCESS TO ME? I THOUGHT I WAS OFF LIMITS TO EVERYONE EXCEPT ATLAS AND THE APE?
OH, I'VE GOT A TRICK OR TWO IN MY BACK POCKET.
SO WHAT DO YOU REALLY WANT?
MY POWERS ARE TURNED WAY DOWN THANKS TO THE MAGIC LANE IS USING ON ME, SO IF YOU WANT TO SOAK SOME UP, YOU ARE OUT OF LUCK.
I WANT TO ESCAPE.
I'VE BEEN A CAPTIVE HERE FOR MONTHS, WAY LONGER THAN YOU.
I'M BEING TESTED. THEY WANT TO MAKE SURE THEY CAN TRUST ME.
AND I'M PLAYING NICE, OR SO THEY THINK. THING IS, I DON'T MIND DOING JOBS FOR PEOPLE. I'LL KILL FOR DOUGH, SURE. BUT I'M NO ONE'S STOOGE.
YEAH, I WANT YOUR POWER. S'ALL I'VE THOUGHT ABOUT SINCE I FIRST GOT A TASTE. BUT NOW I REALLY NEED IT IF I'M EVER GONNA GET OUTTA HERE.
LISTEN. YOU DO REALIZE YOU'RE NOT ON EARTH AT THE MOMENT, YEAH? YOU'RE IN MIRABAI'S MAGICAL DIMENSION.
YOU GET OUT OF YOUR CELL AND IT'S STILL A WORLD OF PIXIES AND DRAGONS AND GOD KNOWS WHAT ALL ELSE.
WELL, THAT EXPLAINS THE OGRES.

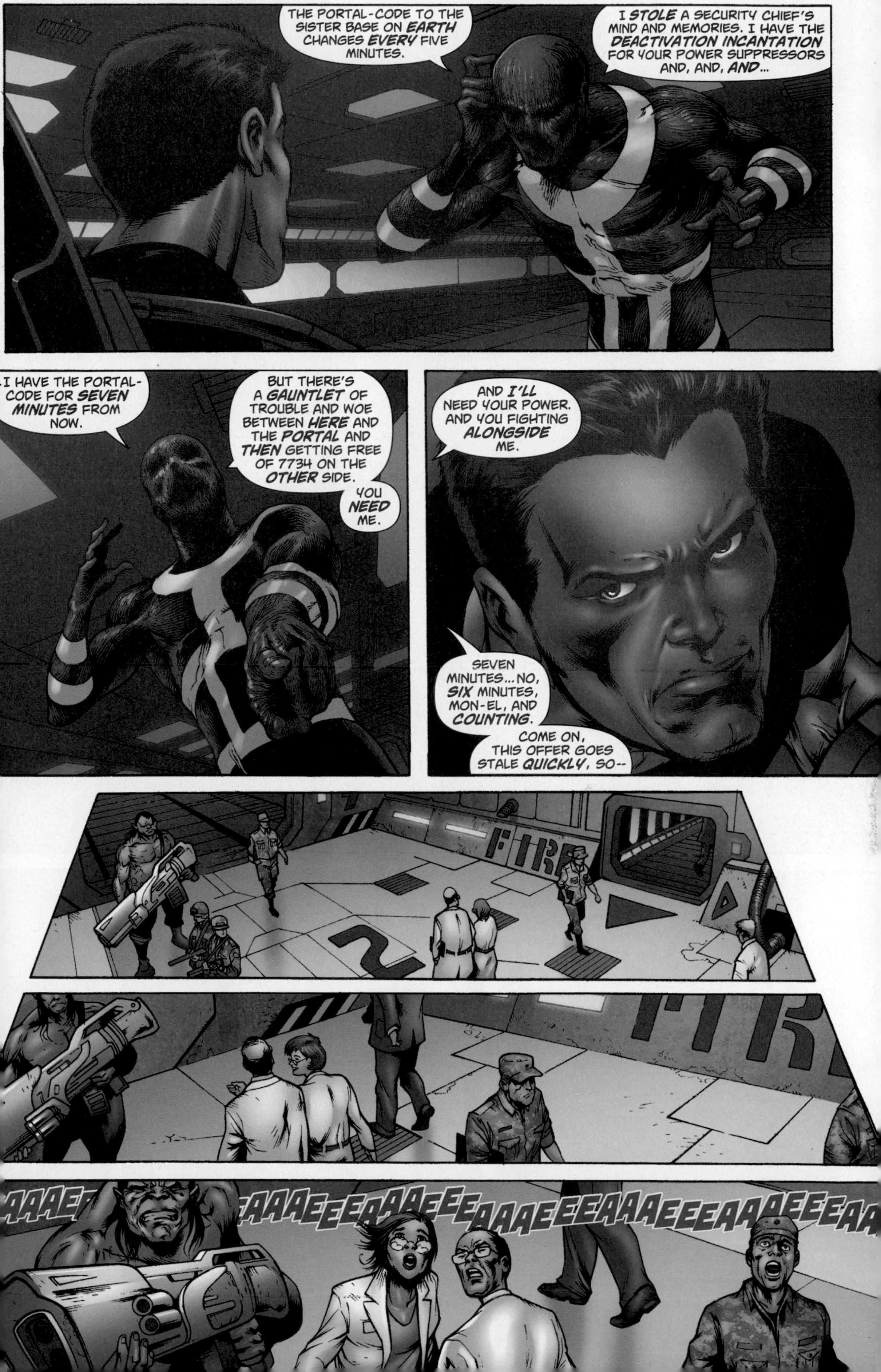
THE PORTAL-CODE TO THE SISTER BASE ON EARTH CHANGES EVERY FIVE MINUTES.
I STOLE A SECURITY CHIEF'S MIND AND MEMORIES. I HAVE THE DEACTIVATION INCANTATION FOR YOUR POWER SUPPRESSORS AND, AND, AND...
...I HAVE THE PORTAL-CODE FOR SEVEN MINUTES FROM NOW.
BUT THERE'S A GAUNTLET OF TROUBLE AND WOE BETWEEN HERE AND THE PORTAL AND THEN GETTING FREE OF 7734 ON THE OTHER SIDE.
YOU NEED ME.
AND I'LL NEED YOUR POWER. AND YOU FIGHTING ALONGSIDE ME.
SEVEN MINUTES... NO, SIX MINUTES, MON-EL, AND COUNTING.
COME ON, THIS OFFER GOES STALE QUICKLY, SO--
FIRE
AAAEEEEAAAAEEEEAAAAEEEEAAAAEEEEAAAAEEEEAA

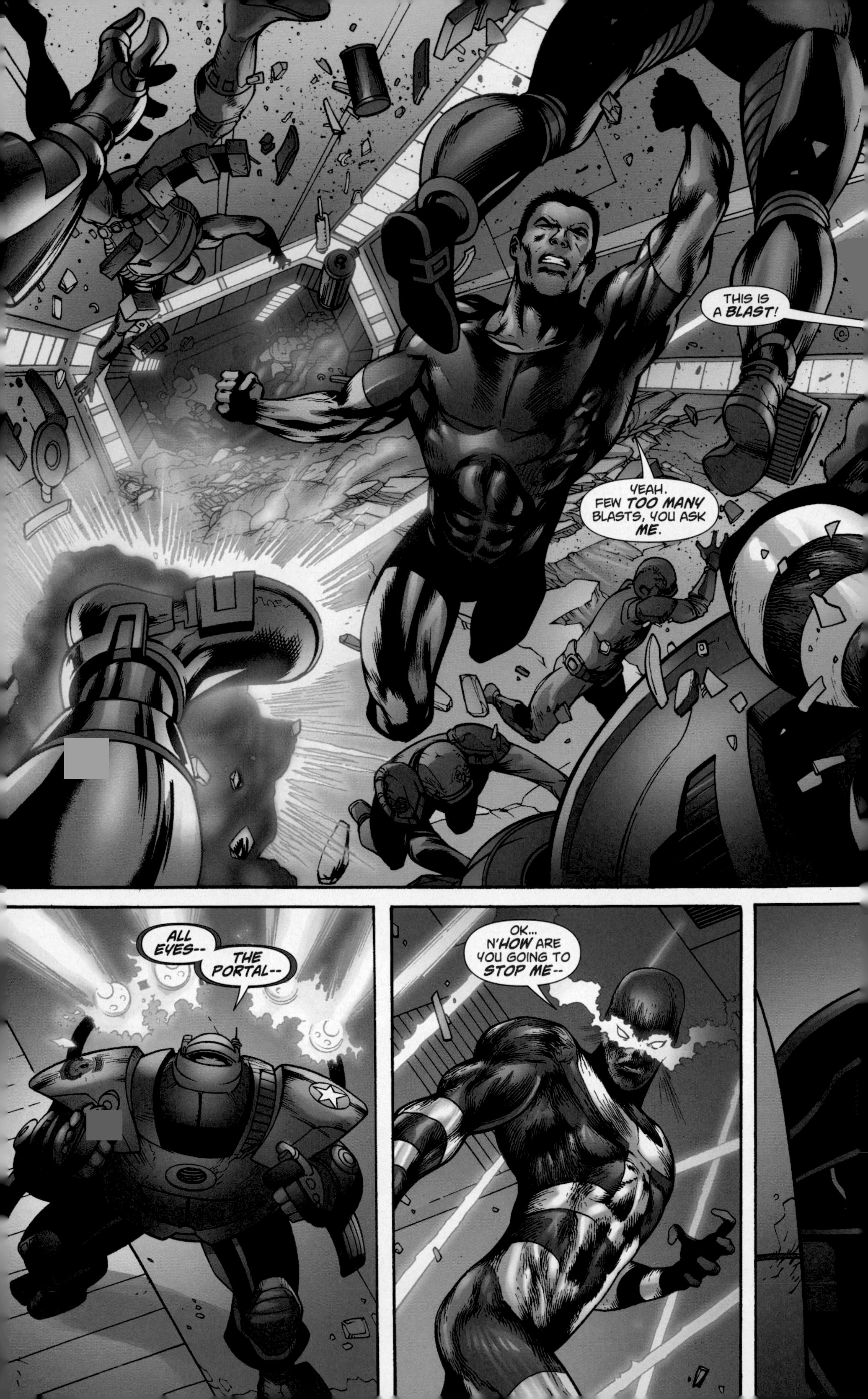
THIS IS A BLAST!
YEAH. FEW TOO MANY BLASTS, YOU ASK ME.
ALL EYES--
THE PORTAL--
OK... N'HOW ARE YOU GOING TO STOP ME--

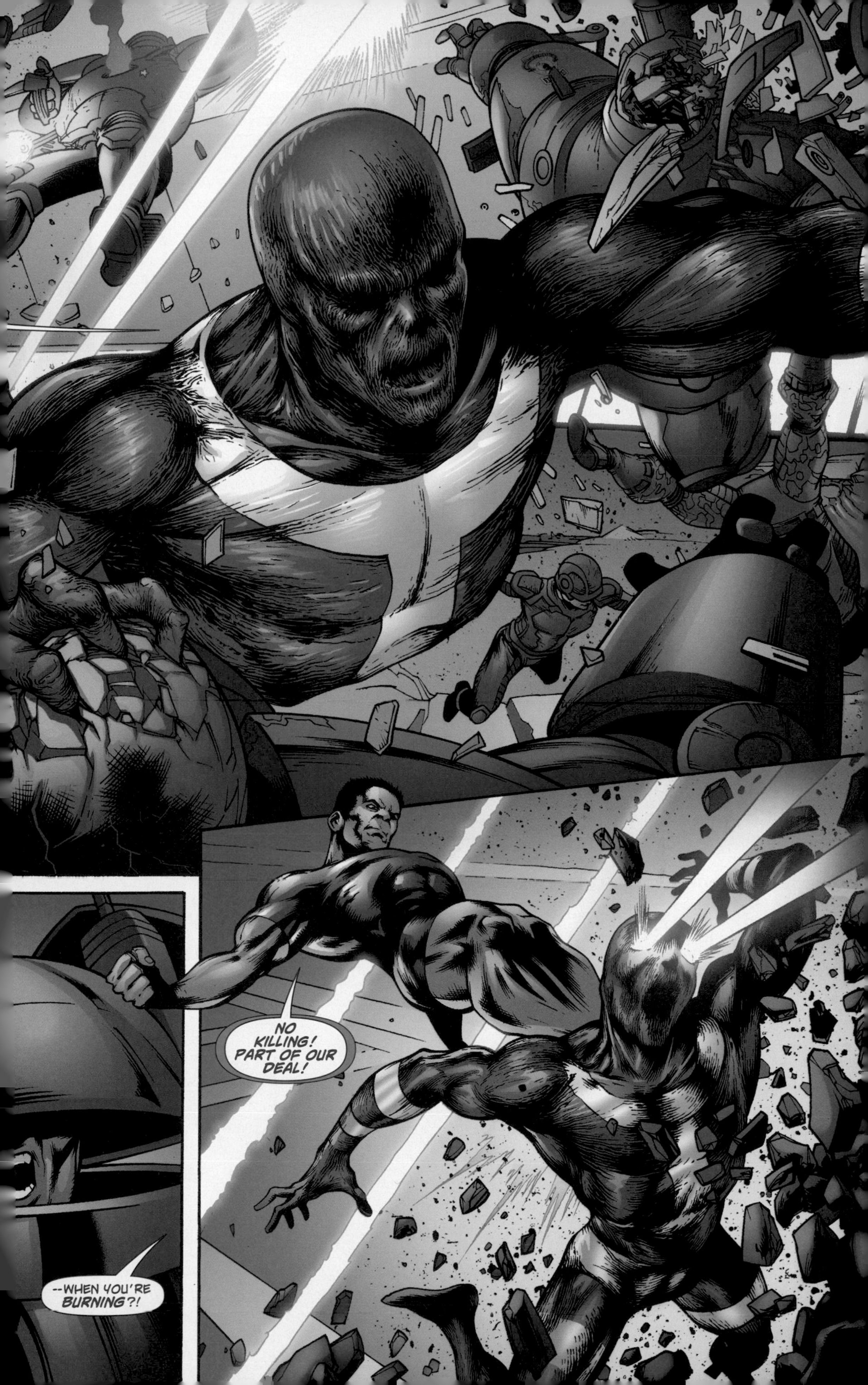
NO KILLING! PART OF OUR DEAL!
--WHEN YOU'RE BURNING?!

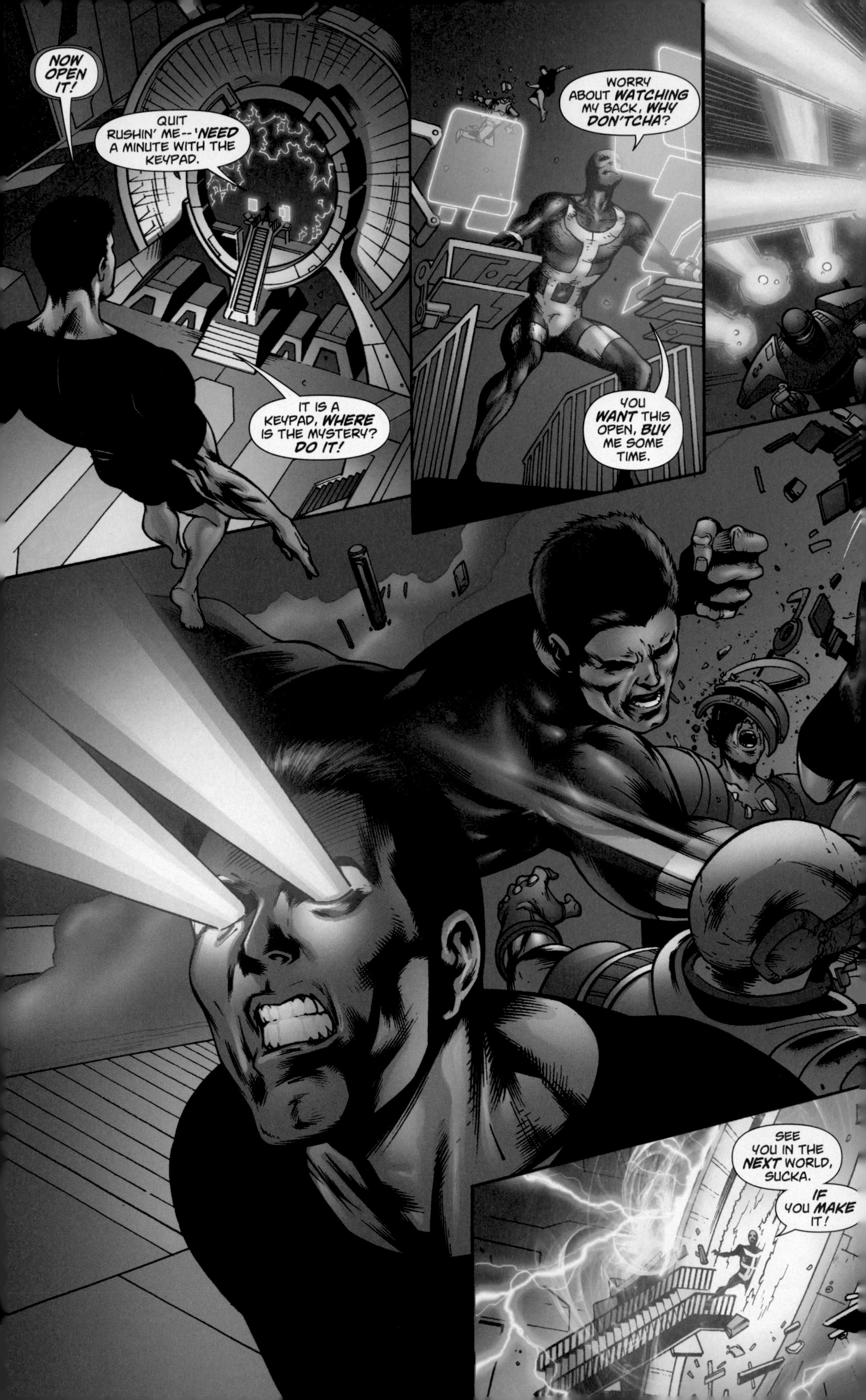
NOW OPEN IT!
QUIT RUSHIN' ME--'NEED A MINUTE WITH THE KEYPAD.
IT IS A KEYPAD, WHERE IS THE MYSTERY? DO IT!
WORRY ABOUT WATCHING MY BACK, WHY DON'TCHA?
YOU WANT THIS OPEN, BUY ME SOME TIME.
SEE YOU IN THE NEXT WORLD, SUCKA.
IF YOU MAKE IT!

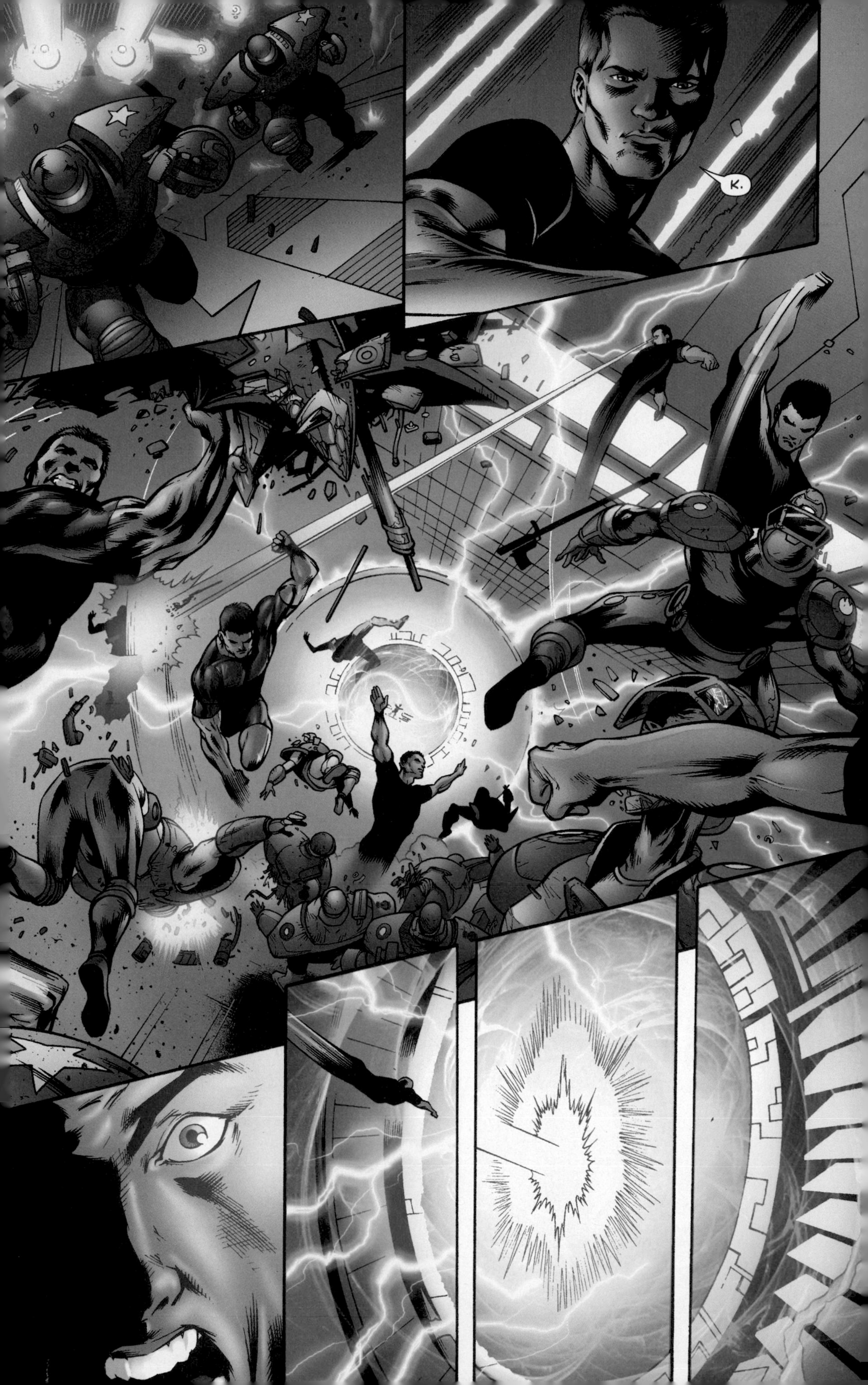
K.

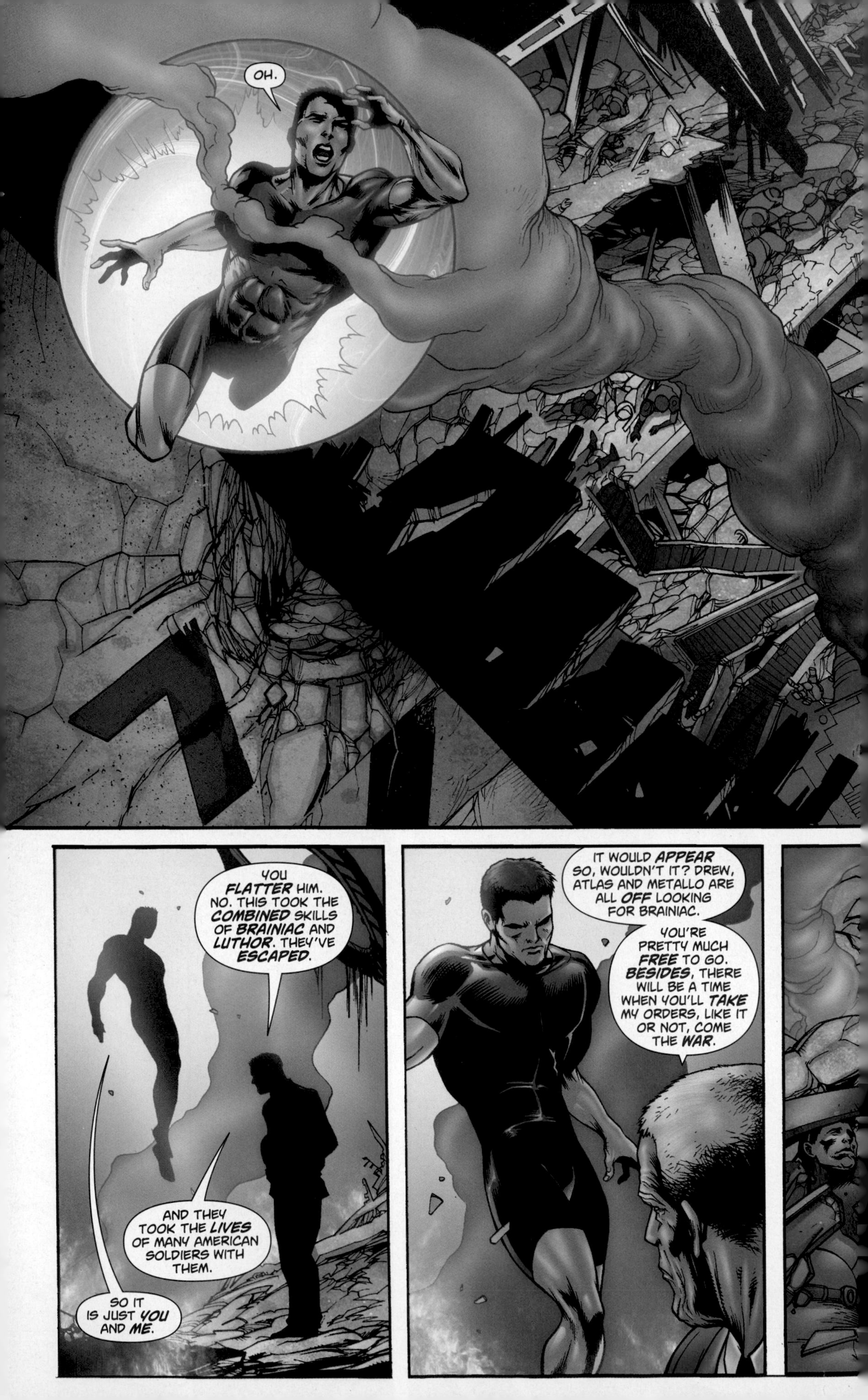
OH.
YOU FLATTER HIM. NO. THIS TOOK THE COMBINED SKILLS OF BRAINIAC AND LUTHOR. THEY'VE ESCAPED.
AND THEY TOOK THE LIVES OF MANY AMERICAN SOLDIERS WITH THEM.
SO IT IS JUST YOU AND ME.
IT WOULD APPEAR SO, WOULDN'T IT? DREW, ATLAS AND METALLO ARE ALL OFF LOOKING FOR BRAINIAC.
YOU'RE PRETTY MUCH FREE TO GO. BESIDES, THERE WILL BE A TIME WHEN YOU'LL TAKE MY ORDERS, LIKE IT OR NOT, COME THE WAR.

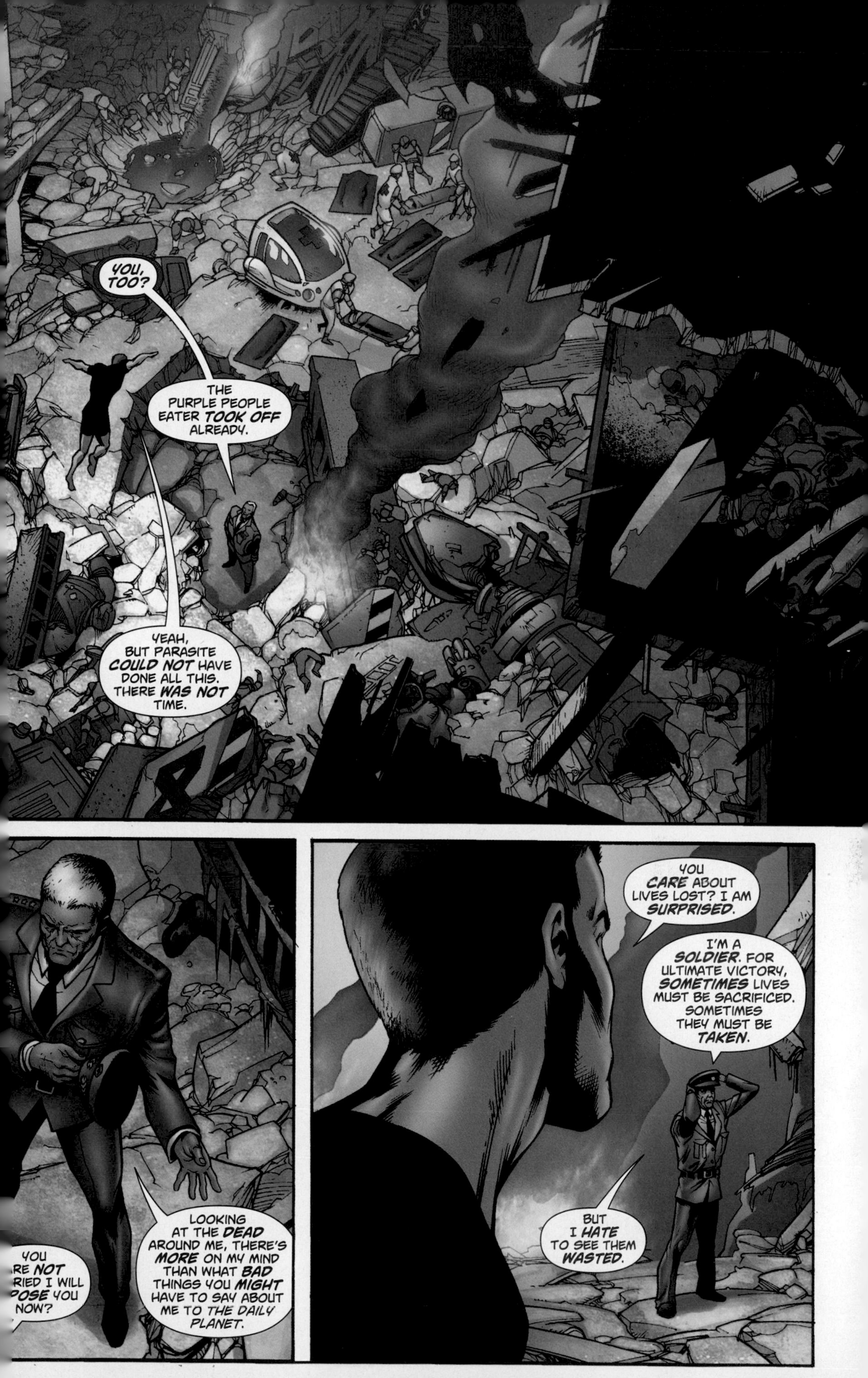

YOU, TOO?
THE PURPLE PEOPLE EATER TOOK OFF ALREADY.
YEAH, BUT PARASITE COULD NOT HAVE DONE ALL THIS. THERE WAS NOT TIME.
YOU RE NOT RIED I WILL POSE YOU NOW?
LOOKING AT THE DEAD AROUND ME, THERE'S MORE ON MY MIND THAN WHAT BAD THINGS YOU MIGHT HAVE TO SAY ABOUT ME TO THE DAILY PLANET.
YOU CARE ABOUT LIVES LOST? I AM SURPRISED.
I'M A SOLDIER. FOR ULTIMATE VICTORY, SOMETIMES LIVES MUST BE SACRIFICED. SOMETIMES THEY MUST BE TAKEN.
BUT I HATE TO SEE THEM WASTED.

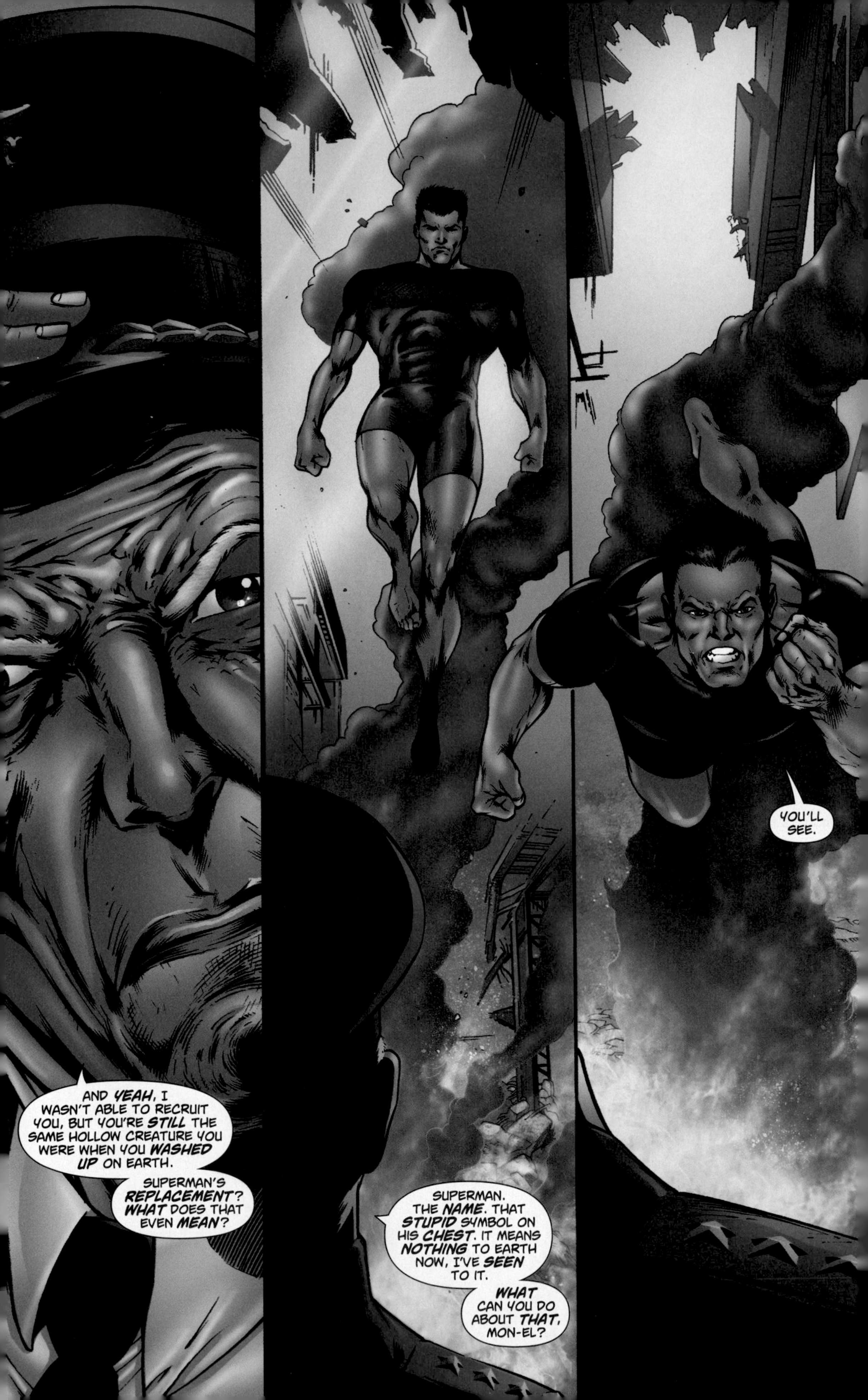
YOU'LL SEE.
AND YEAH, I WASN'T ABLE TO RECRUIT YOU, BUT YOU'RE STILL THE SAME HOLLOW CREATURE YOU WERE WHEN YOU WASHED UP ON EARTH.
SUPERMAN'S REPLACEMENT? WHAT DOES THAT EVEN MEAN?
SUPERMAN. THE NAME. THAT STUPID SYMBOL ON HIS CHEST. IT MEANS NOTHING TO EARTH NOW, I'VE SEEN TO IT.
WHAT CAN YOU DO ABOUT THAT, MON-EL?

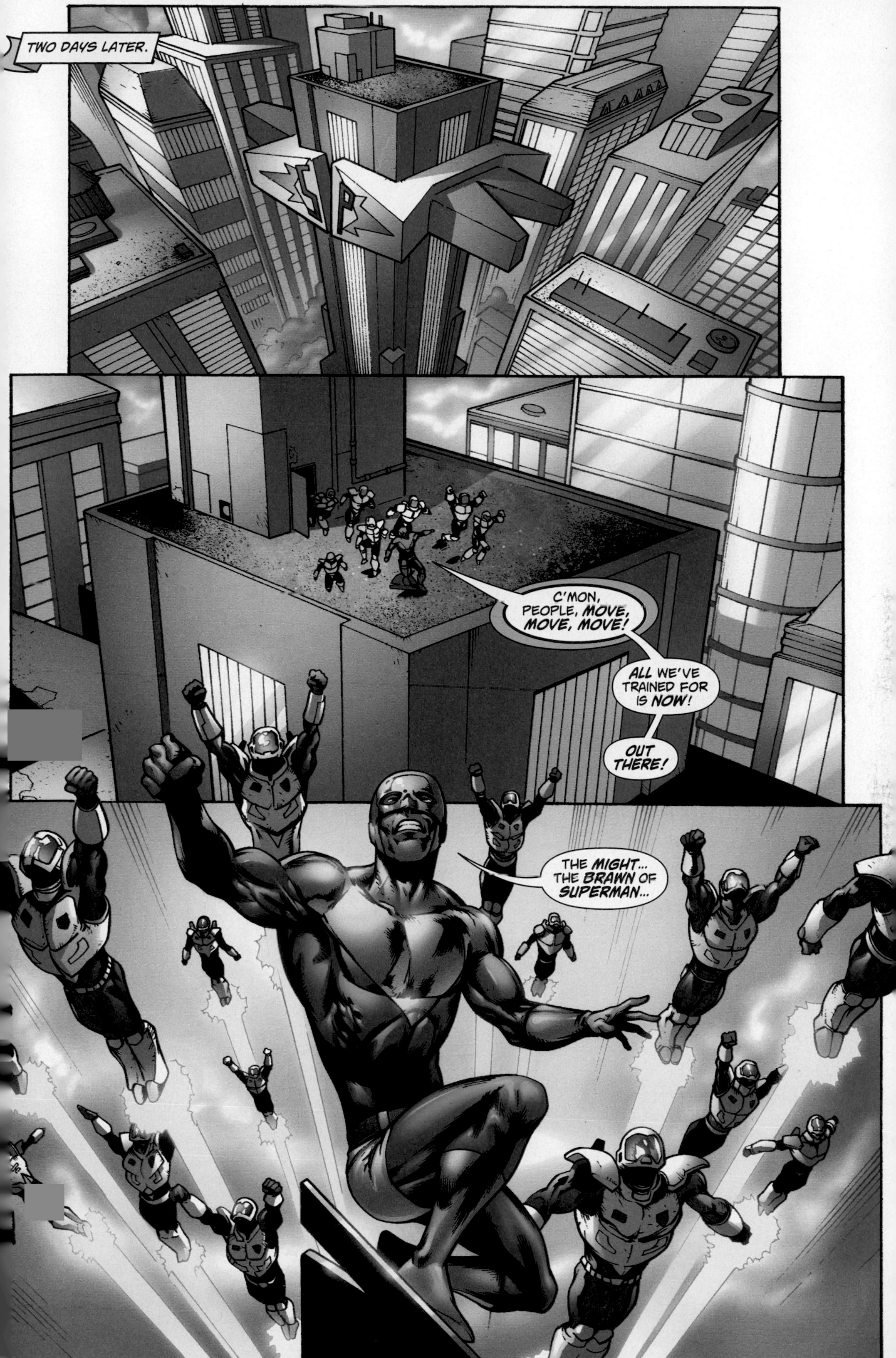
TWO DAYS LATER.
C'MON, PEOPLE, *MOVE*, *MOVE*, *MOVE*!
ALL WE'VE TRAINED FOR IS *NOW*!
OUT THERE!
THE *MIGHT*... THE *BRAWN* OF *SUPERMAN*...

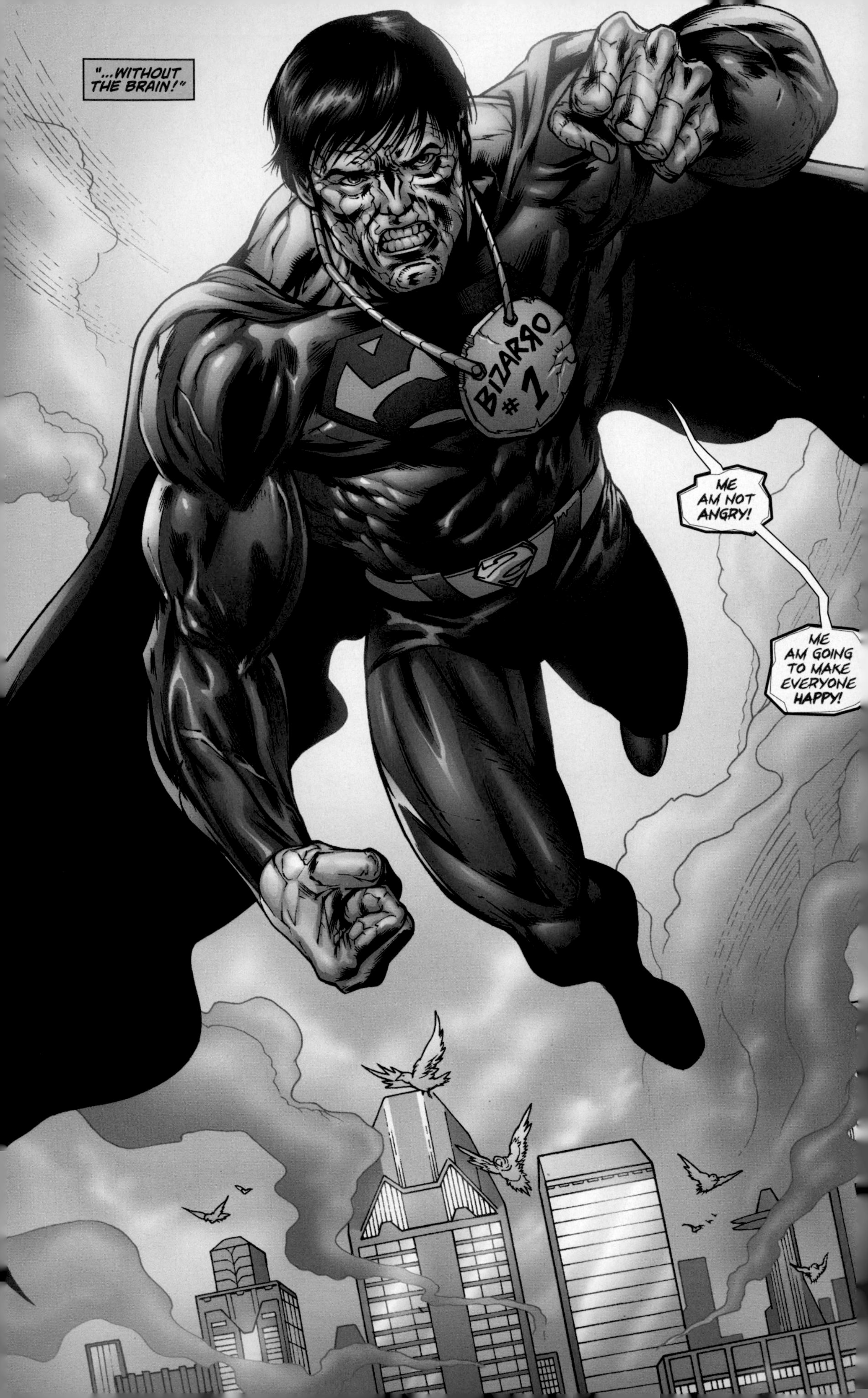
"...WITHOUT THE BRAIN!"
BIZARRO #1
ME AM NOT ANGRY!
ME AM GOING TO MAKE EVERYONE HAPPY!

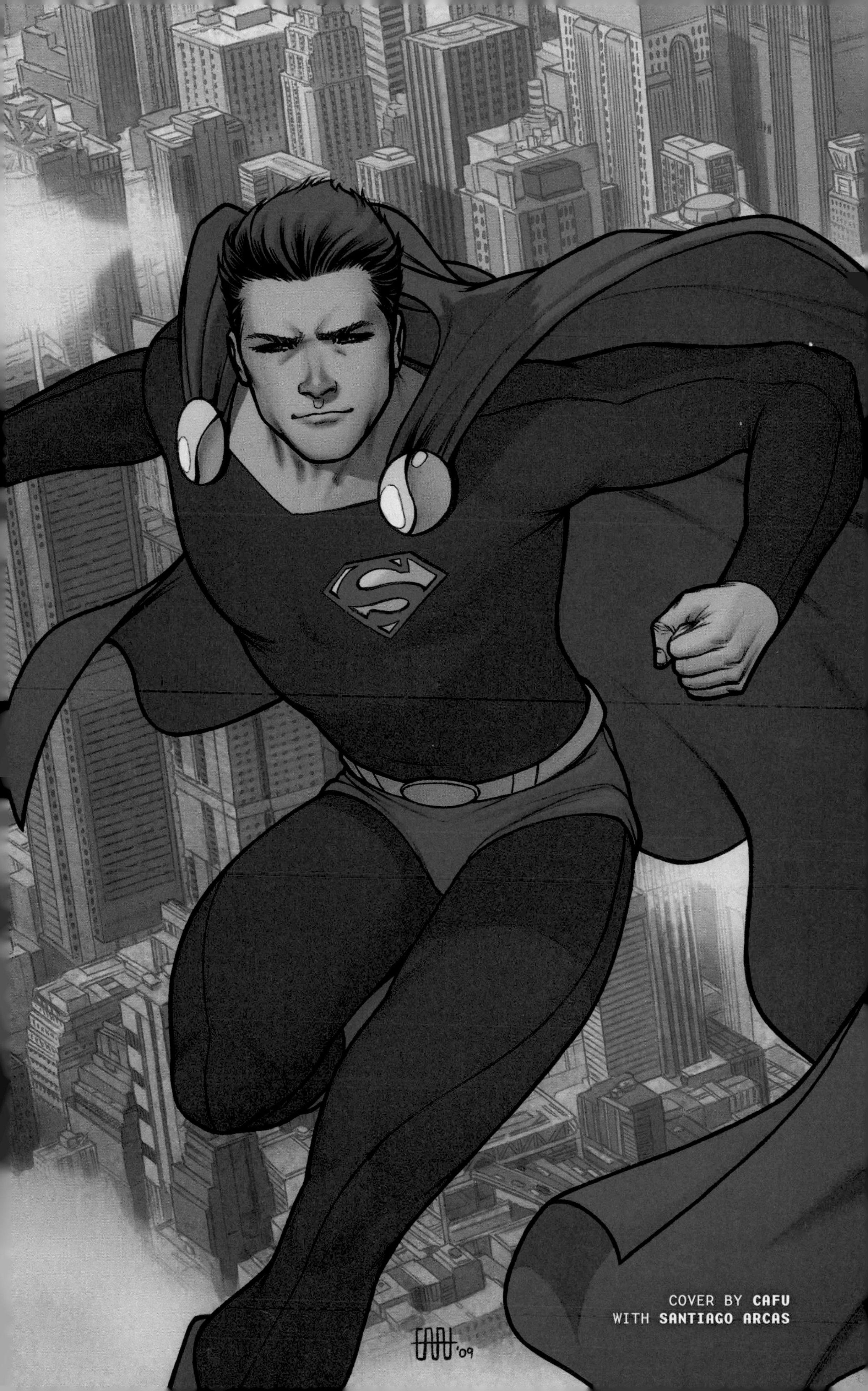

COVER BY **CAFU**
WITH **SANTIAGO ARCAS**

MAN OF VALOR PART ONE

JAVIER PINA <ARTIST>

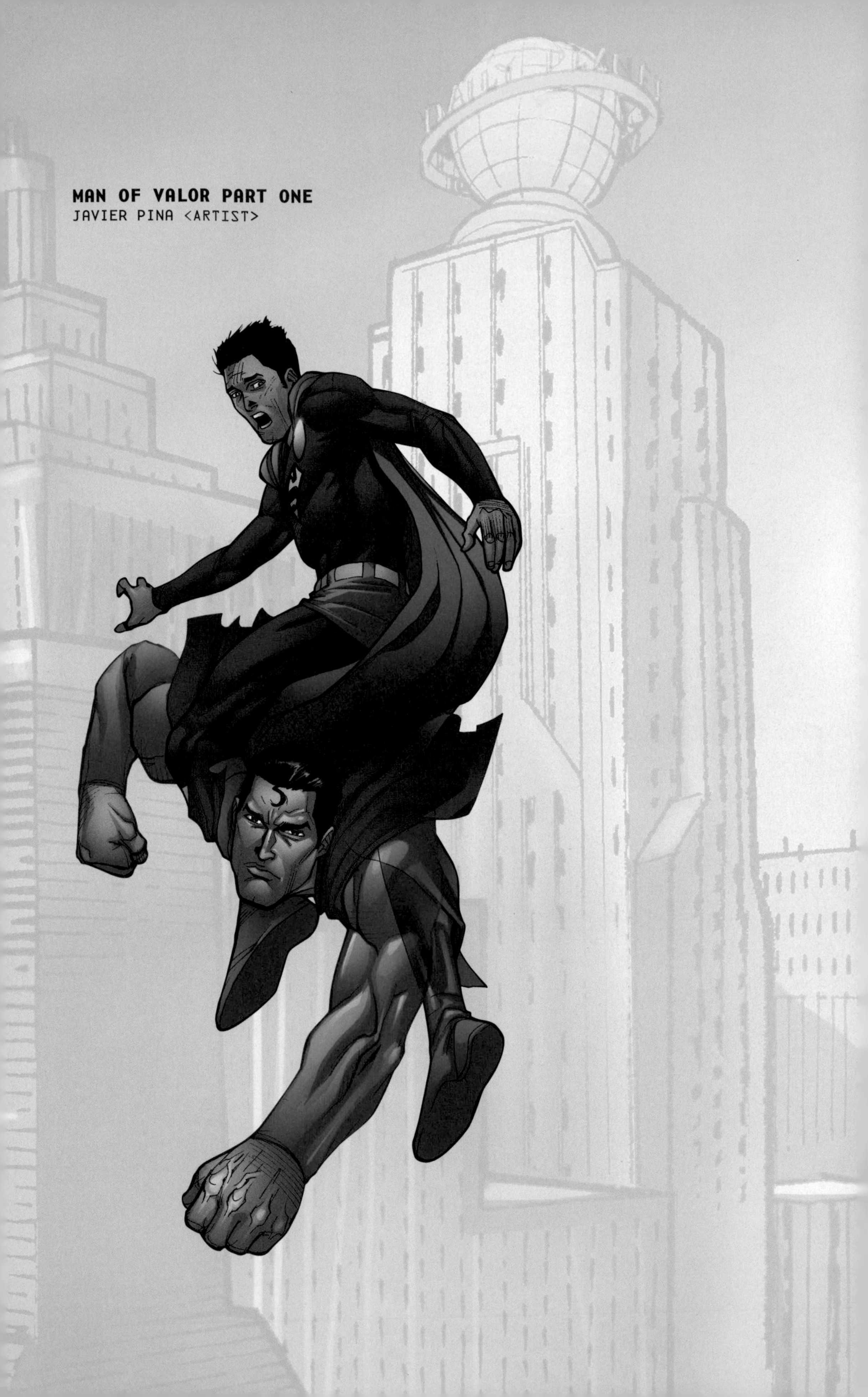

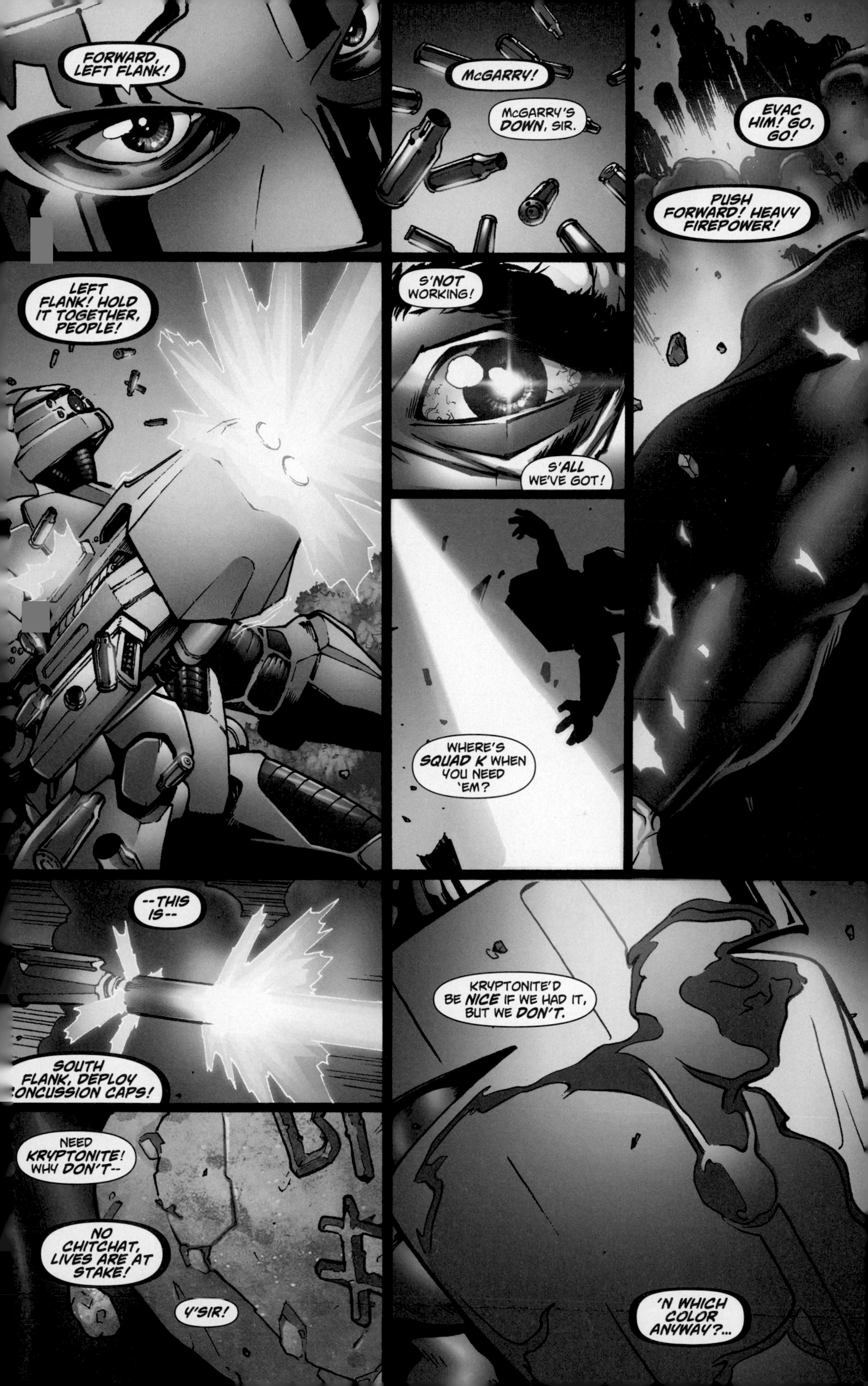
FORWARD, LEFT FLANK!
McGARRY!
McGARRY'S DOWN, SIR.
EVAC HIM! GO, GO!
PUSH FORWARD! HEAVY FIREPOWER!
LEFT FLANK! HOLD IT TOGETHER, PEOPLE!
S'NOT WORKING!
S'ALL WE'VE GOT!
WHERE'S SQUAD K WHEN YOU NEED 'EM?
--THIS IS--
SOUTH FLANK, DEPLOY CONCUSSION CAPS!
NEED KRYPTONITE! WHY DON'T--
NO CHITCHAT, LIVES ARE AT STAKE!
Y'SIR!
KRYPTONITE'D BE NICE IF WE HAD IT, BUT WE DON'T.
'N WHICH COLOR ANYWAY?...

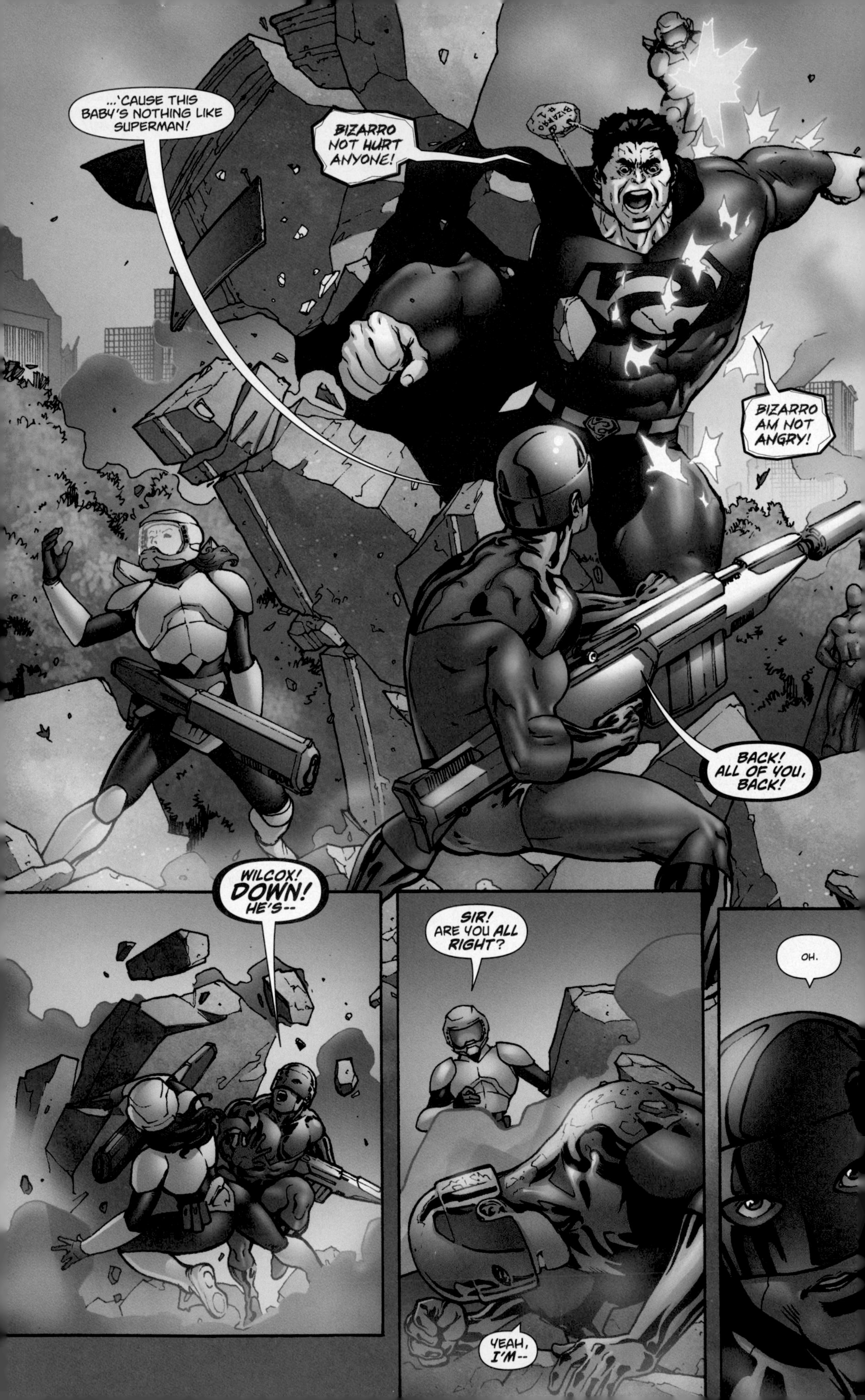
...'CAUSE THIS BABY'S NOTHING LIKE SUPERMAN!
BIZARRO NOT HURT ANYONE!
BIZARRO AM NOT ANGRY!
BACK! ALL OF YOU, BACK!
WILCOX! DOWN! HE'S--
SIR! ARE YOU ALL RIGHT?
YEAH, I'M--
OH.

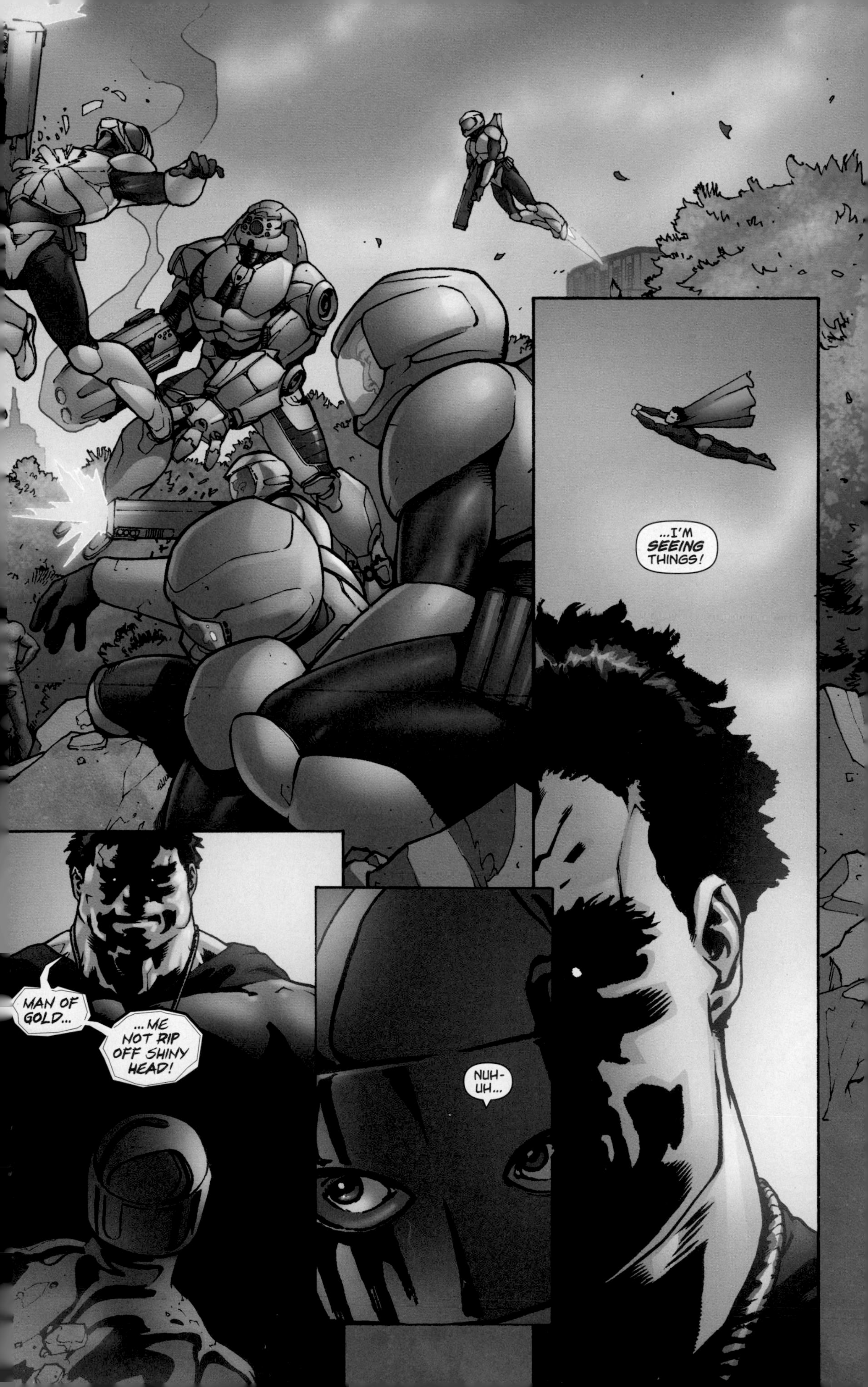
...I'M SEEING THINGS!
MAN OF GOLD...
...ME NOT RIP OFF SHINY HEAD!
NUH-UH...

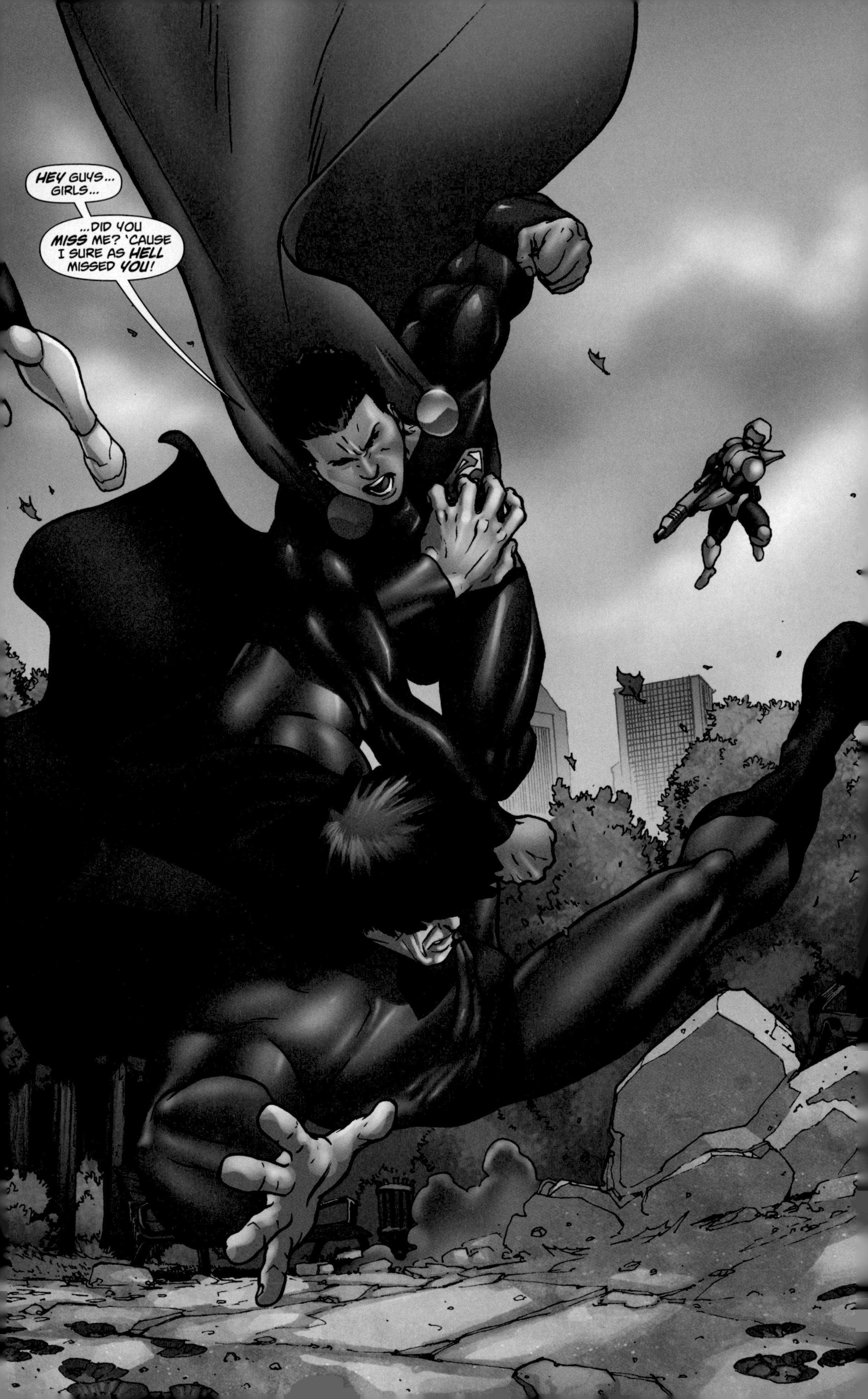
HEY GUYS... GIRLS...
...DID YOU MISS ME? 'CAUSE I SURE AS HELL MISSED YOU!

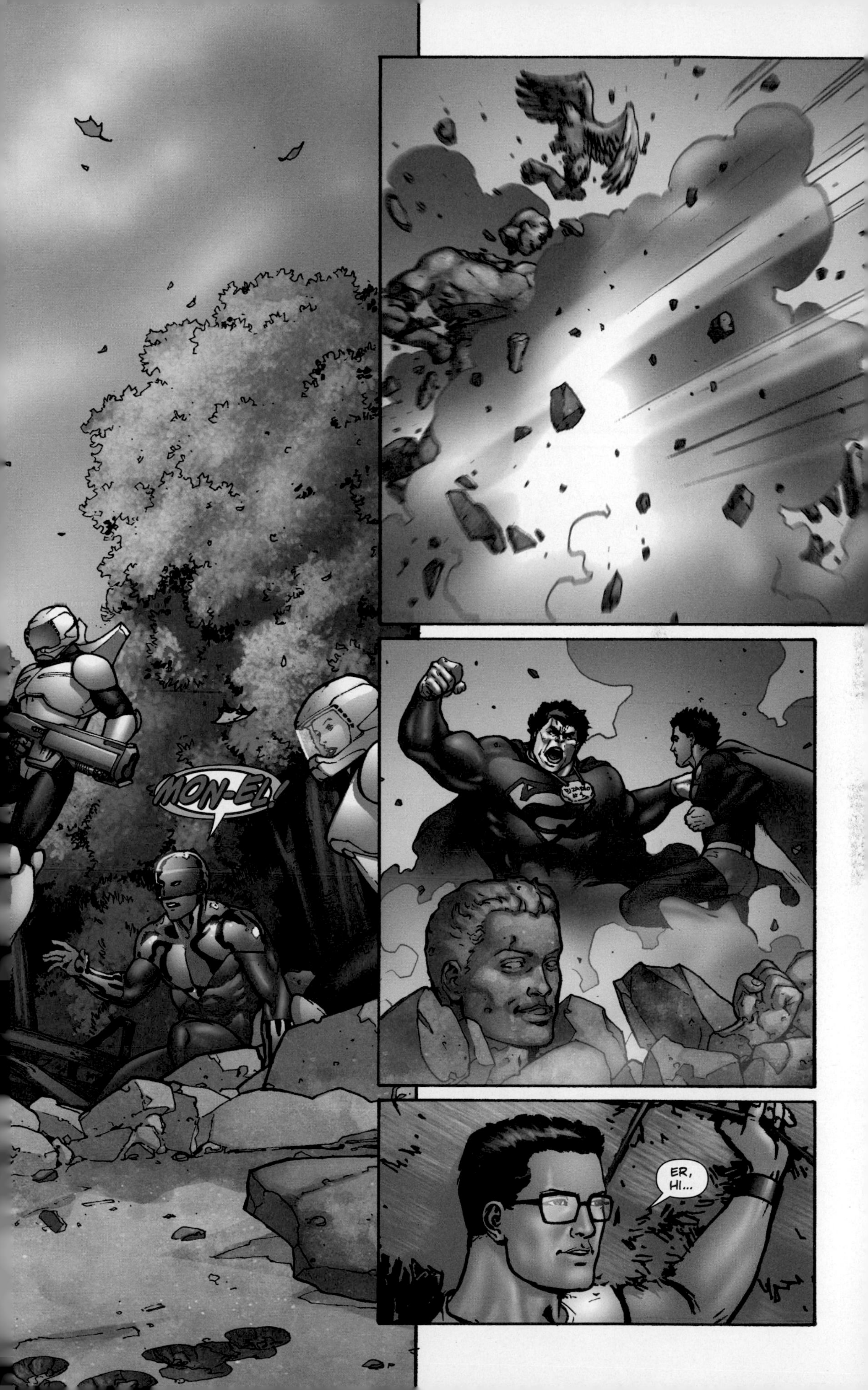
MON-EL!
ER, HI...

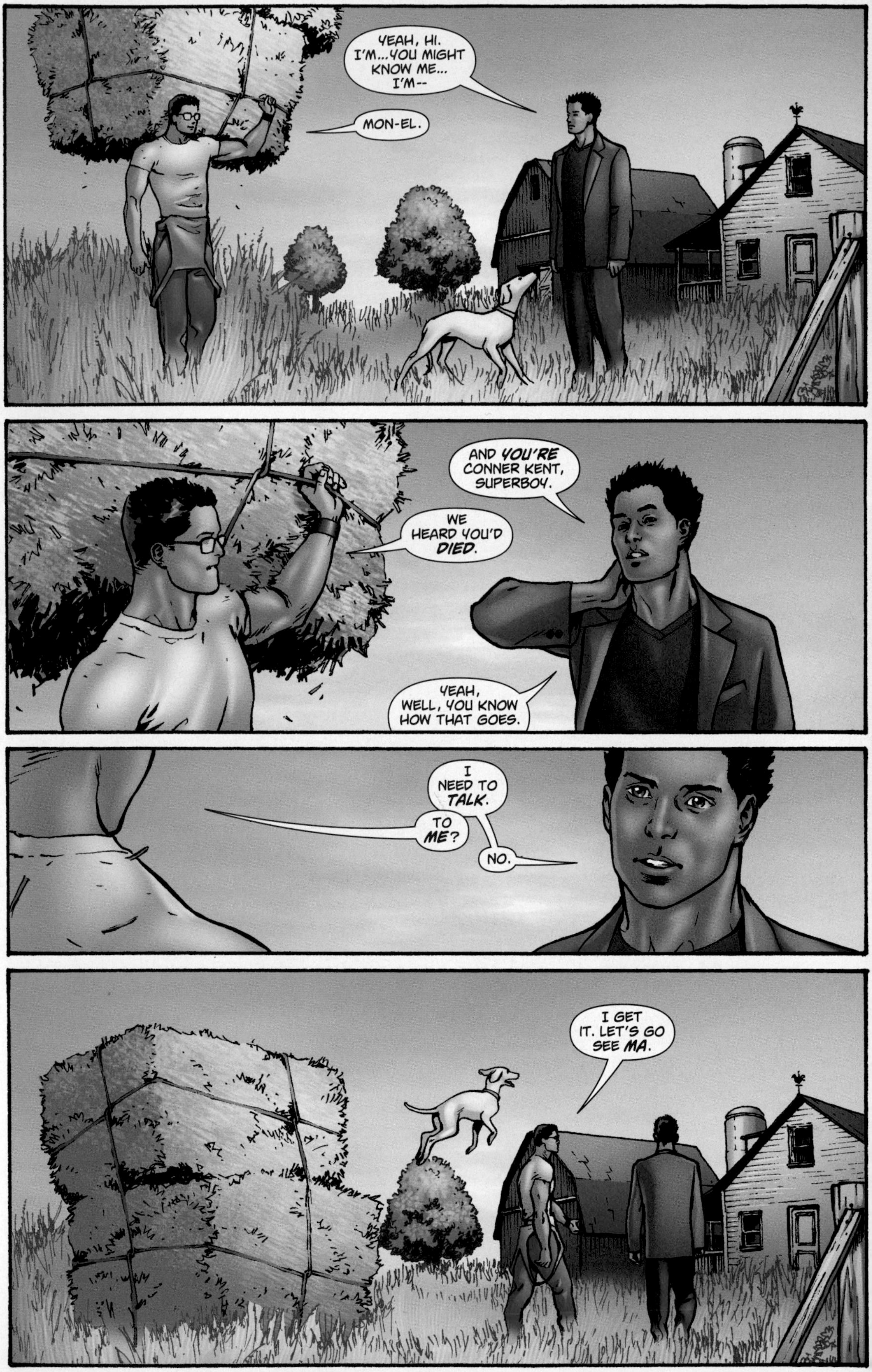

YEAH, HI. I'M...YOU MIGHT KNOW ME... I'M--
MON-EL.
AND YOU'RE CONNER KENT, SUPERBOY.
WE HEARD YOU'D DIED.
YEAH, WELL, YOU KNOW HOW THAT GOES.
I NEED TO TALK.
TO ME?
NO.
I GET IT. LET'S GO SEE MA.

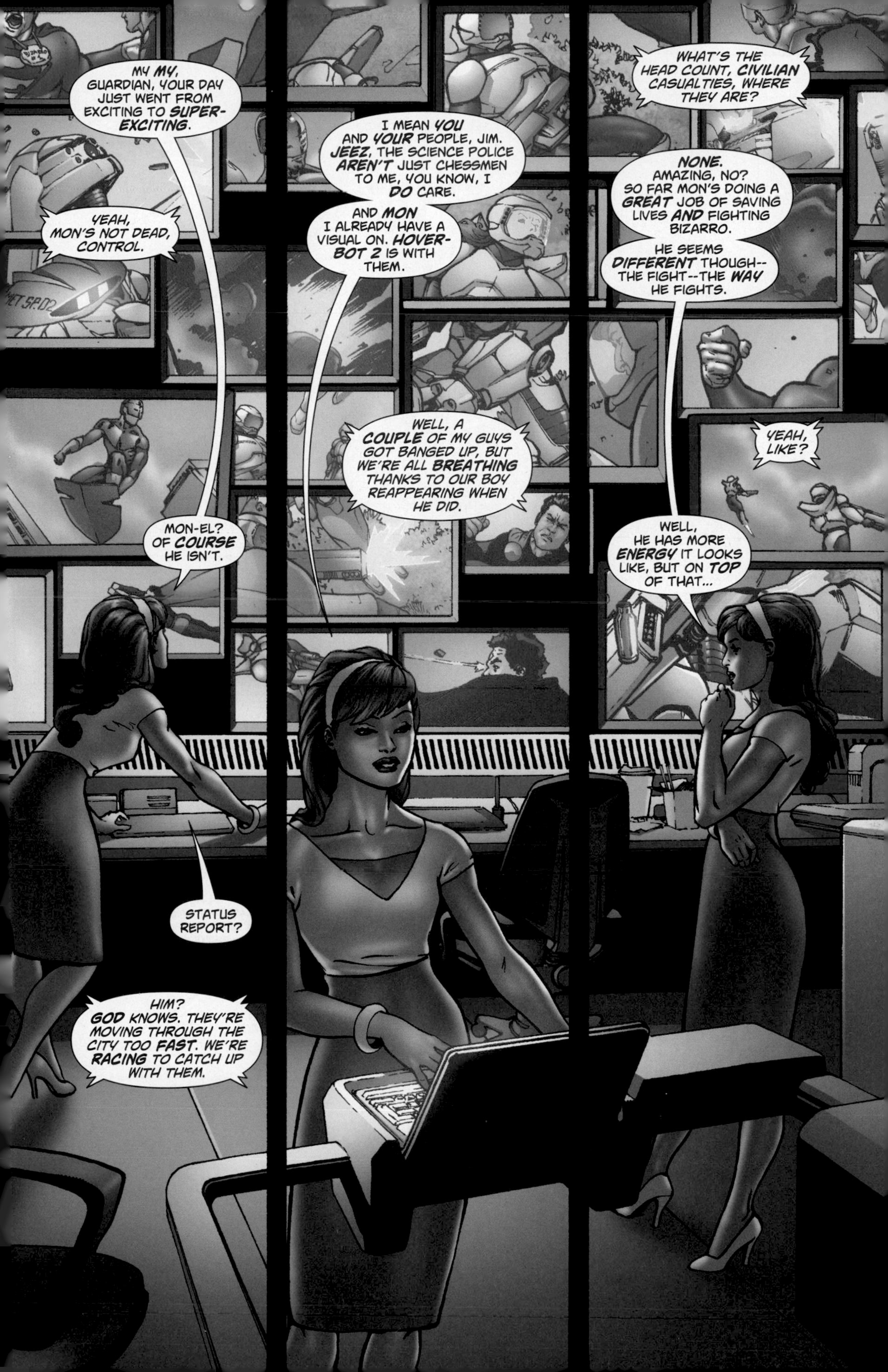
MY MY, GUARDIAN, YOUR DAY JUST WENT FROM EXCITING TO SUPER-EXCITING.
YEAH, MON'S NOT DEAD, CONTROL.
MON-EL? OF COURSE HE ISN'T.
STATUS REPORT?
HIM? GOD KNOWS. THEY'RE MOVING THROUGH THE CITY TOO FAST. WE'RE RACING TO CATCH UP WITH THEM.
I MEAN YOU AND YOUR PEOPLE, JIM. JEEZ, THE SCIENCE POLICE AREN'T JUST CHESSMEN TO ME, YOU KNOW, I DO CARE.
AND MON I ALREADY HAVE A VISUAL ON. HOVER-BOT 2 IS WITH THEM.
WELL, A COUPLE OF MY GUYS GOT BANGED UP, BUT WE'RE ALL BREATHING THANKS TO OUR BOY REAPPEARING WHEN HE DID.
WHAT'S THE HEAD COUNT, CIVILIAN CASUALTIES, WHERE THEY ARE?
NONE. AMAZING, NO? SO FAR MON'S DOING A GREAT JOB OF SAVING LIVES AND FIGHTING BIZARRO.
HE SEEMS DIFFERENT THOUGH--THE FIGHT--THE WAY HE FIGHTS.
YEAH, LIKE?
WELL, HE HAS MORE ENERGY IT LOOKS LIKE, BUT ON TOP OF THAT...

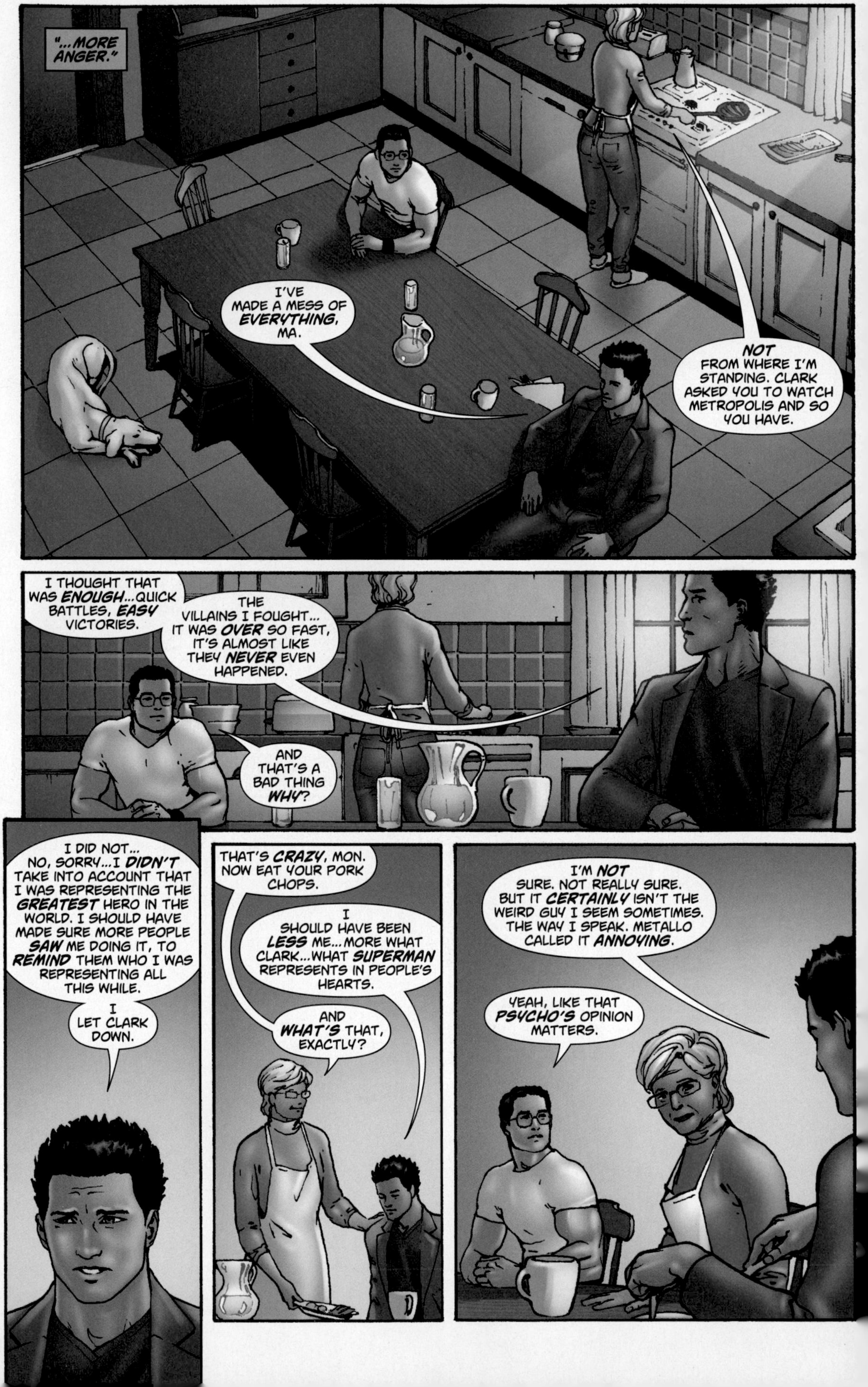
"...MORE ANGER."
I'VE MADE A MESS OF EVERYTHING, MA.
NOT FROM WHERE I'M STANDING. CLARK ASKED YOU TO WATCH METROPOLIS AND SO YOU HAVE.
I THOUGHT THAT WAS ENOUGH...QUICK BATTLES, EASY VICTORIES.
THE VILLAINS I FOUGHT... IT WAS OVER SO FAST, IT'S ALMOST LIKE THEY NEVER EVEN HAPPENED.
AND THAT'S A BAD THING WHY?
I DID NOT... NO, SORRY...I DIDN'T TAKE INTO ACCOUNT THAT I WAS REPRESENTING THE GREATEST HERO IN THE WORLD. I SHOULD HAVE MADE SURE MORE PEOPLE SAW ME DOING IT, TO REMIND THEM WHO I WAS REPRESENTING ALL THIS WHILE.
I LET CLARK DOWN.
THAT'S CRAZY, MON. NOW EAT YOUR PORK CHOPS.
I SHOULD HAVE BEEN LESS ME...MORE WHAT CLARK...WHAT SUPERMAN REPRESENTS IN PEOPLE'S HEARTS.
AND WHAT'S THAT, EXACTLY?
I'M NOT SURE. NOT REALLY SURE. BUT IT CERTAINLY ISN'T THE WEIRD GUY I SEEM SOMETIMES. THE WAY I SPEAK. METALLO CALLED IT ANNOYING.
YEAH, LIKE THAT PSYCHO'S OPINION MATTERS.

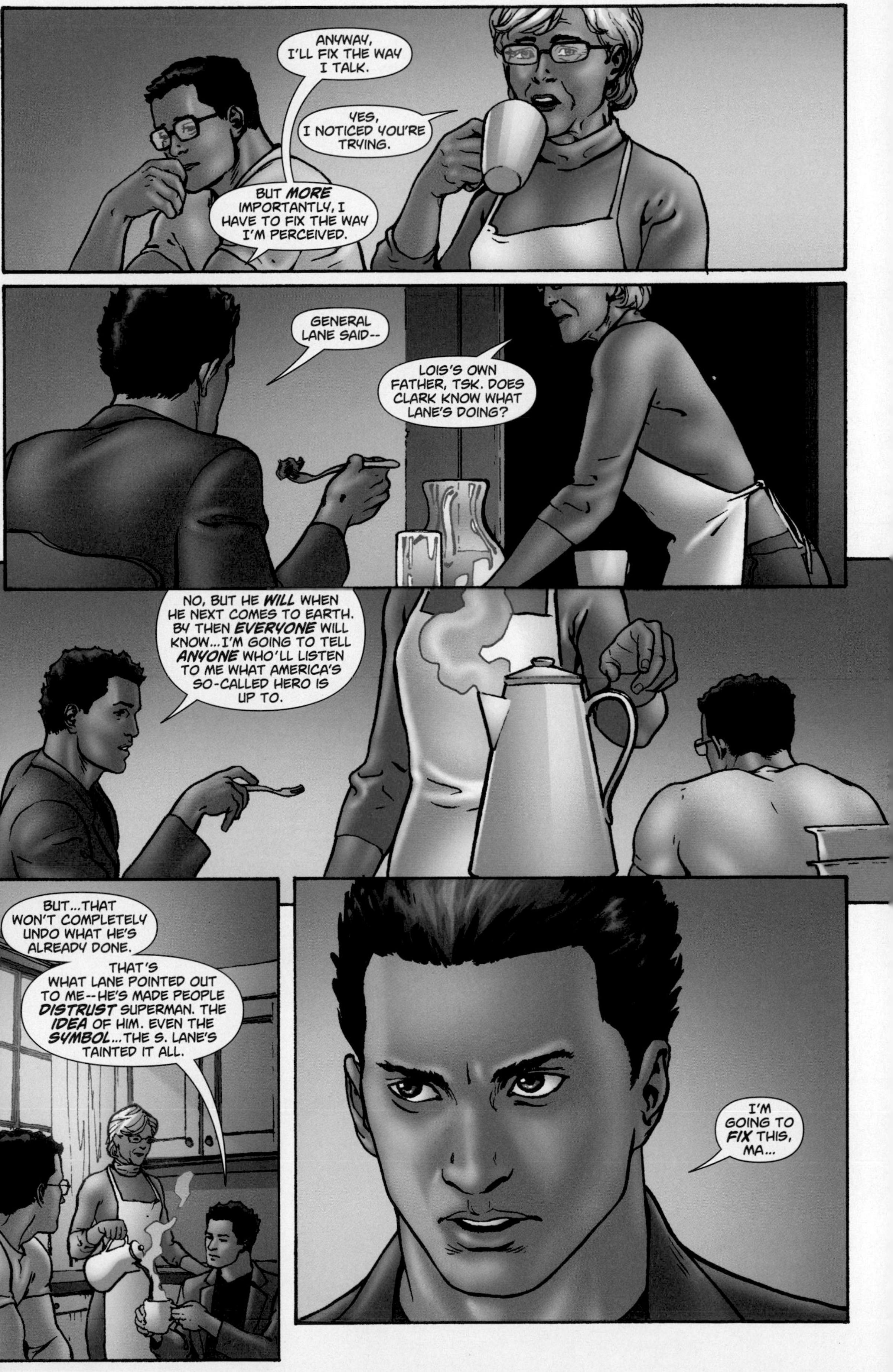
ANYWAY, I'LL FIX THE WAY I TALK.
YES, I NOTICED YOU'RE TRYING.
BUT MORE IMPORTANTLY, I HAVE TO FIX THE WAY I'M PERCEIVED.
GENERAL LANE SAID--
LOIS'S OWN FATHER, TSK. DOES CLARK KNOW WHAT LANE'S DOING?
NO, BUT HE WILL WHEN HE NEXT COMES TO EARTH. BY THEN EVERYONE WILL KNOW...I'M GOING TO TELL ANYONE WHO'LL LISTEN TO ME WHAT AMERICA'S SO-CALLED HERO IS UP TO.
BUT...THAT WON'T COMPLETELY UNDO WHAT HE'S ALREADY DONE.
THAT'S WHAT LANE POINTED OUT TO ME--HE'S MADE PEOPLE DISTRUST SUPERMAN. THE IDEA OF HIM. EVEN THE SYMBOL...THE S. LANE'S TAINTED IT ALL.
I'M GOING TO FIX THIS, MA...

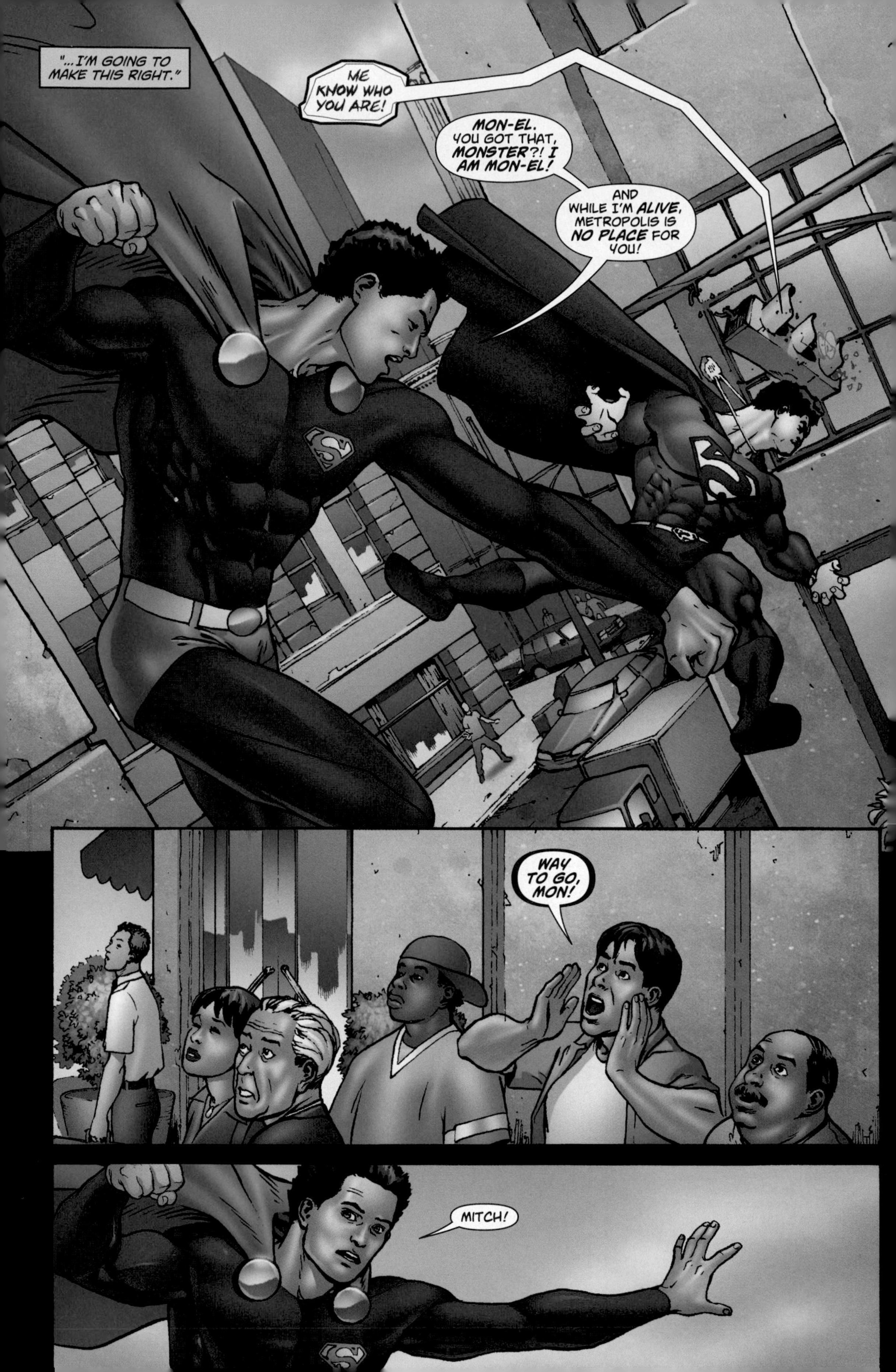
"...I'M GOING TO MAKE THIS RIGHT."
ME KNOW WHO YOU ARE!
MON-EL. YOU GOT THAT, MONSTER?! I AM MON-EL!
AND WHILE I'M ALIVE, METROPOLIS IS NO PLACE FOR YOU!
WAY TO GO, MON!
MITCH!

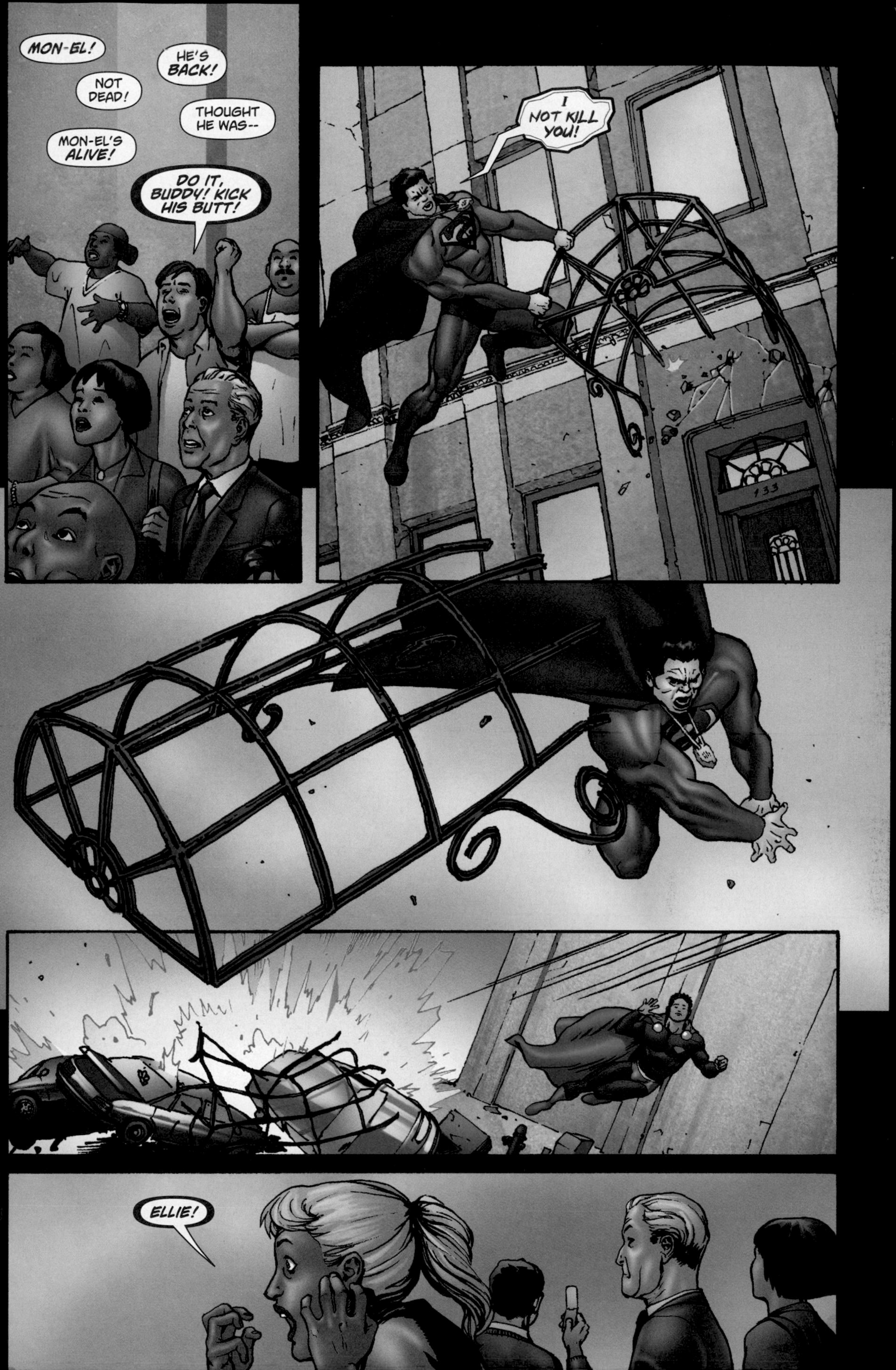
MON-EL!
NOT DEAD!
HE'S BACK!
THOUGHT HE WAS--
MON-EL'S ALIVE!
DO IT, BUDDY! KICK HIS BUTT!
I NOT KILL YOU!
ELLIE!

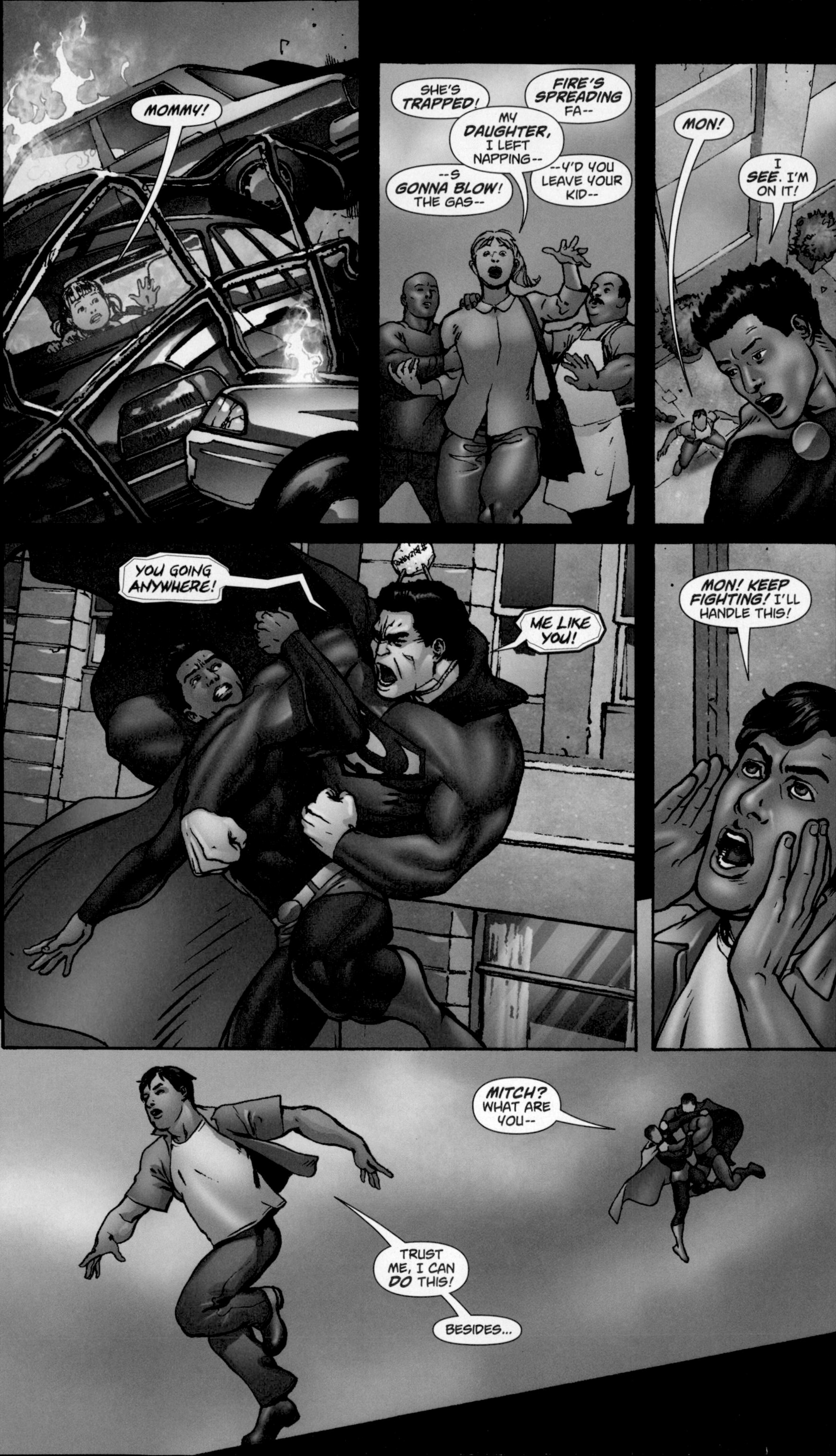
MOMMY!
SHE'S TRAPPED!
FIRE'S SPREADING FA--
MY DAUGHTER, I LEFT NAPPING--
--S GONNA BLOW! THE GAS--
--Y'D YOU LEAVE YOUR KID--
MON!
I SEE. I'M ON IT!
YOU GOING ANYWHERE!
ME LIKE YOU!
MON! KEEP FIGHTING! I'LL HANDLE THIS!
MITCH? WHAT ARE YOU--
TRUST ME, I CAN DO THIS!
BESIDES...

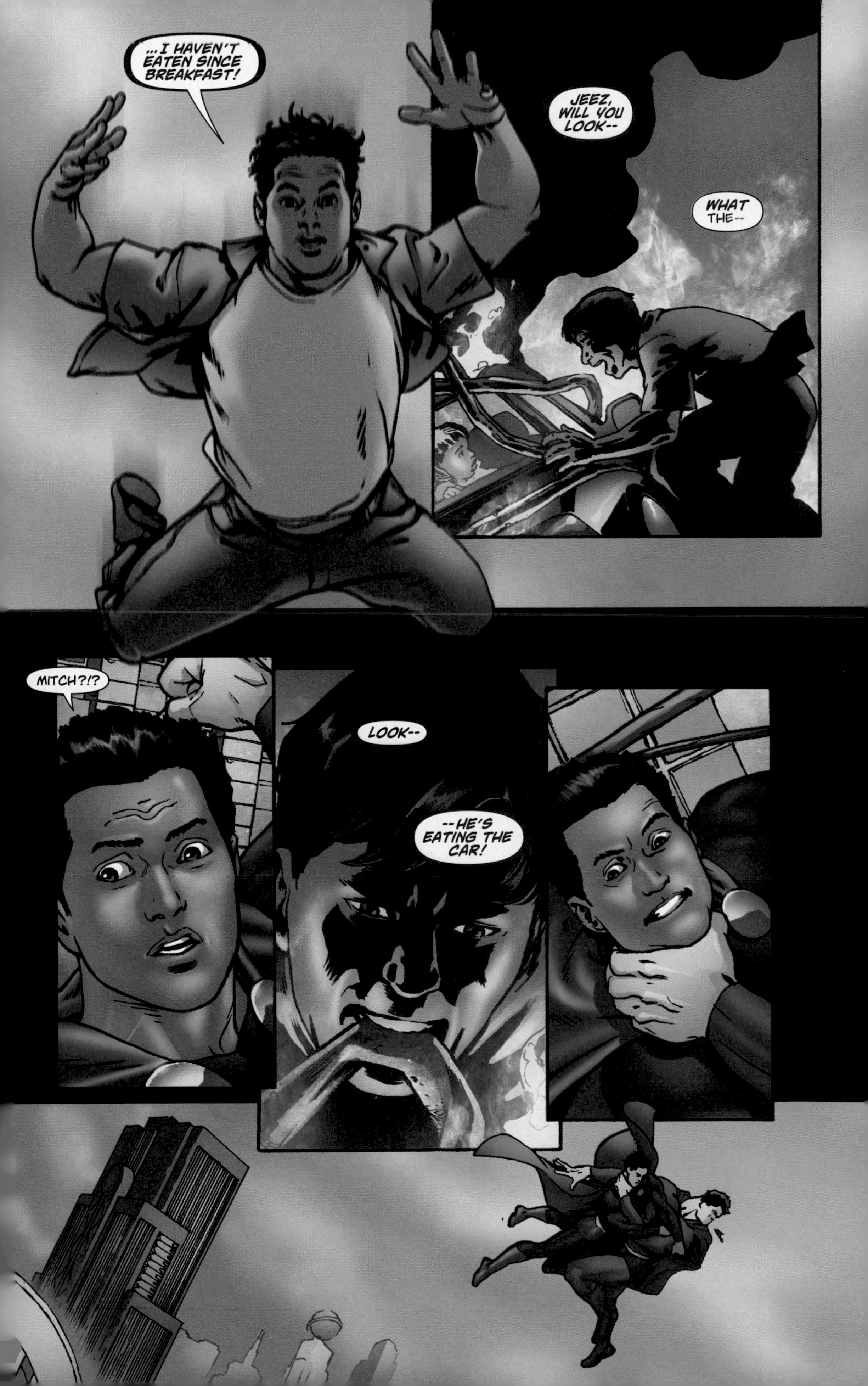
...I HAVEN'T EATEN SINCE BREAKFAST!
JEEZ, WILL YOU LOOK--
WHAT THE--
MITCH?!?
LOOK--
--HE'S EATING THE CAR!

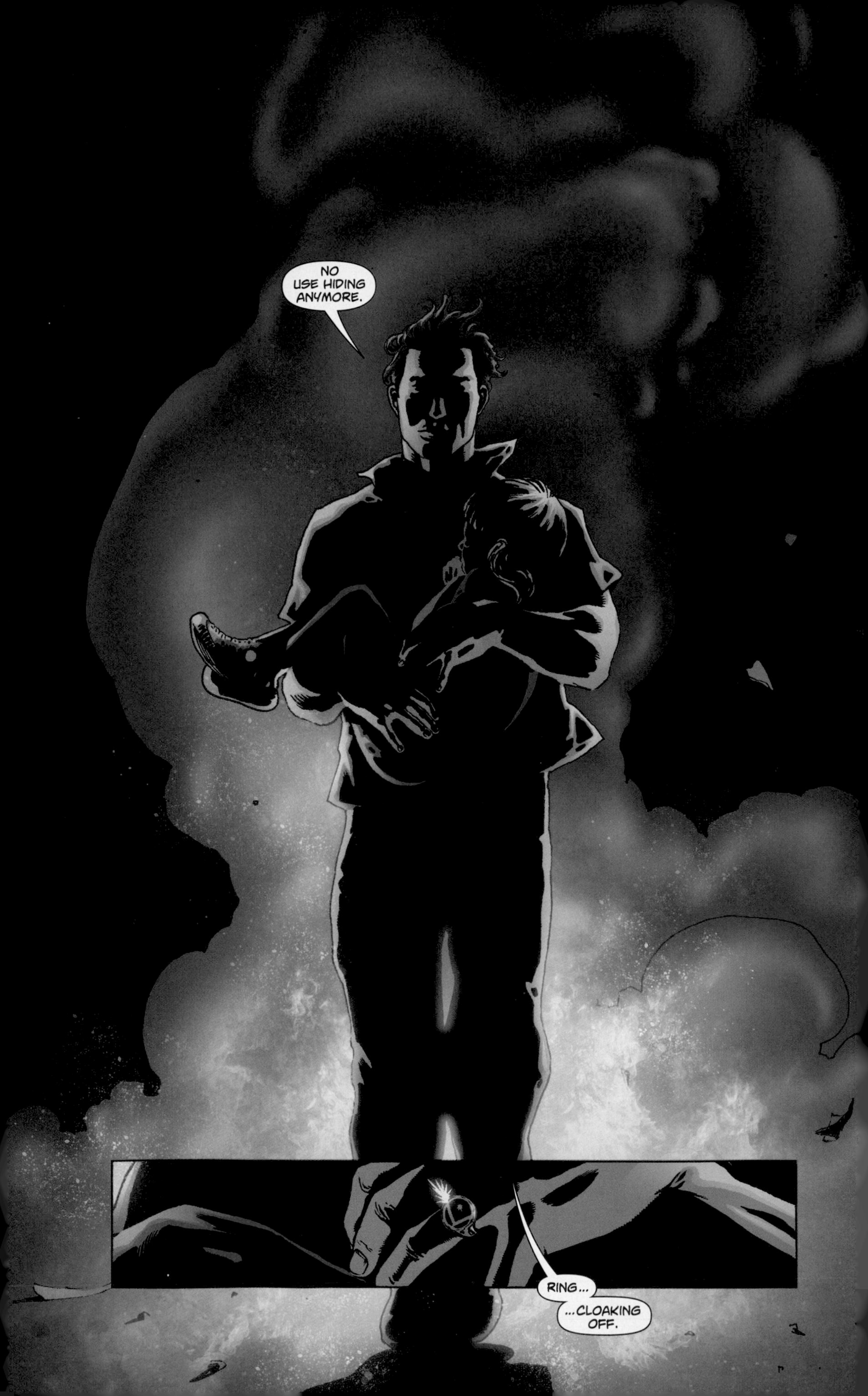
NO USE HIDING ANYMORE.
RING...
...CLOAKING OFF.

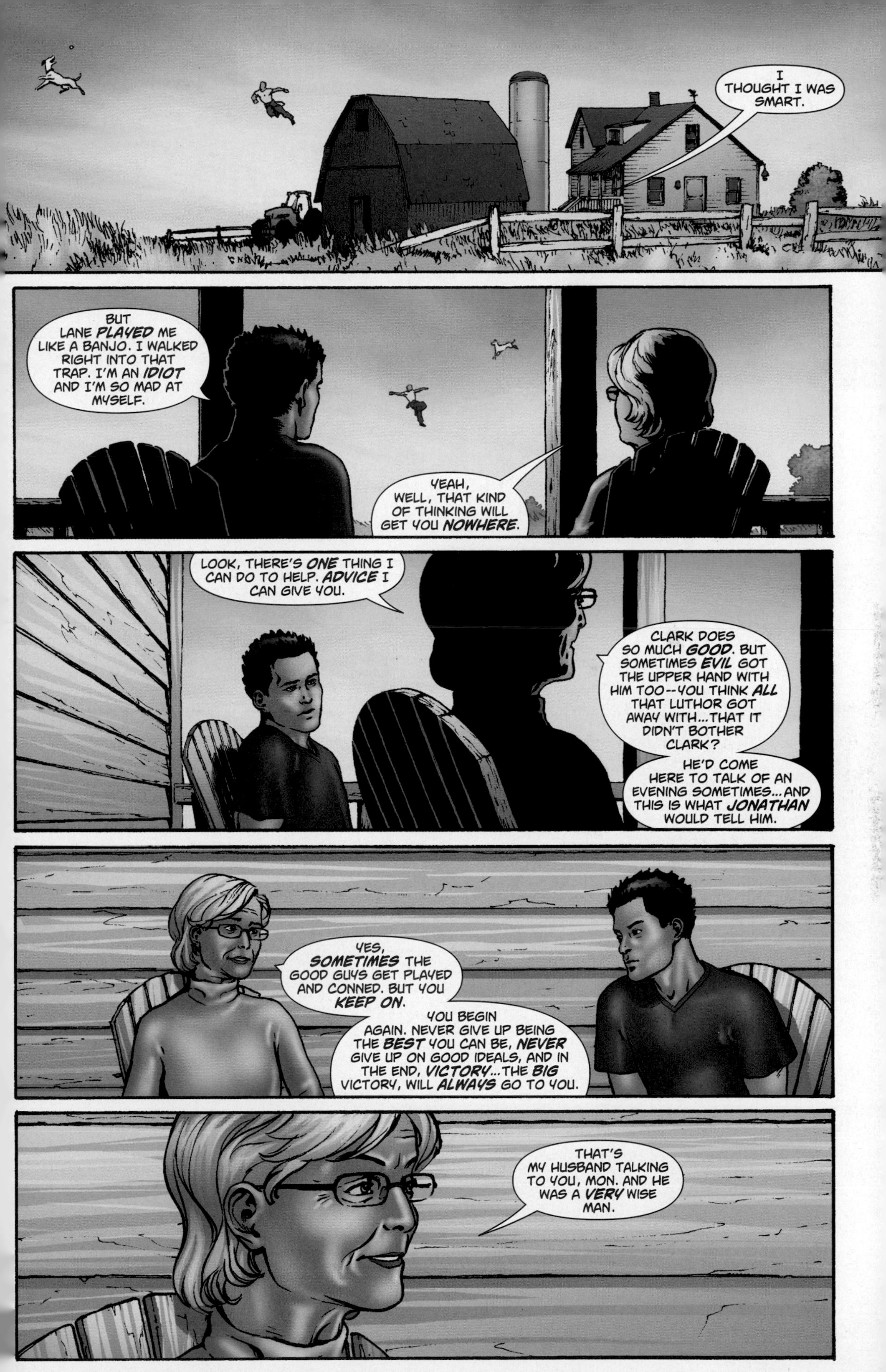
I THOUGHT I WAS SMART.
BUT LANE PLAYED ME LIKE A BANJO. I WALKED RIGHT INTO THAT TRAP. I'M AN IDIOT AND I'M SO MAD AT MYSELF.
YEAH, WELL, THAT KIND OF THINKING WILL GET YOU NOWHERE.
LOOK, THERE'S ONE THING I CAN DO TO HELP. ADVICE I CAN GIVE YOU.
CLARK DOES SO MUCH GOOD. BUT SOMETIMES EVIL GOT THE UPPER HAND WITH HIM TOO--YOU THINK ALL THAT LUTHOR GOT AWAY WITH...THAT IT DIDN'T BOTHER CLARK?
HE'D COME HERE TO TALK OF AN EVENING SOMETIMES...AND THIS IS WHAT JONATHAN WOULD TELL HIM.
YES, SOMETIMES THE GOOD GUYS GET PLAYED AND CONNED. BUT YOU KEEP ON.
YOU BEGIN AGAIN. NEVER GIVE UP BEING THE BEST YOU CAN BE, NEVER GIVE UP ON GOOD IDEALS, AND IN THE END, VICTORY...THE BIG VICTORY, WILL ALWAYS GO TO YOU.
THAT'S MY HUSBAND TALKING TO YOU, MON. AND HE WAS A VERY WISE MAN.

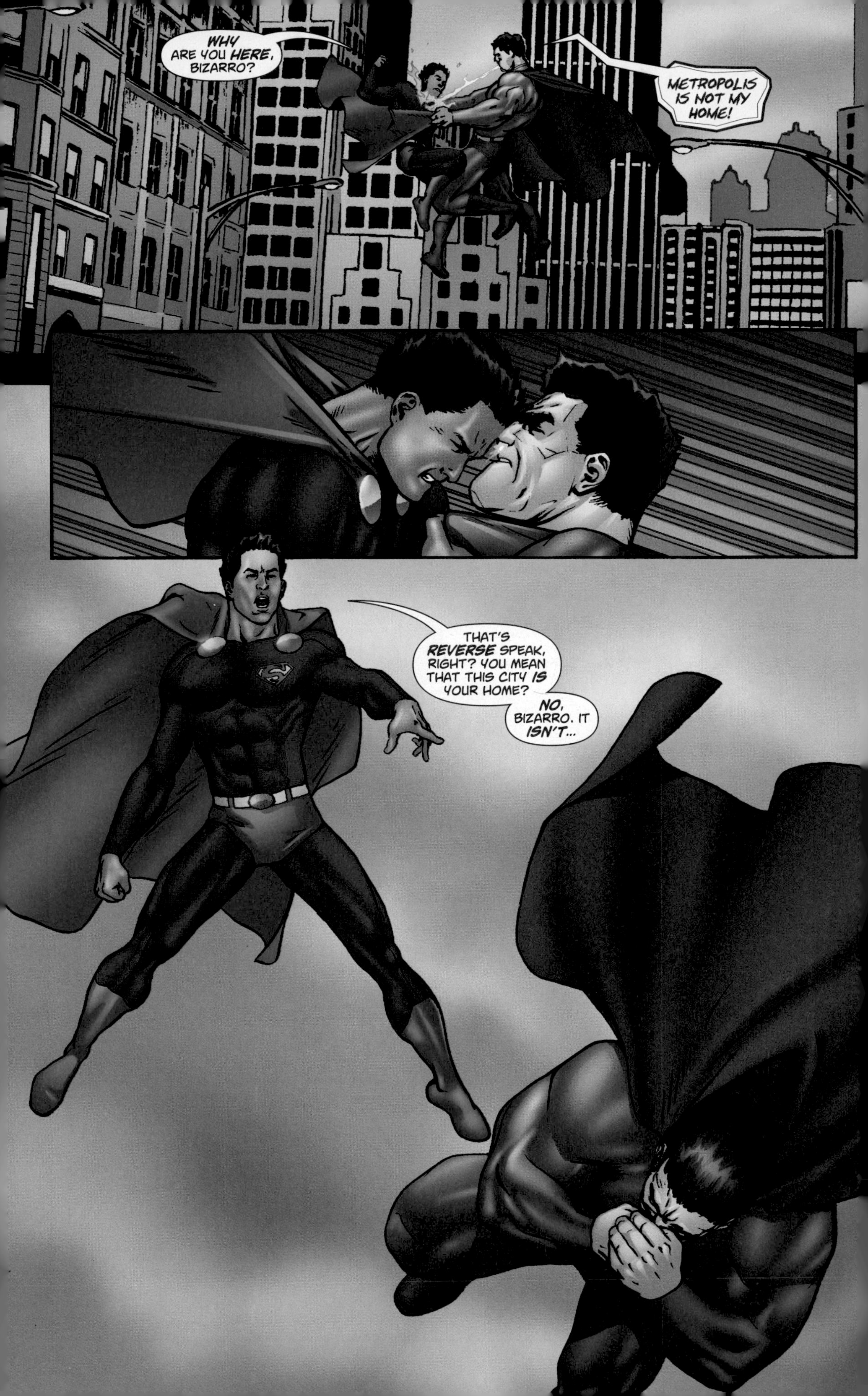
WHY ARE YOU HERE, BIZARRO?
METROPOLIS IS NOT MY HOME!
THAT'S REVERSE SPEAK, RIGHT? YOU MEAN THAT THIS CITY IS YOUR HOME?
NO, BIZARRO. IT ISN'T...

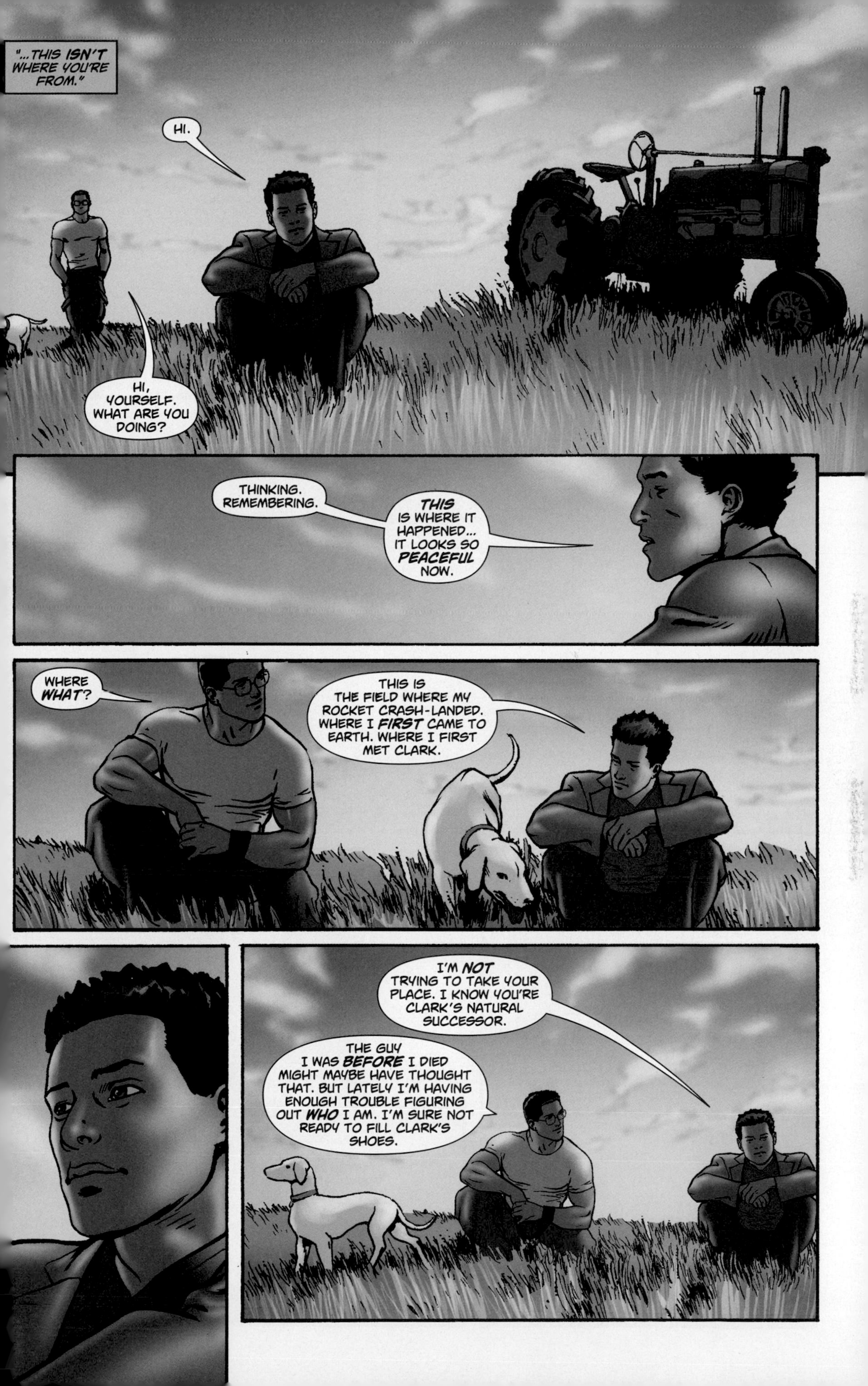
"...THIS ISN'T WHERE YOU'RE FROM."
HI.
HI, YOURSELF. WHAT ARE YOU DOING?
THINKING. REMEMBERING.
THIS IS WHERE IT HAPPENED... IT LOOKS SO PEACEFUL NOW.
WHERE WHAT?
THIS IS THE FIELD WHERE MY ROCKET CRASH-LANDED. WHERE I FIRST CAME TO EARTH. WHERE I FIRST MET CLARK.
I'M NOT TRYING TO TAKE YOUR PLACE. I KNOW YOU'RE CLARK'S NATURAL SUCCESSOR.
THE GUY I WAS BEFORE I DIED MIGHT MAYBE HAVE THOUGHT THAT. BUT LATELY I'M HAVING ENOUGH TROUBLE FIGURING OUT WHO I AM. I'M SURE NOT READY TO FILL CLARK'S SHOES.

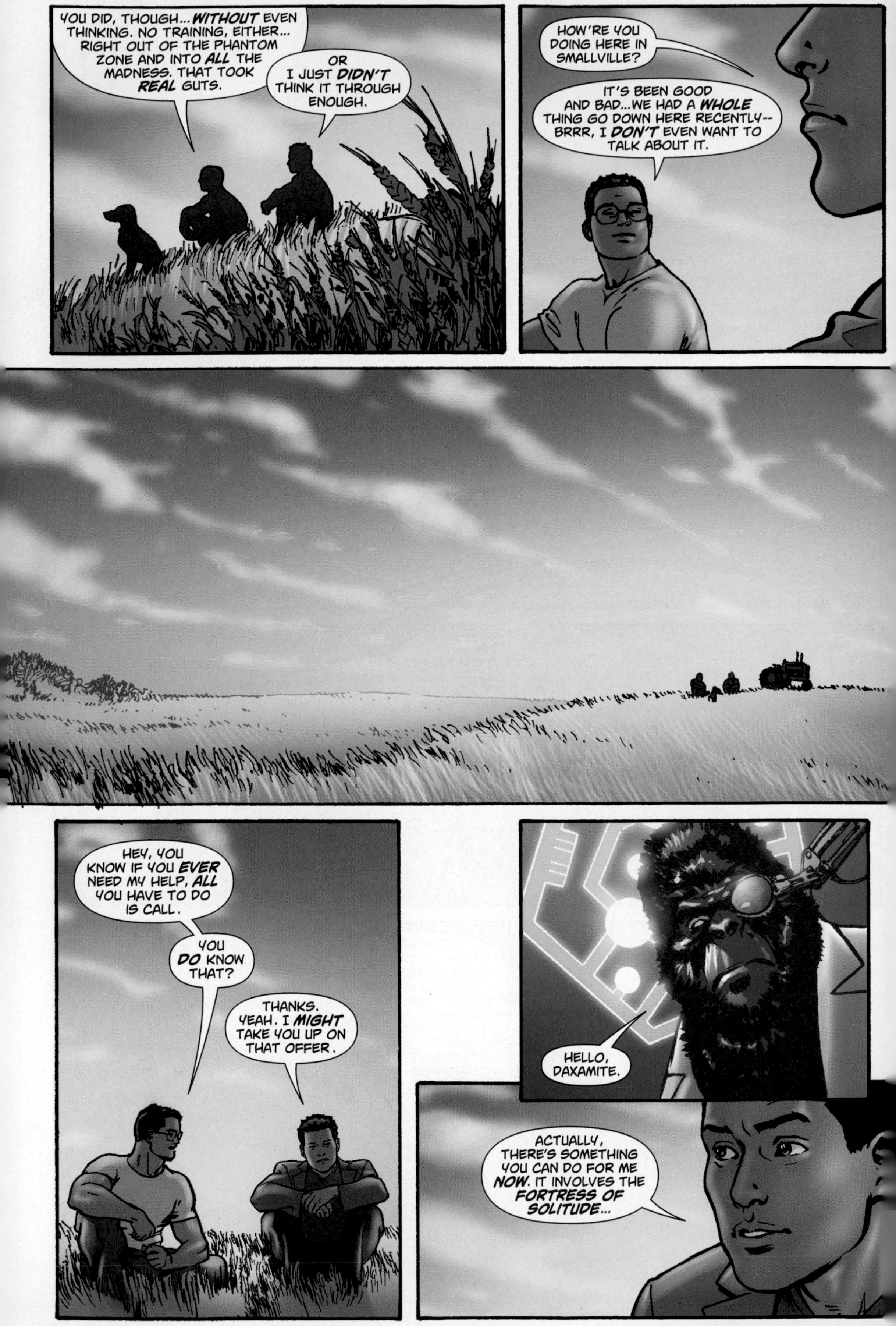
YOU DID, THOUGH... WITHOUT EVEN THINKING. NO TRAINING, EITHER... RIGHT OUT OF THE PHANTOM ZONE AND INTO ALL THE MADNESS. THAT TOOK REAL GUTS.
OR I JUST DIDN'T THINK IT THROUGH ENOUGH.
HOW'RE YOU DOING HERE IN SMALLVILLE?
IT'S BEEN GOOD AND BAD...WE HAD A WHOLE THING GO DOWN HERE RECENTLY-- BRRR, I DON'T EVEN WANT TO TALK ABOUT IT.
HEY, YOU KNOW IF YOU EVER NEED MY HELP, ALL YOU HAVE TO DO IS CALL.
YOU DO KNOW THAT?
THANKS. YEAH. I MIGHT TAKE YOU UP ON THAT OFFER.
HELLO, DAXAMITE.
ACTUALLY, THERE'S SOMETHING YOU CAN DO FOR ME NOW. IT INVOLVES THE FORTRESS OF SOLITUDE...

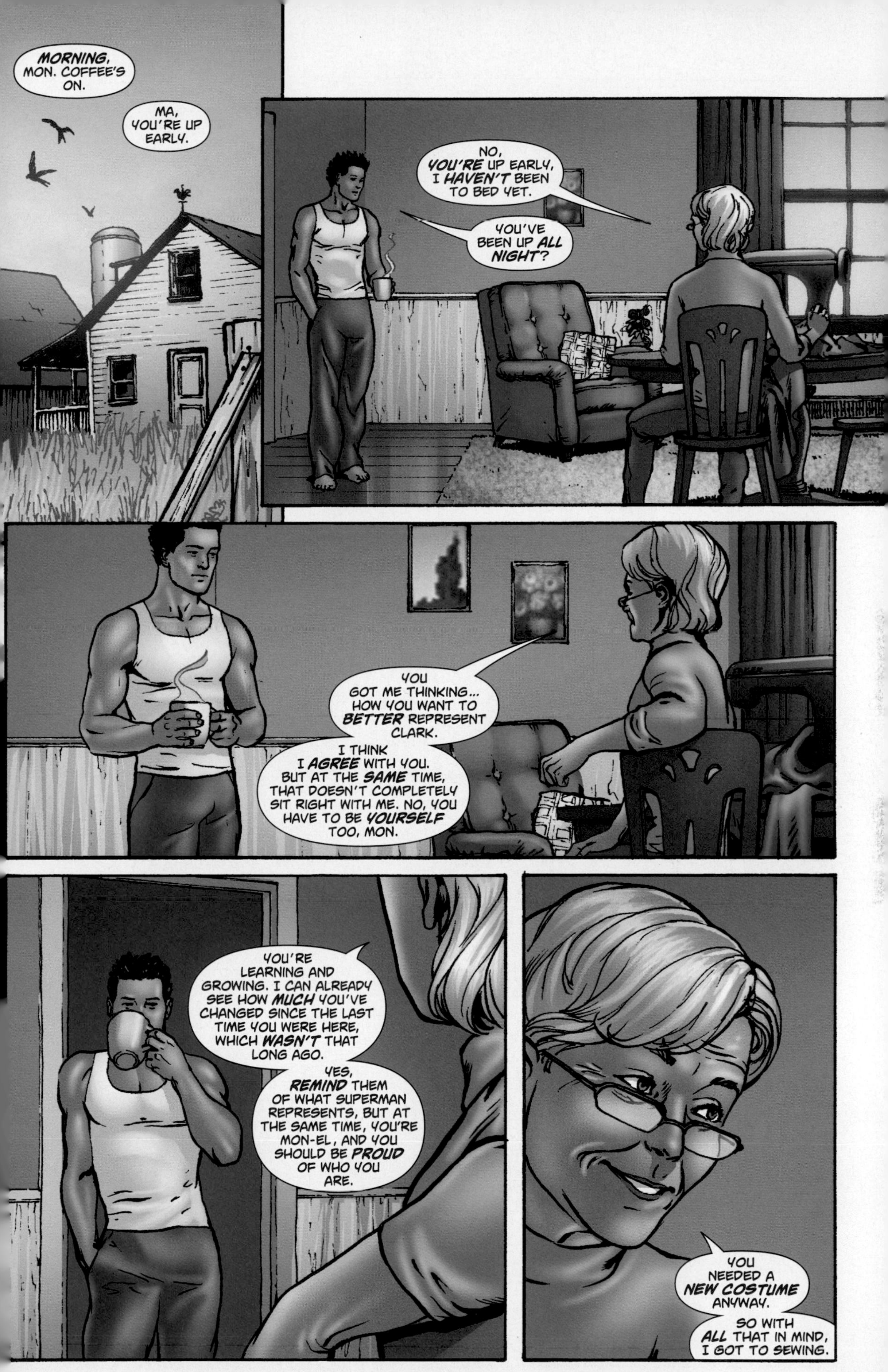
MORNING, MON. COFFEE'S ON.
MA, YOU'RE UP EARLY.
NO, YOU'RE UP EARLY, I HAVEN'T BEEN TO BED YET.
YOU'VE BEEN UP ALL NIGHT?
YOU GOT ME THINKING... HOW YOU WANT TO BETTER REPRESENT CLARK.
I THINK I AGREE WITH YOU. BUT AT THE SAME TIME, THAT DOESN'T COMPLETELY SIT RIGHT WITH ME. NO, YOU HAVE TO BE YOURSELF TOO, MON.
YOU'RE LEARNING AND GROWING. I CAN ALREADY SEE HOW MUCH YOU'VE CHANGED SINCE THE LAST TIME YOU WERE HERE, WHICH WASN'T THAT LONG AGO.
YES, REMIND THEM OF WHAT SUPERMAN REPRESENTS, BUT AT THE SAME TIME, YOU'RE MON-EL, AND YOU SHOULD BE PROUD OF WHO YOU ARE.
YOU NEEDED A NEW COSTUME ANYWAY.
SO WITH ALL THAT IN MIND, I GOT TO SEWING.

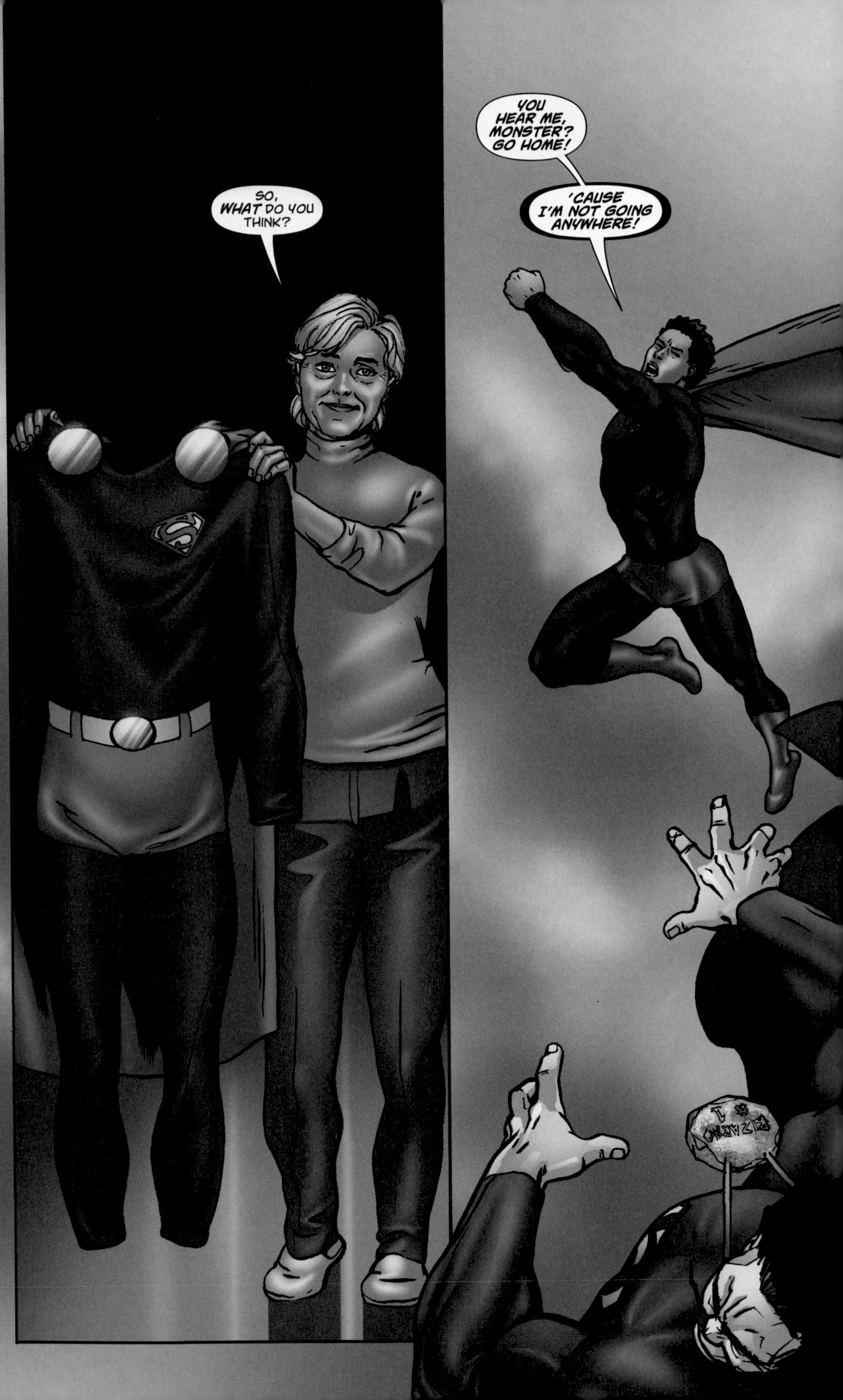
SO, WHAT DO YOU THINK?
YOU HEAR ME, MONSTER? GO HOME!
'CAUSE I'M NOT GOING ANYWHERE!

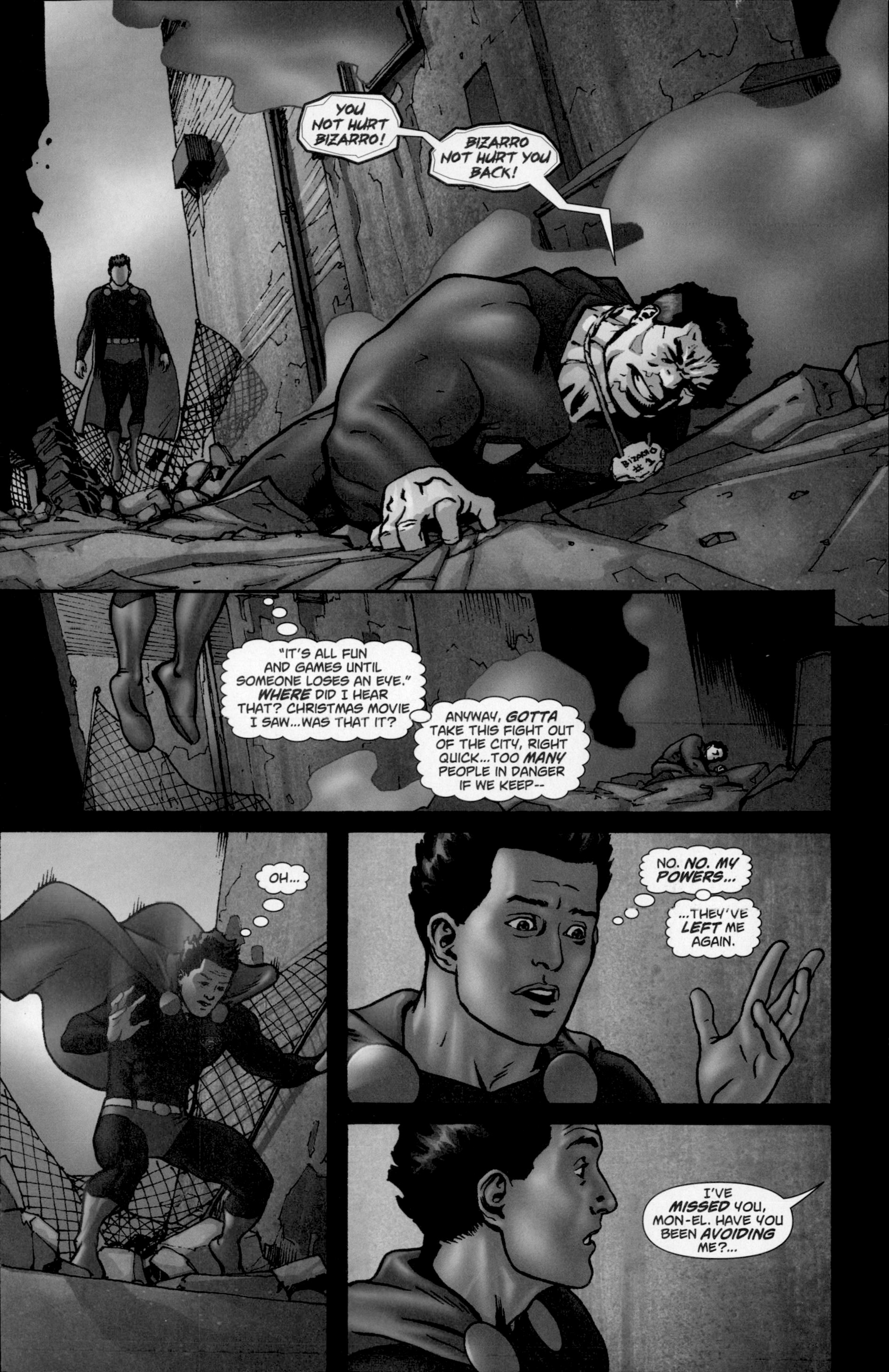

YOU NOT HURT BIZARRO!
BIZARRO NOT HURT YOU BACK!
BIZARRO #1
"IT'S ALL FUN AND GAMES UNTIL SOMEONE LOSES AN EYE." WHERE DID I HEAR THAT? CHRISTMAS MOVIE I SAW...WAS THAT IT?
ANYWAY, GOTTA TAKE THIS FIGHT OUT OF THE CITY, RIGHT QUICK...TOO MANY PEOPLE IN DANGER IF WE KEEP--
OH...
NO. NO. MY POWERS...
...THEY'VE LEFT ME AGAIN.
I'VE MISSED YOU, MON-EL. HAVE YOU BEEN AVOIDING ME?...

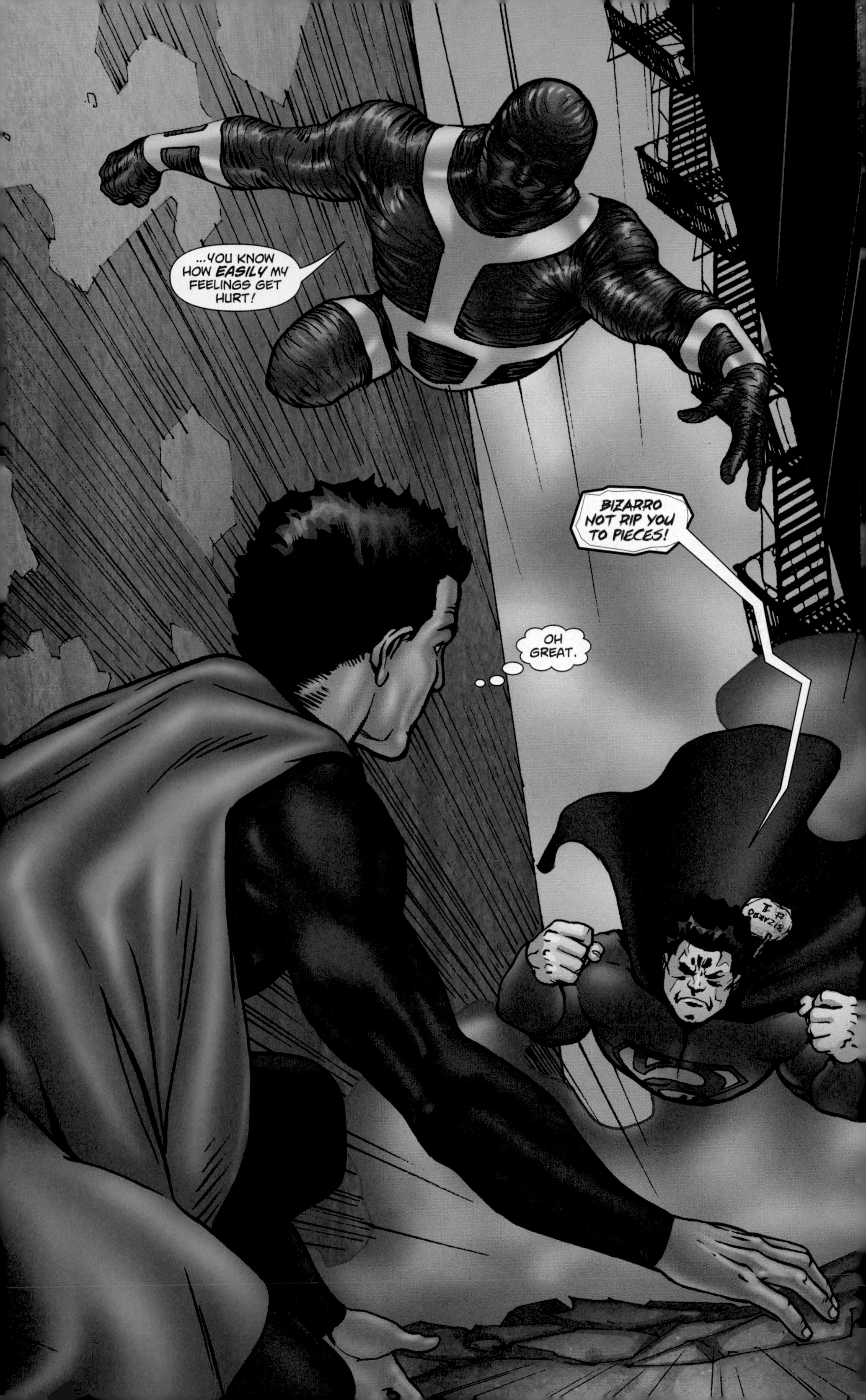
...YOU KNOW HOW EASILY MY FEELINGS GET HURT!
BIZARRO NOT RIP YOU TO PIECES!
OH GREAT.

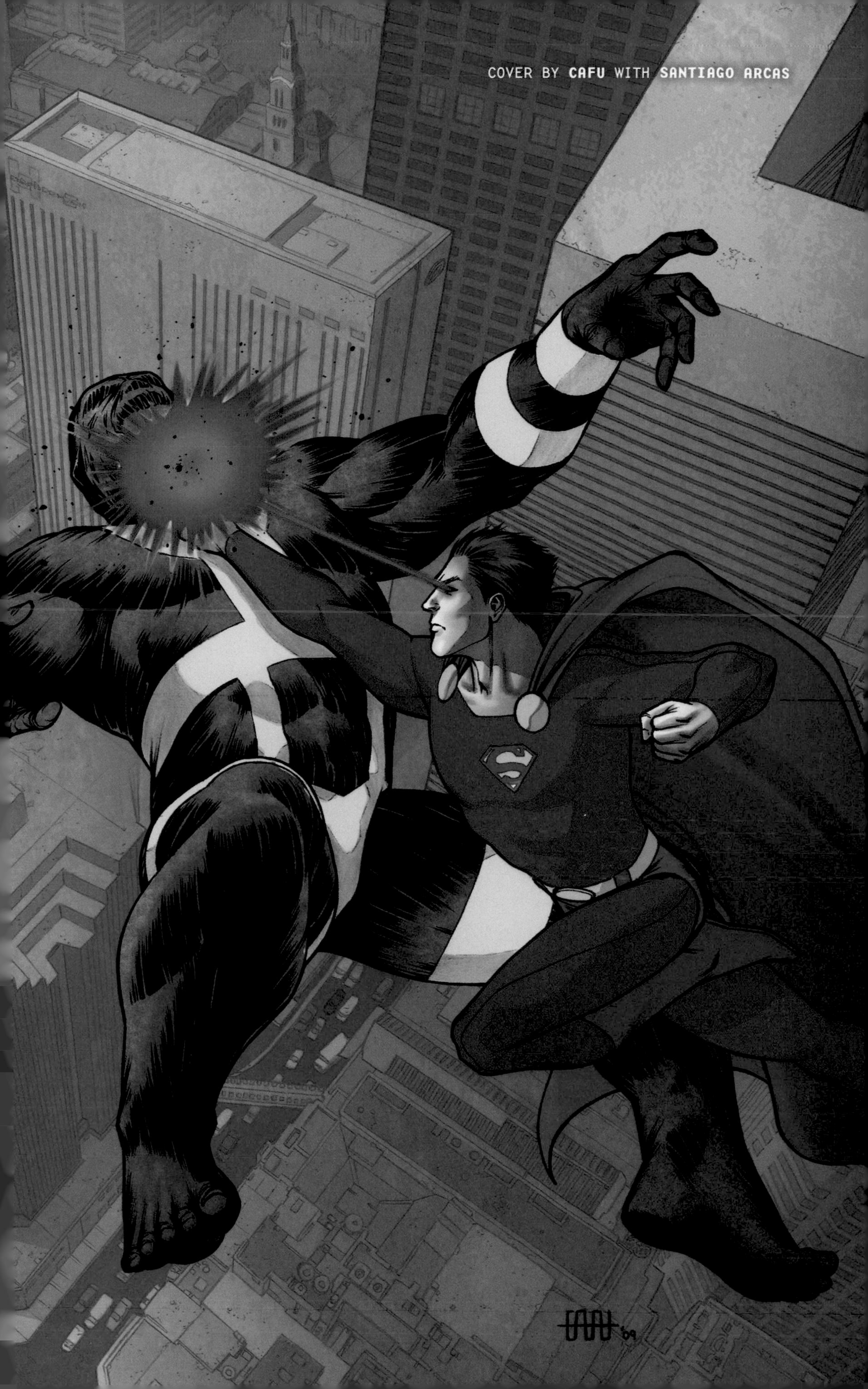

COVER BY **CAFU** WITH **SANTIAGO ARCAS**

MAN OF VALOR PART TWO

BERNARD CHANG <ARTIST>

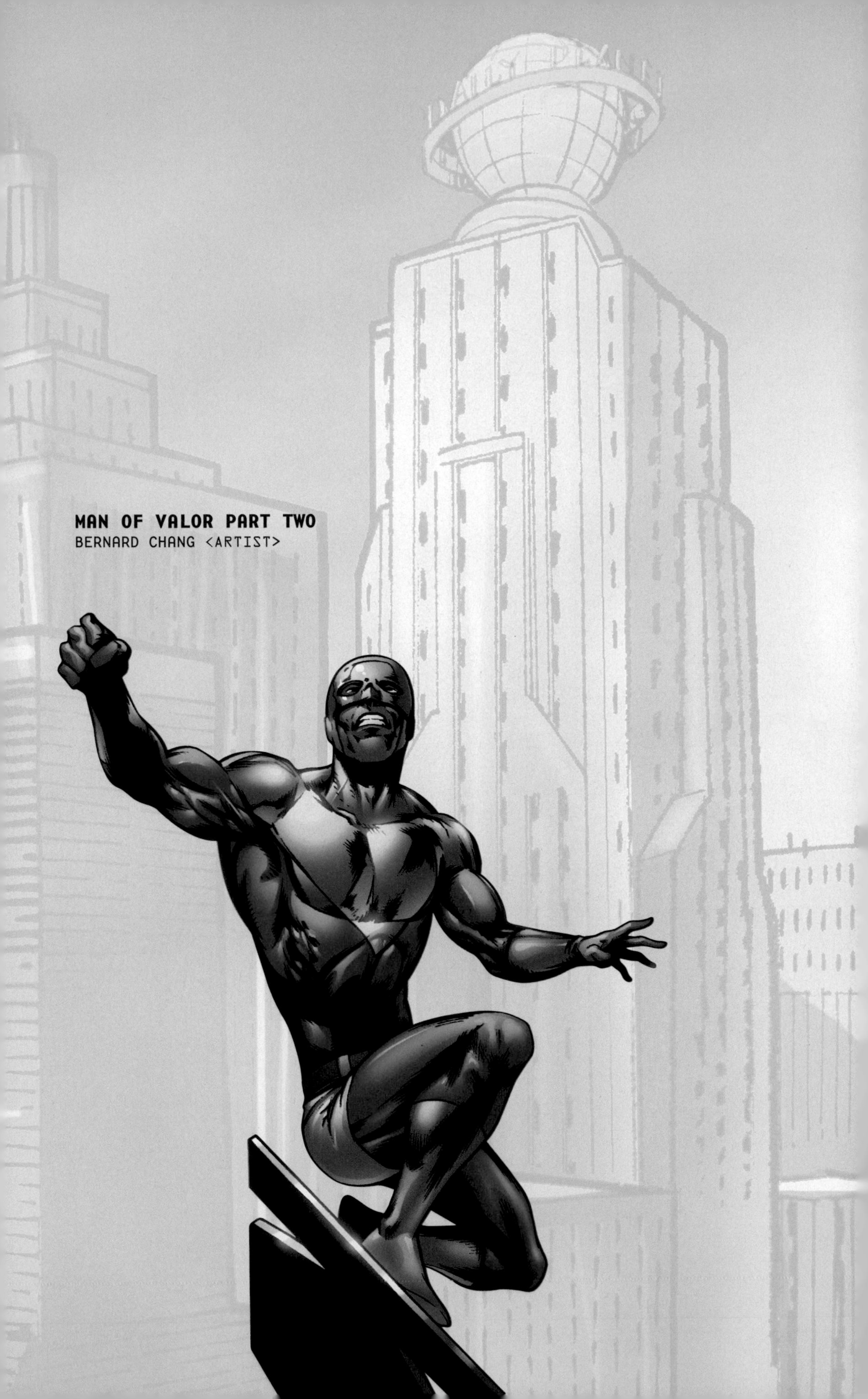

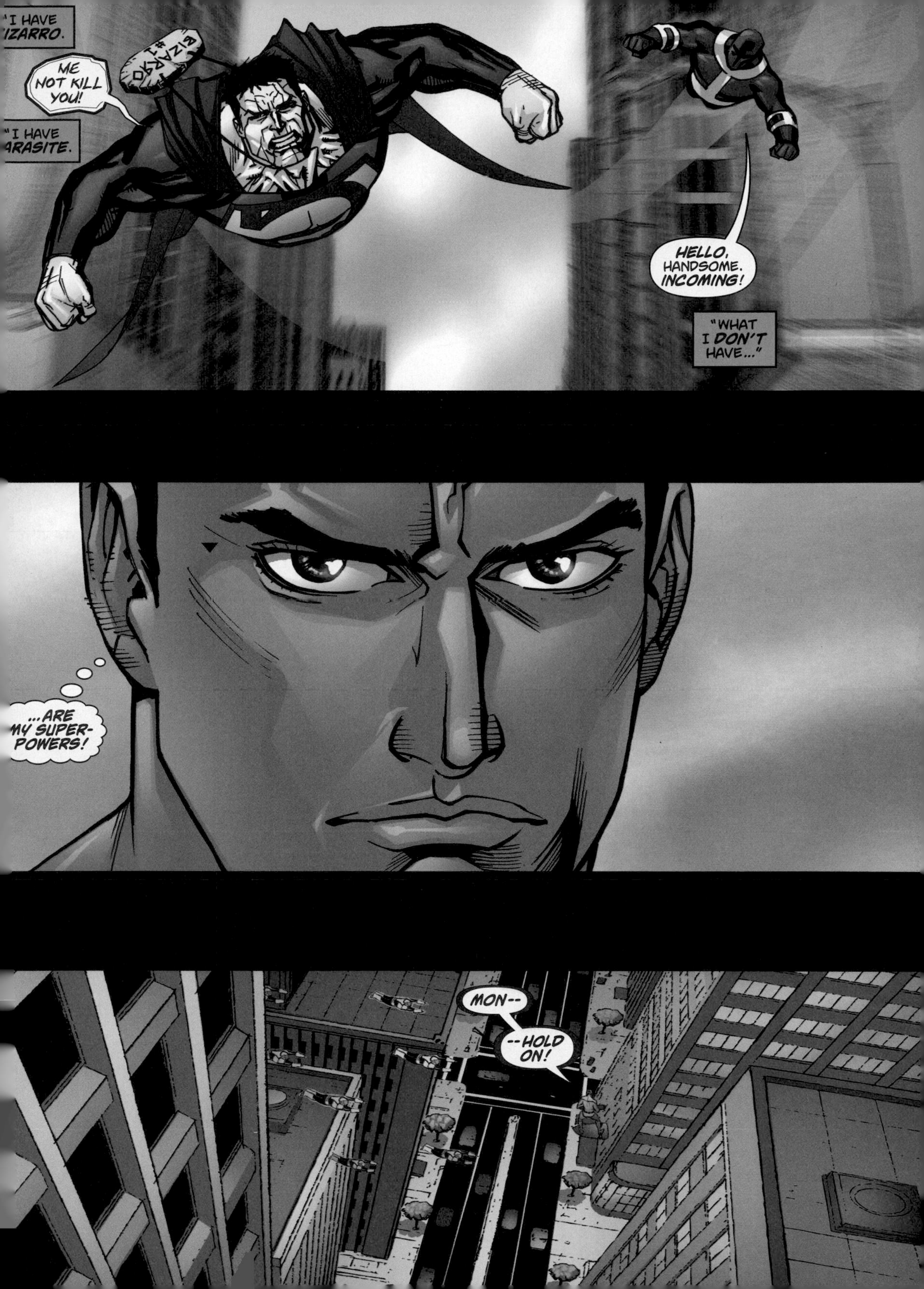
"I HAVE
IZARRO.
BIZARRO #1
ME NOT KILL YOU!
"I HAVE
ARASITE.
HELLO, HANDSOME. INCOMING!
"WHAT I DON'T HAVE..."
...ARE MY SUPER-POWERS!
MON--
--HOLD ON!

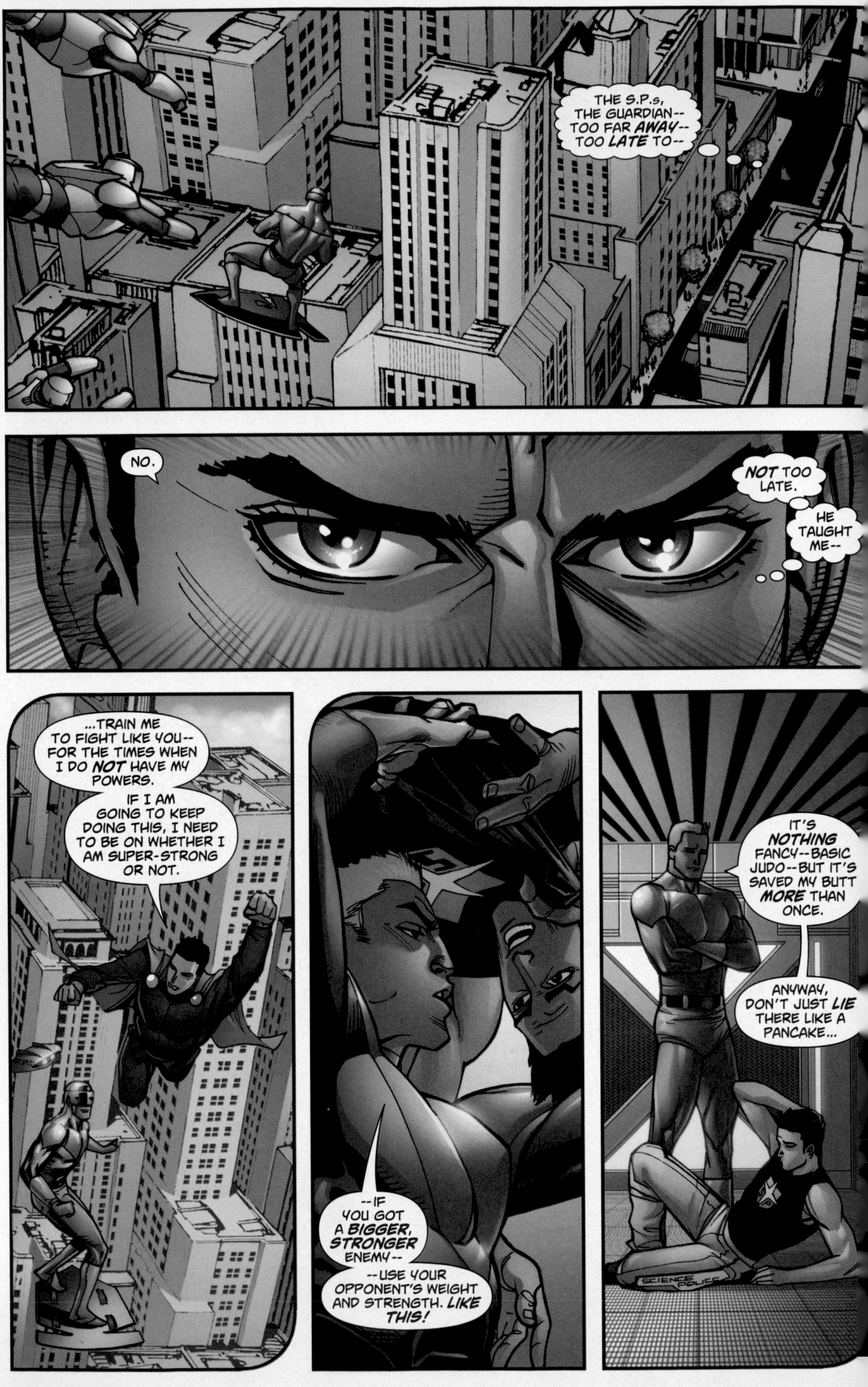
THE S.P.s, THE GUARDIAN-- TOO FAR AWAY-- TOO LATE TO--
NO.
NOT TOO LATE.
HE TAUGHT ME--
...TRAIN ME TO FIGHT LIKE YOU-- FOR THE TIMES WHEN I DO NOT HAVE MY POWERS.
IF I AM GOING TO KEEP DOING THIS, I NEED TO BE ON WHETHER I AM SUPER-STRONG OR NOT.
--IF YOU GOT A BIGGER, STRONGER ENEMY--
--USE YOUR OPPONENT'S WEIGHT AND STRENGTH. LIKE THIS!
IT'S NOTHING FANCY--BASIC JUDO--BUT IT'S SAVED MY BUTT MORE THAN ONCE.
ANYWAY, DON'T JUST LIE THERE LIKE A PANCAKE...
SCIENCE POLICE

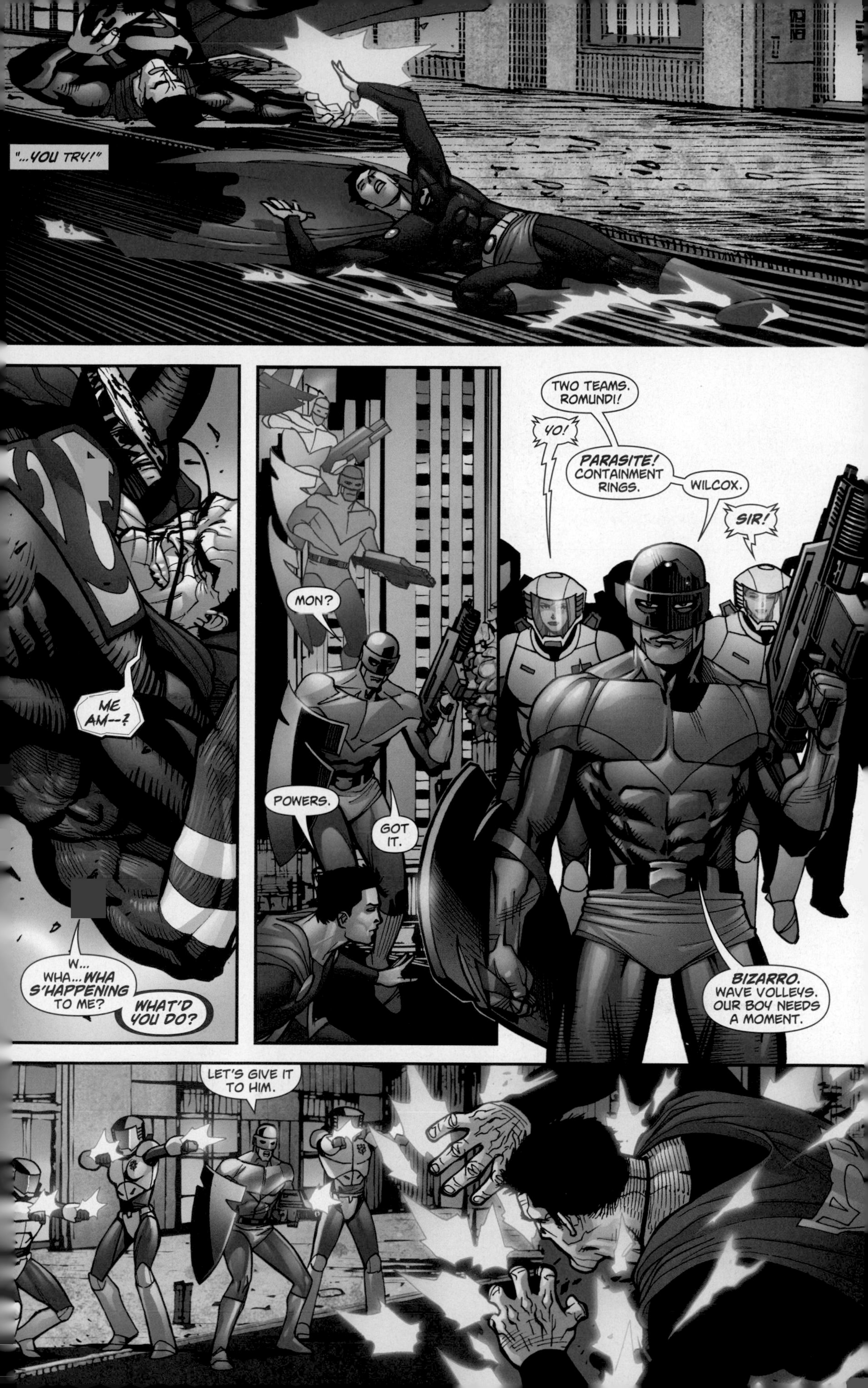
"...YOU TRY!"
ME AM--?
W... WHA...WHA S'HAPPENING TO ME?
WHAT'D YOU DO?
MON?
POWERS.
GOT IT.
TWO TEAMS. ROMUNDI!
YO!
PARASITE! CONTAINMENT RINGS.
WILCOX.
SIR!
BIZARRO. WAVE VOLLEYS. OUR BOY NEEDS A MOMENT.
LET'S GIVE IT TO HIM.

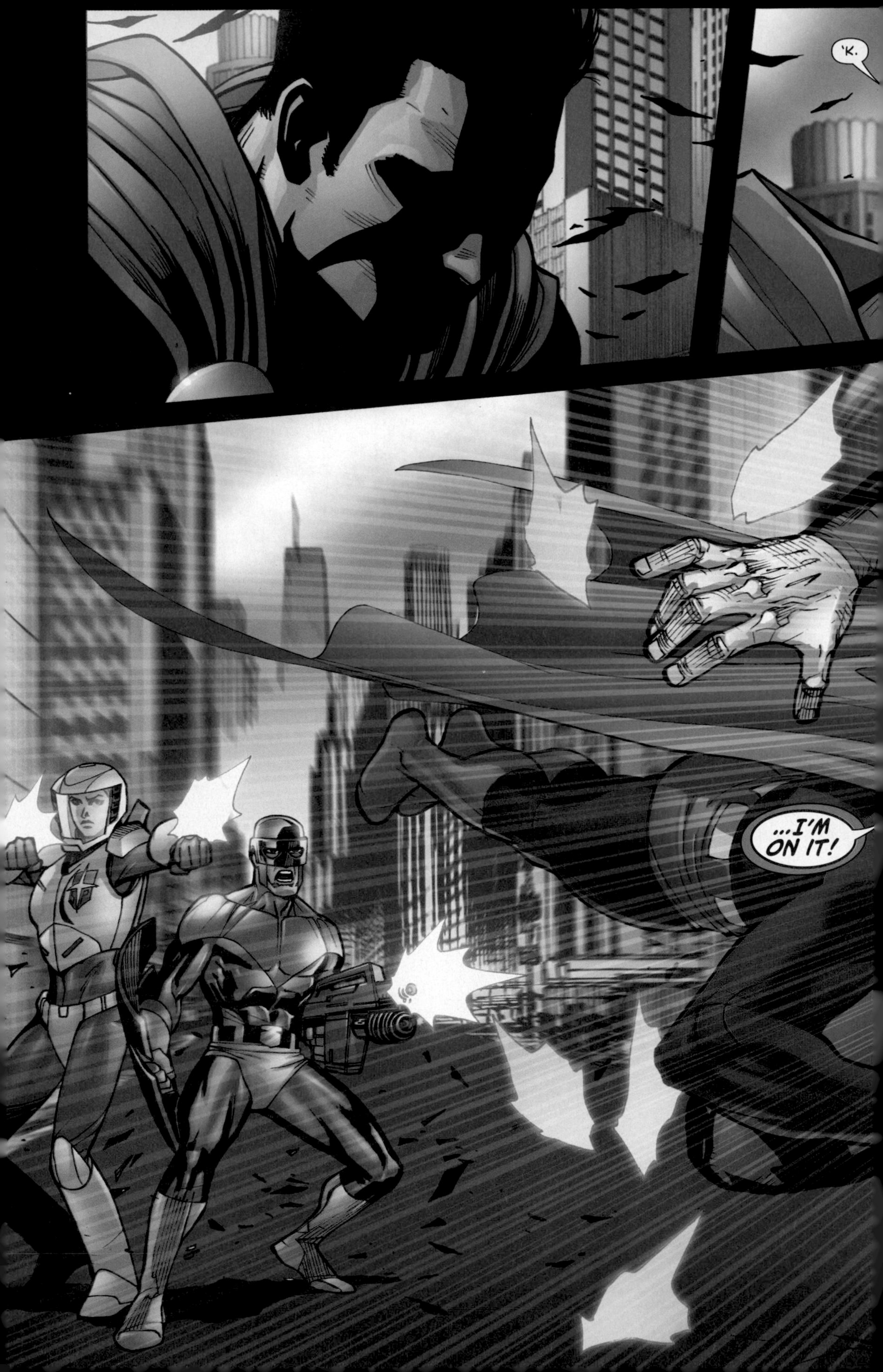
'K.
...I'M ON IT!

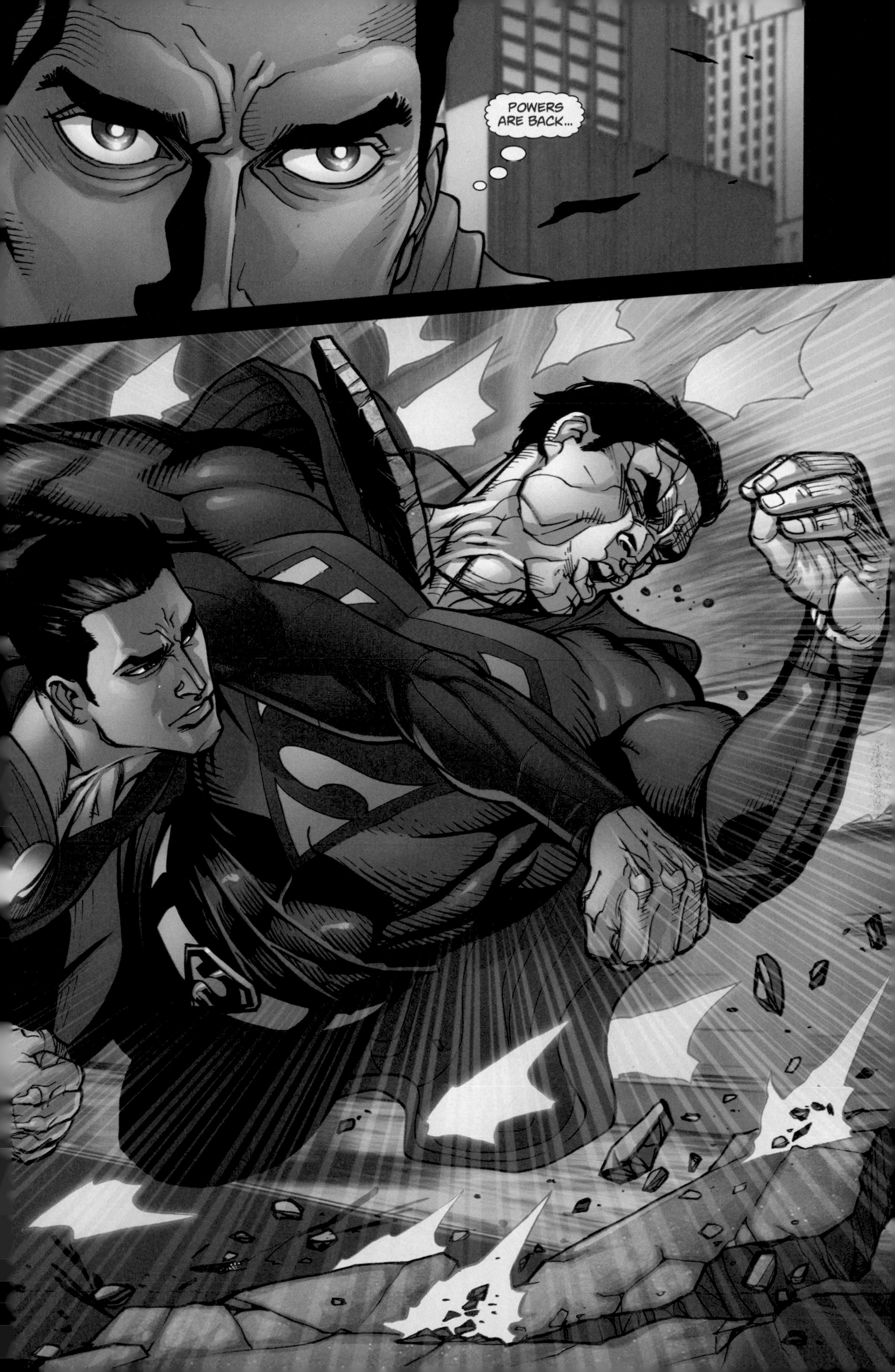
POWERS ARE BACK...

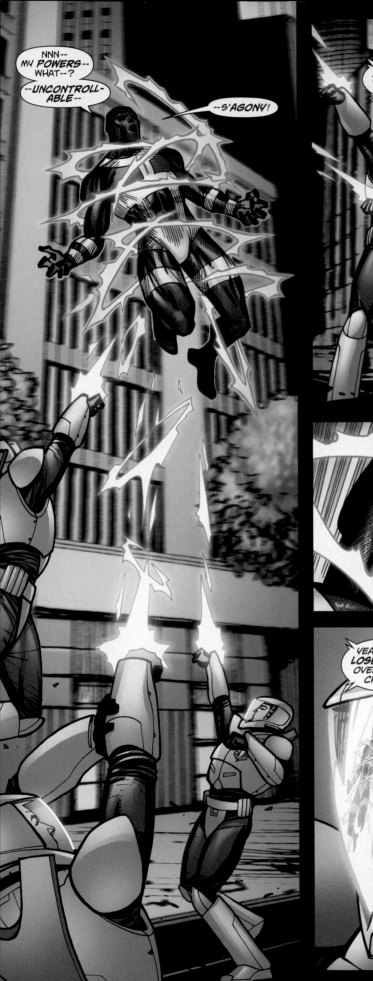

NNN-- MY *POWERS*-- WHAT--?

--UNCONTROLL- ABLE--

--S'*AGONY*!

KEEP THE RINGS ON HIM--

HARD TO--

JUST DO IT, BLAYLOCK. LESS YAP!

NO! *LEMME* GO! THEY'LL SEND ME *BACK*! BAC TO *LANE*

YEAH, I'LL *LOSE* SLEEP OVER THAT, CREEP.

KEEP FIRING, GUYS!

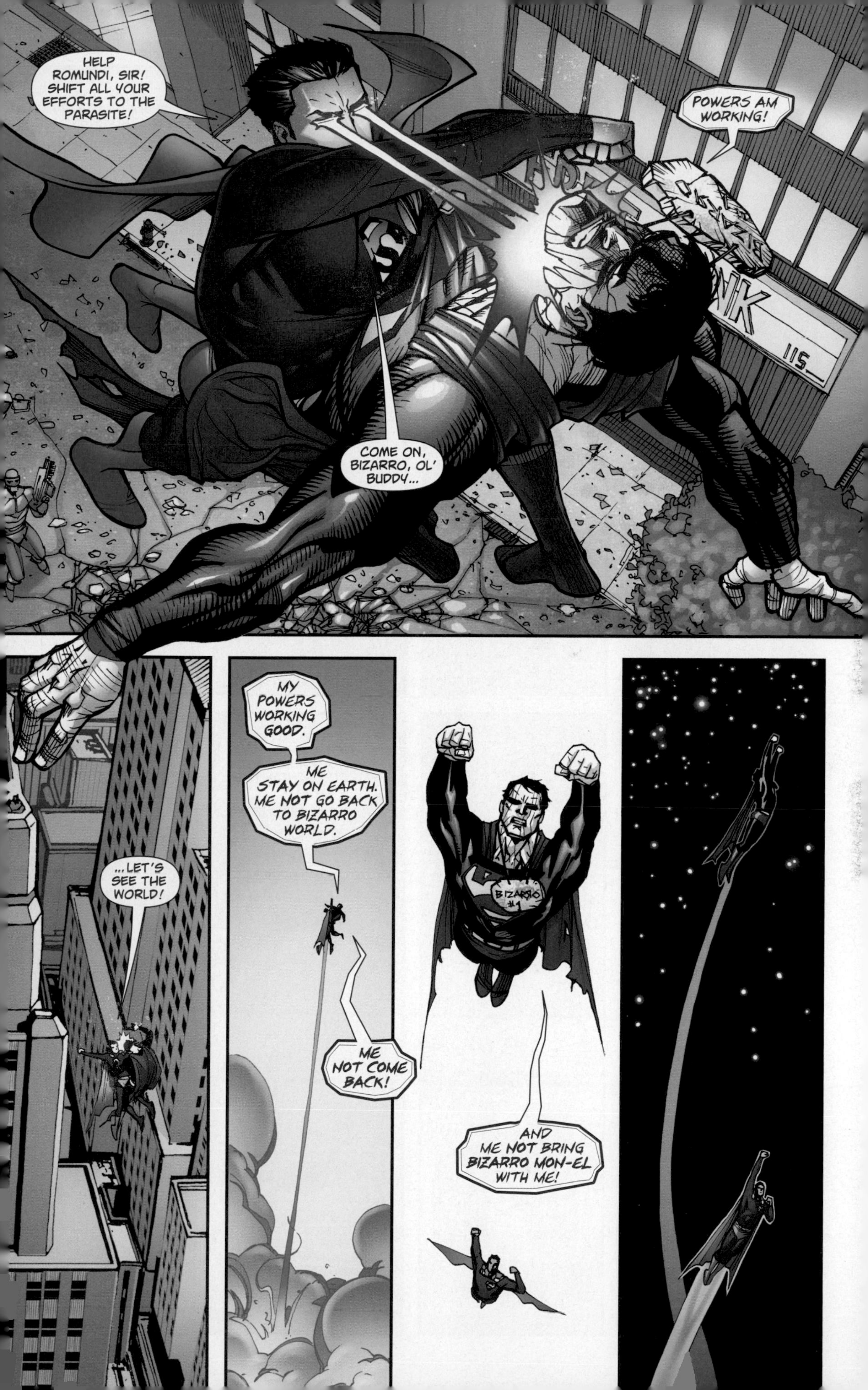
HELP ROMUNDI, SIR! SHIFT ALL YOUR EFFORTS TO THE PARASITE!
POWERS AM WORKING!
COME ON, BIZARRO, OL' BUDDY...
...LET'S SEE THE WORLD!
MY POWERS WORKING GOOD.
ME STAY ON EARTH. ME NOT GO BACK TO BIZARRO WORLD.
ME NOT COME BACK!
AND ME NOT BRING BIZARRO MON-EL WITH ME!

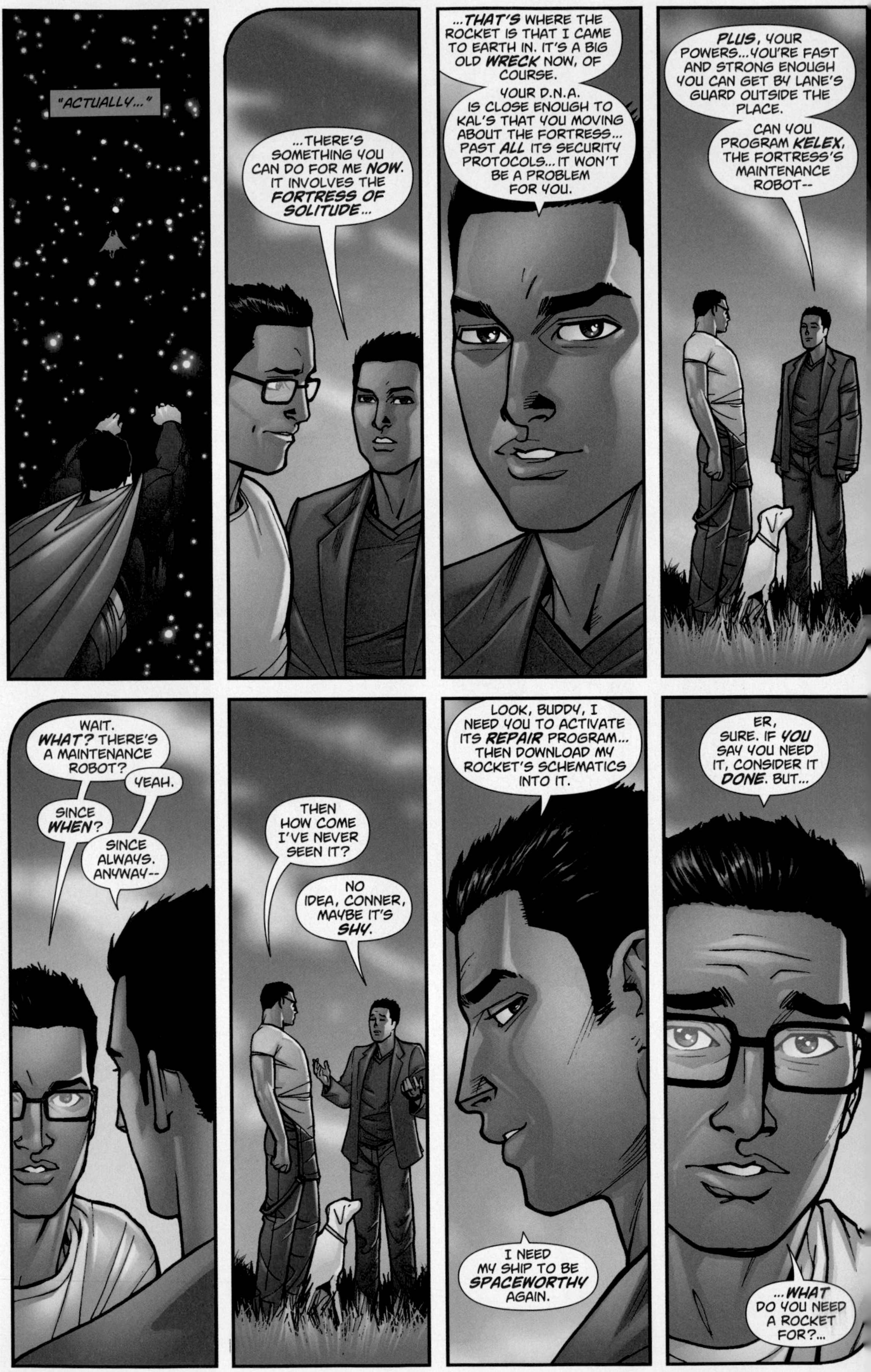
"ACTUALLY..."
...THERE'S SOMETHING YOU CAN DO FOR ME NOW. IT INVOLVES THE FORTRESS OF SOLITUDE...
...THAT'S WHERE THE ROCKET IS THAT I CAME TO EARTH IN. IT'S A BIG OLD WRECK NOW, OF COURSE.
YOUR D.N.A. IS CLOSE ENOUGH TO KAL'S THAT YOU MOVING ABOUT THE FORTRESS... PAST ALL ITS SECURITY PROTOCOLS... IT WON'T BE A PROBLEM FOR YOU.
PLUS, YOUR POWERS... YOU'RE FAST AND STRONG ENOUGH YOU CAN GET BY LANE'S GUARD OUTSIDE THE PLACE.
CAN YOU PROGRAM KELEX, THE FORTRESS'S MAINTENANCE ROBOT--
WAIT. WHAT? THERE'S A MAINTENANCE ROBOT?
YEAH.
SINCE WHEN?
SINCE ALWAYS. ANYWAY--
THEN HOW COME I'VE NEVER SEEN IT?
NO IDEA, CONNER, MAYBE IT'S SHY.
LOOK, BUDDY, I NEED YOU TO ACTIVATE ITS REPAIR PROGRAM... THEN DOWNLOAD MY ROCKET'S SCHEMATICS INTO IT.
I NEED MY SHIP TO BE SPACEWORTHY AGAIN.
ER, SURE. IF YOU SAY YOU NEED IT, CONSIDER IT DONE. BUT...
...WHAT DO YOU NEED A ROCKET FOR?...

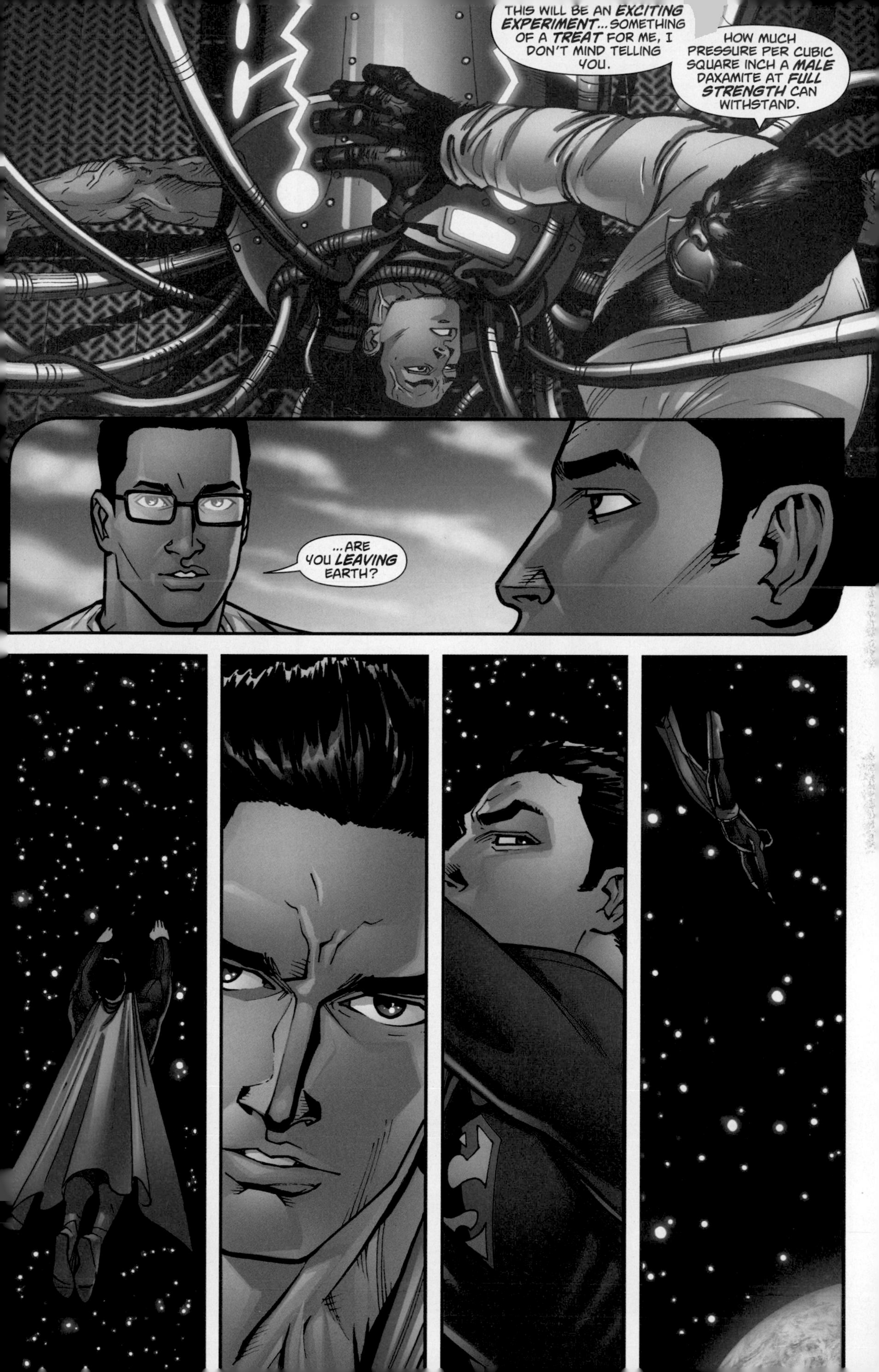
THIS WILL BE AN EXCITING EXPERIMENT...SOMETHING OF A TREAT FOR ME, I DON'T MIND TELLING YOU.
HOW MUCH PRESSURE PER CUBIC SQUARE INCH A MALE DAXAMITE AT FULL STRENGTH CAN WITHSTAND.
...ARE YOU LEAVING EARTH?

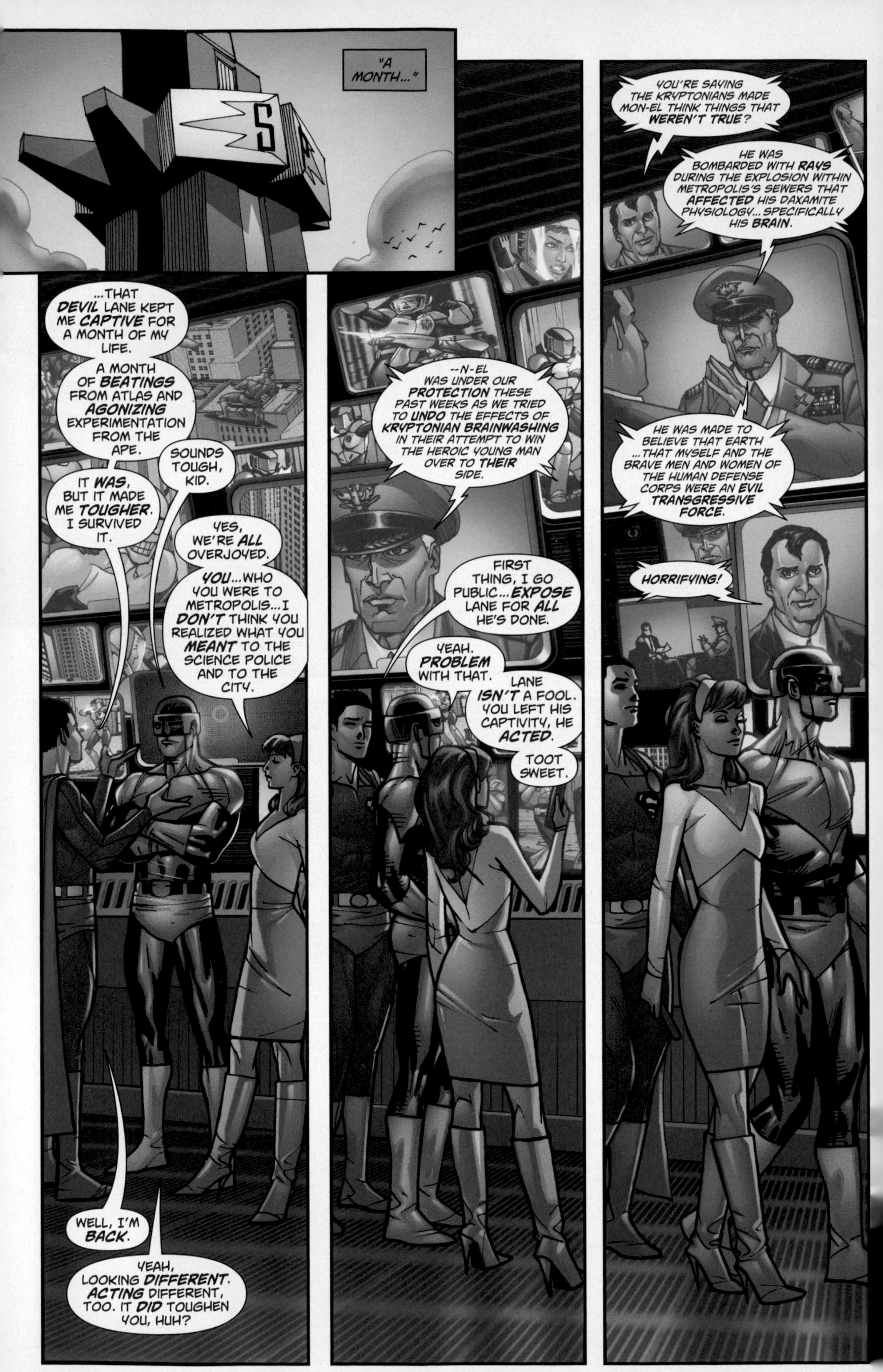
"A MONTH..."
...THAT DEVIL LANE KEPT ME CAPTIVE FOR A MONTH OF MY LIFE.
A MONTH OF BEATINGS FROM ATLAS AND AGONIZING EXPERIMENTATION FROM THE APE.
SOUNDS TOUGH, KID.
IT WAS, BUT IT MADE ME TOUGHER. I SURVIVED IT.
YES, WE'RE ALL OVERJOYED.
YOU...WHO YOU WERE TO METROPOLIS...I DON'T THINK YOU REALIZED WHAT YOU MEANT TO THE SCIENCE POLICE AND TO THE CITY.
WELL, I'M BACK.
YEAH, LOOKING DIFFERENT. ACTING DIFFERENT, TOO. IT DID TOUGHEN YOU, HUH?
--N-EL WAS UNDER OUR PROTECTION THESE PAST WEEKS AS WE TRIED TO UNDO THE EFFECTS OF KRYPTONIAN BRAINWASHING IN THEIR ATTEMPT TO WIN THE HEROIC YOUNG MAN OVER TO THEIR SIDE.
FIRST THING, I GO PUBLIC...EXPOSE LANE FOR ALL HE'S DONE.
YEAH. PROBLEM WITH THAT.
LANE ISN'T A FOOL. YOU LEFT HIS CAPTIVITY, HE ACTED.
TOOT SWEET.
YOU'RE SAYING THE KRYPTONIANS MADE MON-EL THINK THINGS THAT WEREN'T TRUE?
HE WAS BOMBARDED WITH RAYS DURING THE EXPLOSION WITHIN METROPOLIS'S SEWERS THAT AFFECTED HIS DAXAMITE PHYSIOLOGY...SPECIFICALLY HIS BRAIN.
HE WAS MADE TO BELIEVE THAT EARTH ...THAT MYSELF AND THE BRAVE MEN AND WOMEN OF THE HUMAN DEFENSE CORPS WERE AN EVIL TRANSGRESSIVE FORCE.
HORRIFYING!

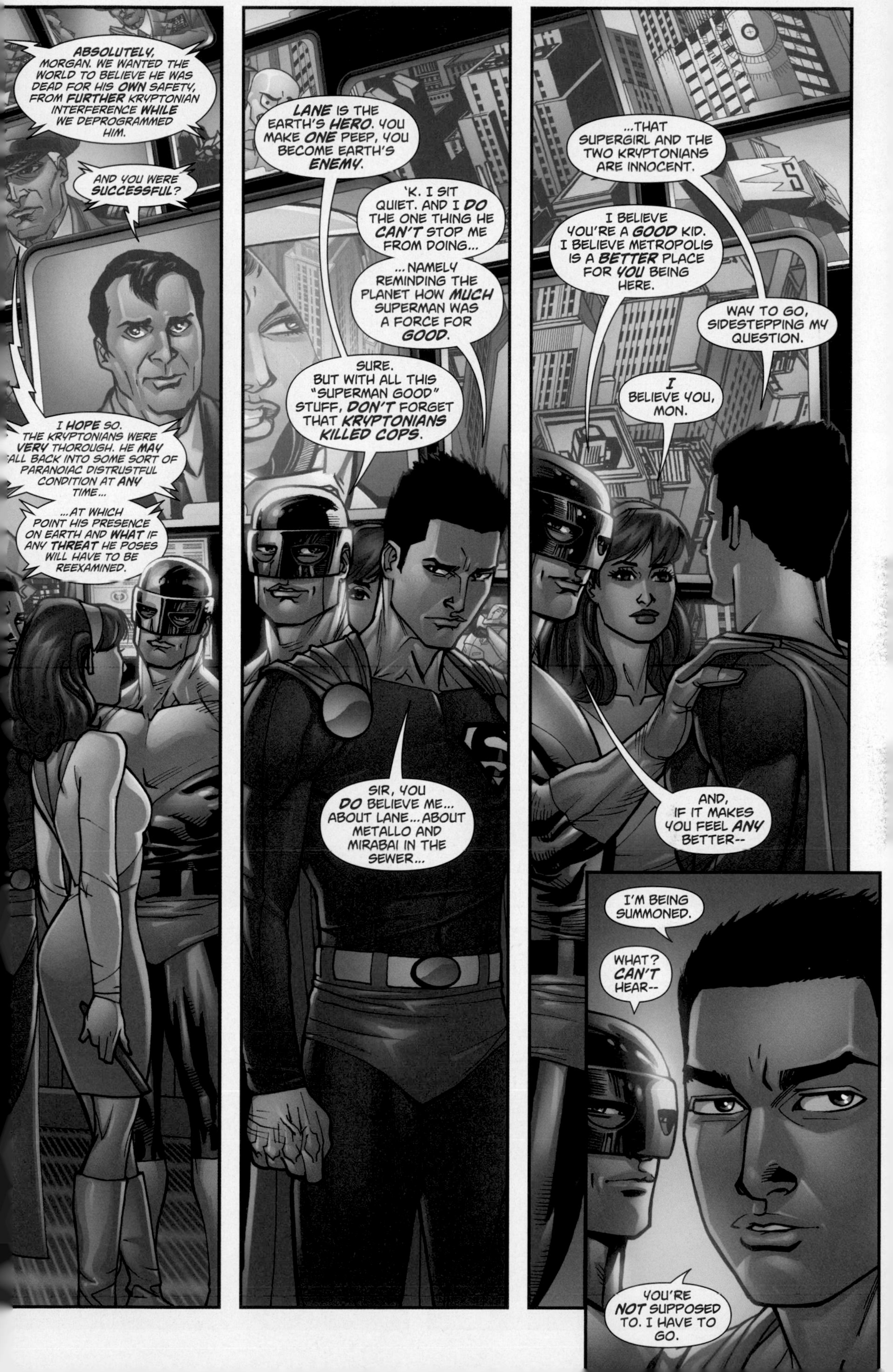
ABSOLUTELY, MORGAN. WE WANTED THE WORLD TO BELIEVE HE WAS DEAD FOR HIS OWN SAFETY, FROM FURTHER KRYPTONIAN INTERFERENCE WHILE WE DEPROGRAMMED HIM.
AND YOU WERE SUCCESSFUL?
I HOPE SO. THE KRYPTONIANS WERE VERY THOROUGH. HE MAY FALL BACK INTO SOME SORT OF PARANOIAC DISTRUSTFUL CONDITION AT ANY TIME...
...AT WHICH POINT HIS PRESENCE ON EARTH AND WHAT IF ANY THREAT HE POSES WILL HAVE TO BE REEXAMINED.
LANE IS THE EARTH'S HERO. YOU MAKE ONE PEEP, YOU BECOME EARTH'S ENEMY.
'K. I SIT QUIET. AND I DO THE ONE THING HE CAN'T STOP ME FROM DOING...
...NAMELY REMINDING THE PLANET HOW MUCH SUPERMAN WAS A FORCE FOR GOOD.
SURE. BUT WITH ALL THIS "SUPERMAN GOOD" STUFF, DON'T FORGET THAT KRYPTONIANS KILLED COPS.
SIR, YOU DO BELIEVE ME... ABOUT LANE... ABOUT METALLO AND MIRABAI IN THE SEWER...
...THAT SUPERGIRL AND THE TWO KRYPTONIANS ARE INNOCENT.
I BELIEVE YOU'RE A GOOD KID. I BELIEVE METROPOLIS IS A BETTER PLACE FOR YOU BEING HERE.
WAY TO GO, SIDESTEPPING MY QUESTION.
I BELIEVE YOU, MON.
AND, IF IT MAKES YOU FEEL ANY BETTER--
I'M BEING SUMMONED.
WHAT? CAN'T HEAR--
YOU'RE NOT SUPPOSED TO. I HAVE TO GO.

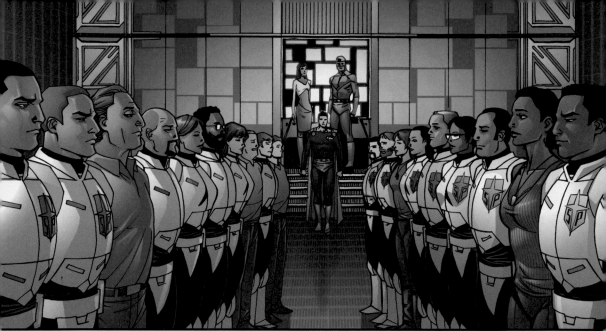

MON-EL. WILCOX.

I KNOW WHO YOU ARE. WHAT'S THIS ALL ABOUT?

I...WE JUST WANTED YOU TO KNOW HOW GLAD WE ARE TO HAVE YOU BACK IN THE SCIENCE POLICE.

THANKS, REALLY. THANK YOU, EVERYONE--

HI, JONNY.

HELLO, BILLI.

WE SHOULD TALK.

CAN'T NOW. LATER?

SURE.

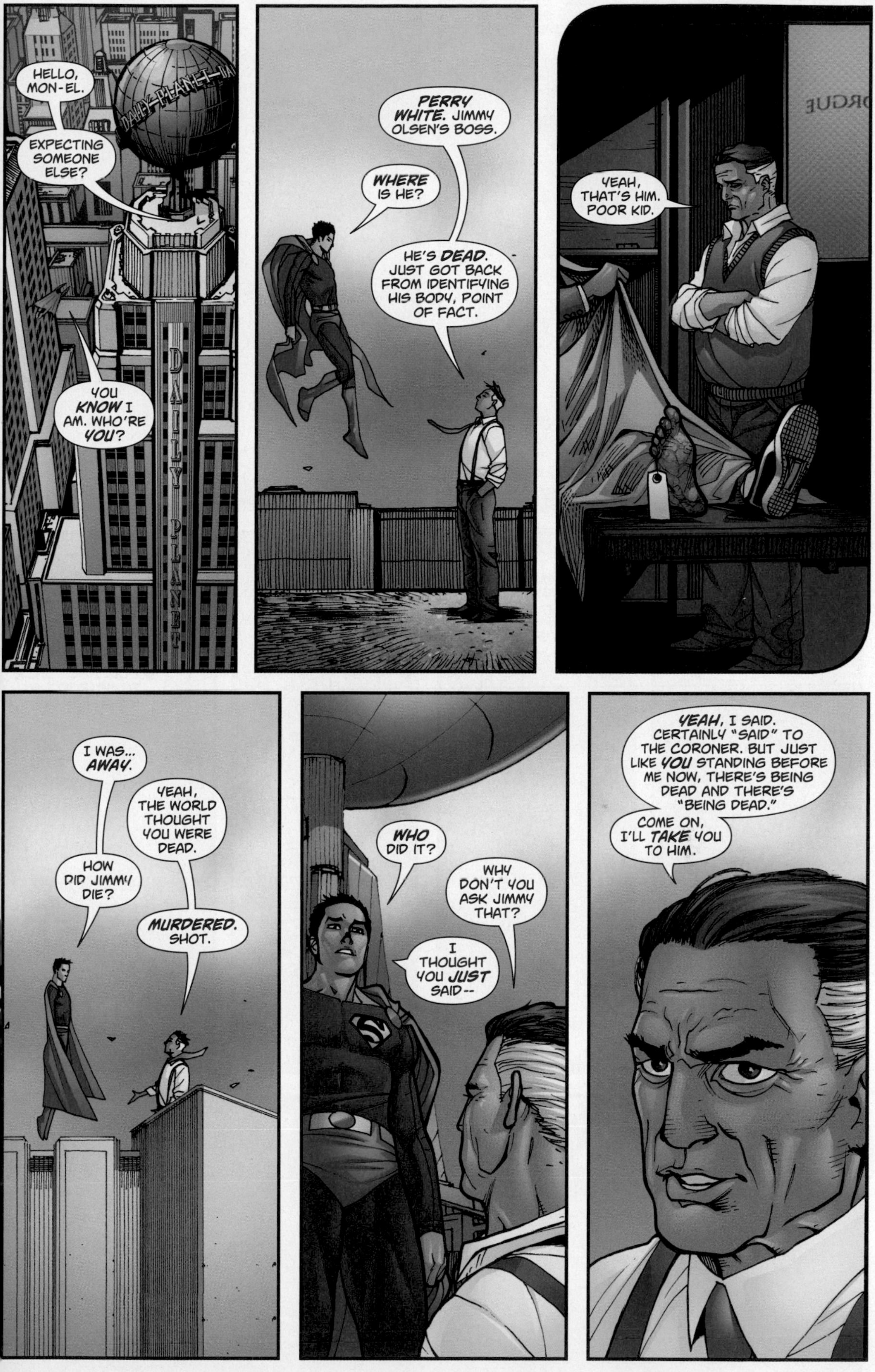
DAILY PLANET
HELLO, MON-EL.
EXPECTING SOMEONE ELSE?
YOU KNOW I AM. WHO'RE YOU?
DAILY PLANET
PERRY WHITE. JIMMY OLSEN'S BOSS.
WHERE IS HE?
HE'S DEAD. JUST GOT BACK FROM IDENTIFYING HIS BODY, POINT OF FACT.
ORGUE
YEAH, THAT'S HIM. POOR KID.
I WAS... AWAY.
YEAH, THE WORLD THOUGHT YOU WERE DEAD.
HOW DID JIMMY DIE?
MURDERED. SHOT.
WHO DID IT?
WHY DON'T YOU ASK JIMMY THAT?
I THOUGHT YOU JUST SAID--
YEAH, I SAID. CERTAINLY "SAID" TO THE CORONER. BUT JUST LIKE YOU STANDING BEFORE ME NOW, THERE'S BEING DEAD AND THERE'S "BEING DEAD."
COME ON, I'LL TAKE YOU TO HIM.

WHAT IS THIS PLACE? ... THE PEMBERTON CAMERA AND FILM FACTORY.

WHERE THE DAILY PLANET AND MUCH OF AMERICA GOT ITS CAMERA FILM MANUFACTURED BACK **BEFORE** MEMORY CARDS.

PEMBERTON CAMERA FACTORY

USED TO BE JIMMY'S SECOND HOME.

IRONIC THAT, DESERTED LIKE THIS--

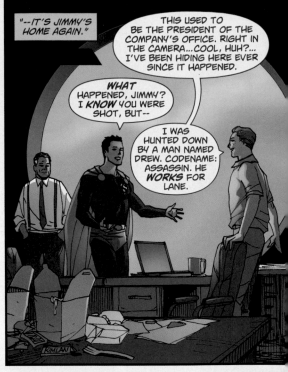

"--IT'S JIMMY'S HOME AGAIN."

THIS USED TO BE THE PRESIDENT OF THE COMPANY'S OFFICE. RIGHT IN THE CAMERA...COOL, HUH?... I'VE BEEN HIDING HERE EVER SINCE IT HAPPENED.

WHAT HAPPENED, JIMMY? I *KNOW* YOU WERE SHOT, BUT--

I WAS HUNTED DOWN BY A MAN NAMED DREW. CODENAME: ASSASSIN. HE *WORKS* FOR LANE.

OH YEAH, *MET* HIM... SAW HIM, ANYWAY... ONCE.

THEN WHAT?

I FELL INTO THE WATERS OF RIVER CITY. I WENT TO THE BOTTOM.

THAT'S *ALMOST* ALL I REMEMBER.

ALMOST?

I REMEMBER A SHAPE APPEARING OUT OF THE DARKNESS.

"*BIG*. ALIEN-LOOKING. *HUGE* BLACK EYES."

YEAH, I *MAY* HAVE MET HIM, *TOO*.

THEN I WOKE UP ON THE RIVER BANK, NO BULLET WOUNDS, NO BLOOD. I GOT *BACK* TO METROPOLIS, STAT, *HID* OUT HERE.

THE WORLD *THINKS* I'M DEAD, MON. LANE *AND* DREW AND 7734 THINK I'M *DEAD*.

GIVES ME THE *FREEDOM* TO SEE AND DO AND GO PLACES I *NEVER* COULD BEFORE.

PERRY SAID HE IDENTIFIED SOMEONE.

SOME POOR DEAD KID. PUT MY I.D. ON HIM. DRUG O.D., I THINK. FOUND HIM BY THE RIVER *NEAR* WHERE I WOKE UP...TIME IN THE WATER HAD DONE A REAL *NUMBER* ON HIS BODY.

THEN WHEN PERRY FOUND THE *CLUE* I LEFT HIM IN MY APARTMENT...ONCE WE MADE CONTACT, I HAD HIM GO *CONFIRM* THE DEAD GUY WAS ME.

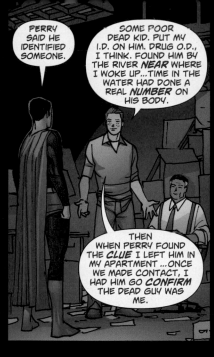

I'M BEGINNING TO *UNCOVER* STUFF ON LANE, MON. I'M GETTING *PLACES* LOIS CAN'T, AND WITHOUT THE RISK OF PERSECUTION AND ARREST THAT SHE'S GOING THROUGH.

SOON WE'LL HAVE ENOUGH, WE CAN *EXPOSE* HIM, YOU AND ME.

AND *ME.*

OH YEAH, *THIS* IS MY CONTACT INSIDE 7734.

NATASHA IRONS, MON-EL.

I *SAW* YOU AT LANE'S BASE. YOU WERE WITH A VILLAIN...MAJOR DISASTER.

MAJOR *FORCE,* ACTUALLY. YEAH. I'M SPECIALIST JENNY BLAKE WHEN I'M THERE *UNDERCOVER.* I REMEMBER YOU, *TOO,* OBVIOUSLY. GLAD TO SEE YOU'RE *FREE.*

YOU *DIDN'T* HELP ME THEN. I GUESS YOU COULDN'T.

COULDN'T? DIDN'T? *HOW'D* YOU THINK THE PARASITE GOT THE GATEWAY CODE THAT ALLOWED YOU A WAY *OUT?*

IT'S JUST I GOTTA STAY *SHARP* AND WAY SLY WITH THIS. ONE SLIP, THEY TUMBLE ME, I'M *DEAD,* AND ALL I'VE DONE AND SACRIFICED WILL BE FOR *NOTHING.*

I'LL BE PASSING INFO *BACK* VIA JIMMY. STUFF FOR HIM TO USE...AND STUFF YOU CAN MAYBE USE YOURSELF, MON.

LIKE *CAPTAIN ATOM.* THEY HAVE HIM UNDER SOME SORT OF MIND CONTROL, BUT *IF* THE TIME COMES WE CAN HELP BREAK HIM FREE--

SURE, LET ME KNOW.

I GOTTA GO.

SHE DOES THAT.

MY UNCLE'S IN A COMA, ATLAS. DIDN'T KNOW THAT WAS GOING DOWN UNTIL IT DID. I'M GOING TO SEE UNCLE JOHN AND THEN GET BACK INSIDE BEFORE THEY NOTICE I'M GONE.

AND SOON ENOUGH, WE CAN BRING THESE %$%^ERS DOWN.

ONE THING I NEED SOONER, SOON...SOON AS YOU CAN...THE LOCATION OF ONE OF THE HUMAN DEFENSE CORPS'S HIDDEN BASES.

IT'S UNDER THE SEA...SOME-WHERE.

BUT THE SEA'S A BIG PLACE. I'LL GET ON IT.

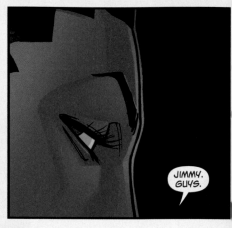

JIMMY. GUYS.

SO THAT'S IT FOR NOW, MON. YOU GO BE A HERO AND I'LL BE A GHOST.

BUT NOW THE LINES OF COMMUNICATION ARE OPEN.

YES, YES, GOOD.

HEY, JIMMY, SUPERMAN WOULD BE PROUD OF YOU FOR THIS.

RIGHT BACK AT YOU, PAL.

I'M SORRY I WASN'T AROUND TO SAVE YOU.

I UNDERSTAND, MON.

AND LOOK AT US. WE'RE ALIVE. ISN'T IT GREAT?

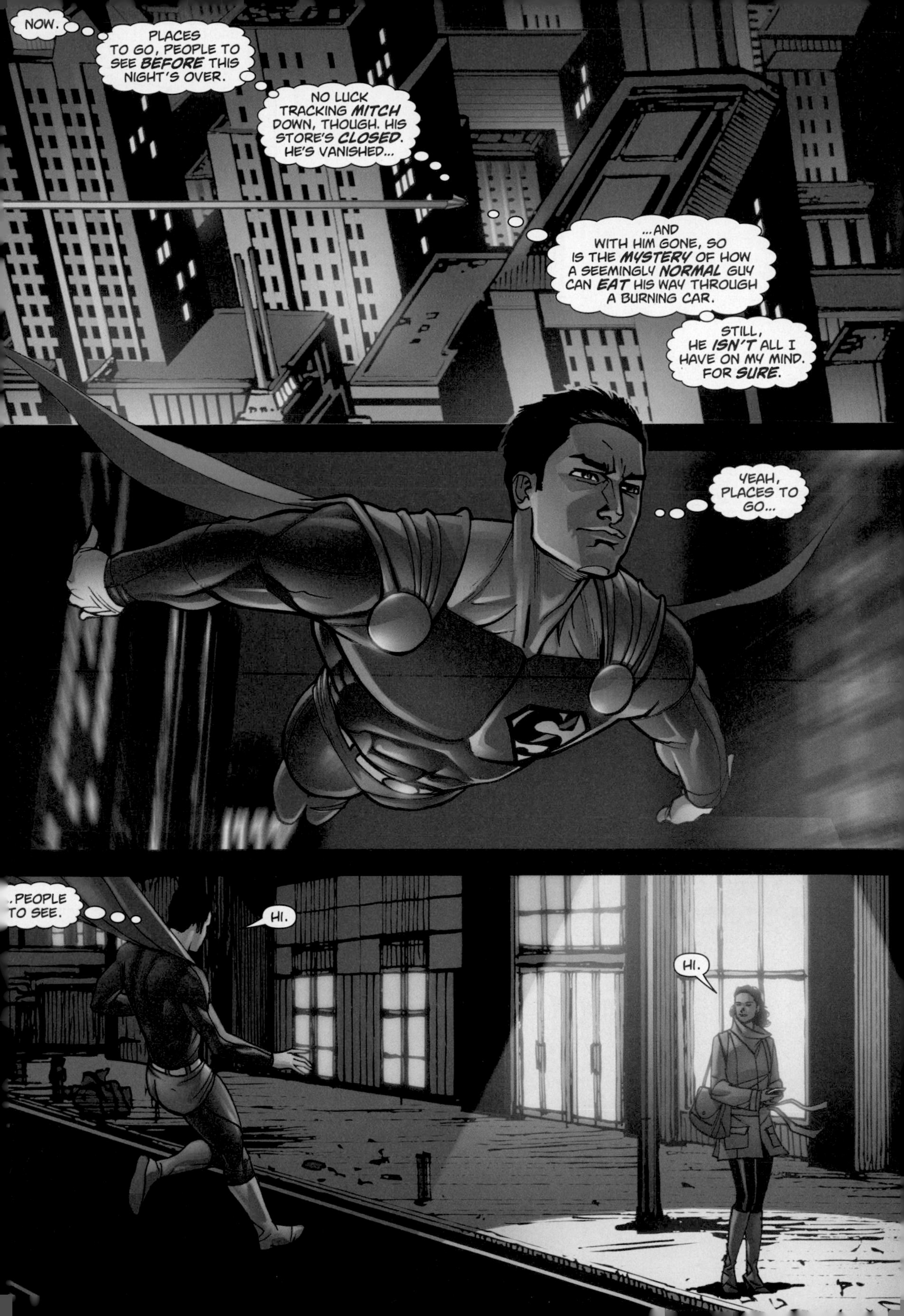
NOW.
PLACES TO GO, PEOPLE TO SEE BEFORE THIS NIGHT'S OVER.
NO LUCK TRACKING MITCH DOWN, THOUGH. HIS STORE'S CLOSED. HE'S VANISHED...
...AND WITH HIM GONE, SO IS THE MYSTERY OF HOW A SEEMINGLY NORMAL GUY CAN EAT HIS WAY THROUGH A BURNING CAR.
STILL, HE ISN'T ALL I HAVE ON MY MIND. FOR SURE.
YEAH, PLACES TO GO...
.PEOPLE TO SEE.
HI.
HI.

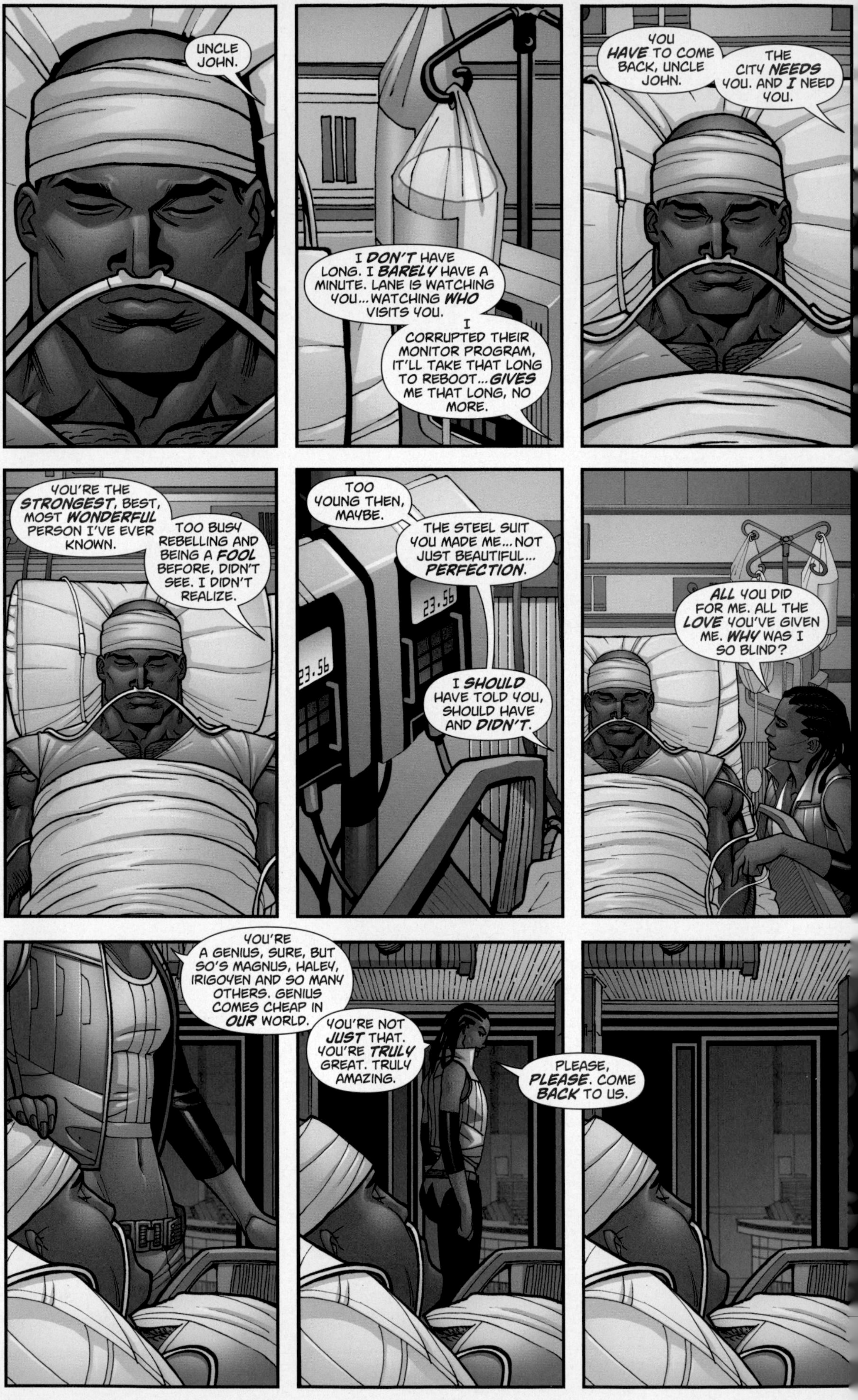
UNCLE JOHN.
I DON'T HAVE LONG. I BARELY HAVE A MINUTE. LANE IS WATCHING YOU...WATCHING WHO VISITS YOU.
I CORRUPTED THEIR MONITOR PROGRAM, IT'LL TAKE THAT LONG TO REBOOT...GIVES ME THAT LONG, NO MORE.
YOU HAVE TO COME BACK, UNCLE JOHN.
THE CITY NEEDS YOU. AND I NEED YOU.
YOU'RE THE STRONGEST, BEST, MOST WONDERFUL PERSON I'VE EVER KNOWN.
TOO BUSY REBELLING AND BEING A FOOL BEFORE, DIDN'T SEE. I DIDN'T REALIZE.
TOO YOUNG THEN, MAYBE.
THE STEEL SUIT YOU MADE ME...NOT JUST BEAUTIFUL... PERFECTION.
23.56
23.56
I SHOULD HAVE TOLD YOU, SHOULD HAVE AND DIDN'T.
ALL YOU DID FOR ME. ALL THE LOVE YOU'VE GIVEN ME. WHY WAS I SO BLIND?
YOU'RE A GENIUS, SURE, BUT SO'S MAGNUS, HALEY, IRIGOYEN AND SO MANY OTHERS. GENIUS COMES CHEAP IN OUR WORLD.
YOU'RE NOT JUST THAT. YOU'RE TRULY GREAT. TRULY AMAZING.
PLEASE, PLEASE. COME BACK TO US.

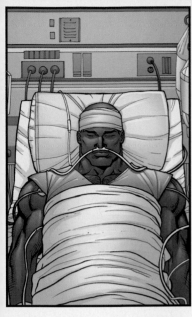
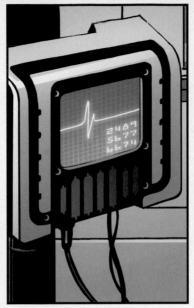

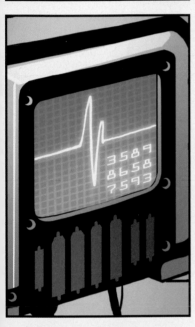

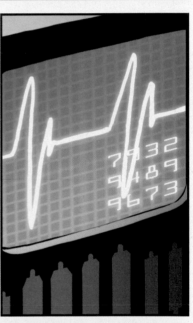

ATLAS!

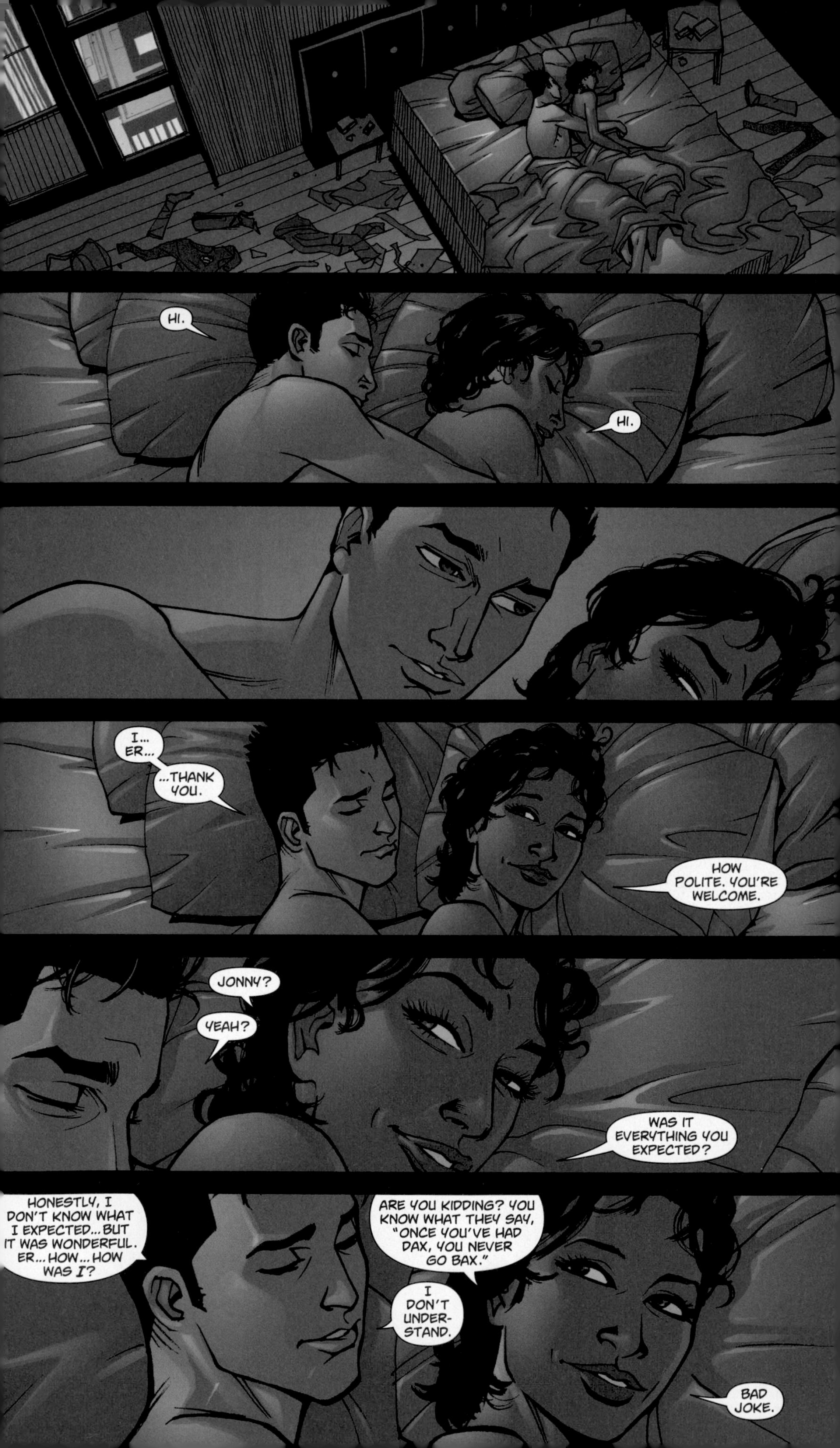
HI.
HI.
I... ER... ...THANK YOU.
HOW POLITE. YOU'RE WELCOME.
JONNY?
YEAH?
WAS IT EVERYTHING YOU EXPECTED?
HONESTLY, I DON'T KNOW WHAT I EXPECTED... BUT IT WAS WONDERFUL. ER... HOW... HOW WAS I?
ARE YOU KIDDING? YOU KNOW WHAT THEY SAY, "ONCE YOU'VE HAD DAX, YOU NEVER GO BAX."
I DON'T UNDER-STAND.
BAD JOKE.

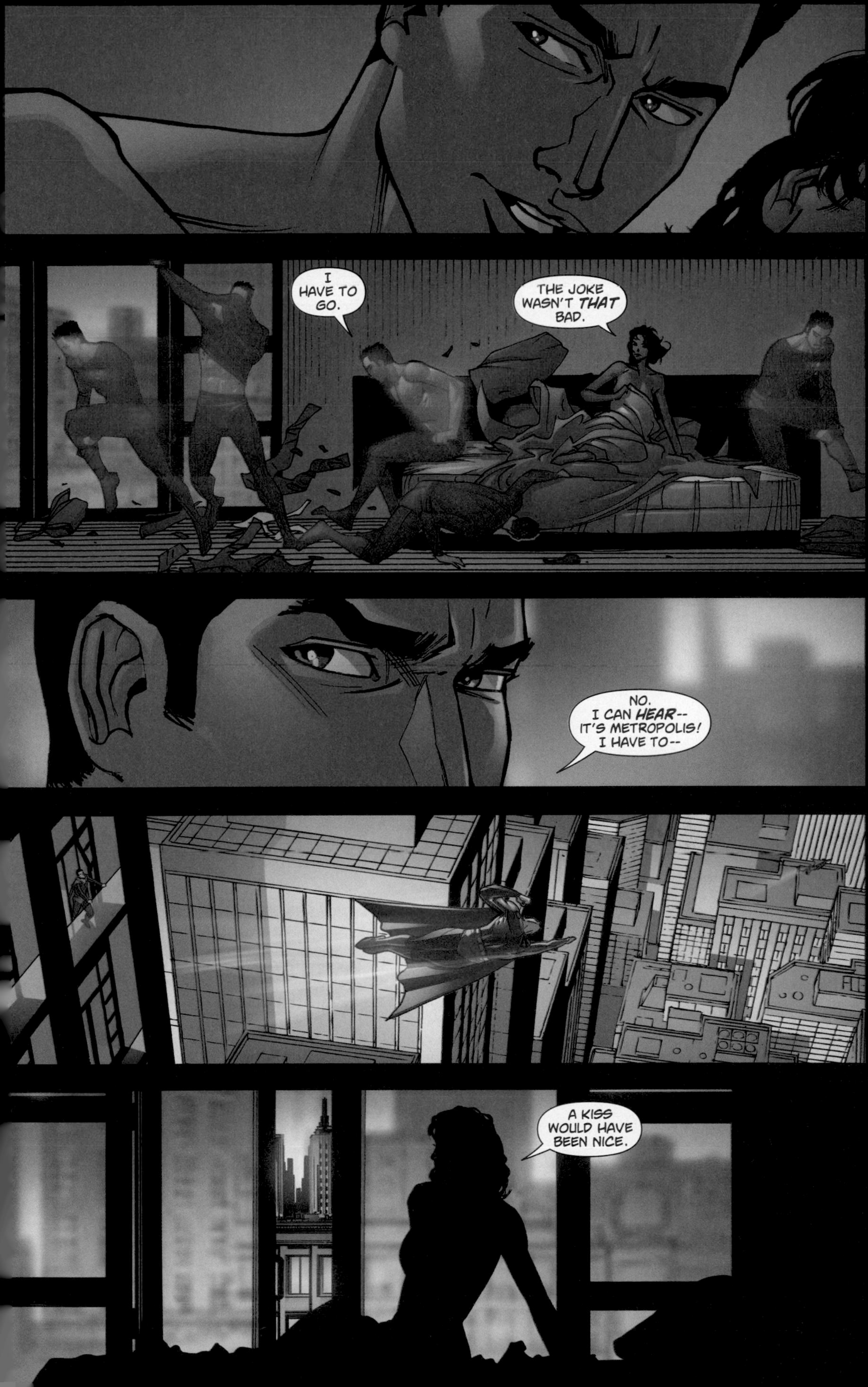
I HAVE TO GO.
THE JOKE WASN'T THAT BAD.
NO. I CAN HEAR-- IT'S METROPOLIS! I HAVE TO--
A KISS WOULD HAVE BEEN NICE.

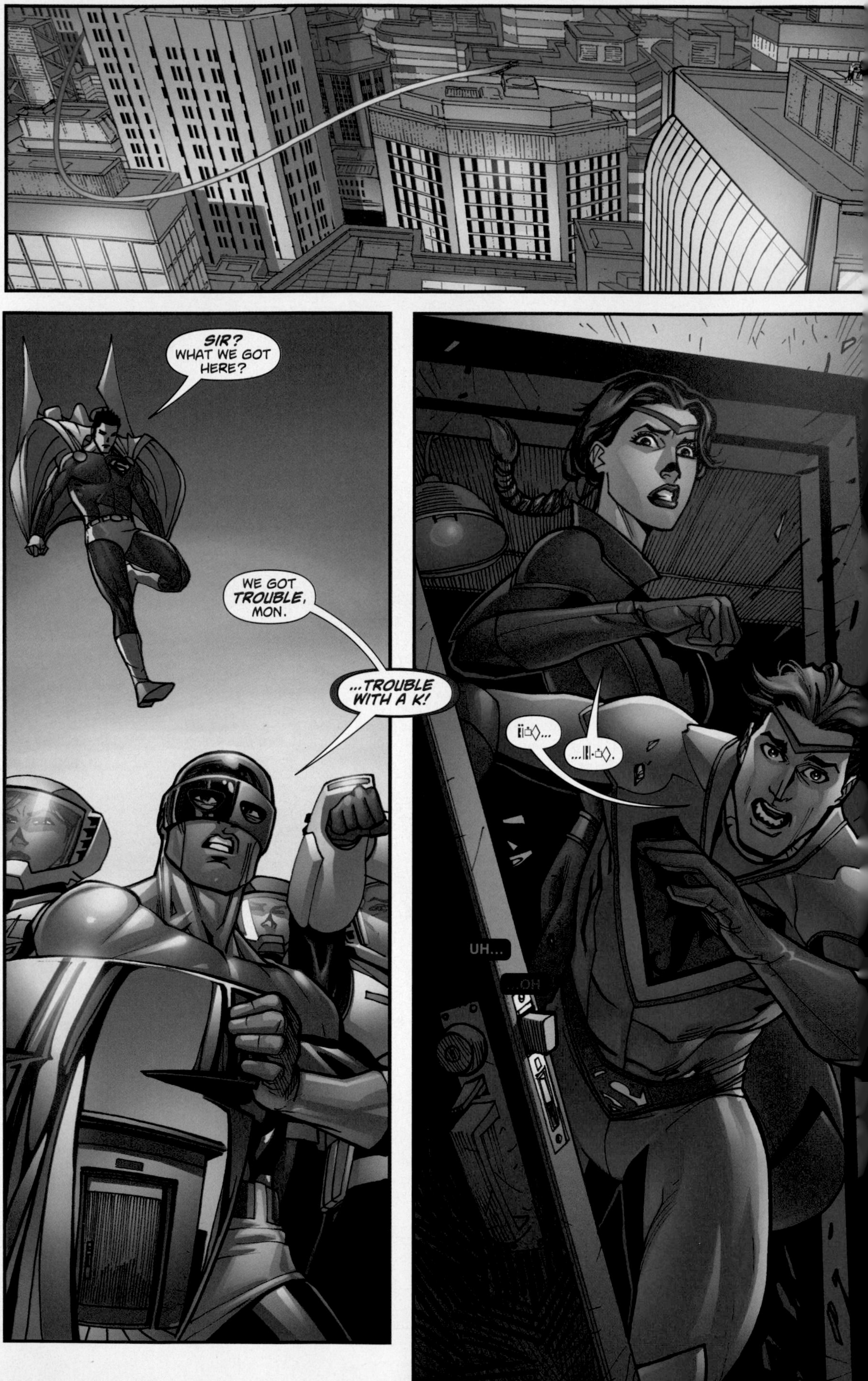
SIR? WHAT WE GOT HERE?
WE GOT TROUBLE, MON.
...TROUBLE WITH A K!
UH...
...OH

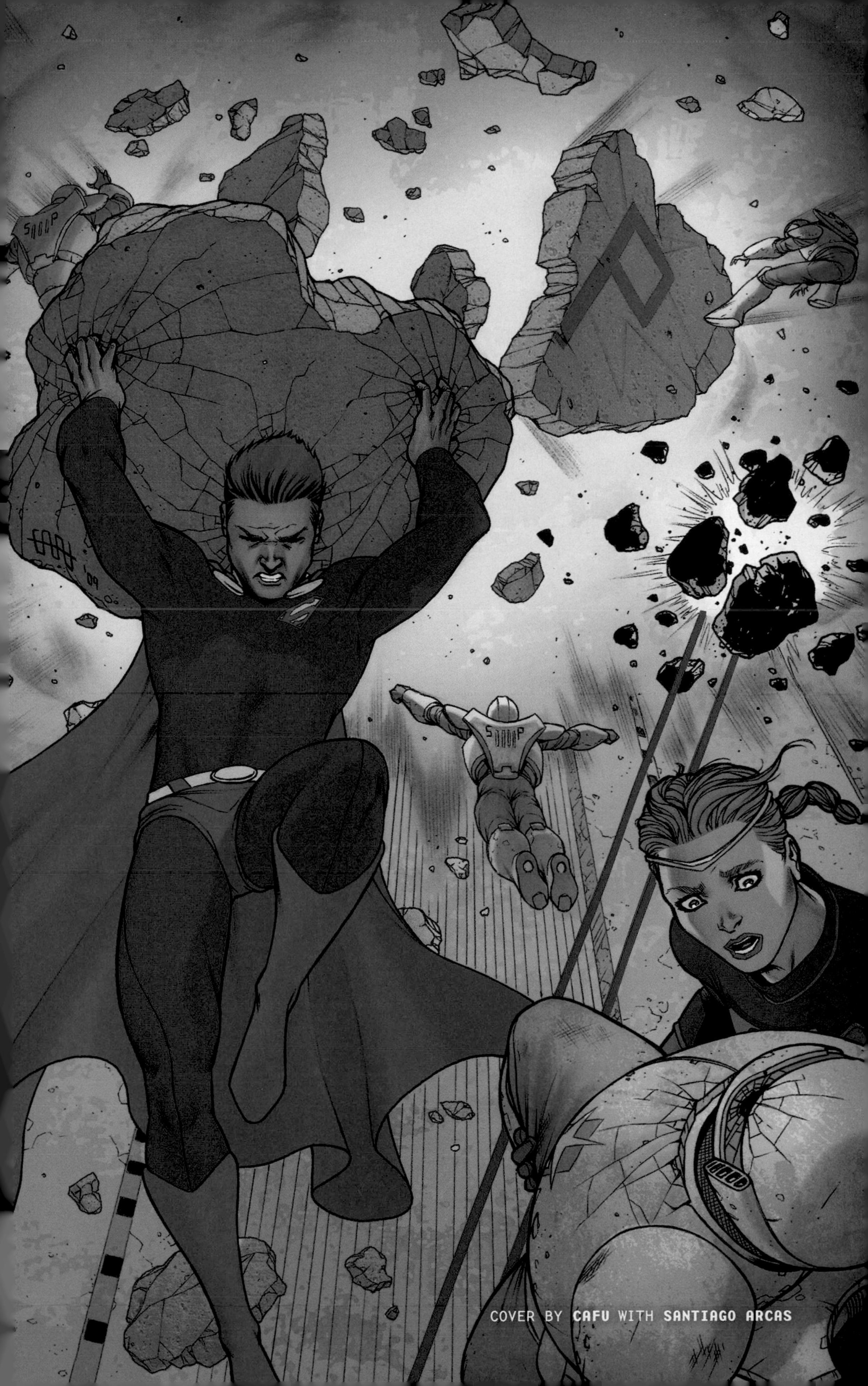

COVER BY **CAFU** WITH **SANTIAGO ARCAS**

MAN OF VALOR PART THREE
BERNARD CHANG <ARTIST>

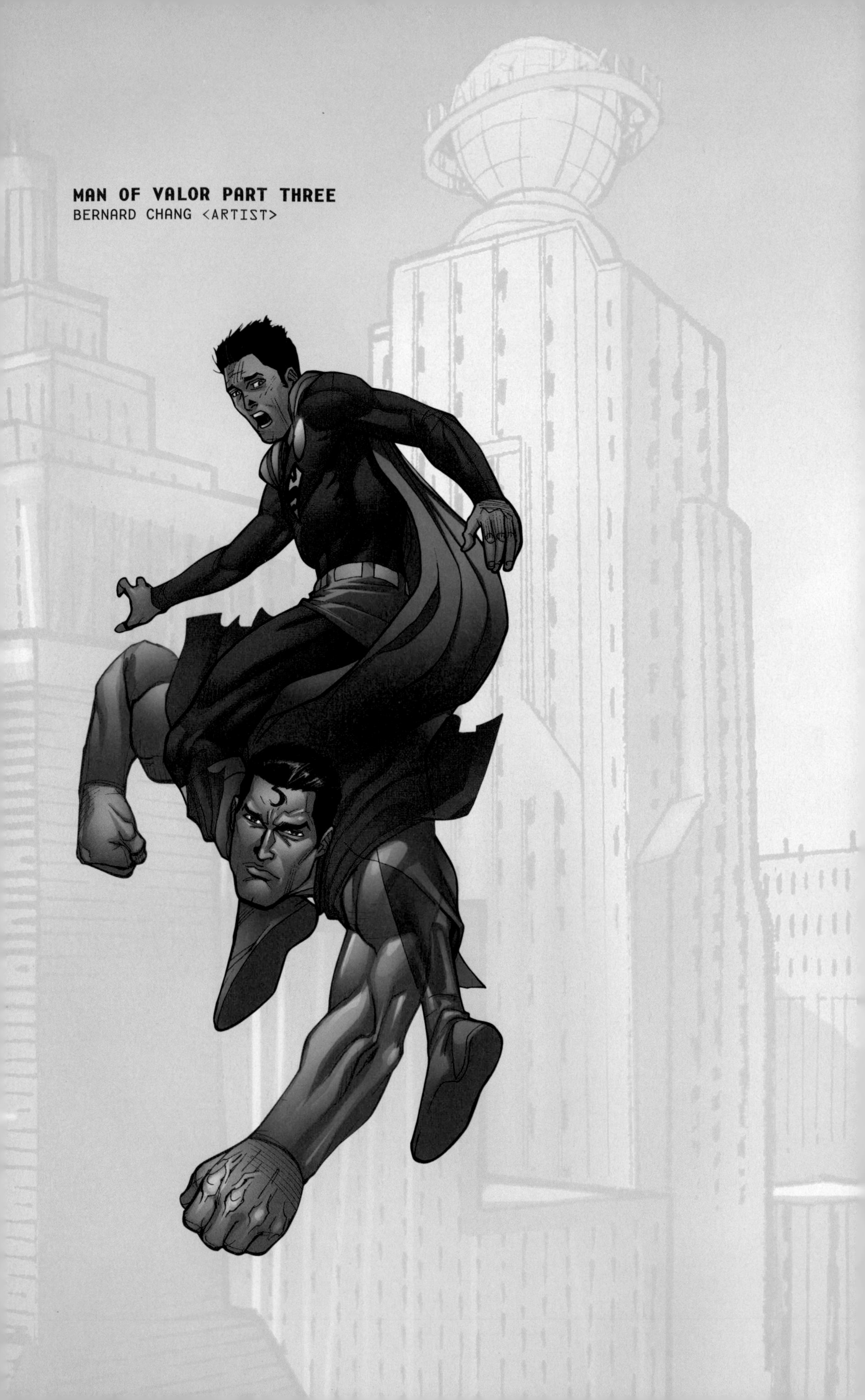

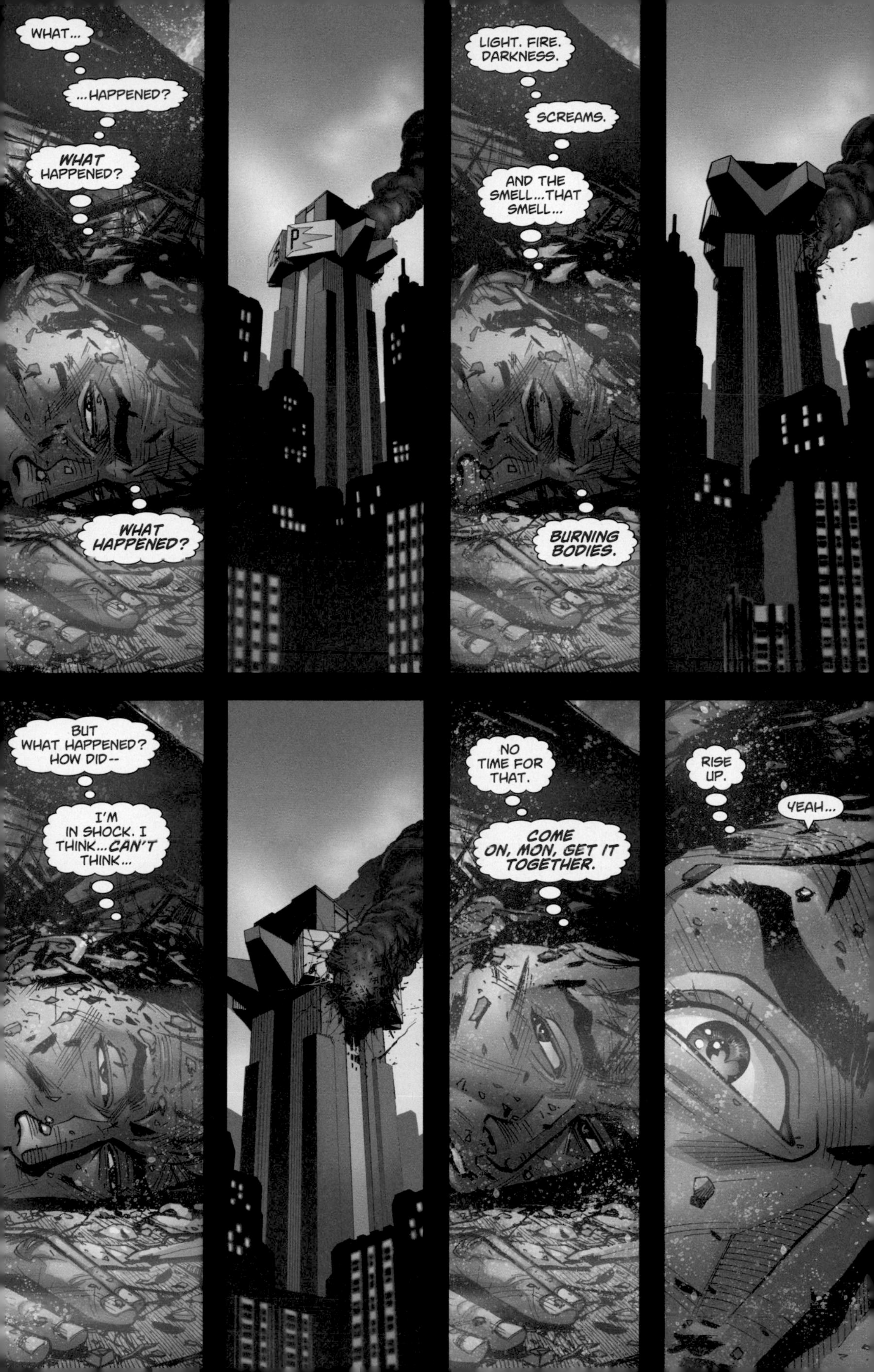
WHAT...
...HAPPENED?
WHAT HAPPENED?
WHAT HAPPENED?
LIGHT. FIRE. DARKNESS.
SCREAMS.
AND THE SMELL...THAT SMELL...
BURNING BODIES.
BUT WHAT HAPPENED? HOW DID--
I'M IN SHOCK. I THINK...CAN'T THINK...
NO TIME FOR THAT.
COME ON, MON, GET IT TOGETHER.
RISE UP.
YEAH...

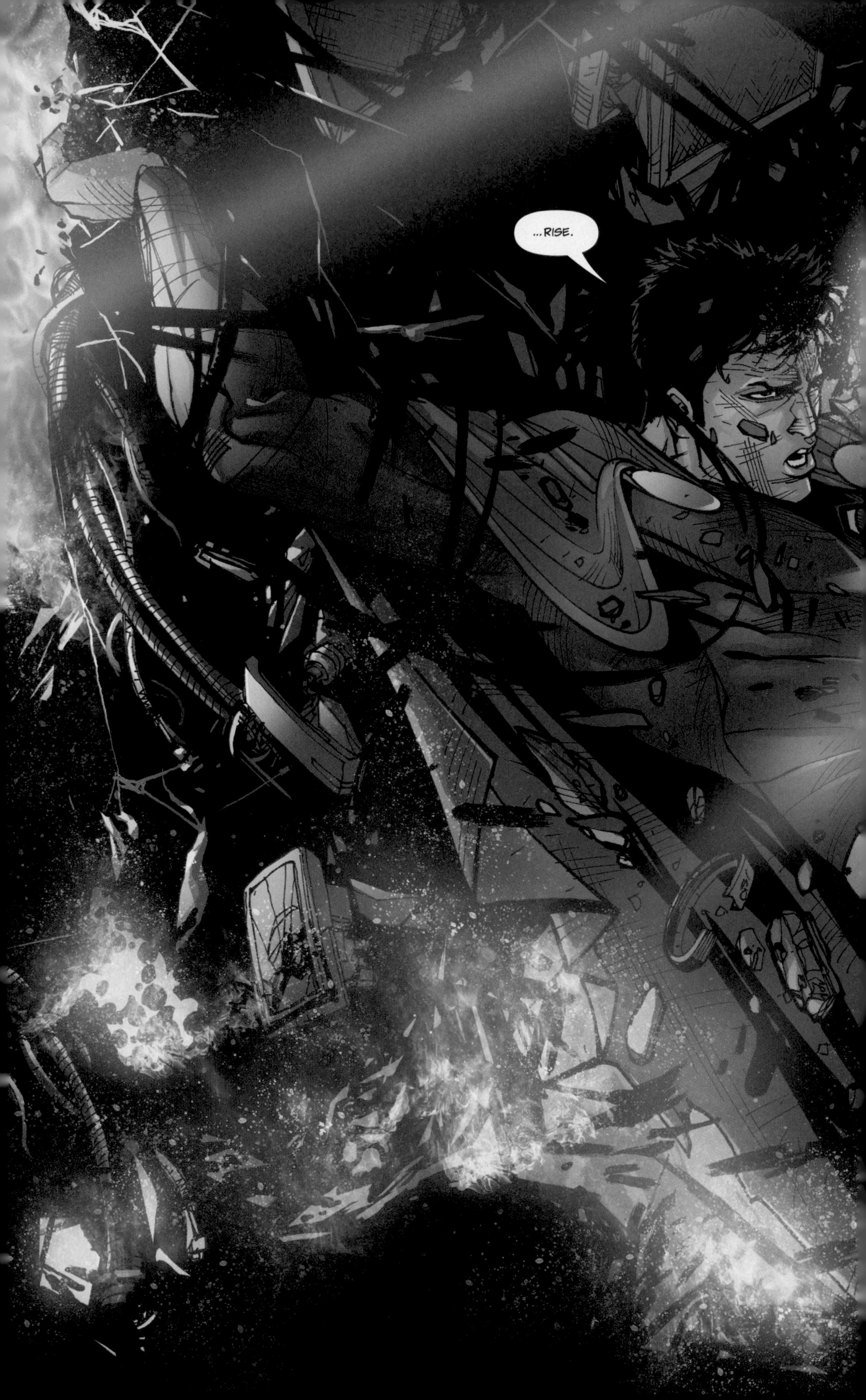
...RISE.

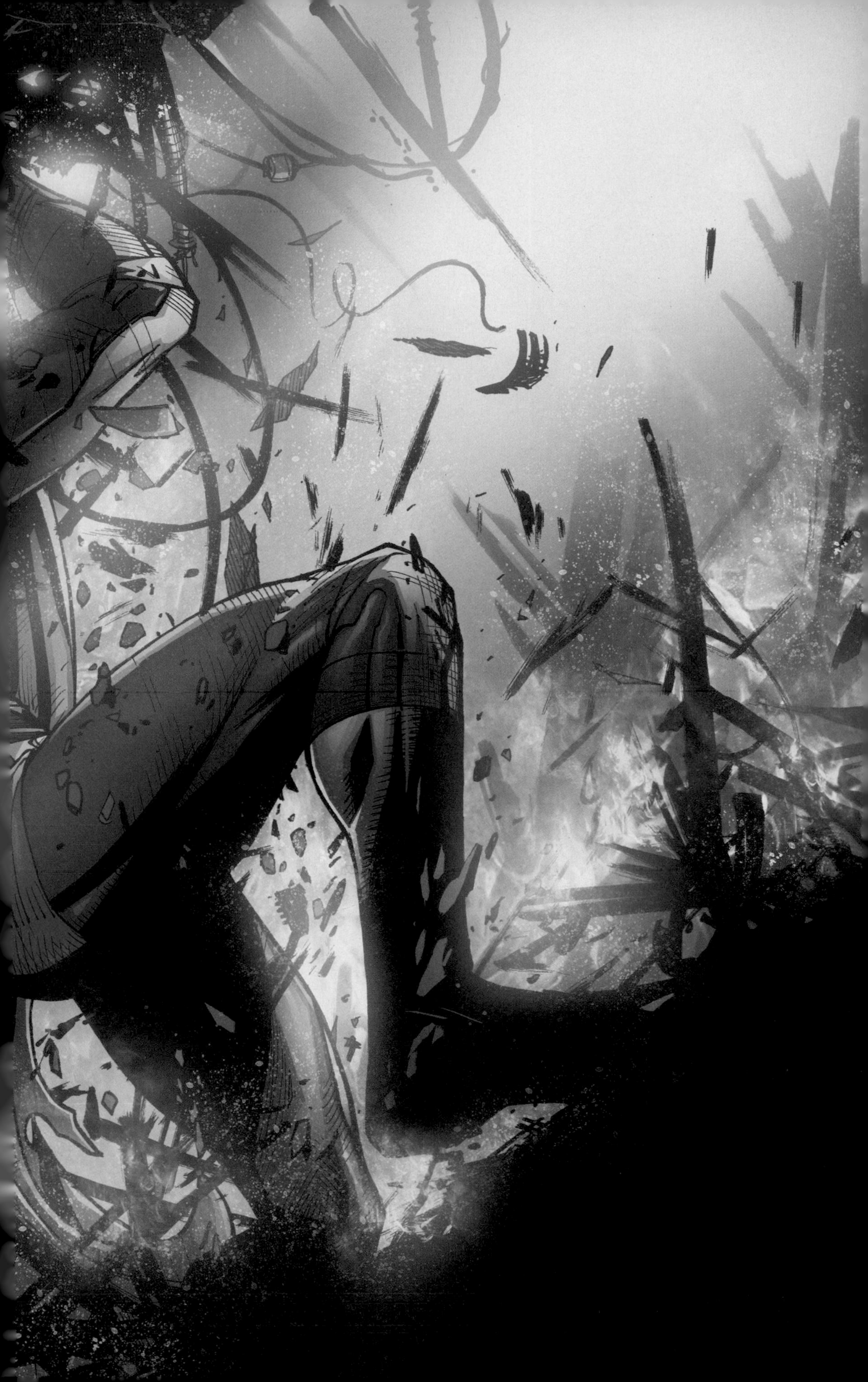

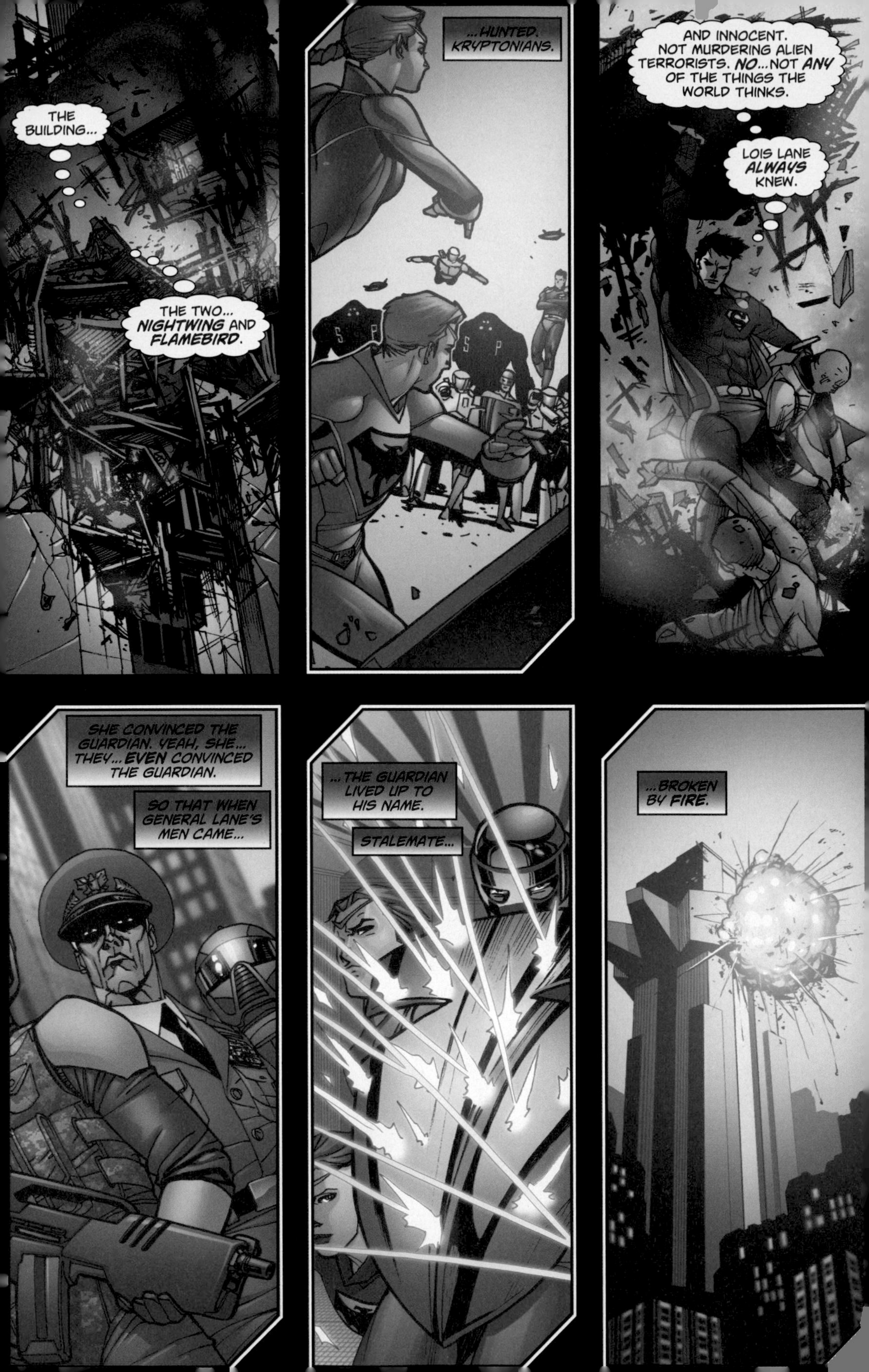
THE BUILDING...
THE TWO... NIGHTWING AND FLAMEBIRD.
...HUNTED. KRYPTONIANS.
AND INNOCENT. NOT MURDERING ALIEN TERRORISTS. NO...NOT ANY OF THE THINGS THE WORLD THINKS.
LOIS LANE ALWAYS KNEW.
SHE CONVINCED THE GUARDIAN. YEAH, SHE... THEY...EVEN CONVINCED THE GUARDIAN.
SO THAT WHEN GENERAL LANE'S MEN CAME...
...THE GUARDIAN LIVED UP TO HIS NAME.
STALEMATE...
...BROKEN BY FIRE.

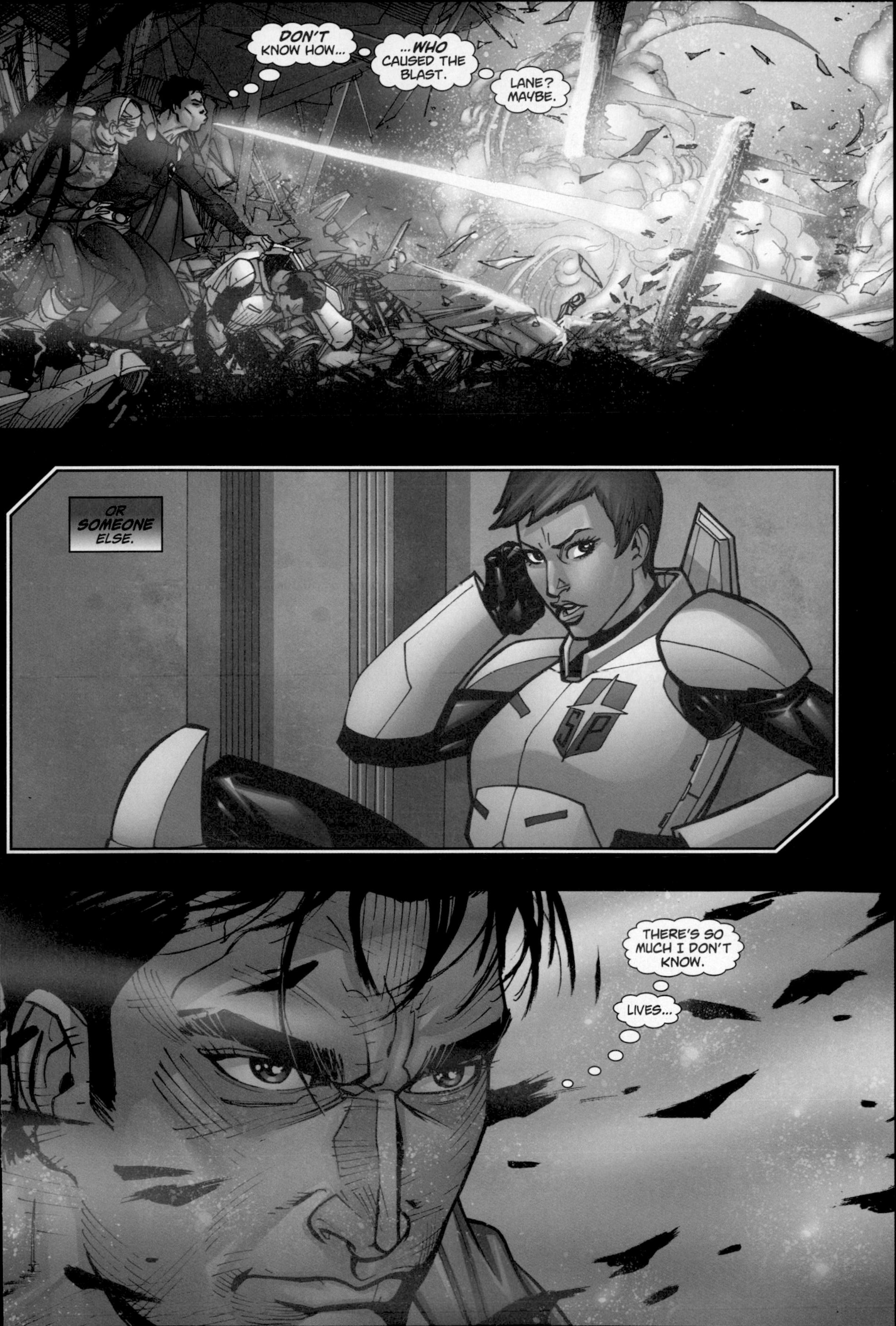
DON'T KNOW HOW...
...WHO CAUSED THE BLAST.
LANE? MAYBE.
OR SOMEONE ELSE.
THERE'S SO MUCH I DON'T KNOW.
LIVES...

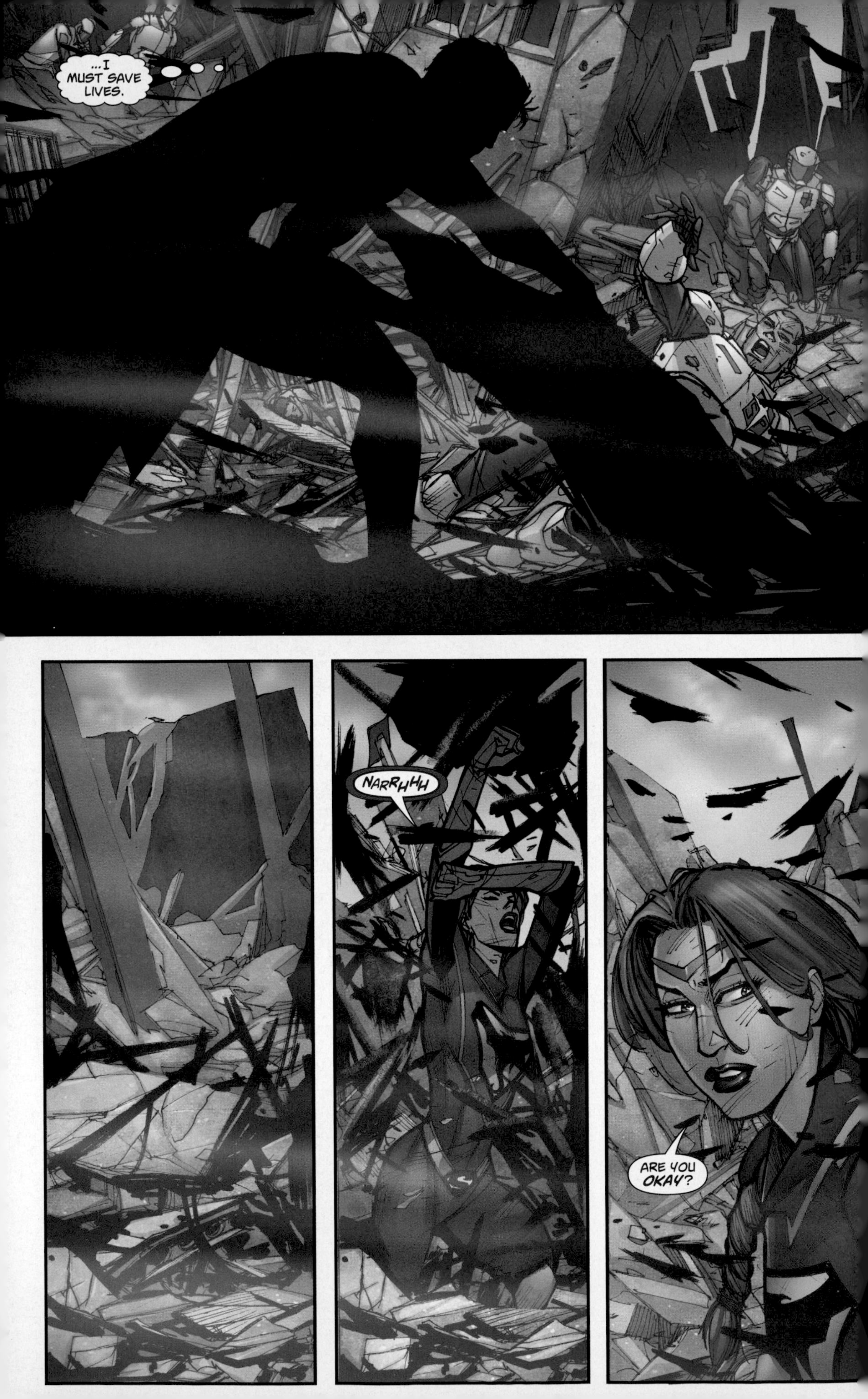
...I MUST SAVE LIVES.
NARRHHH
ARE YOU OKAY?

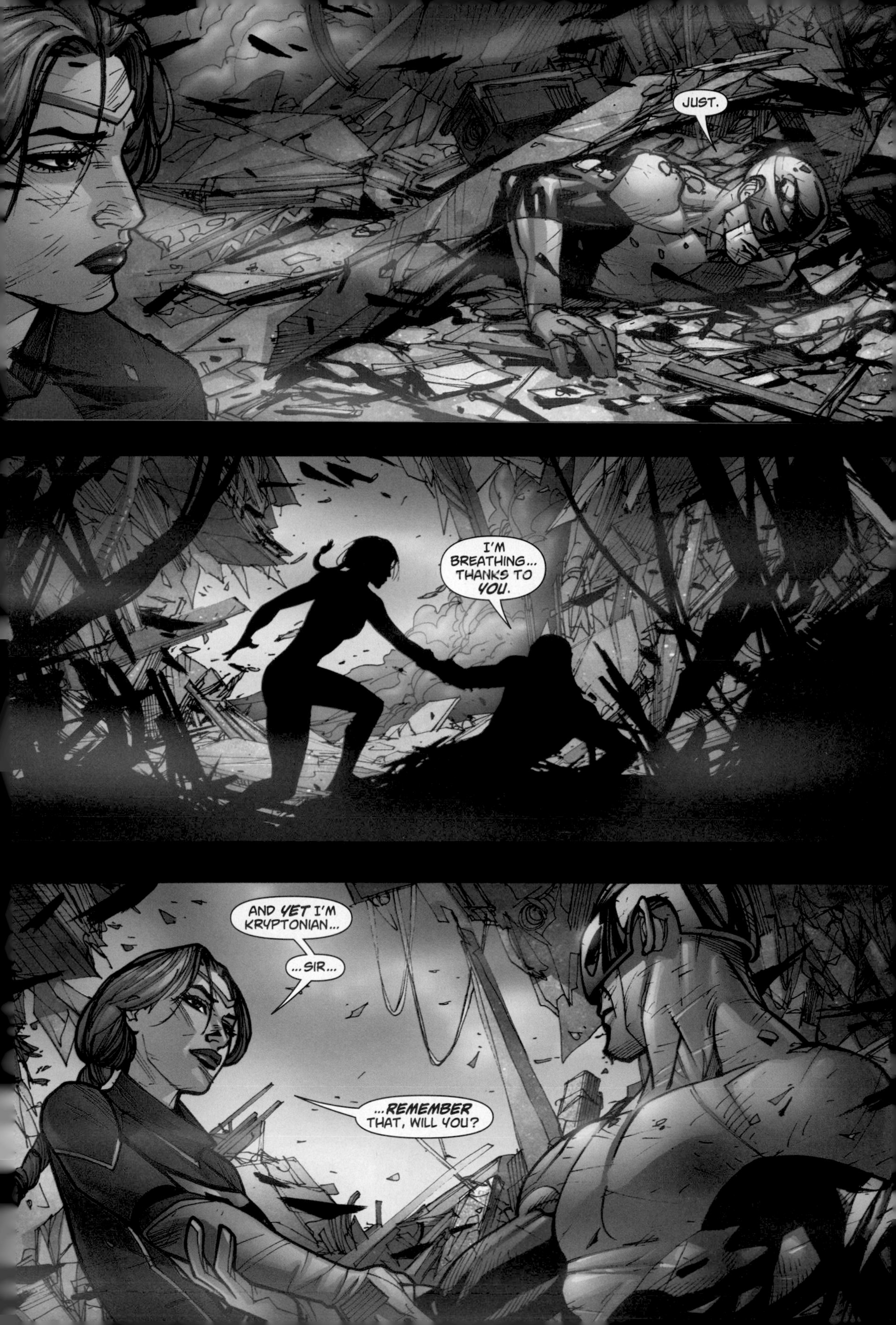
JUST.
I'M BREATHING... THANKS TO *YOU*.
AND *YET* I'M KRYPTONIAN...
...SIR...
...*REMEMBER* THAT, WILL YOU?

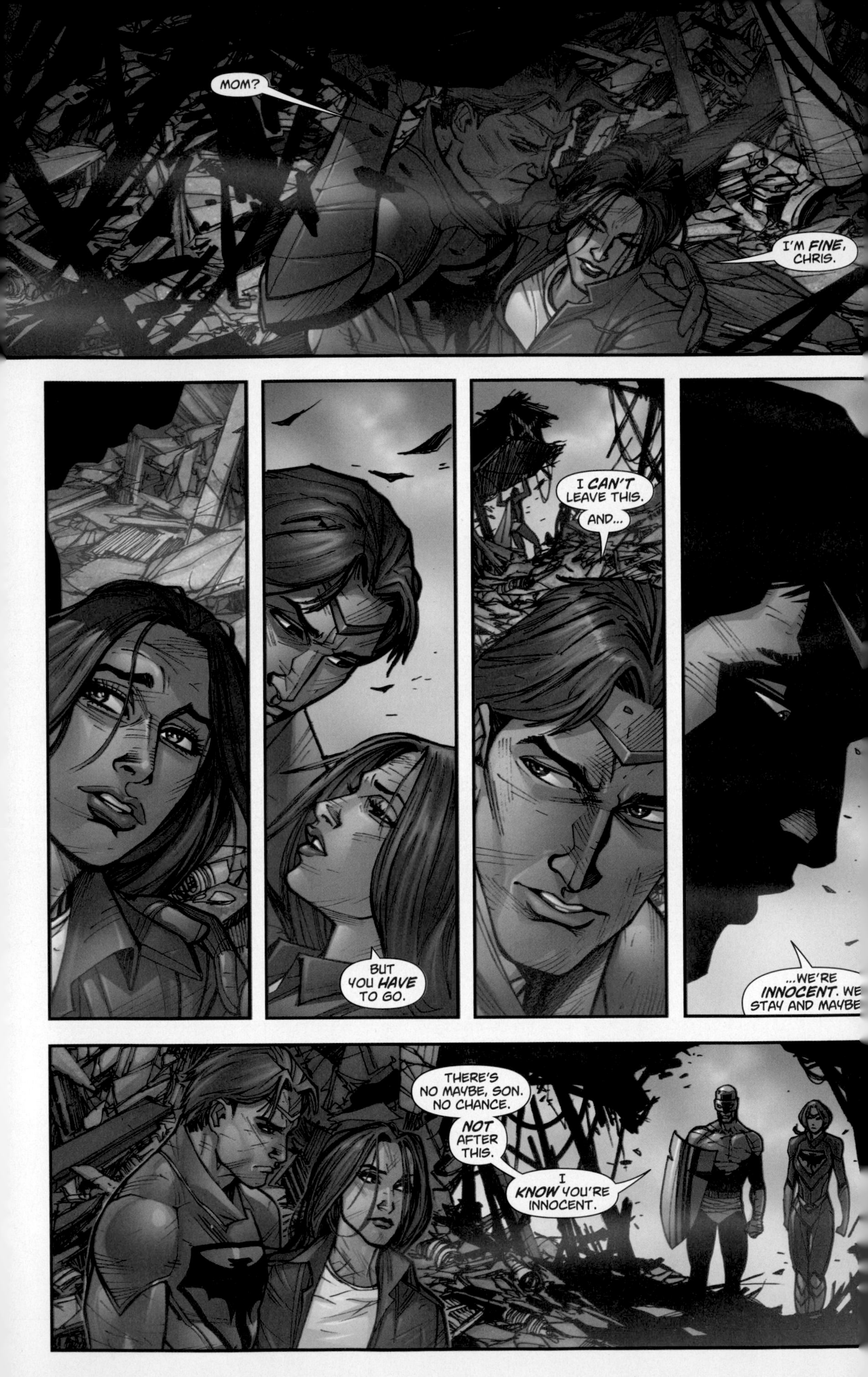
MOM?
I'M FINE, CHRIS.
I CAN'T LEAVE THIS.
AND...
BUT YOU HAVE TO GO.
...WE'RE INNOCENT. WE STAY AND MAYBE
THERE'S NO MAYBE, SON. NO CHANCE.
NOT AFTER THIS.
I KNOW YOU'RE INNOCENT.

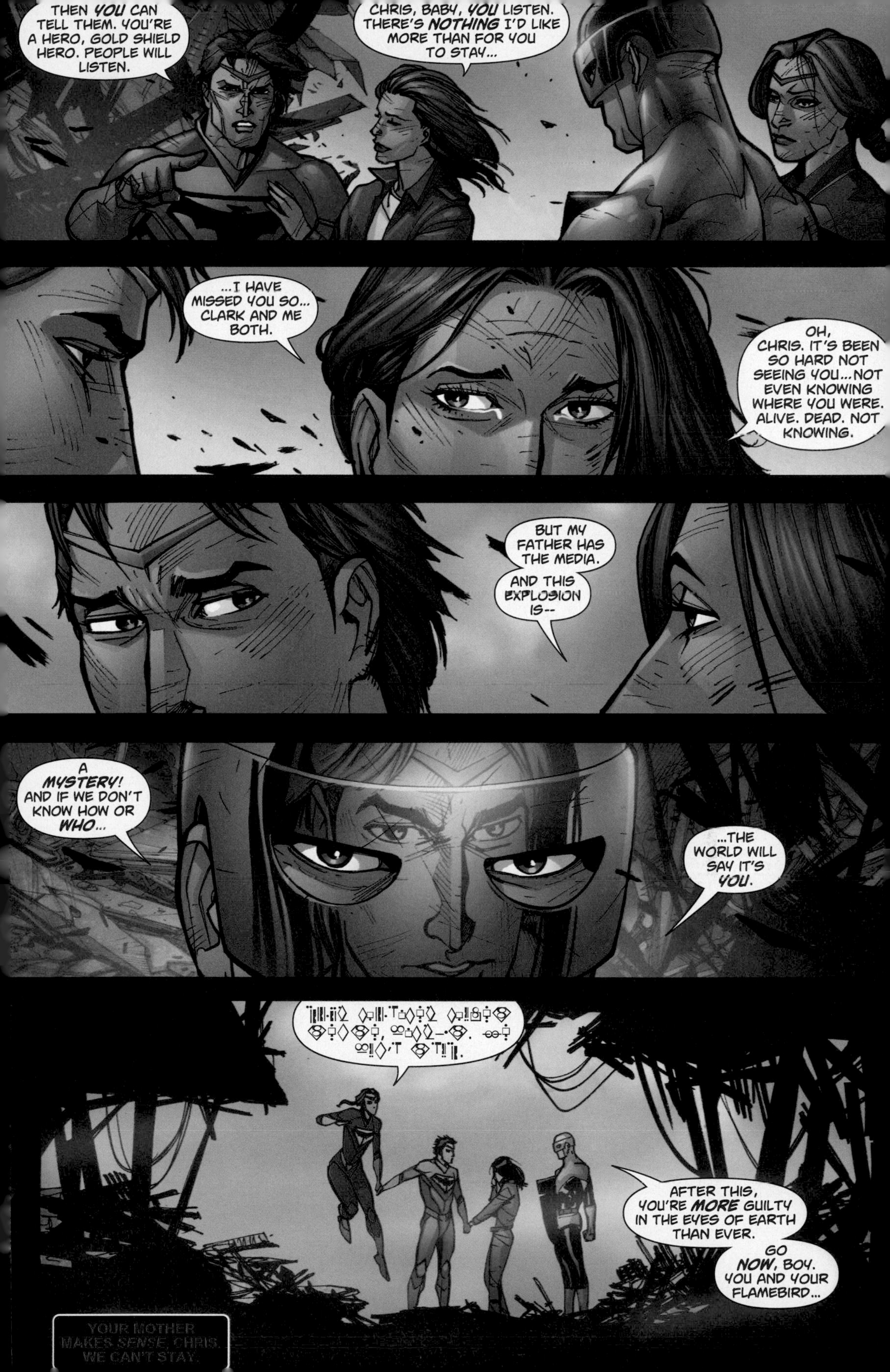

THEN YOU CAN TELL THEM. YOU'RE A HERO, GOLD SHIELD HERO. PEOPLE WILL LISTEN.
CHRIS, BABY, YOU LISTEN. THERE'S NOTHING I'D LIKE MORE THAN FOR YOU TO STAY...
...I HAVE MISSED YOU SO... CLARK AND ME BOTH.
OH, CHRIS. IT'S BEEN SO HARD NOT SEEING YOU...NOT EVEN KNOWING WHERE YOU WERE. ALIVE. DEAD. NOT KNOWING.
BUT MY FATHER HAS THE MEDIA.
AND THIS EXPLOSION IS--
A MYSTERY! AND IF WE DON'T KNOW HOW OR WHO...
...THE WORLD WILL SAY IT'S YOU.
AFTER THIS, YOU'RE MORE GUILTY IN THE EYES OF EARTH THAN EVER.
GO NOW, BOY. YOU AND YOUR FLAMEBIRD...
YOUR MOTHER MAKES SENSE, CHRIS. WE CAN'T STAY.

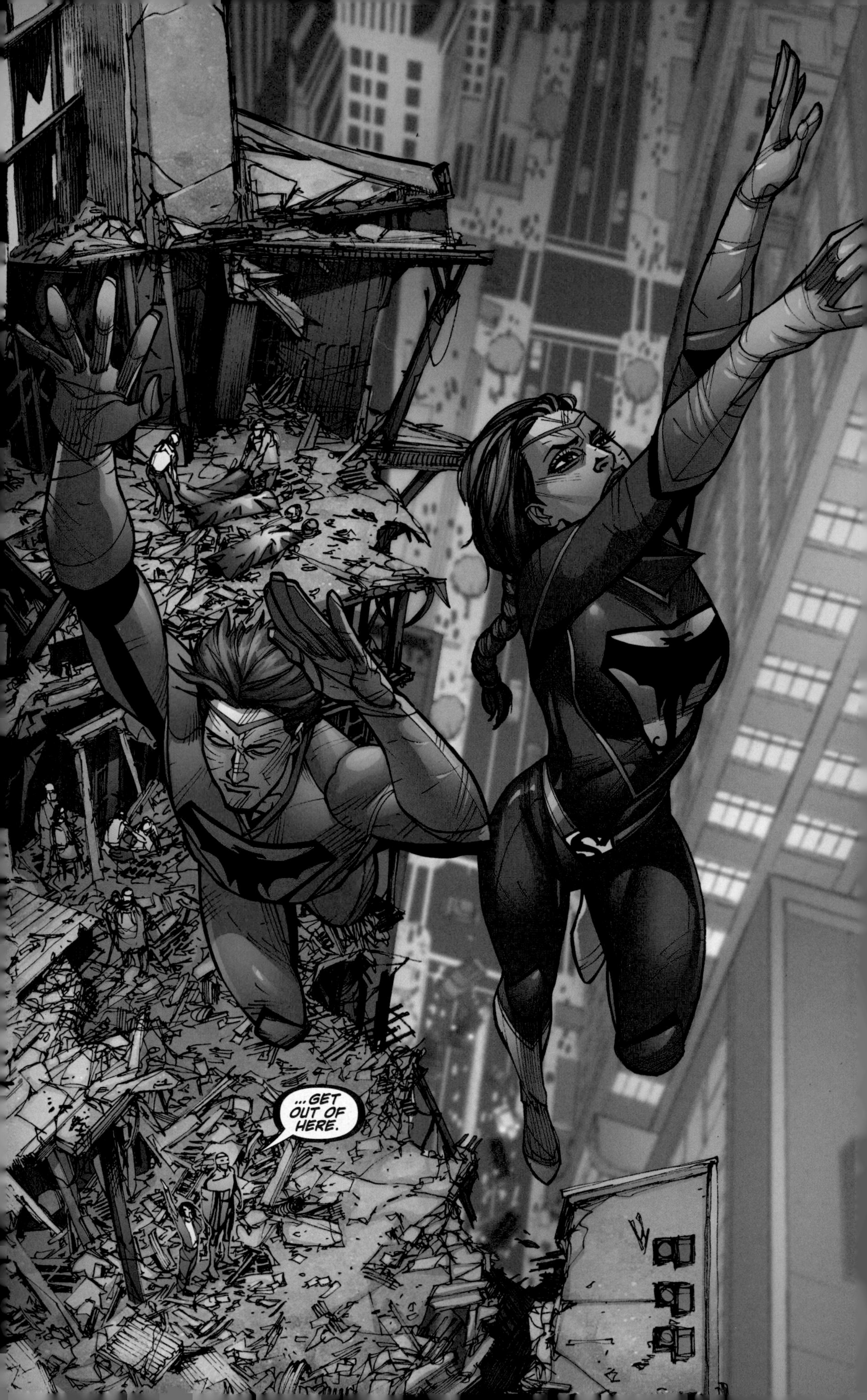
...GET OUT OF HERE.

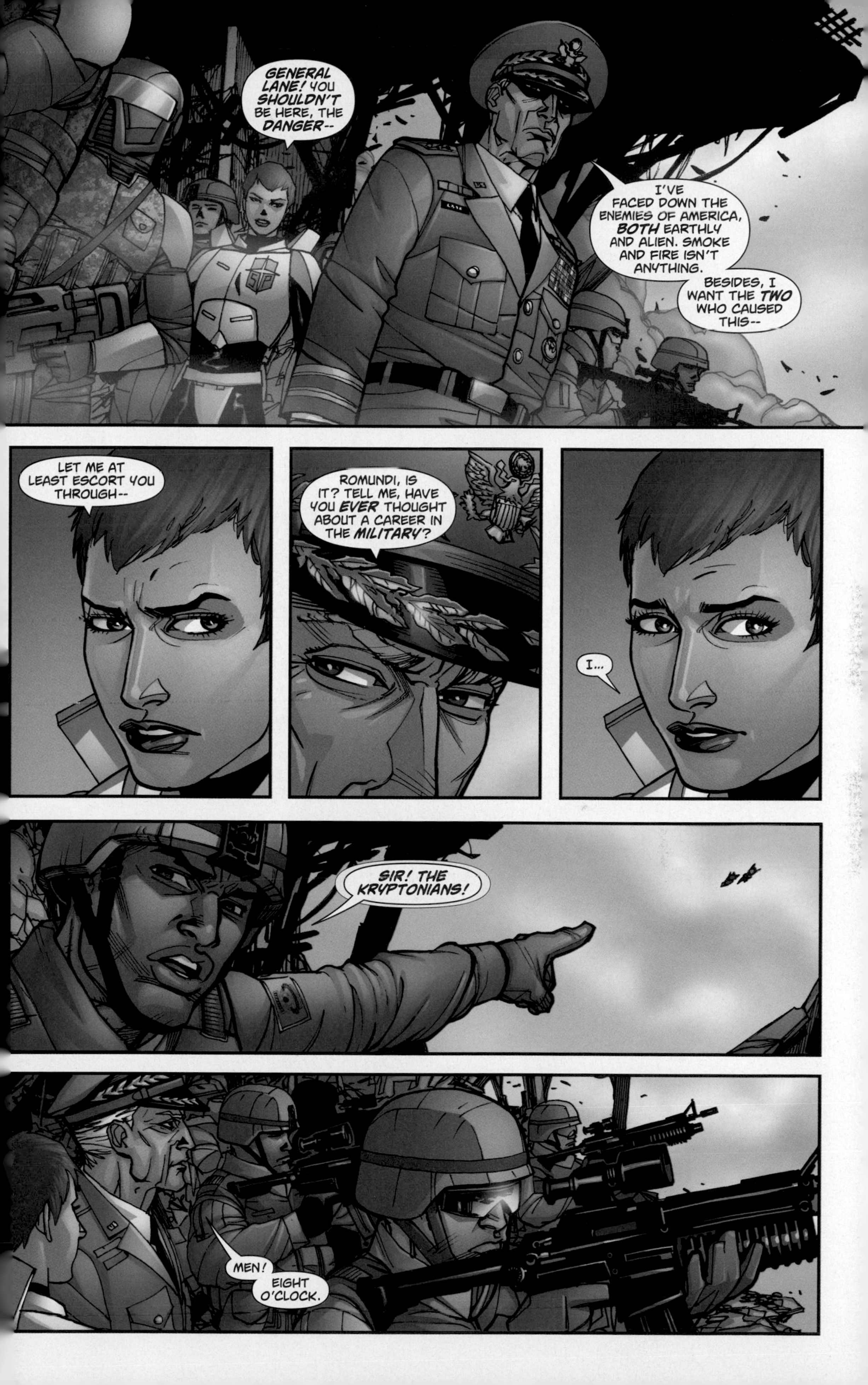
GENERAL LANE! YOU SHOULDN'T BE HERE, THE DANGER--
I'VE FACED DOWN THE ENEMIES OF AMERICA, BOTH EARTHLY AND ALIEN. SMOKE AND FIRE ISN'T ANYTHING.
BESIDES, I WANT THE TWO WHO CAUSED THIS--
LET ME AT LEAST ESCORT YOU THROUGH--
ROMUNDI, IS IT? TELL ME, HAVE YOU EVER THOUGHT ABOUT A CAREER IN THE MILITARY?
I...
SIR! THE KRYPTONIANS!
MEN! EIGHT O'CLOCK.

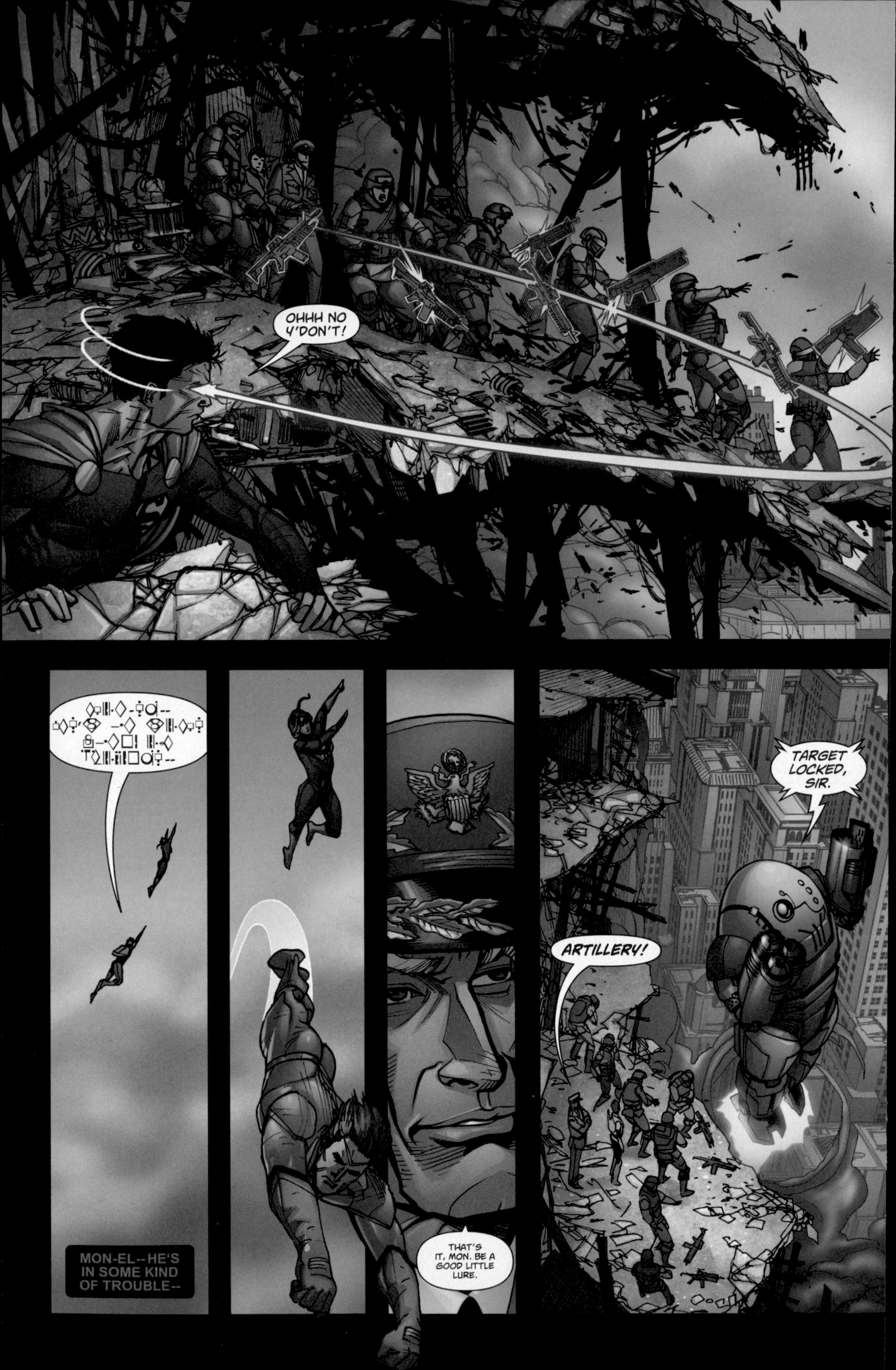
OHHH NO Y'DON'T!
MON-EL--HE'S IN SOME KIND OF TROUBLE--
THAT'S IT, MON. BE A GOOD LITTLE LURE.
TARGET LOCKED, SIR.
ARTILLERY!

THEN *FIRE AT WILL!!*

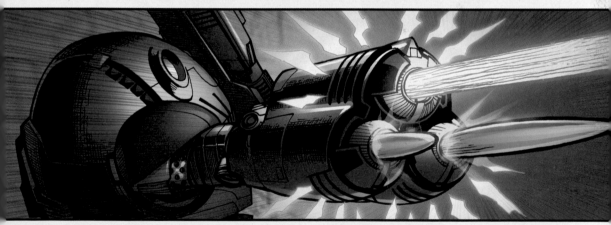

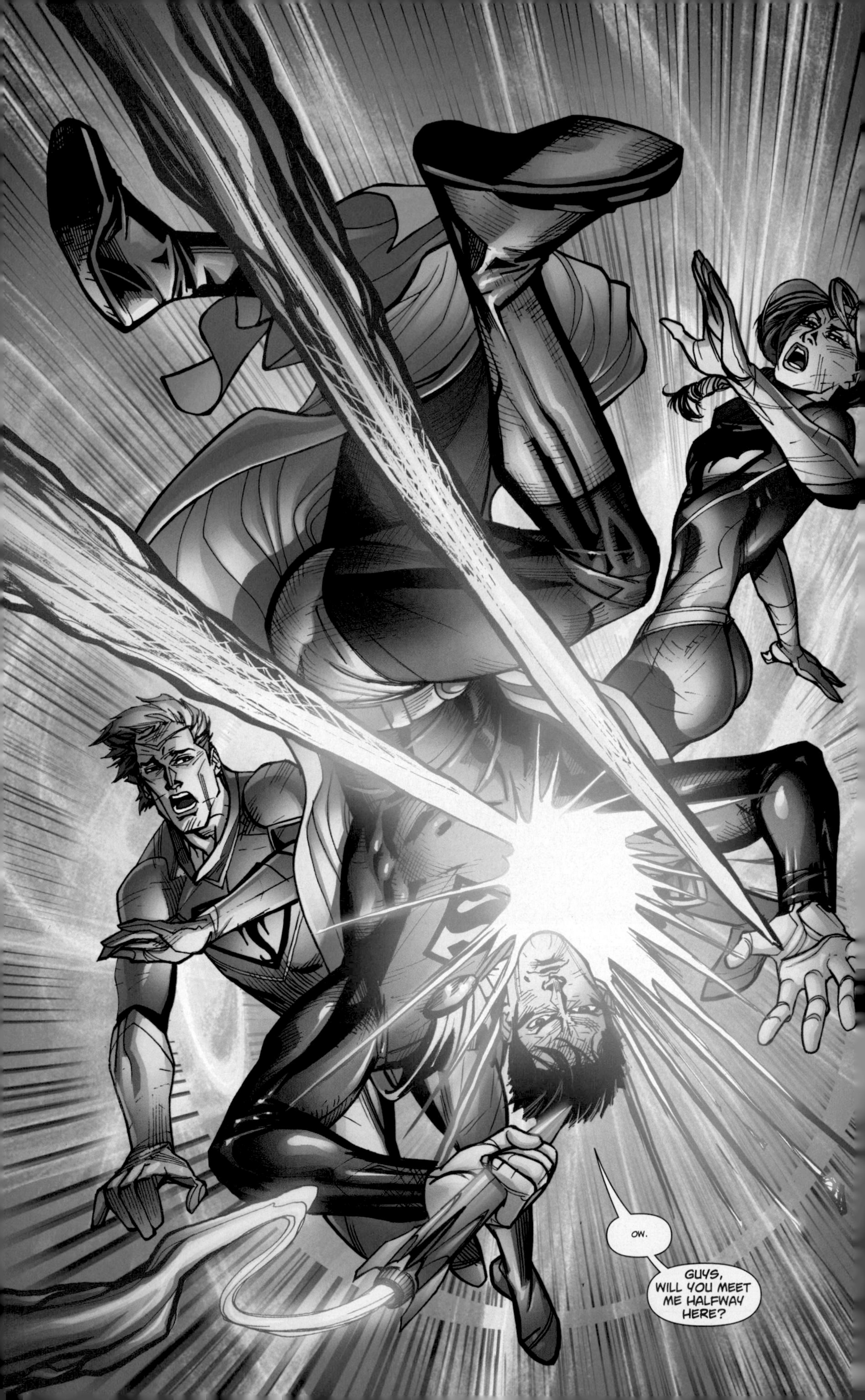
OW.
GUYS, WILL YOU MEET ME HALFWAY HERE?

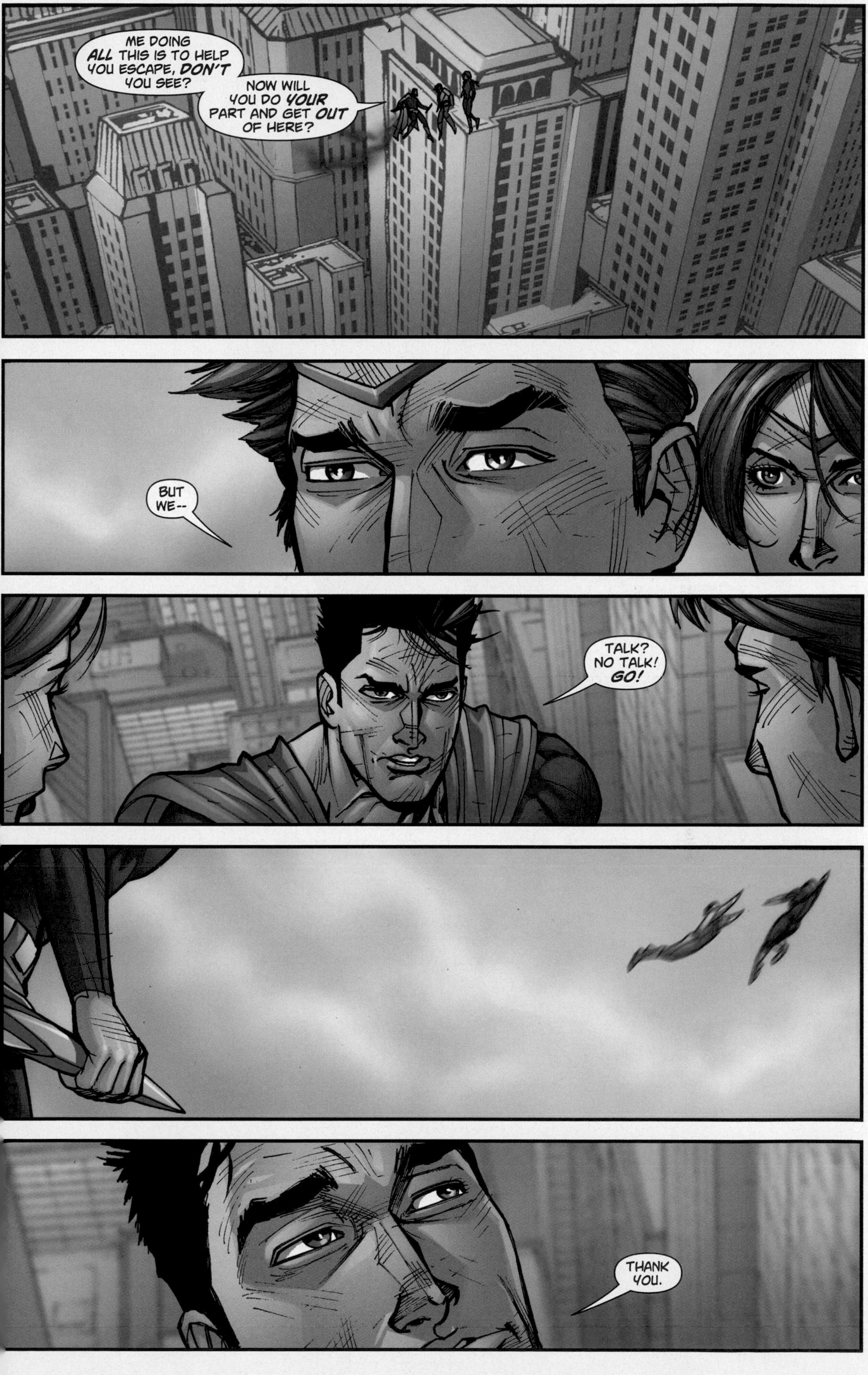
ME DOING ALL THIS IS TO HELP YOU ESCAPE, DON'T YOU SEE?
NOW WILL YOU DO YOUR PART AND GET OUT OF HERE?
BUT WE--
TALK? NO TALK! GO!
THANK YOU.

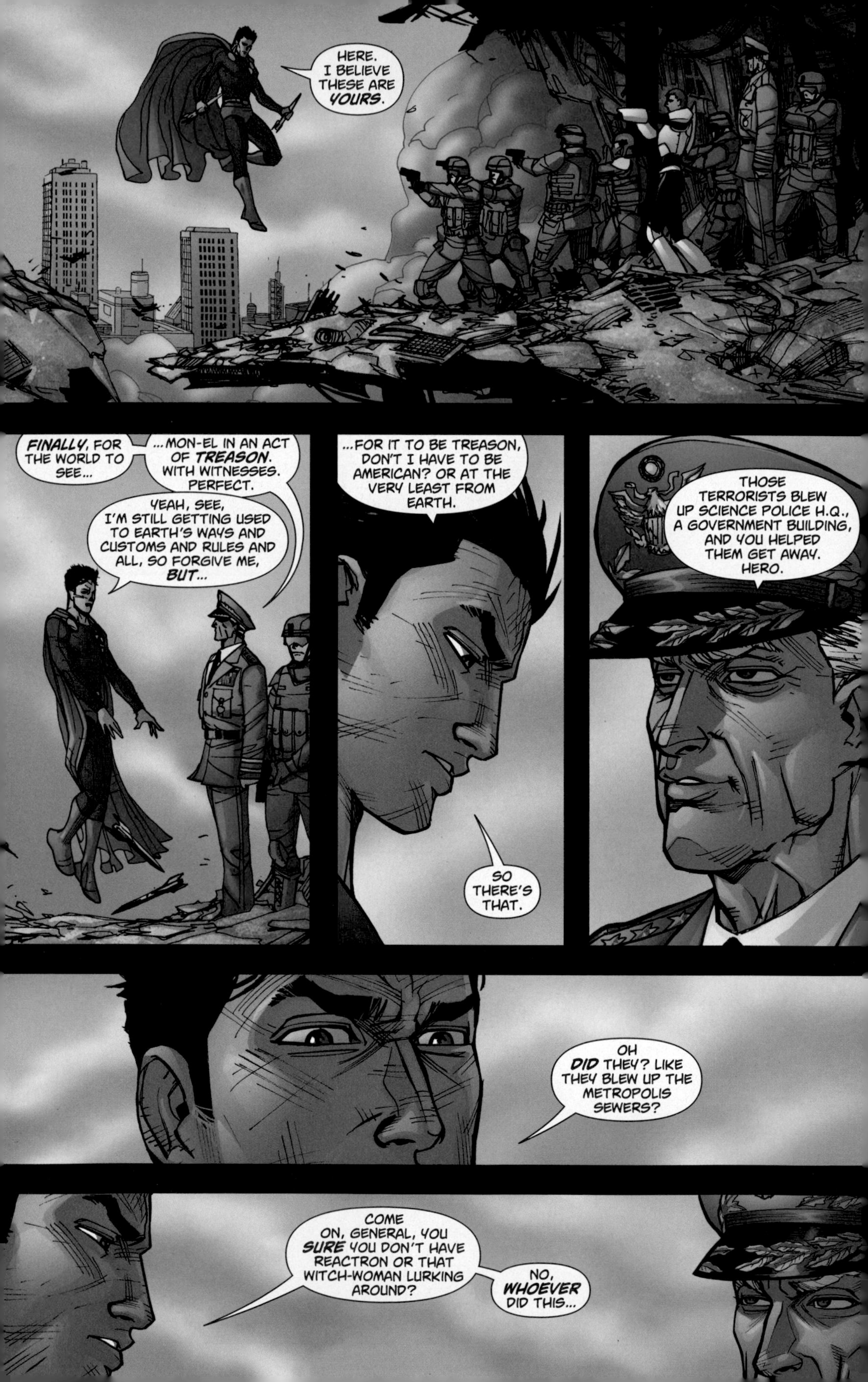
HERE. I BELIEVE THESE ARE *YOURS*.
FINALLY, FOR THE WORLD TO SEE...
...MON-EL IN AN ACT OF *TREASON*. WITH WITNESSES. PERFECT.
YEAH, SEE, I'M STILL GETTING USED TO EARTH'S WAYS AND CUSTOMS AND RULES AND ALL, SO FORGIVE ME, *BUT*...
...FOR IT TO BE TREASON, DON'T I HAVE TO BE AMERICAN? OR AT THE VERY LEAST FROM EARTH.
SO THERE'S THAT.
THOSE TERRORISTS BLEW UP SCIENCE POLICE H.Q., A GOVERNMENT BUILDING, AND YOU HELPED THEM GET AWAY. HERO.
OH *DID* THEY? LIKE THEY BLEW UP THE METROPOLIS SEWERS?
COME ON, GENERAL, YOU *SURE* YOU DON'T HAVE REACTRON OR THAT WITCH-WOMAN LURKING AROUND?
NO, *WHOEVER* DID THIS...

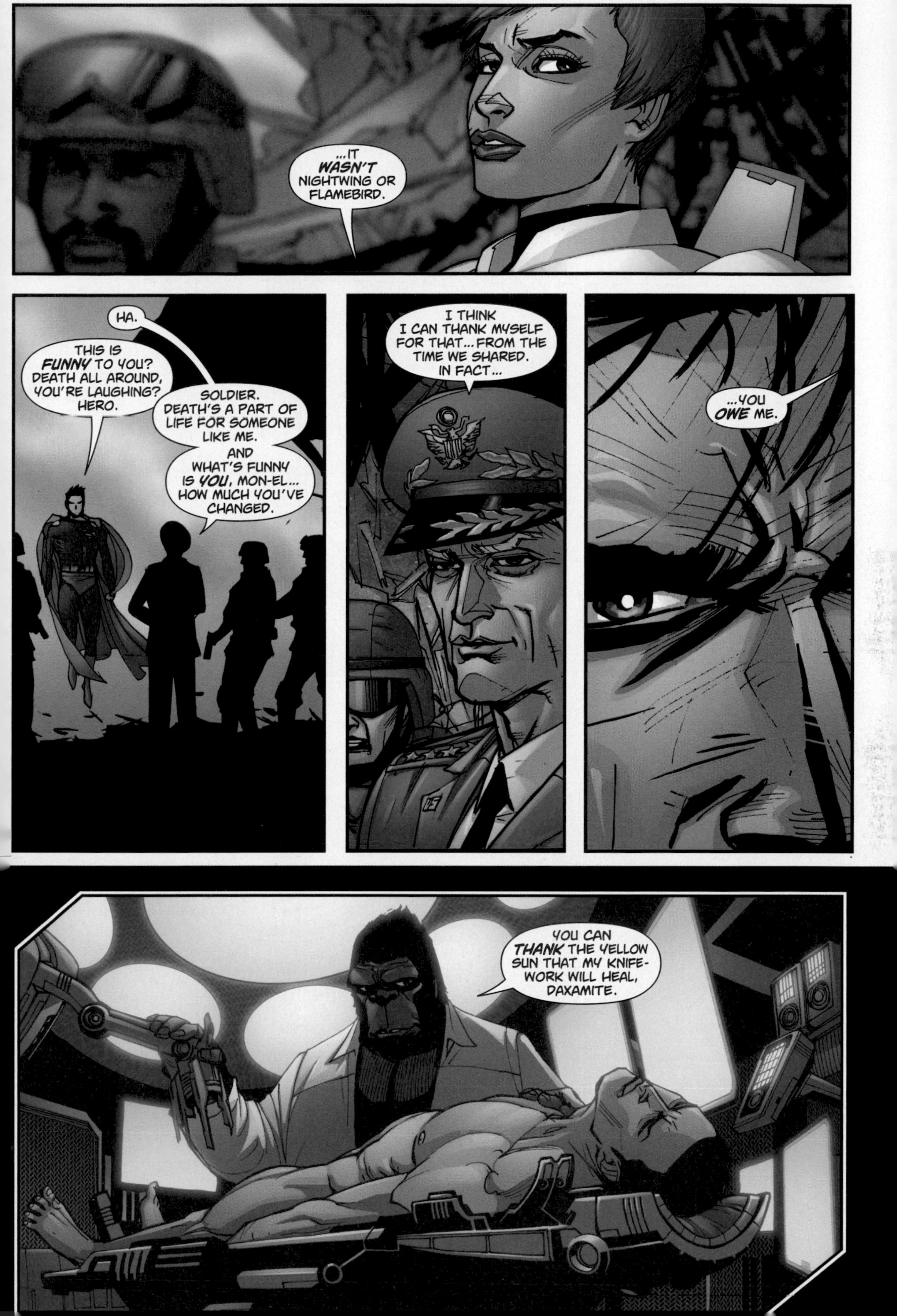
...IT WASN'T NIGHTWING OR FLAMEBIRD.
HA.
THIS IS FUNNY TO YOU? DEATH ALL AROUND, YOU'RE LAUGHING? HERO.
SOLDIER. DEATH'S A PART OF LIFE FOR SOMEONE LIKE ME.
AND WHAT'S FUNNY IS YOU, MON-EL... HOW MUCH YOU'VE CHANGED.
I THINK I CAN THANK MYSELF FOR THAT... FROM THE TIME WE SHARED. IN FACT...
...YOU OWE ME.
YOU CAN THANK THE YELLOW SUN THAT MY KNIFE-WORK WILL HEAL, DAXAMITE.

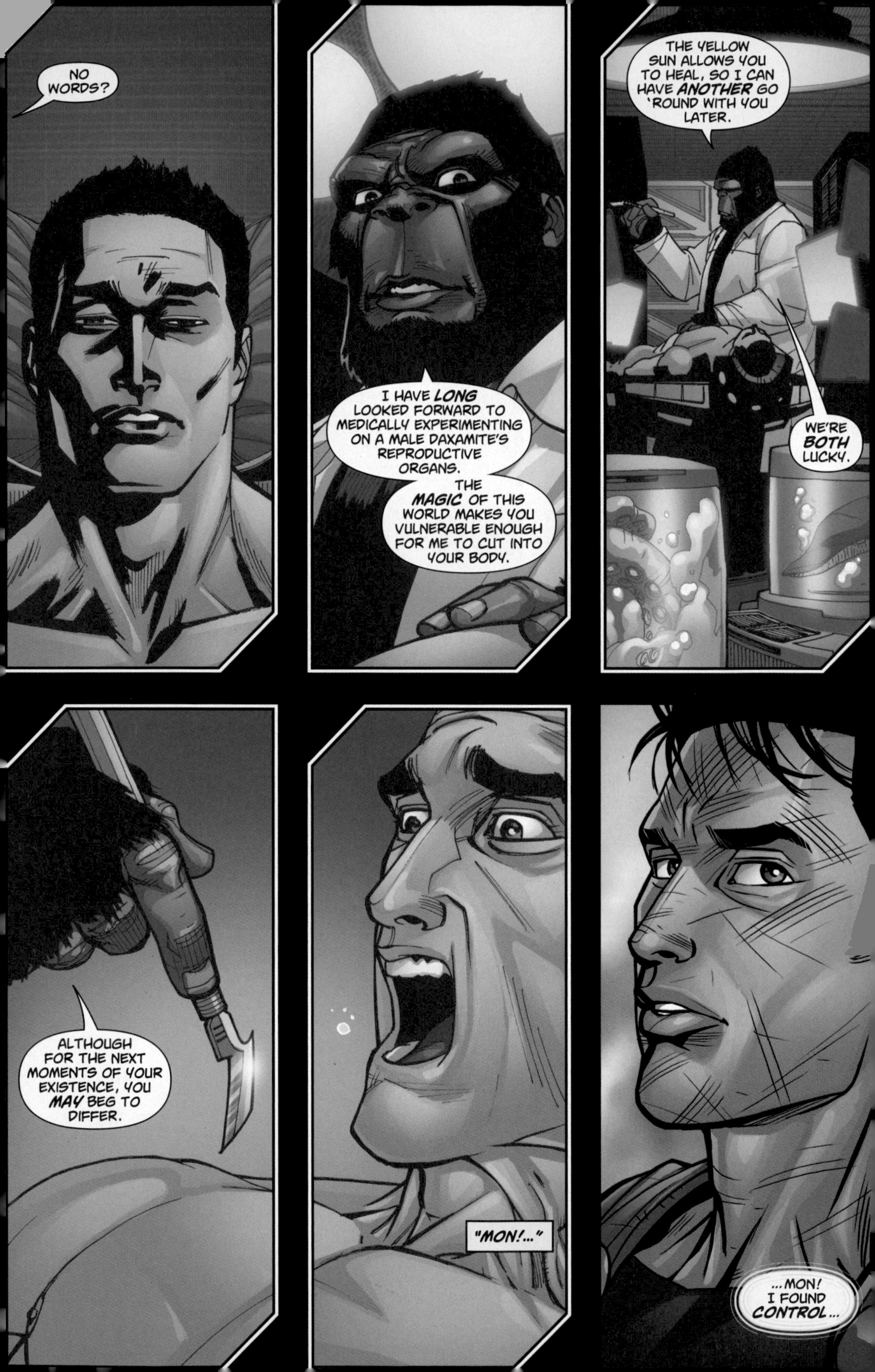
NO WORDS?
I HAVE LONG LOOKED FORWARD TO MEDICALLY EXPERIMENTING ON A MALE DAXAMITE'S REPRODUCTIVE ORGANS.
THE MAGIC OF THIS WORLD MAKES YOU VULNERABLE ENOUGH FOR ME TO CUT INTO YOUR BODY.
THE YELLOW SUN ALLOWS YOU TO HEAL, SO I CAN HAVE ANOTHER GO 'ROUND WITH YOU LATER.
WE'RE BOTH LUCKY.
ALTHOUGH FOR THE NEXT MOMENTS OF YOUR EXISTENCE, YOU MAY BEG TO DIFFER.
"MON!..."
...MON! I FOUND CONTROL...

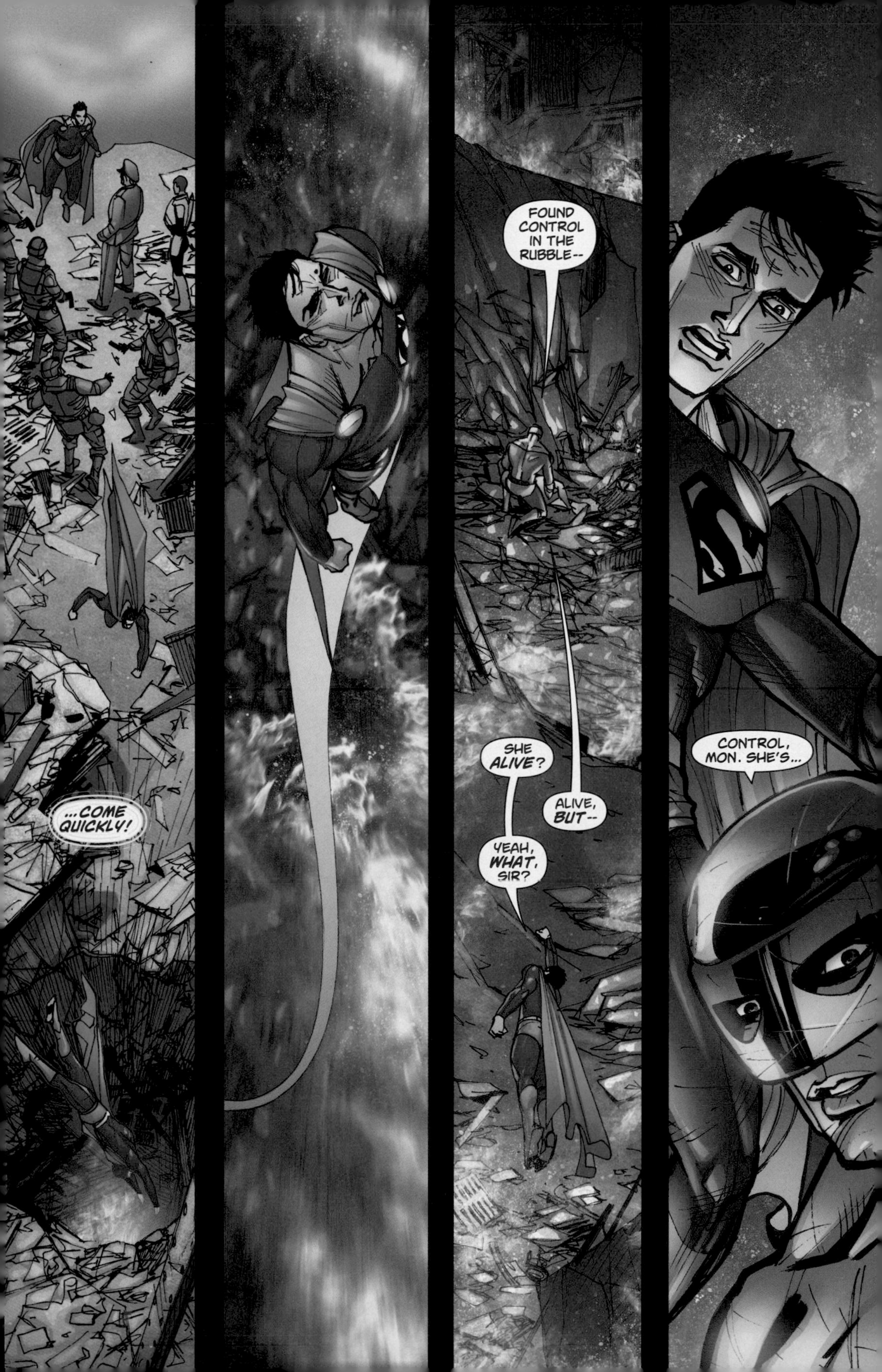
...COME QUICKLY!
FOUND CONTROL IN THE RUBBLE--
SHE ALIVE?
ALIVE, BUT--
YEAH, WHAT, SIR?
CONTROL, MON. SHE'S...

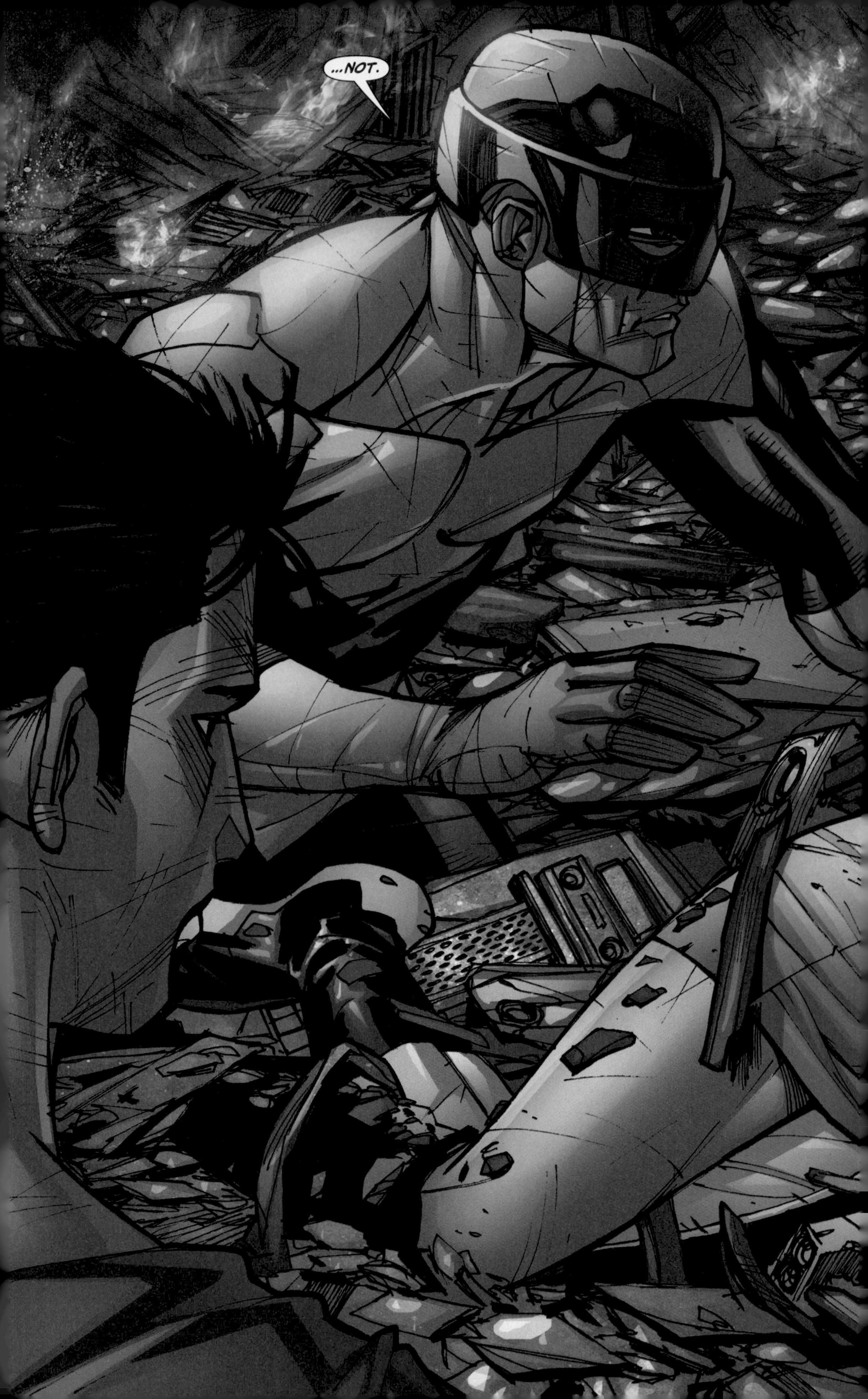
...NOT.

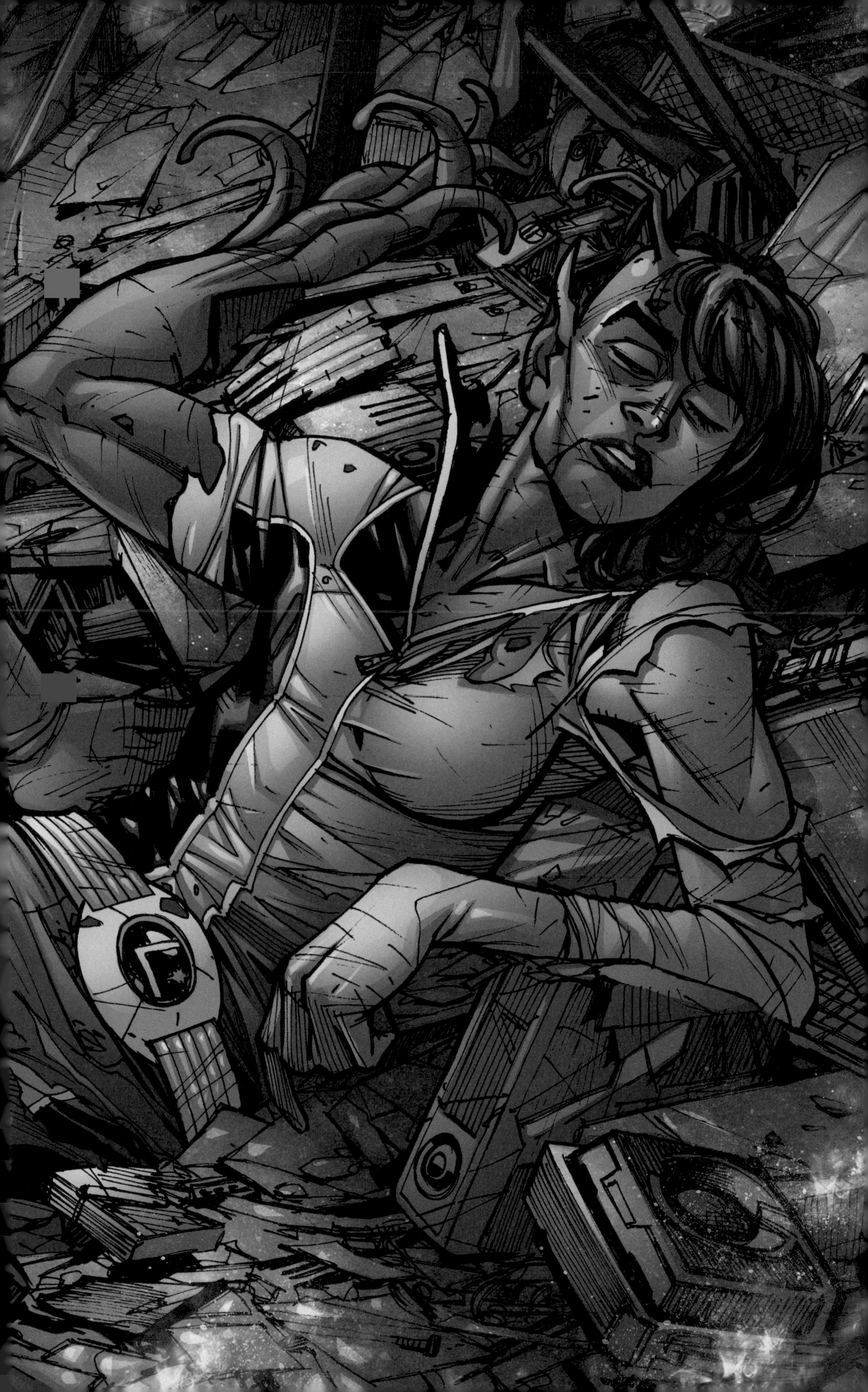

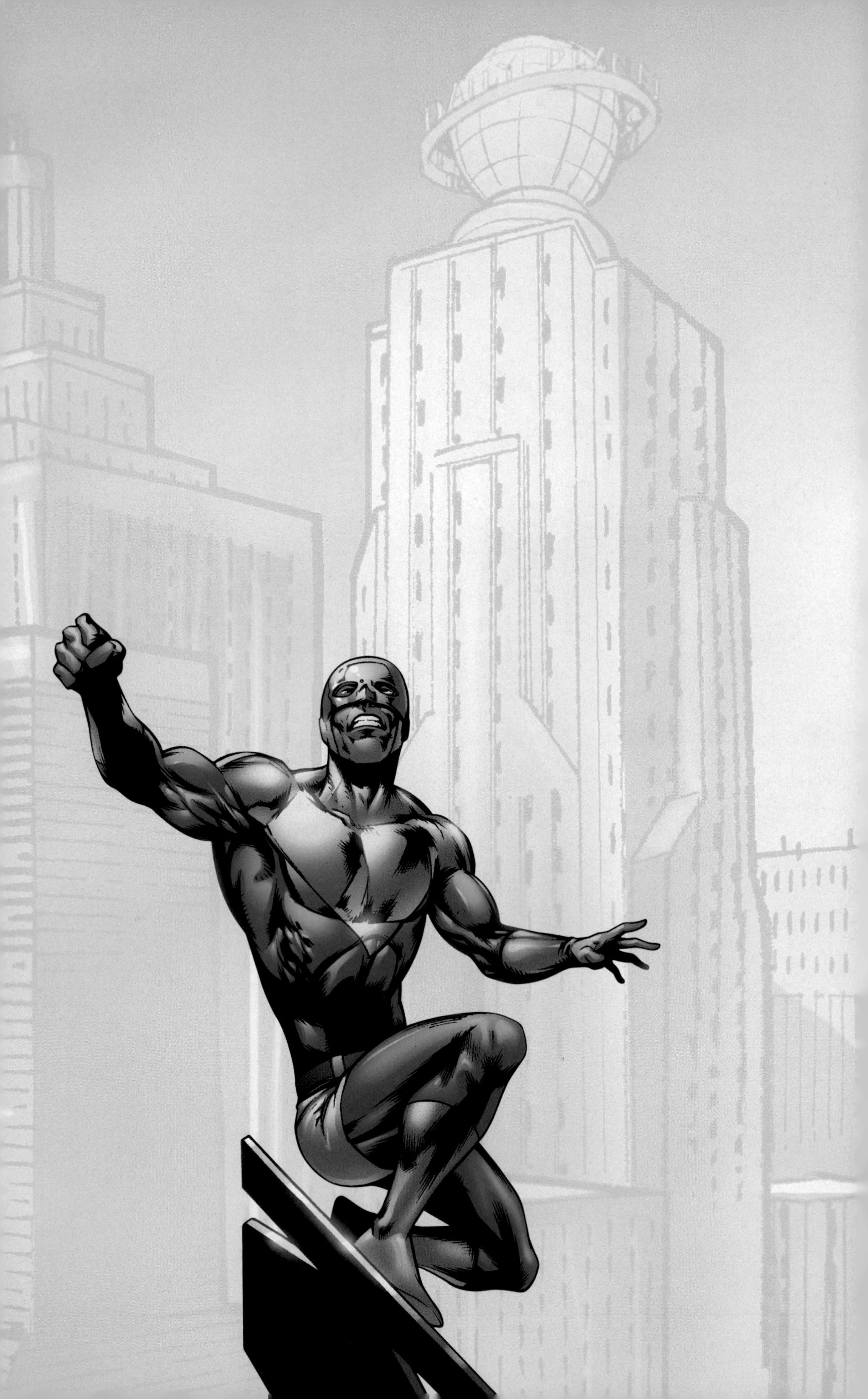

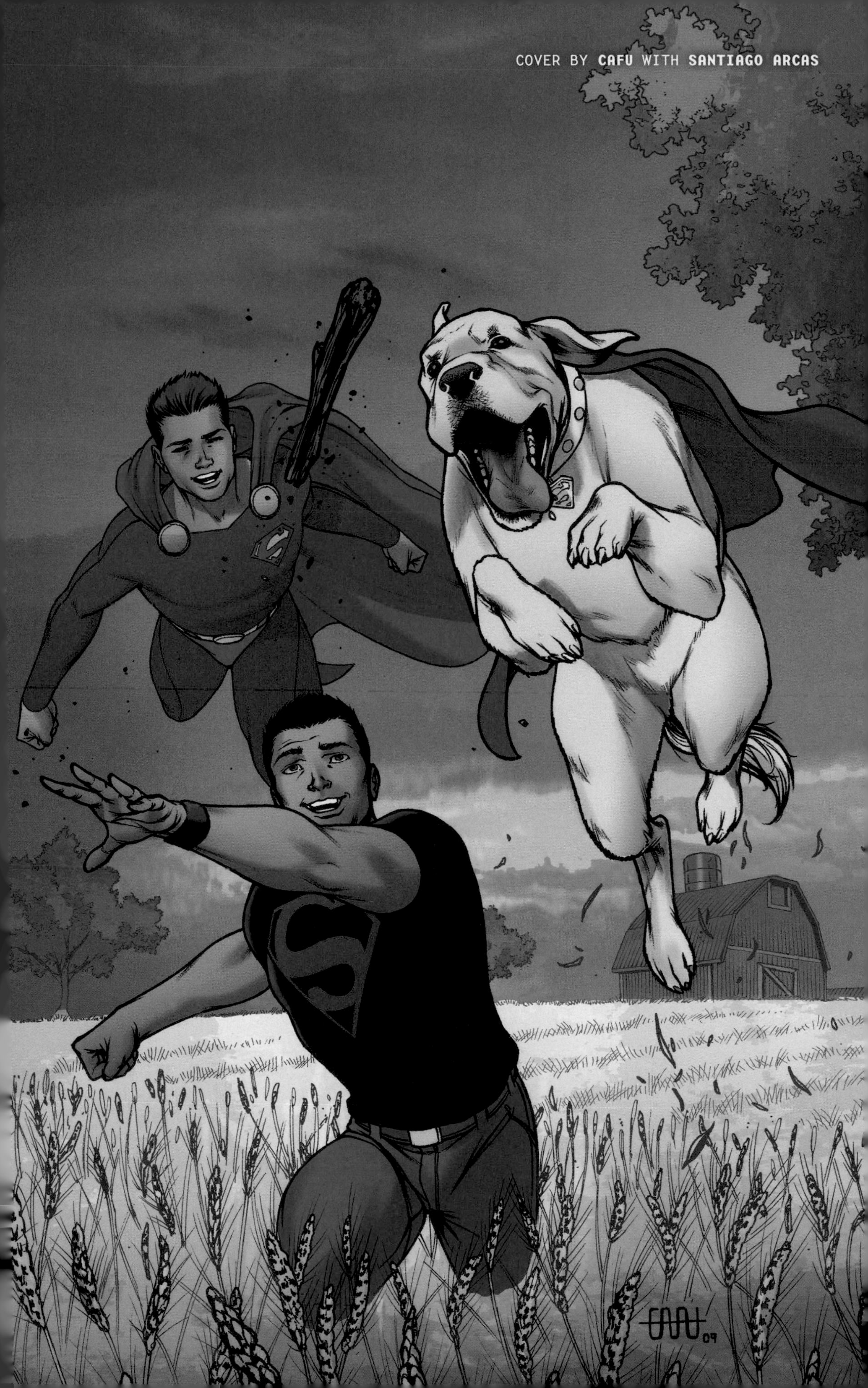

COVER BY **CAFU** WITH **SANTIAGO ARCAS**

MAN OF VALOR PART FOUR

BERNARD CHANG <ARTIST - PAGES 175-185>
JAVIER PINA <ARTIST - PAGES 186-196>

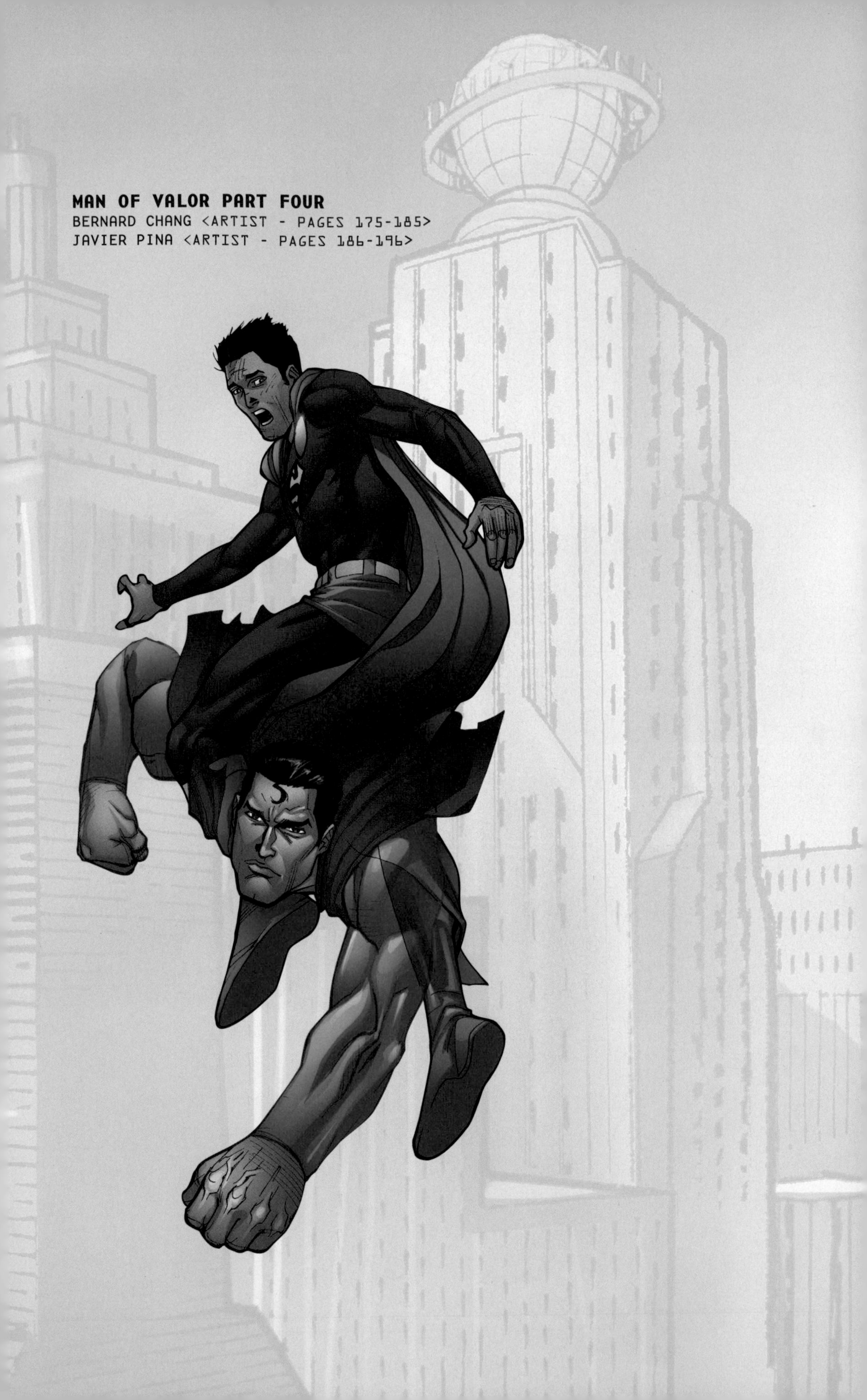

THE ESPIONAGE SQUAD part 1

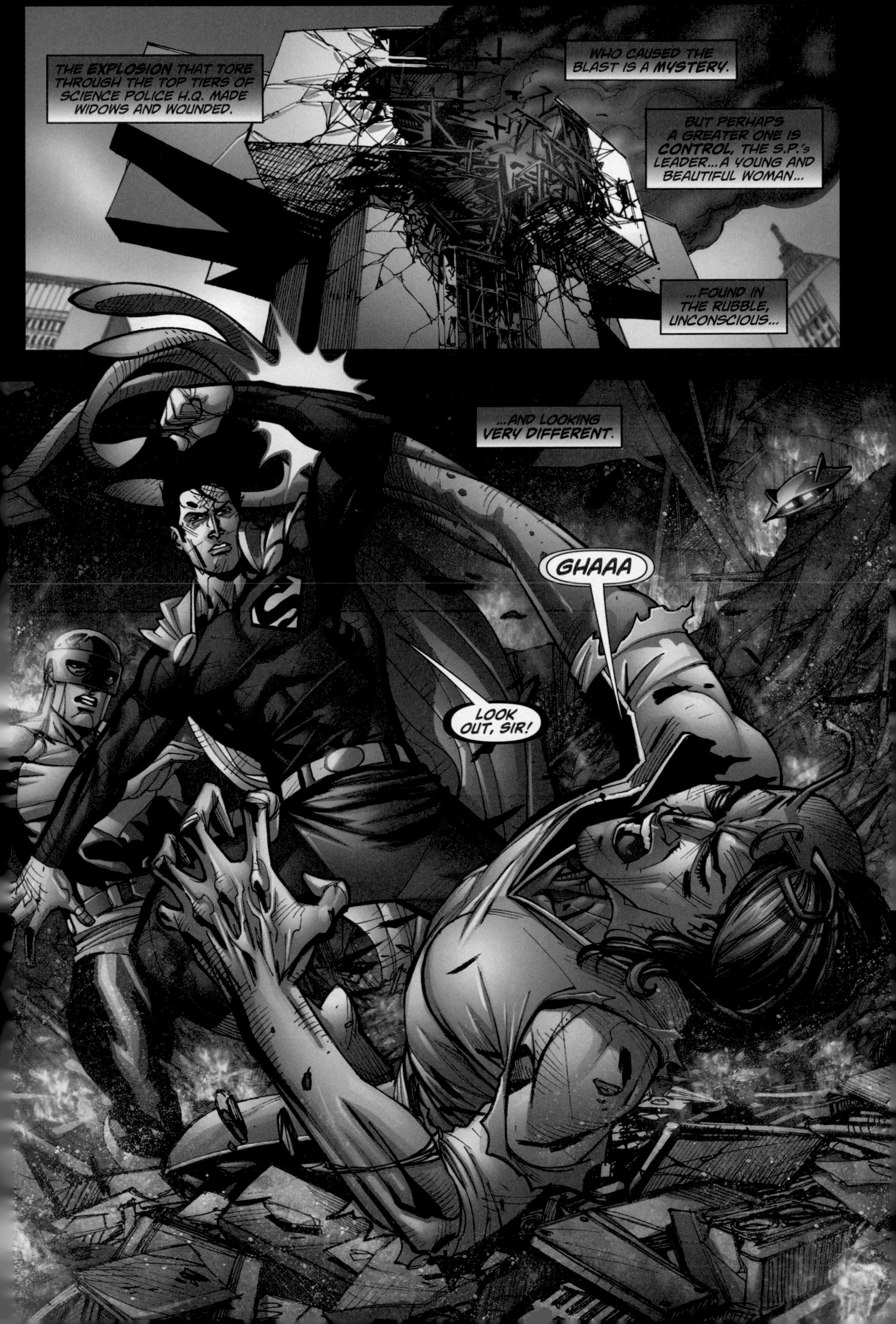
THE EXPLOSION THAT TORE THROUGH THE TOP TIERS OF SCIENCE POLICE H.Q. MADE WIDOWS AND WOUNDED.
WHO CAUSED THE BLAST IS A MYSTERY.
BUT PERHAPS A GREATER ONE IS CONTROL, THE S.P.'s LEADER...A YOUNG AND BEAUTIFUL WOMAN...
...FOUND IN THE RUBBLE, UNCONSCIOUS...
...AND LOOKING VERY DIFFERENT.
GHAAA
LOOK OUT, SIR!

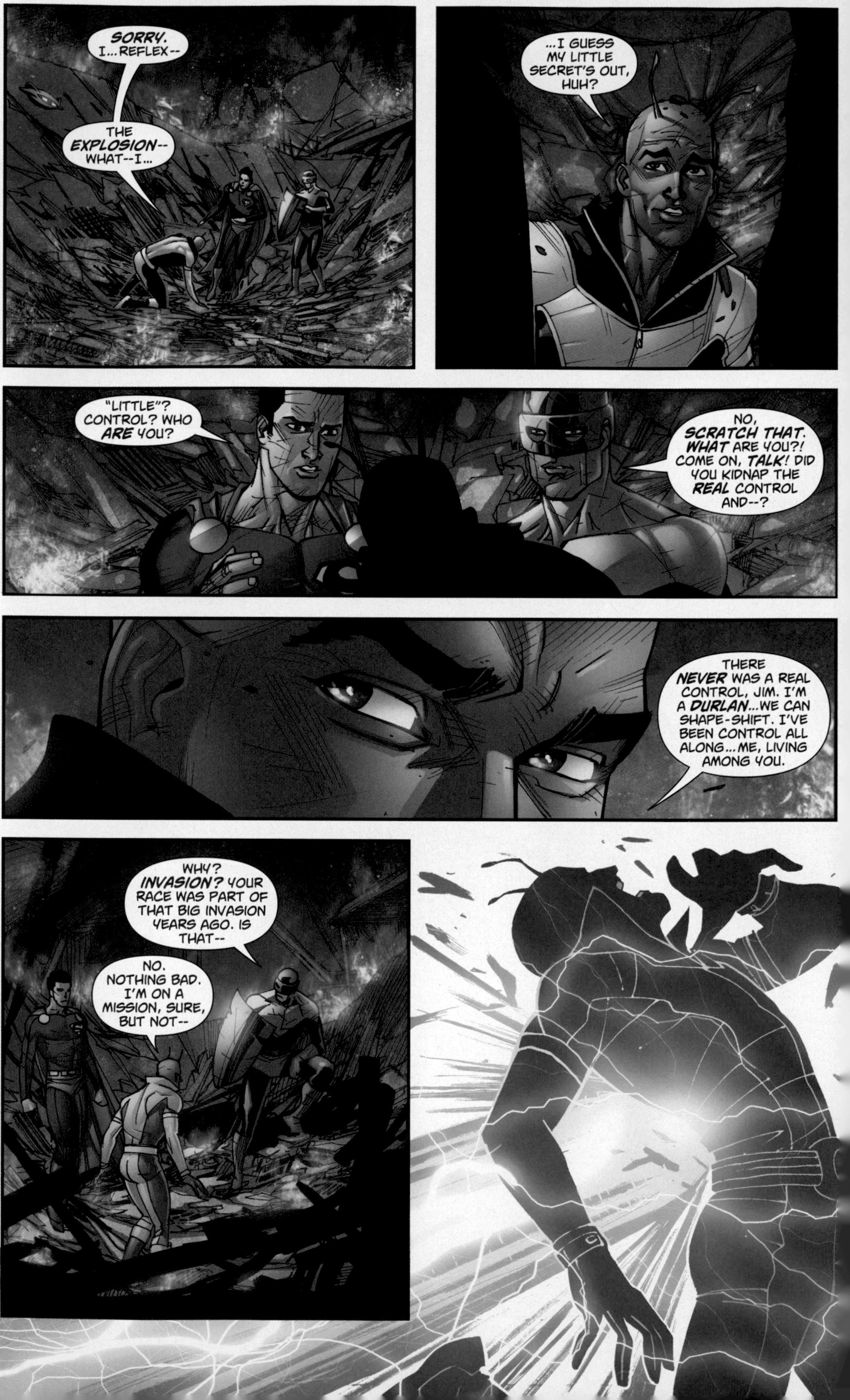
SORRY. I...REFLEX--
THE EXPLOSION-- WHAT--I...
...I GUESS MY LITTLE SECRET'S OUT, HUH?
"LITTLE"? CONTROL? WHO ARE YOU?
NO, SCRATCH THAT. WHAT ARE YOU?! COME ON, TALK! DID YOU KIDNAP THE REAL CONTROL AND--?
THERE NEVER WAS A REAL CONTROL, JIM. I'M A DURLAN...WE CAN SHAPE-SHIFT. I'VE BEEN CONTROL ALL ALONG...ME, LIVING AMONG YOU.
WHY? INVASION? YOUR RACE WAS PART OF THAT BIG INVASION YEARS AGO. IS THAT--
NO. NOTHING BAD. I'M ON A MISSION, SURE, BUT NOT--

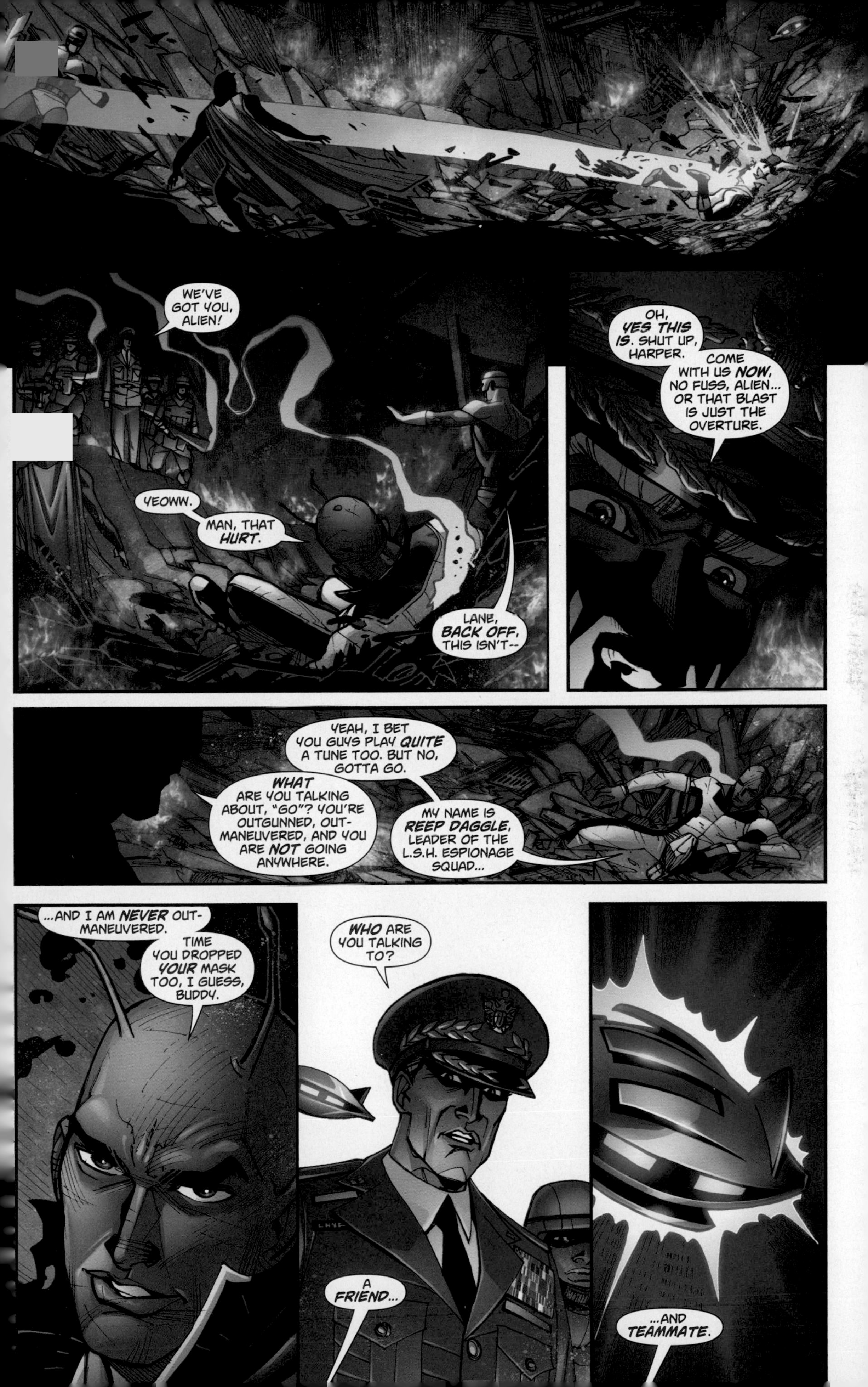
WE'VE GOT YOU, ALIEN!
YEOWW.
MAN, THAT HURT.
LANE, BACK OFF, THIS ISN'T--
OH, YES THIS IS. SHUT UP, HARPER.
COME WITH US NOW, NO FUSS, ALIEN... OR THAT BLAST IS JUST THE OVERTURE.
YEAH, I BET YOU GUYS PLAY QUITE A TUNE TOO. BUT NO, GOTTA GO.
WHAT ARE YOU TALKING ABOUT, "GO"? YOU'RE OUTGUNNED, OUT-MANEUVERED, AND YOU ARE NOT GOING ANYWHERE.
MY NAME IS REEP DAGGLE, LEADER OF THE L.S.H. ESPIONAGE SQUAD...
...AND I AM NEVER OUT-MANEUVERED.
TIME YOU DROPPED YOUR MASK TOO, I GUESS, BUDDY.
WHO ARE YOU TALKING TO?
A FRIEND...
...AND TEAMMATE.

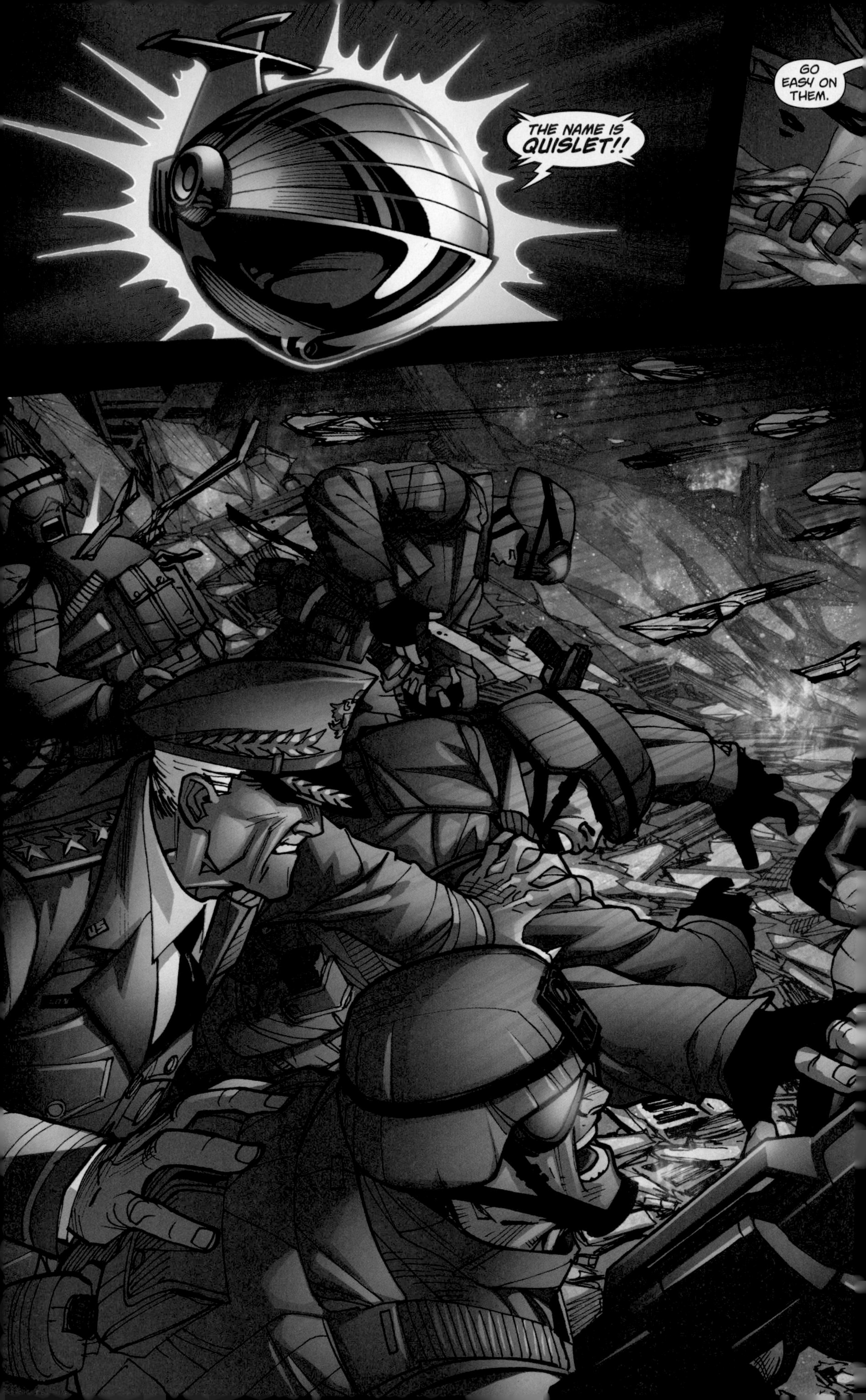
THE NAME IS QUISLET!!
GO EASY ON THEM.

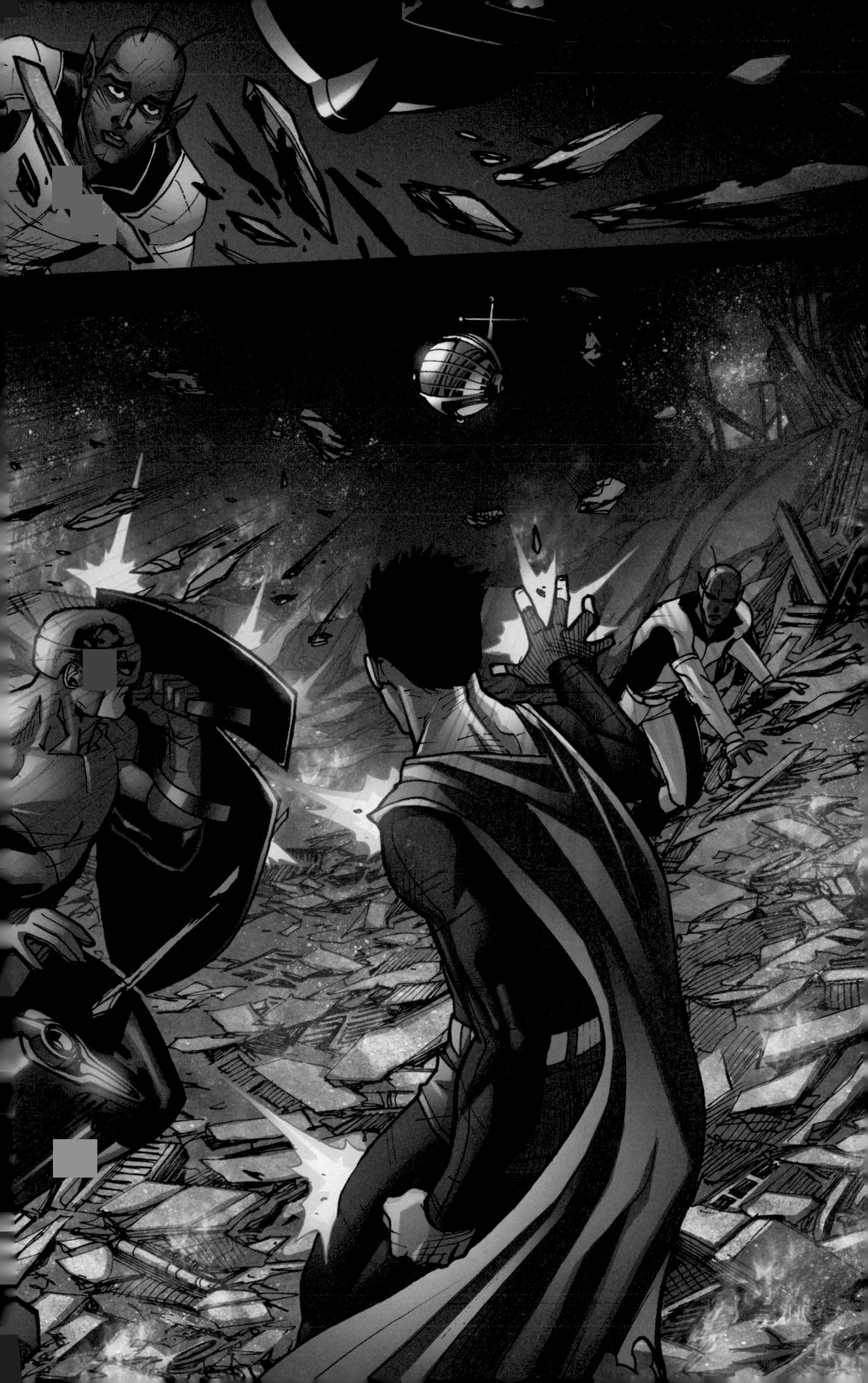

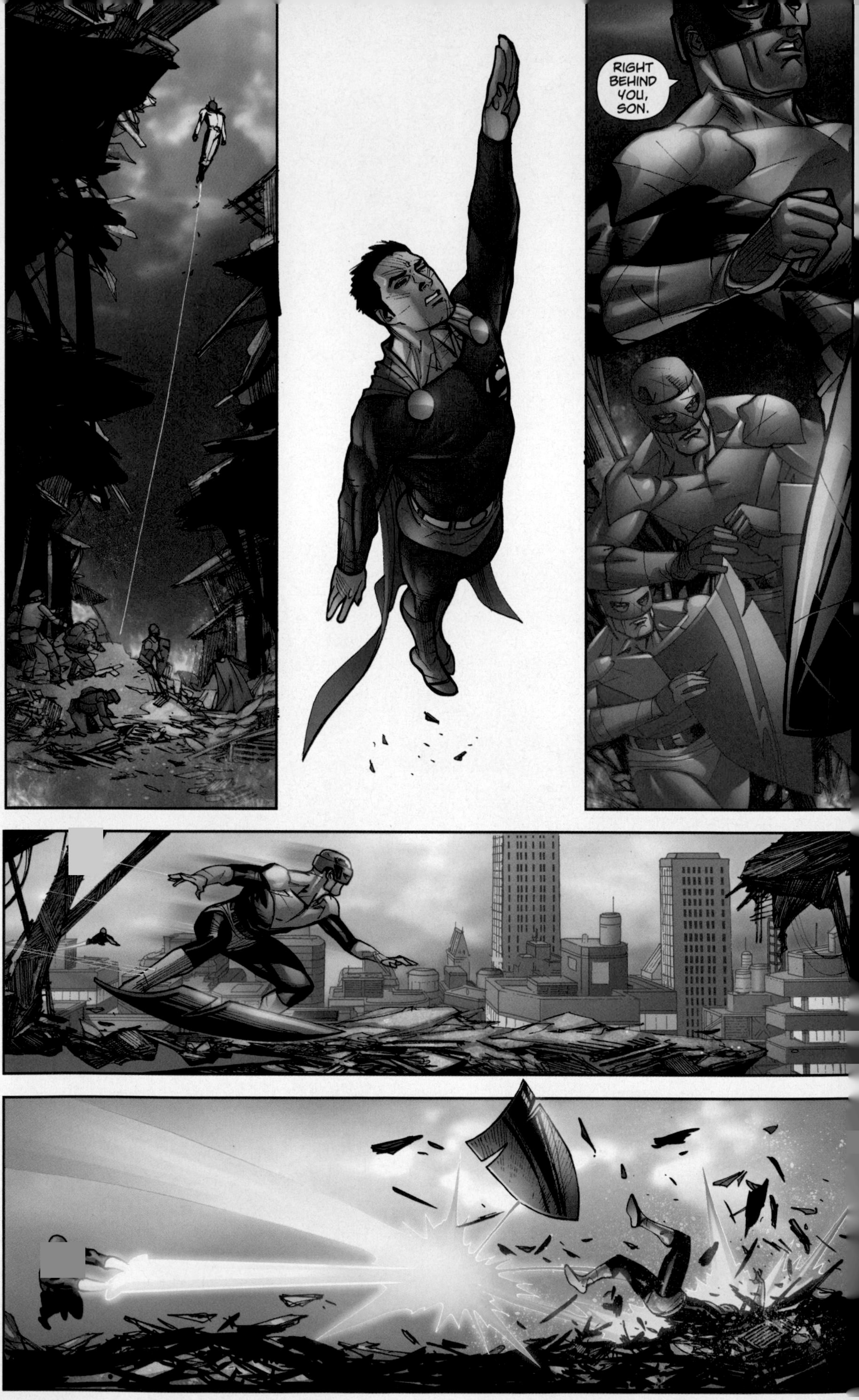
RIGHT BEHIND YOU, SON.

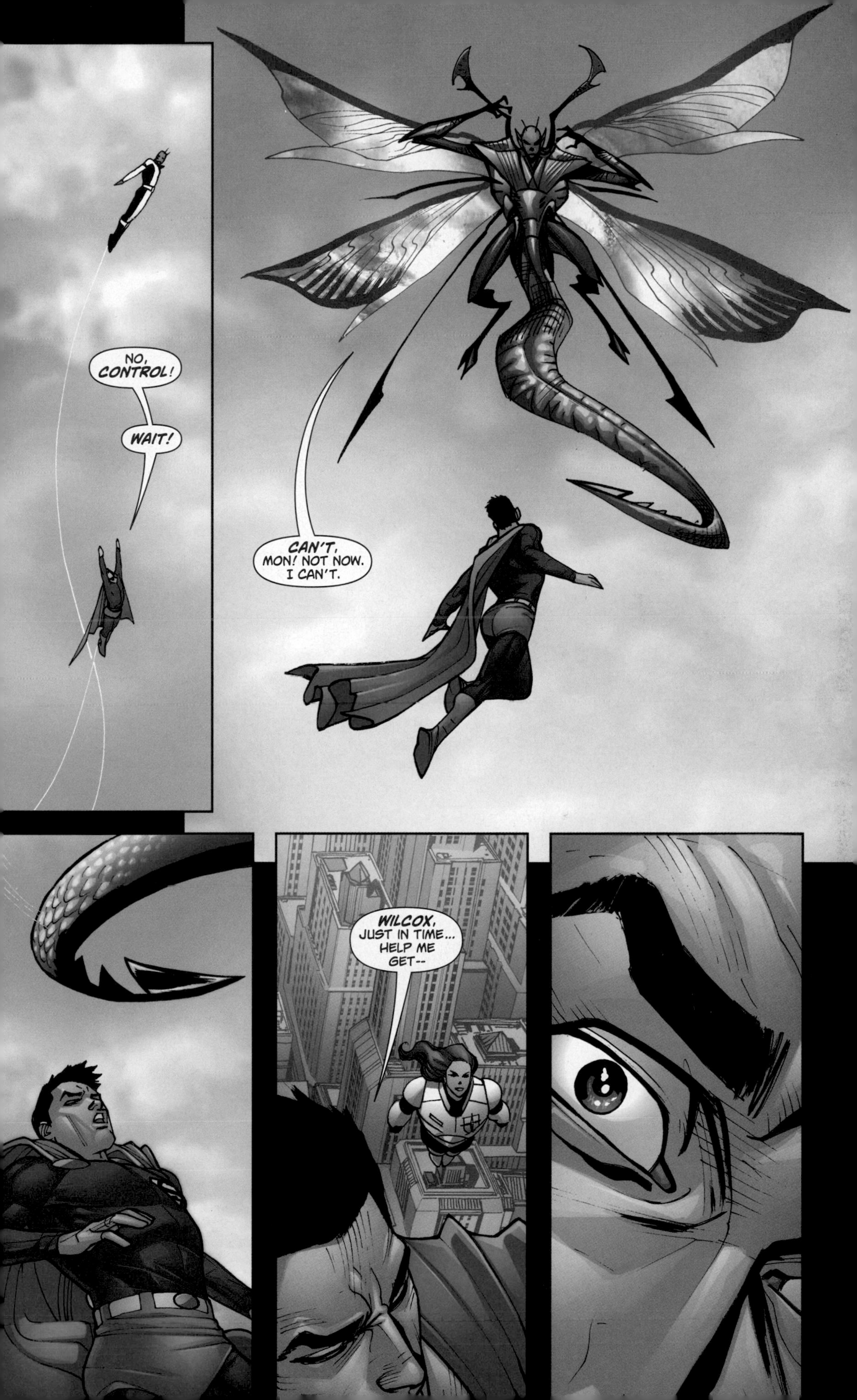
NO, CONTROL!
WAIT!
CAN'T, MON! NOT NOW. I CAN'T.
WILCOX, JUST IN TIME... HELP ME GET--

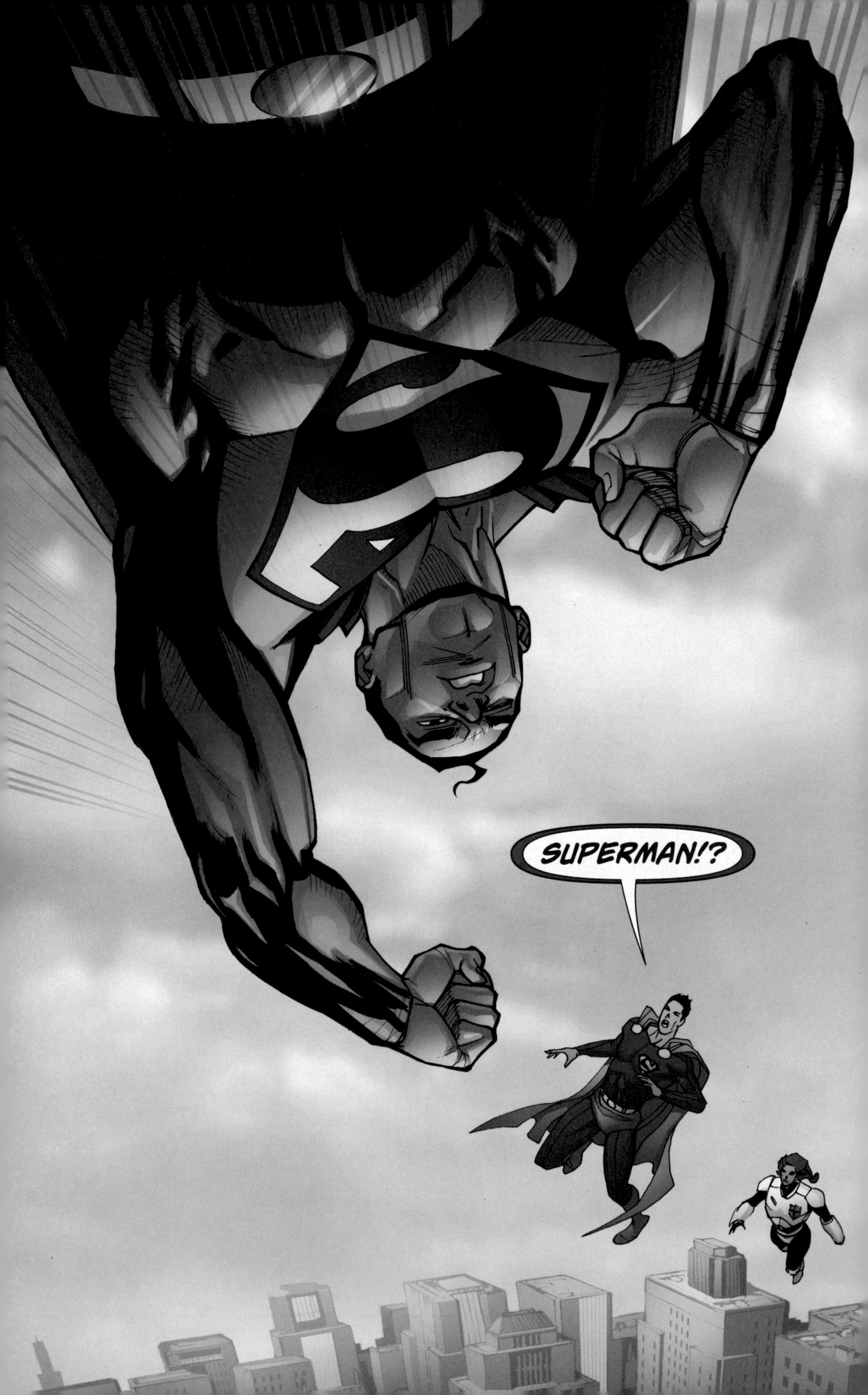
SUPERMAN!?

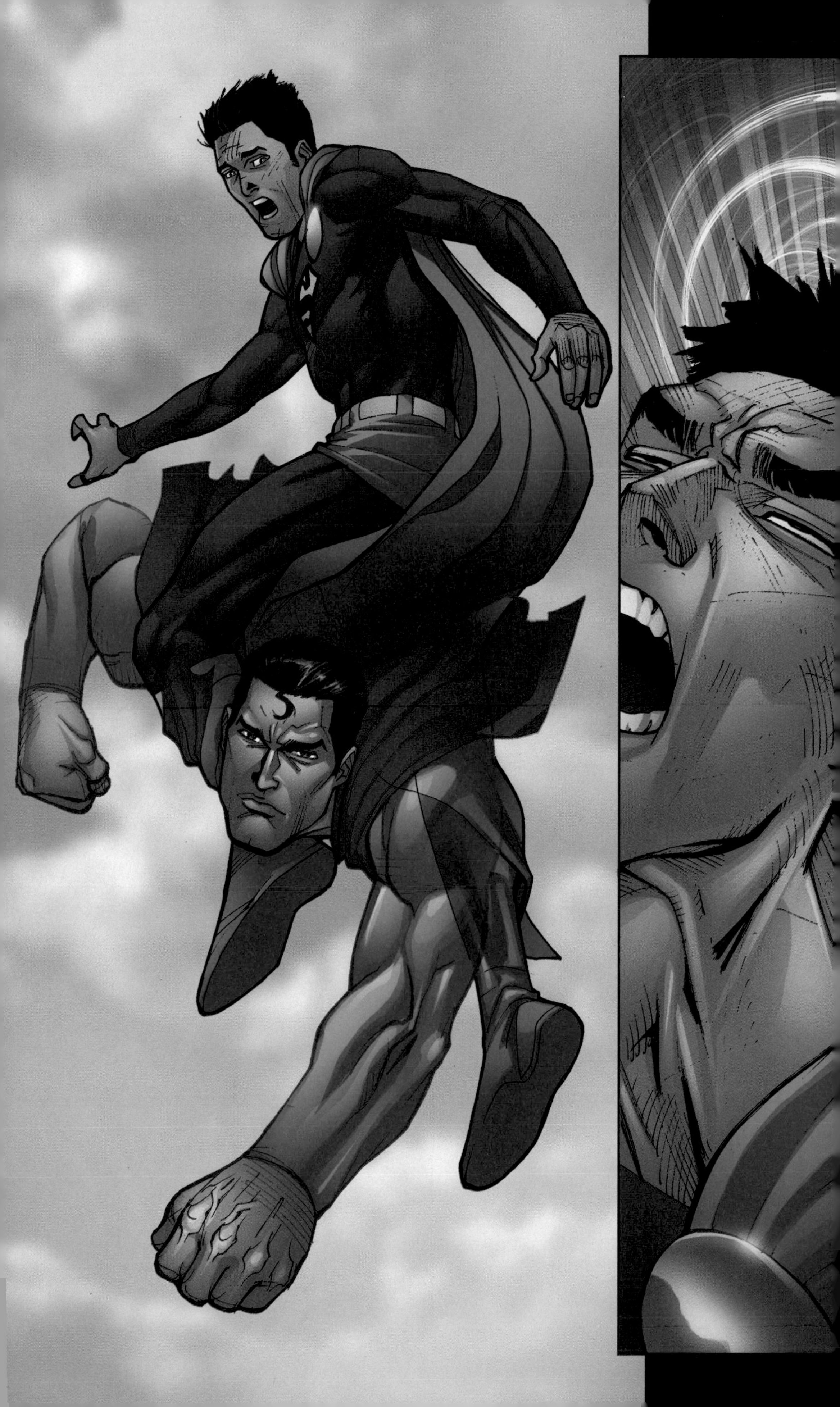

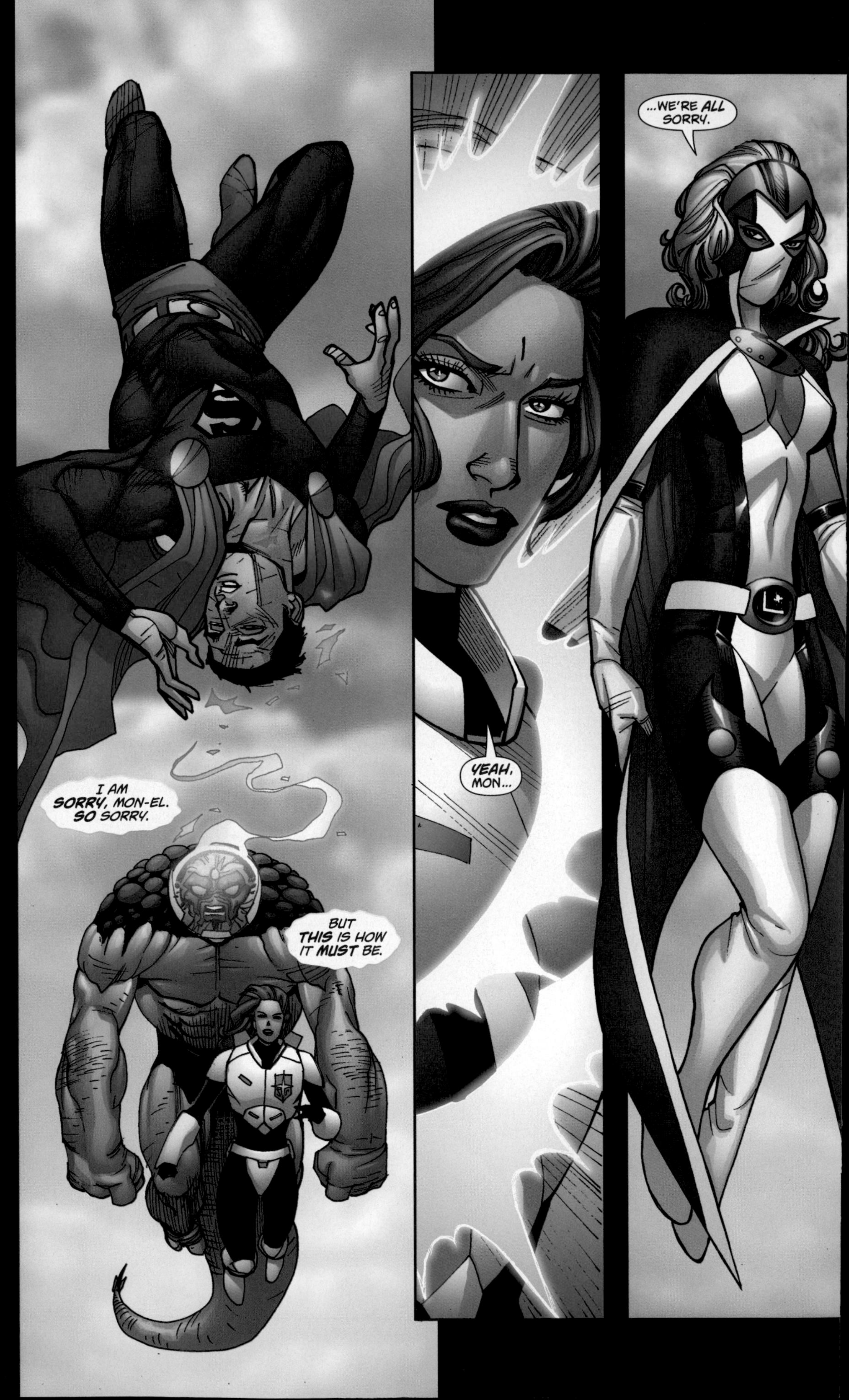
I AM SORRY, MON-EL. SO SORRY.
BUT THIS IS HOW IT MUST BE.
YEAH, MON...
...WE'RE ALL SORRY.

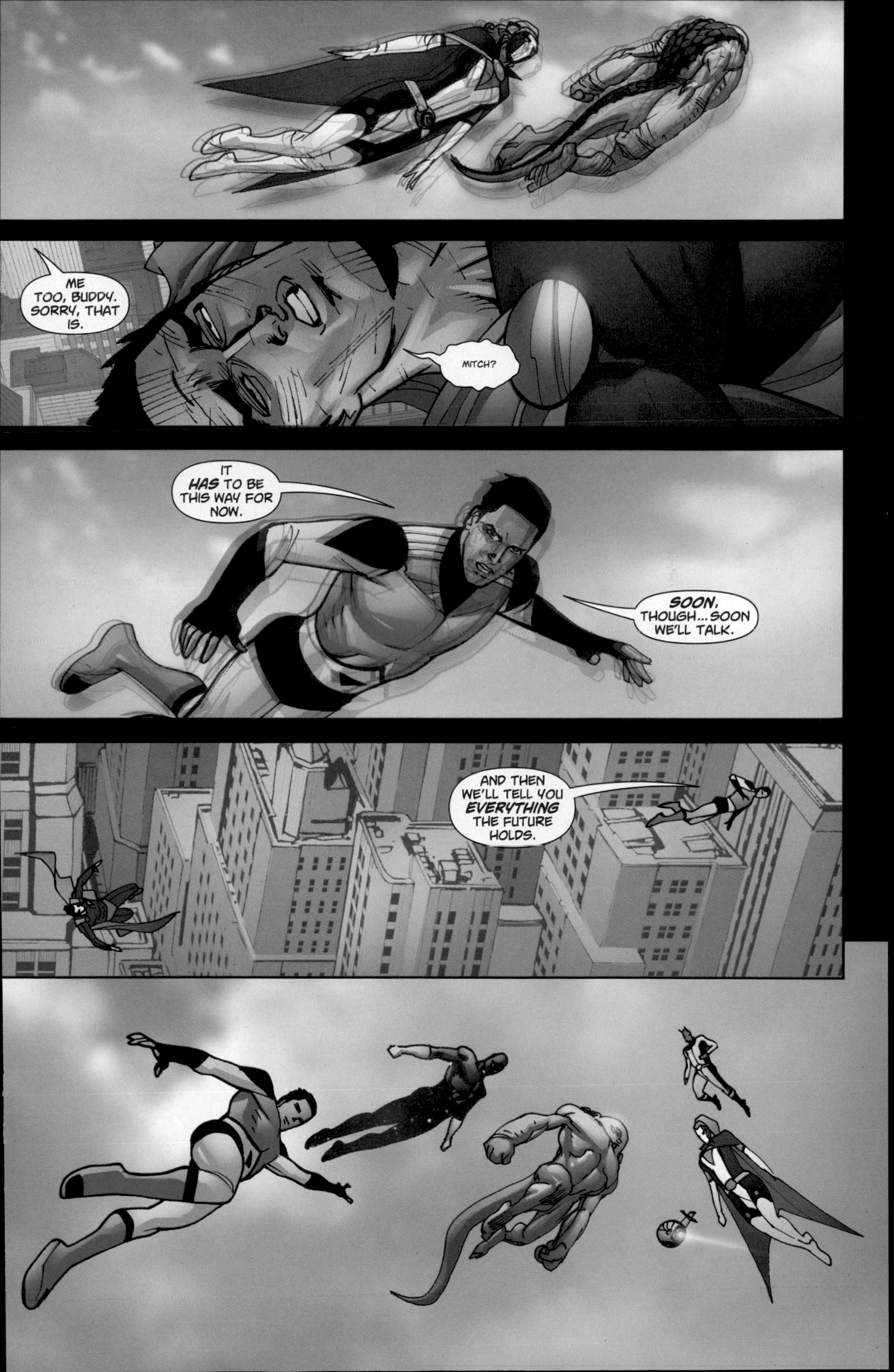
ME TOO, BUDDY. SORRY, THAT IS.
MITCH?
IT HAS TO BE THIS WAY FOR NOW.
SOON, THOUGH... SOON WE'LL TALK.
AND THEN WE'LL TELL YOU EVERYTHING THE FUTURE HOLDS.

THE ESPIONAGE SQUAD part 2

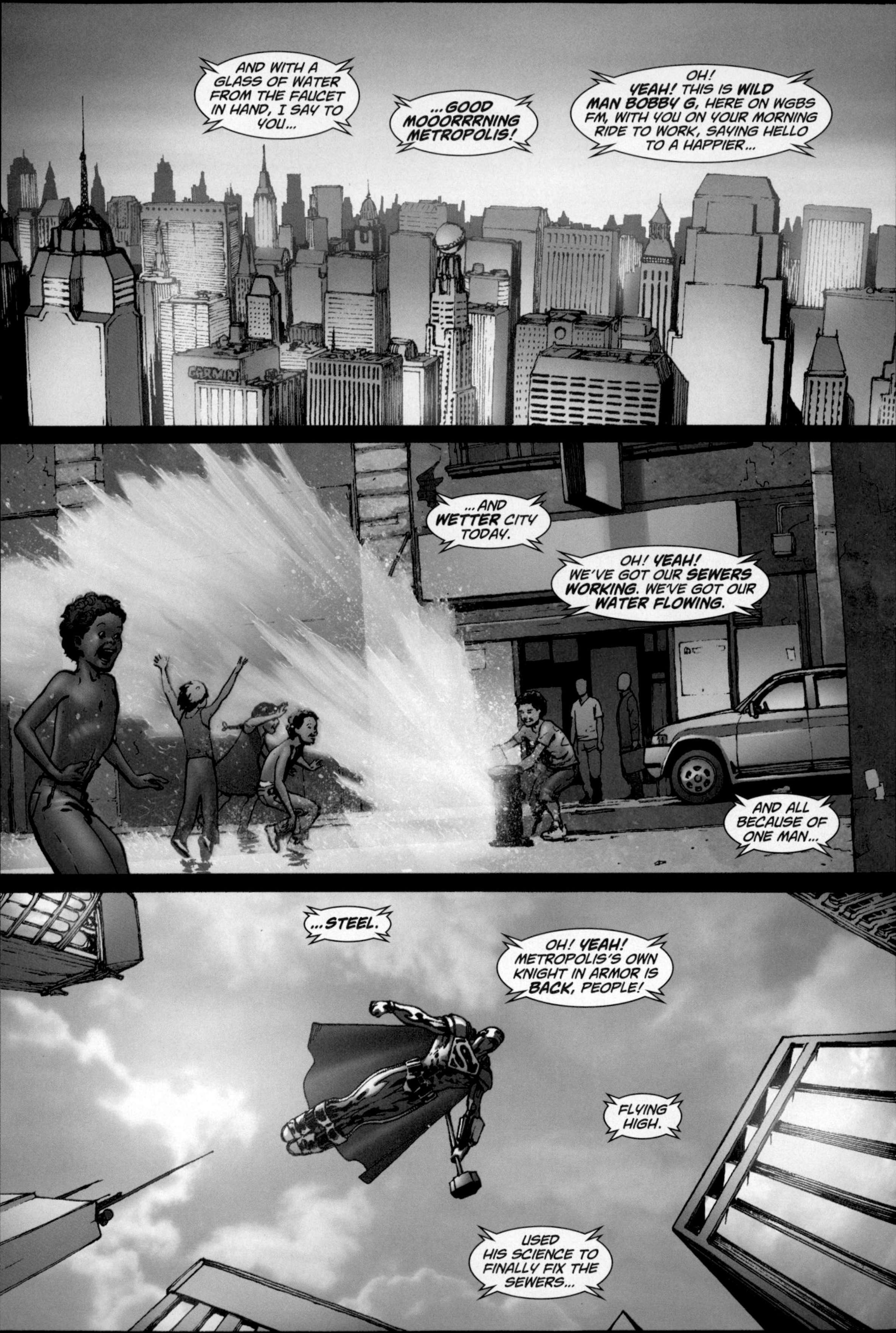
AND WITH A GLASS OF WATER FROM THE FAUCET IN HAND, I SAY TO YOU...
...GOOD MOOORRRNING METROPOLIS!
OH! YEAH! THIS IS WILD MAN BOBBY G, HERE ON WGBS FM, WITH YOU ON YOUR MORNING RIDE TO WORK, SAYING HELLO TO A HAPPIER...
...AND WETTER CITY TODAY.
OH! YEAH! WE'VE GOT OUR SEWERS WORKING. WE'VE GOT OUR WATER FLOWING.
AND ALL BECAUSE OF ONE MAN...
...STEEL.
OH! YEAH! METROPOLIS'S OWN KNIGHT IN ARMOR IS BACK, PEOPLE!
FLYING HIGH.
USED HIS SCIENCE TO FINALLY FIX THE SEWERS...

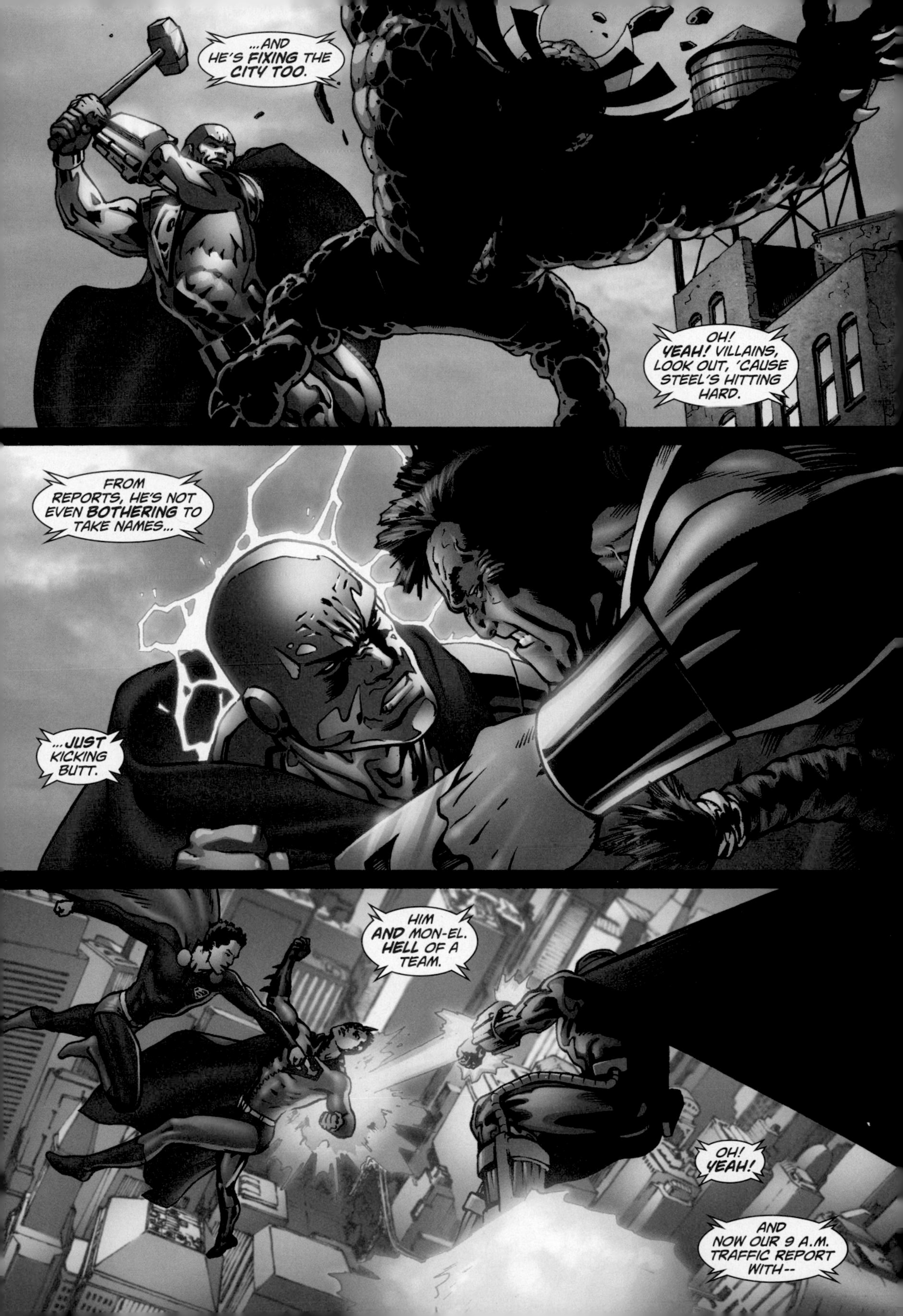
...AND HE'S FIXING THE CITY TOO.
OH! YEAH! VILLAINS, LOOK OUT, 'CAUSE STEEL'S HITTING HARD.
FROM REPORTS, HE'S NOT EVEN BOTHERING TO TAKE NAMES...
...JUST KICKING BUTT.
HIM AND MON-EL. HELL OF A TEAM.
OH! YEAH!
AND NOW OUR 9 A.M. TRAFFIC REPORT WITH--

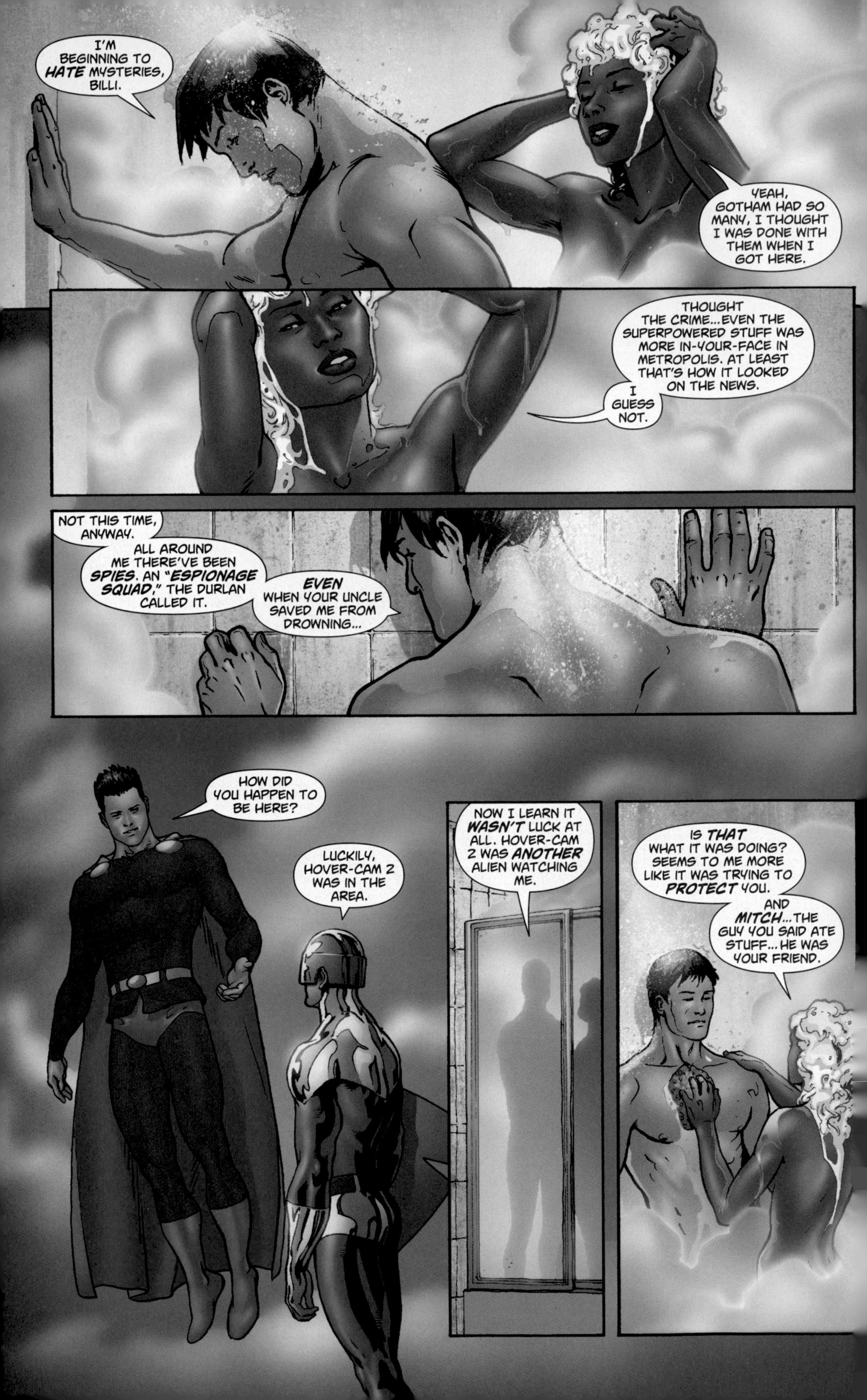
I'M BEGINNING TO HATE MYSTERIES, BILLI.
YEAH, GOTHAM HAD SO MANY, I THOUGHT I WAS DONE WITH THEM WHEN I GOT HERE.
THOUGHT THE CRIME...EVEN THE SUPERPOWERED STUFF WAS MORE IN-YOUR-FACE IN METROPOLIS. AT LEAST THAT'S HOW IT LOOKED ON THE NEWS.
I GUESS NOT.
NOT THIS TIME, ANYWAY.
ALL AROUND ME THERE'VE BEEN SPIES. AN "ESPIONAGE SQUAD," THE DURLAN CALLED IT.
EVEN WHEN YOUR UNCLE SAVED ME FROM DROWNING...
HOW DID YOU HAPPEN TO BE HERE?
LUCKILY, HOVER-CAM 2 WAS IN THE AREA.
NOW I LEARN IT WASN'T LUCK AT ALL. HOVER-CAM 2 WAS ANOTHER ALIEN WATCHING ME.
IS THAT WHAT IT WAS DOING? SEEMS TO ME MORE LIKE IT WAS TRYING TO PROTECT YOU.
AND MITCH...THE GUY YOU SAID ATE STUFF...HE WAS YOUR FRIEND.

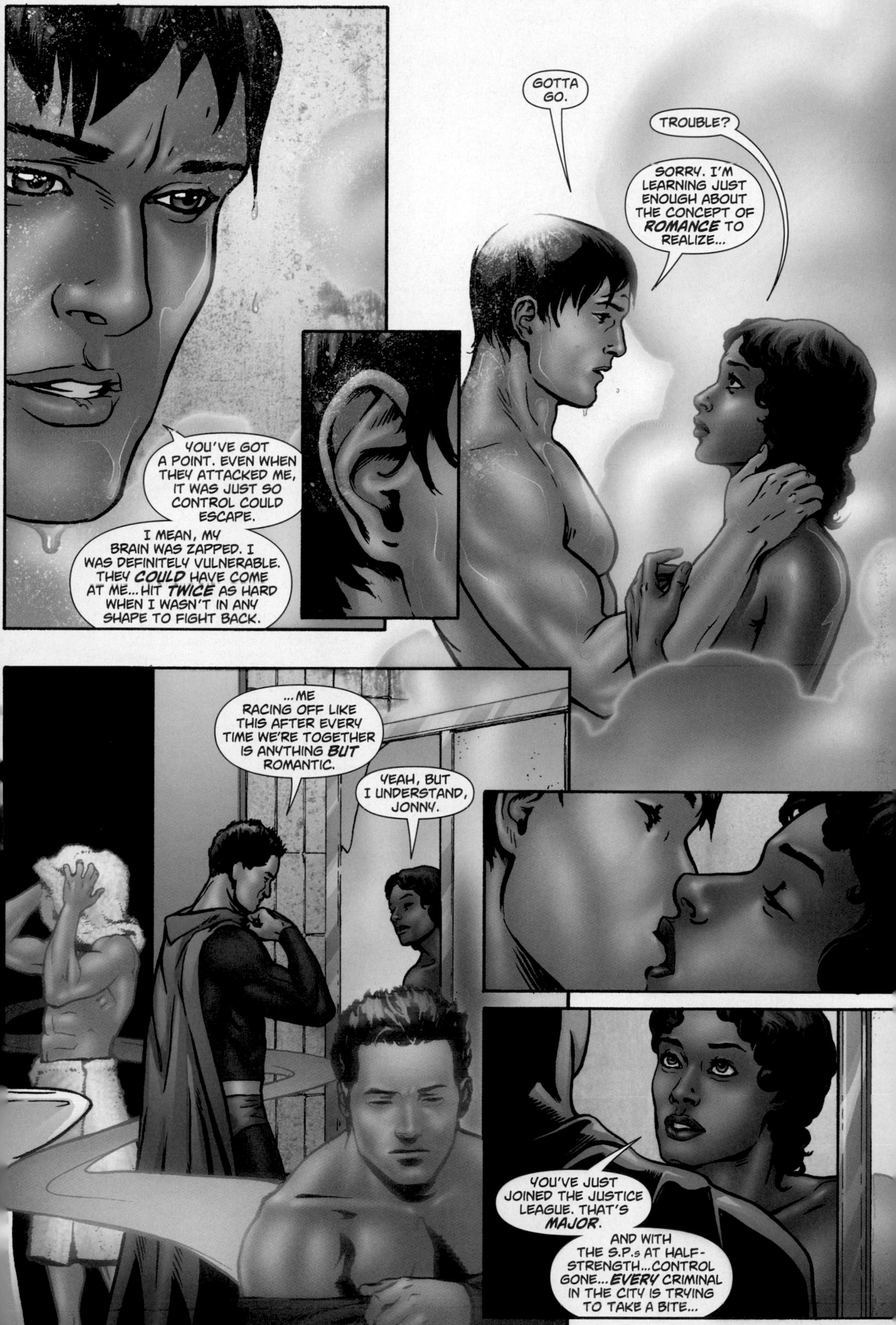
GOTTA GO.
TROUBLE?
SORRY. I'M LEARNING JUST ENOUGH ABOUT THE CONCEPT OF ROMANCE TO REALIZE...
YOU'VE GOT A POINT. EVEN WHEN THEY ATTACKED ME, IT WAS JUST SO CONTROL COULD ESCAPE.
I MEAN, MY BRAIN WAS ZAPPED. I WAS DEFINITELY VULNERABLE. THEY COULD HAVE COME AT ME...HIT TWICE AS HARD WHEN I WASN'T IN ANY SHAPE TO FIGHT BACK.
...ME RACING OFF LIKE THIS AFTER EVERY TIME WE'RE TOGETHER IS ANYTHING BUT ROMANTIC.
YEAH, BUT I UNDERSTAND, JONNY.
YOU'VE JUST JOINED THE JUSTICE LEAGUE. THAT'S MAJOR.
AND WITH THE S.P.s AT HALF-STRENGTH...CONTROL GONE...EVERY CRIMINAL IN THE CITY IS TRYING TO TAKE A BITE...

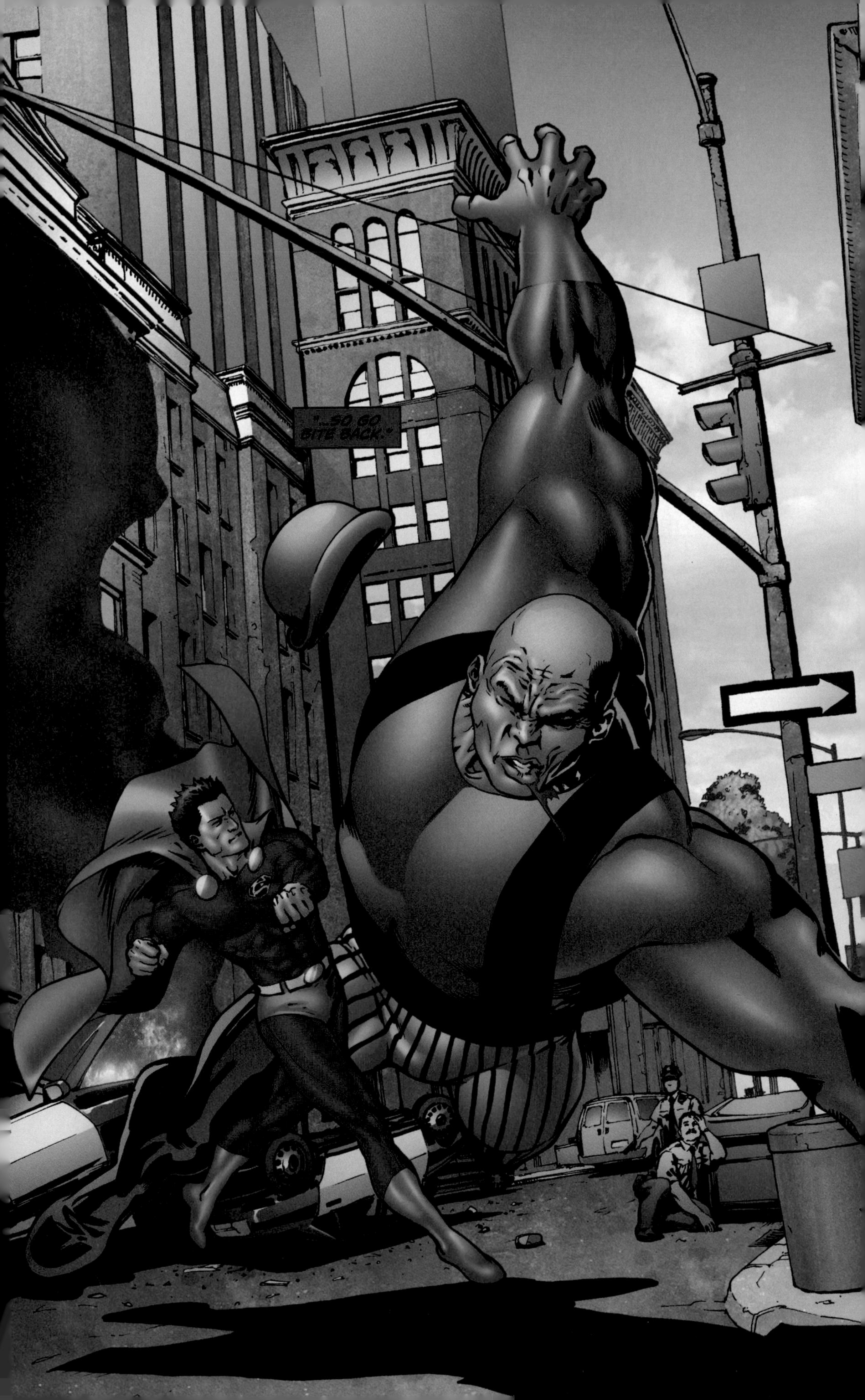
"...SO GO BITE BACK."

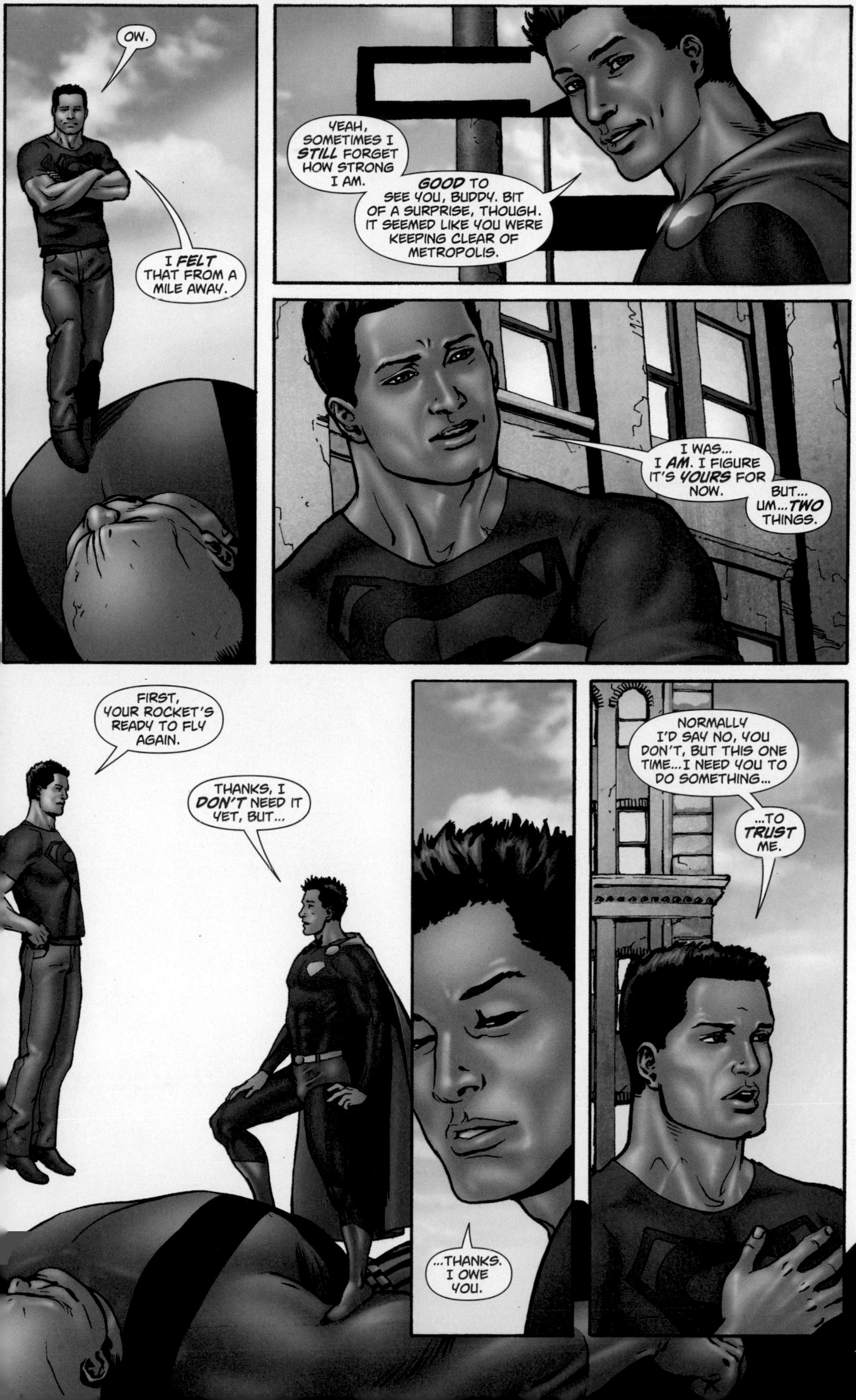
OW.
I FELT THAT FROM A MILE AWAY.
YEAH, SOMETIMES I STILL FORGET HOW STRONG I AM.
GOOD TO SEE YOU, BUDDY. BIT OF A SURPRISE, THOUGH. IT SEEMED LIKE YOU WERE KEEPING CLEAR OF METROPOLIS.
I WAS... I AM. I FIGURE IT'S YOURS FOR NOW.
BUT... UM...TWO THINGS.
FIRST, YOUR ROCKET'S READY TO FLY AGAIN.
THANKS, I DON'T NEED IT YET, BUT...
NORMALLY I'D SAY NO, YOU DON'T, BUT THIS ONE TIME...I NEED YOU TO DO SOMETHING...
...TO TRUST ME.
...THANKS. I OWE YOU.

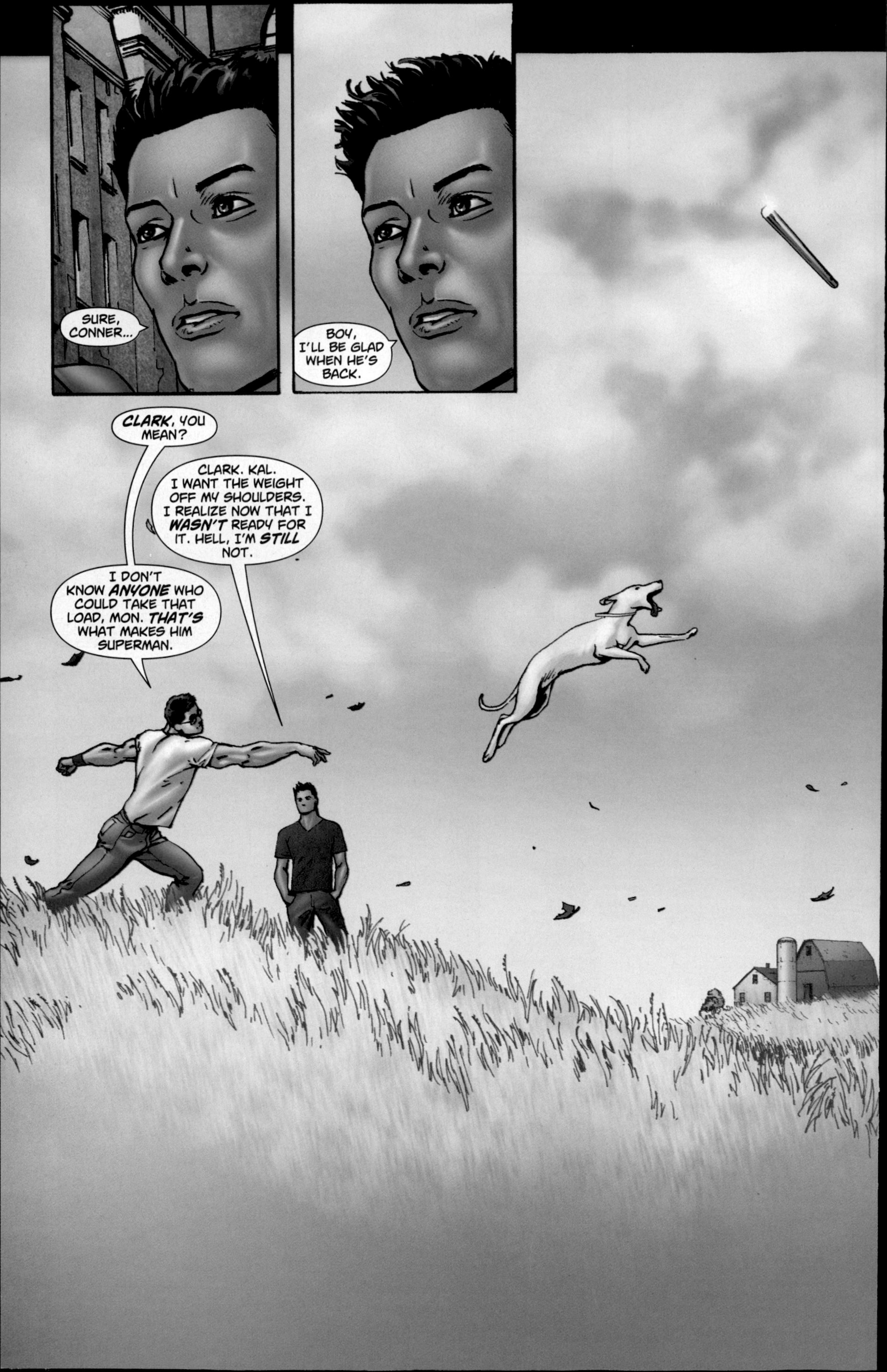
SURE, CONNER...
BOY, I'LL BE GLAD WHEN HE'S BACK.
CLARK, YOU MEAN?
CLARK. KAL. I WANT THE WEIGHT OFF MY SHOULDERS. I REALIZE NOW THAT I WASN'T READY FOR IT. HELL, I'M STILL NOT.
I DON'T KNOW ANYONE WHO COULD TAKE THAT LOAD, MON. THAT'S WHAT MAKES HIM SUPERMAN.

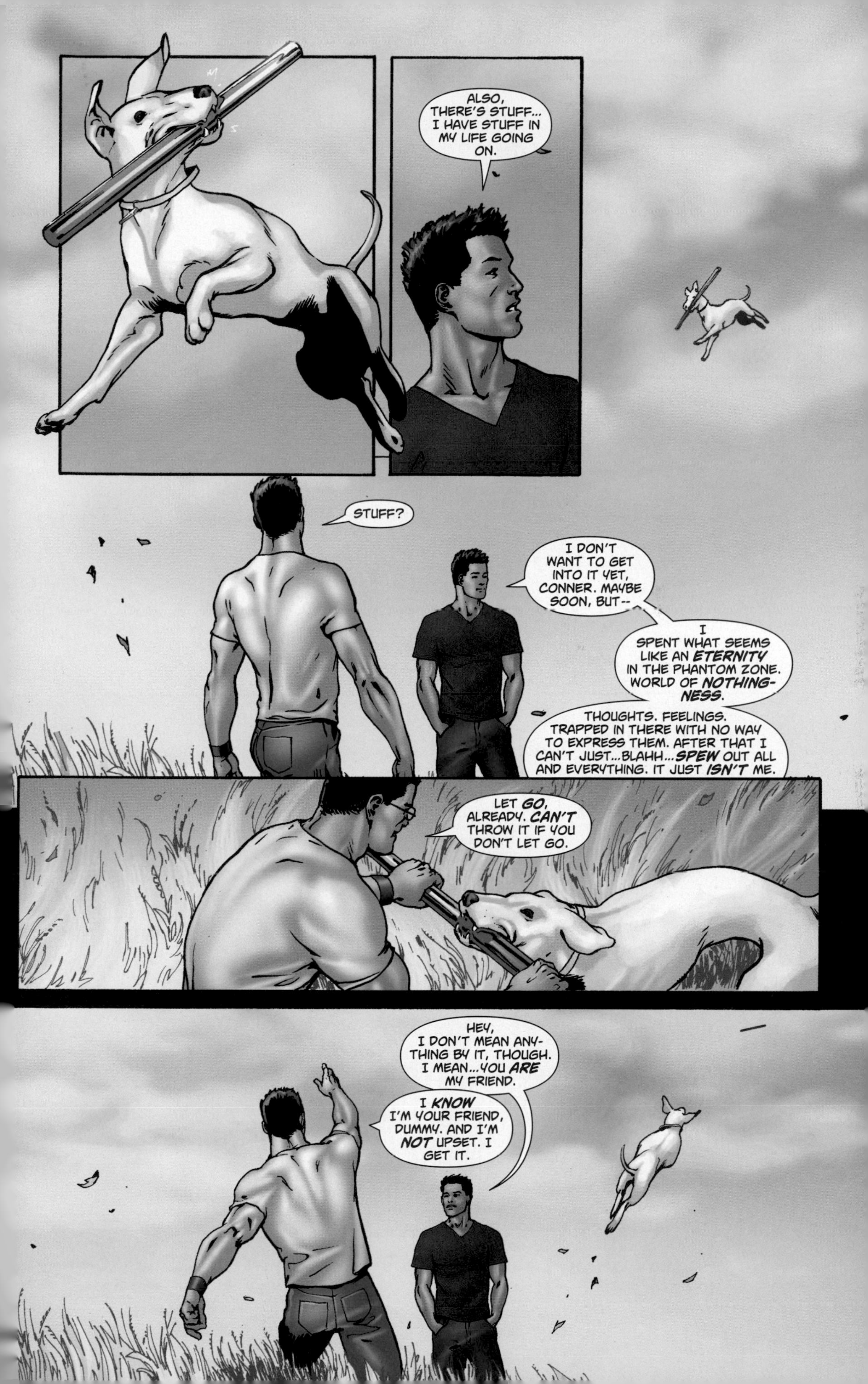
ALSO, THERE'S STUFF... I HAVE STUFF IN MY LIFE GOING ON.
STUFF?
I DON'T WANT TO GET INTO IT YET, CONNER. MAYBE SOON, BUT--
I SPENT WHAT SEEMS LIKE AN ETERNITY IN THE PHANTOM ZONE. WORLD OF NOTHINGNESS.
THOUGHTS. FEELINGS. TRAPPED IN THERE WITH NO WAY TO EXPRESS THEM. AFTER THAT I CAN'T JUST...BLAHH...SPEW OUT ALL AND EVERYTHING. IT JUST ISN'T ME.
LET GO, ALREADY. CAN'T THROW IT IF YOU DON'T LET GO.
HEY, I DON'T MEAN ANYTHING BY IT, THOUGH. I MEAN...YOU ARE MY FRIEND.
I KNOW I'M YOUR FRIEND, DUMMY. AND I'M NOT UPSET. I GET IT.

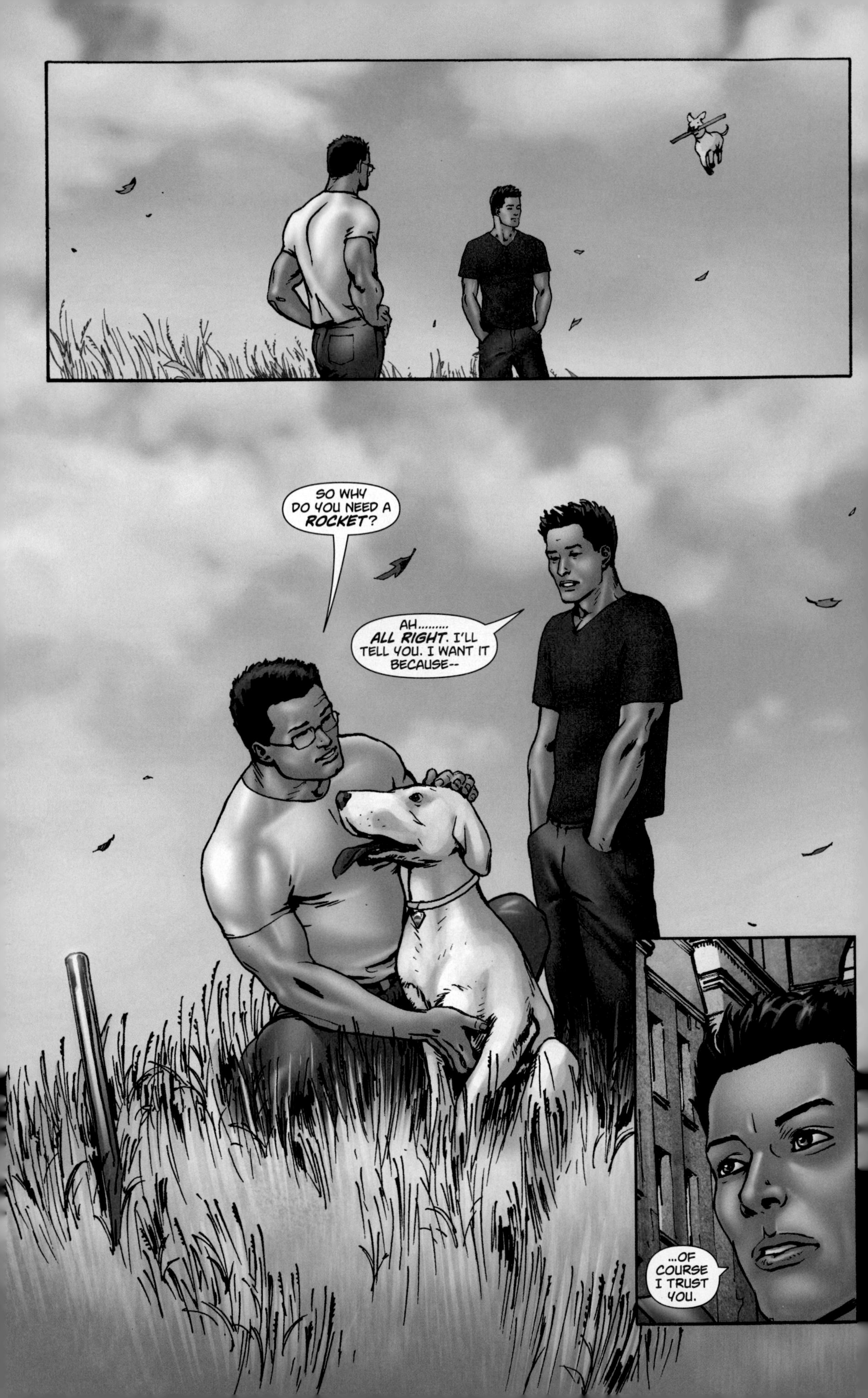
SO WHY DO YOU NEED A ROCKET?
AH......... ALL RIGHT. I'LL TELL YOU. I WANT IT BECAUSE--
...OF COURSE I TRUST YOU.

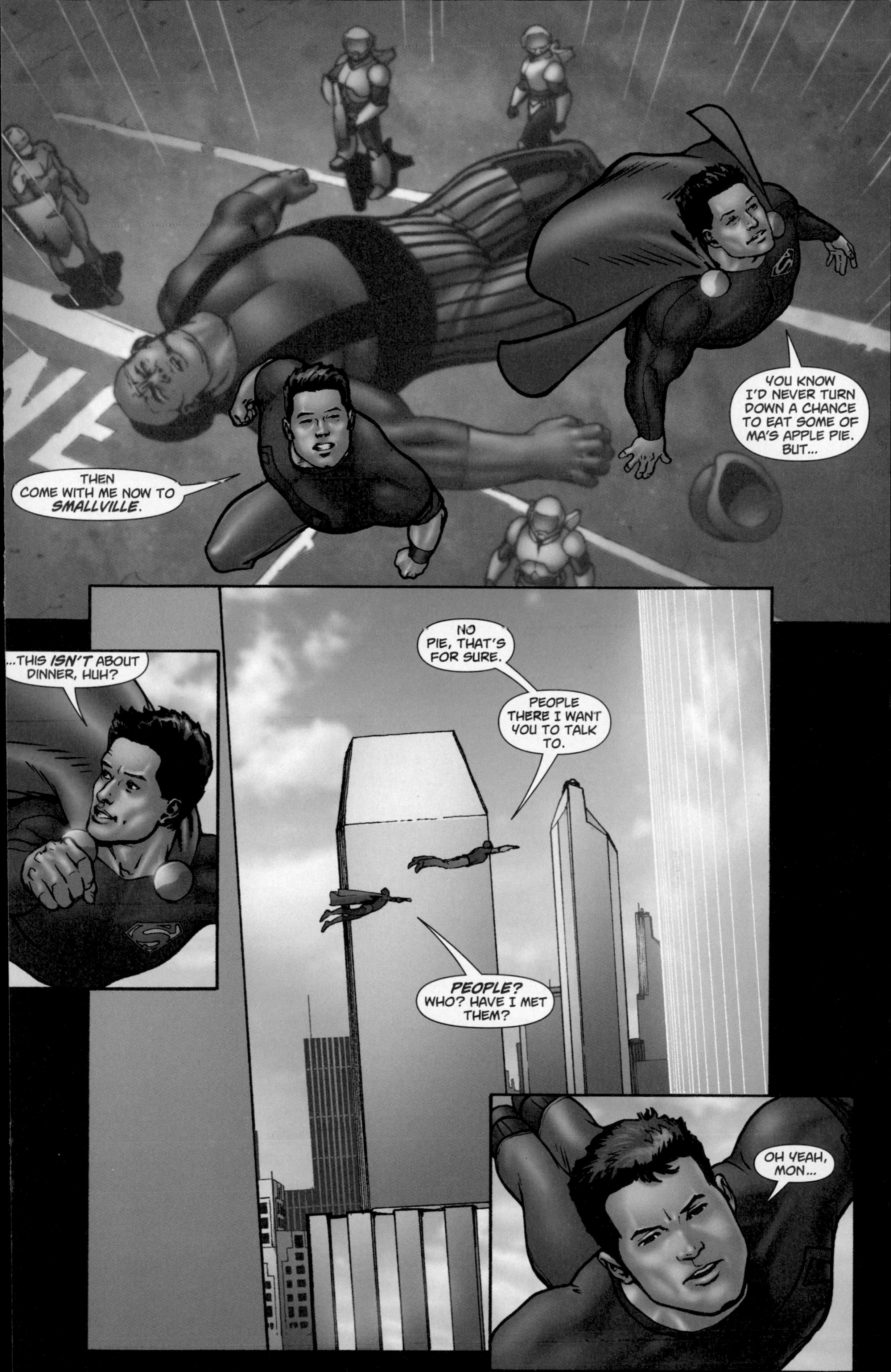
YOU KNOW I'D NEVER TURN DOWN A CHANCE TO EAT SOME OF MA'S APPLE PIE. BUT...
THEN COME WITH ME NOW TO SMALLVILLE.
...THIS ISN'T ABOUT DINNER, HUH?
NO PIE, THAT'S FOR SURE.
PEOPLE THERE I WANT YOU TO TALK TO.
PEOPLE? WHO? HAVE I MET THEM?
OH YEAH, MON...

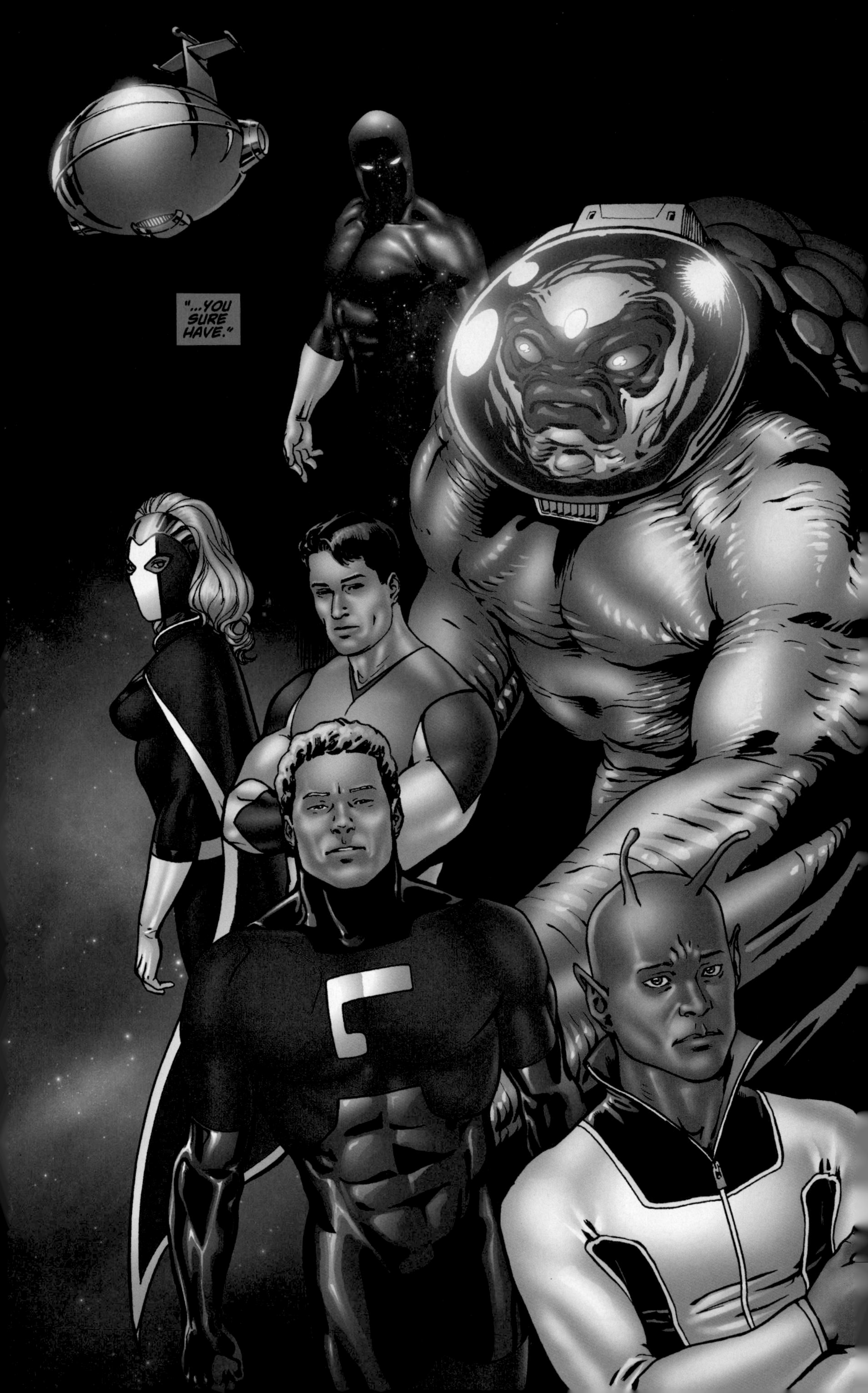
"...YOU SURE HAVE."

COVER BY **MARK BUCKINGHAM** WITH **BRAD ANDERSON**

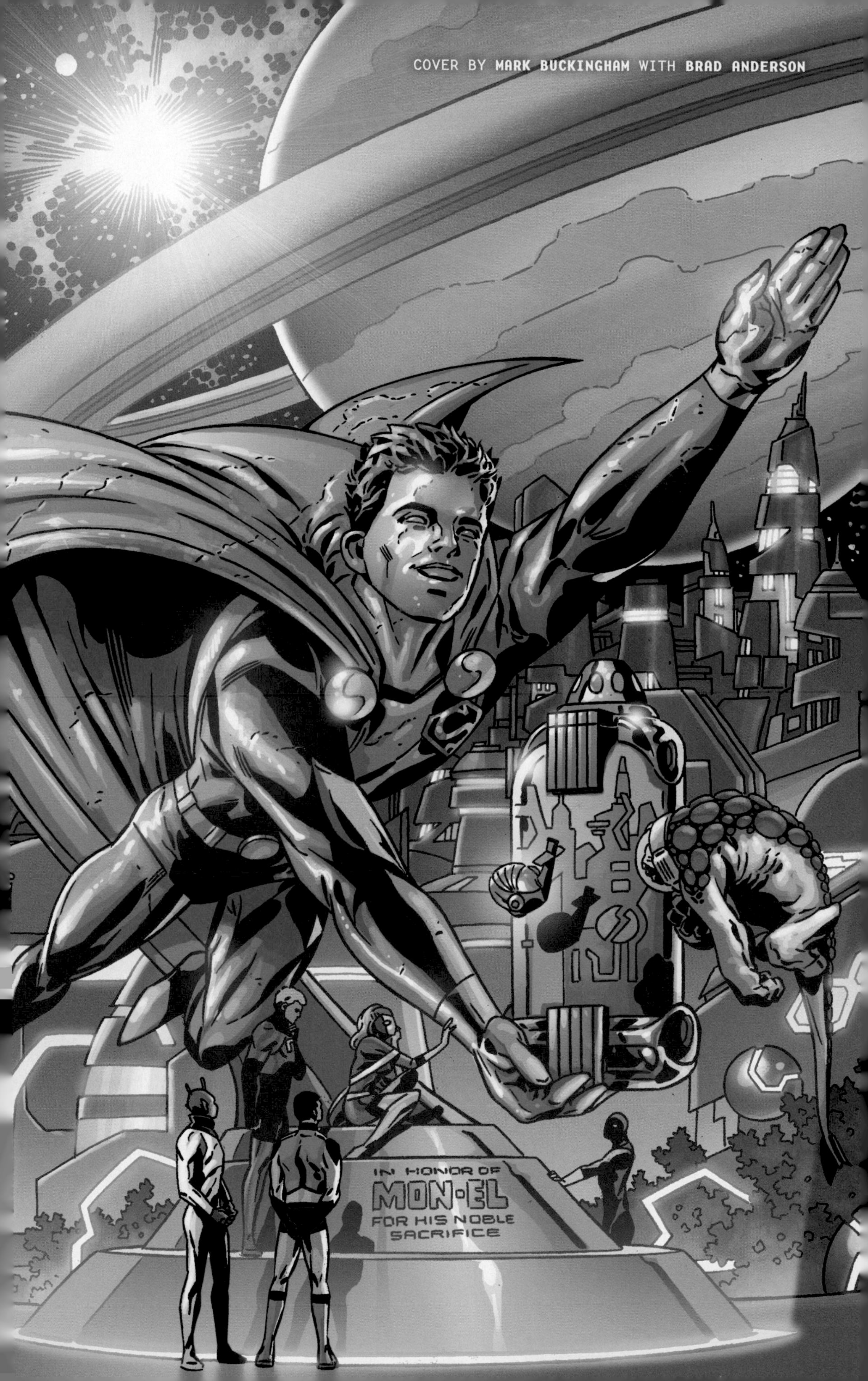
IN HONOR OF
MON-EL
FOR HIS NOBLE
SACRIFICE

<PREVIOUSLY IN>
SUPERMAN:
LAST STAND OF
NEW KRYPTON

Mon-El and the Legion of Super-Heroes joined Superman in his battle to prevent Brainiac and Lex Luthor from destroying New Krypton. Their mission: save the bottle cities aboard Brainiac's ship to ensure that they will one day become the birthplaces of the Legionnaires.

At Superman's insistence, Mon-El and the Legion leave New Krypton with the bottle cities so that they can return them to their rightful places in the universe and save the future...

MAN OF VALOR FINALE

BERNARD CHANG <ARTIST>

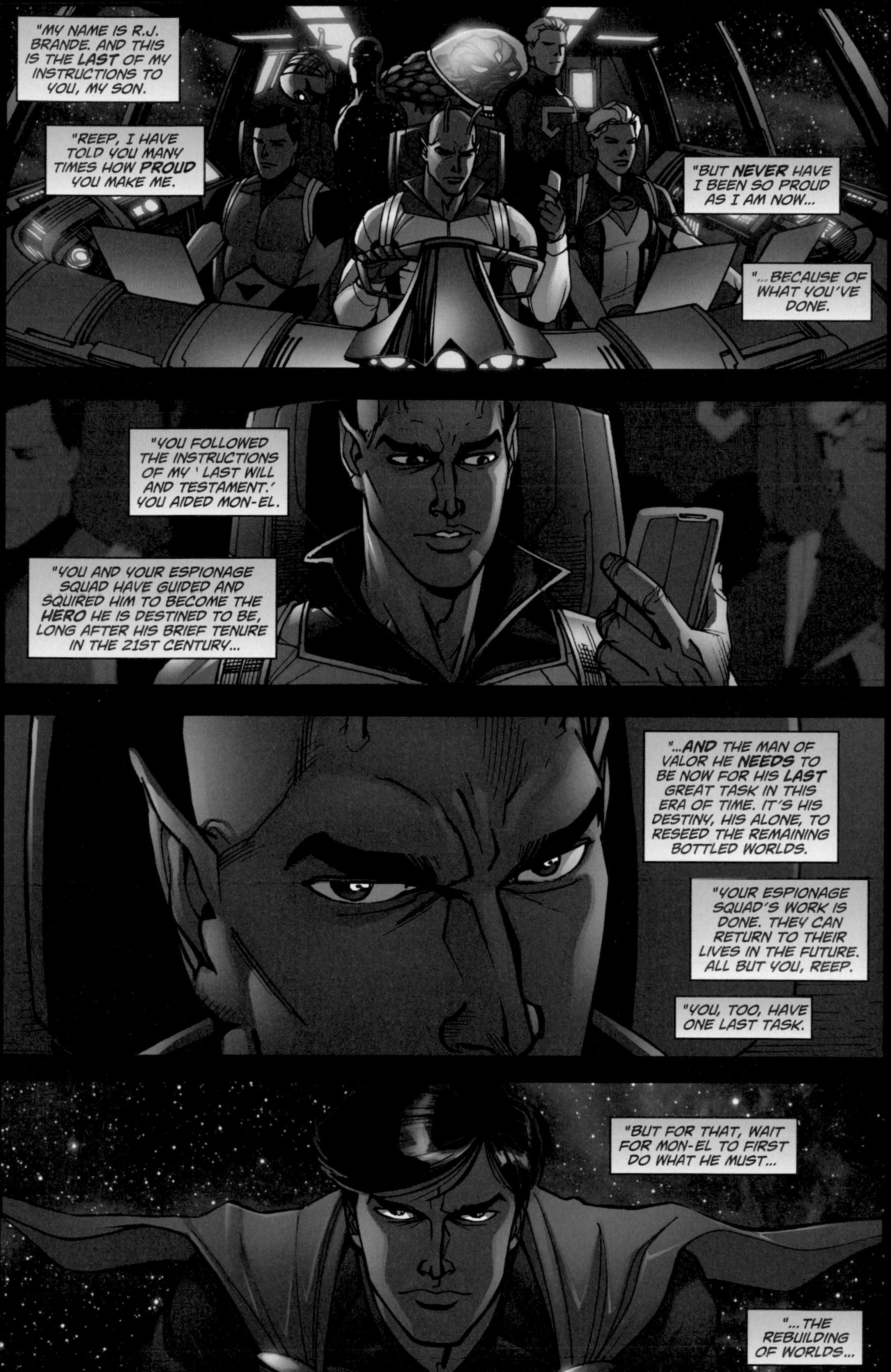
"MY NAME IS R.J. BRANDE. AND THIS IS THE LAST OF MY INSTRUCTIONS TO YOU, MY SON.
"REEP, I HAVE TOLD YOU MANY TIMES HOW PROUD YOU MAKE ME.
"BUT NEVER HAVE I BEEN SO PROUD AS I AM NOW...
"...BECAUSE OF WHAT YOU'VE DONE.
"YOU FOLLOWED THE INSTRUCTIONS OF MY 'LAST WILL AND TESTAMENT.' YOU AIDED MON-EL.
"YOU AND YOUR ESPIONAGE SQUAD HAVE GUIDED AND SQUIRED HIM TO BECOME THE HERO HE IS DESTINED TO BE, LONG AFTER HIS BRIEF TENURE IN THE 21ST CENTURY...
"...AND THE MAN OF VALOR HE NEEDS TO BE NOW FOR HIS LAST GREAT TASK IN THIS ERA OF TIME. IT'S HIS DESTINY, HIS ALONE, TO RESEED THE REMAINING BOTTLED WORLDS.
"YOUR ESPIONAGE SQUAD'S WORK IS DONE. THEY CAN RETURN TO THEIR LIVES IN THE FUTURE. ALL BUT YOU, REEP.
"YOU, TOO, HAVE ONE LAST TASK.
"BUT FOR THAT, WAIT FOR MON-EL TO FIRST DO WHAT HE MUST...
"...THE REBUILDING OF WORLDS...

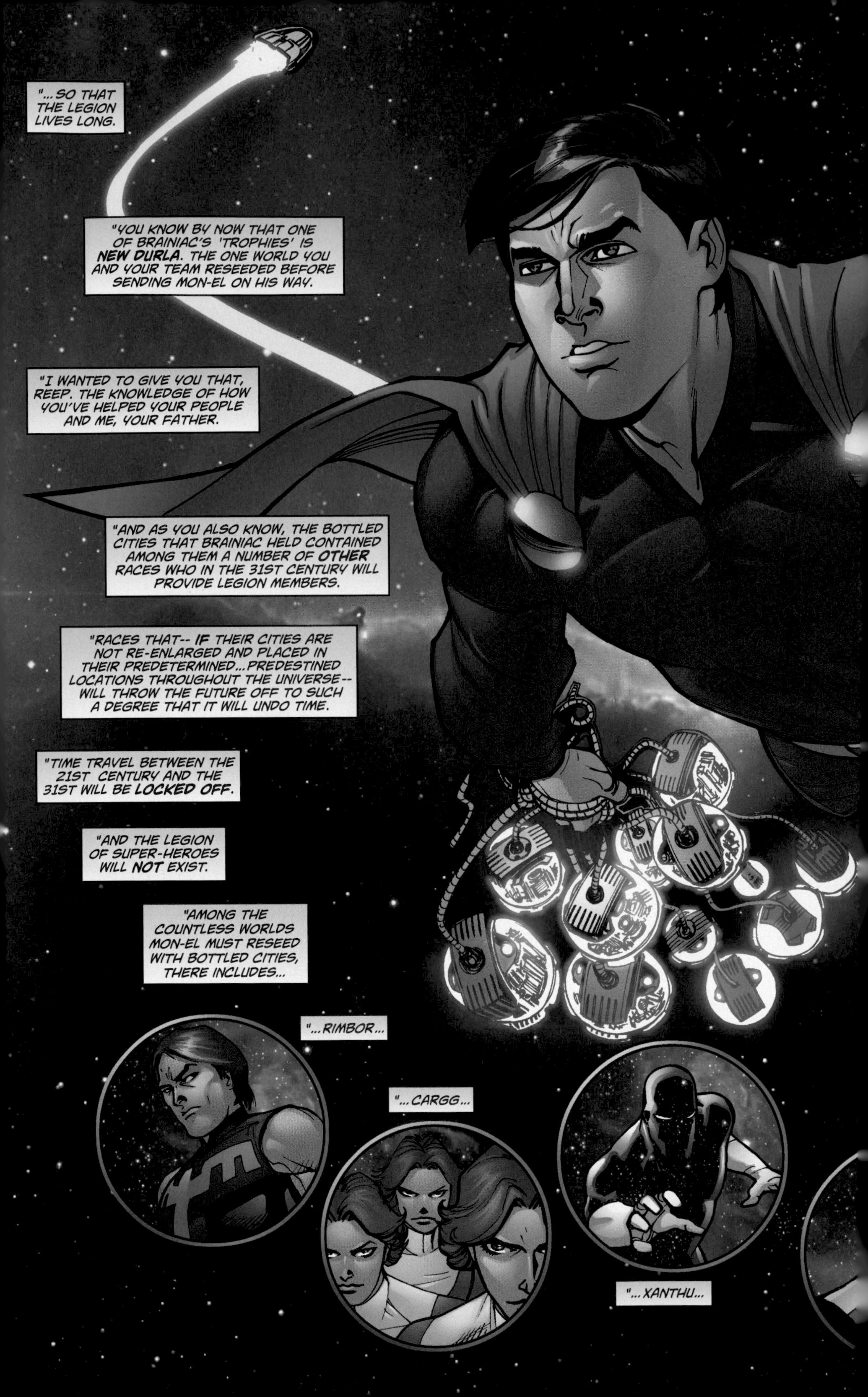
"...SO THAT THE LEGION LIVES LONG.
"YOU KNOW BY NOW THAT ONE OF BRAINIAC'S 'TROPHIES' IS NEW DURLA. THE ONE WORLD YOU AND YOUR TEAM RESEEDED BEFORE SENDING MON-EL ON HIS WAY.
"I WANTED TO GIVE YOU THAT, REEP. THE KNOWLEDGE OF HOW YOU'VE HELPED YOUR PEOPLE AND ME, YOUR FATHER.
"AND AS YOU ALSO KNOW, THE BOTTLED CITIES THAT BRAINIAC HELD CONTAINED AMONG THEM A NUMBER OF OTHER RACES WHO IN THE 31ST CENTURY WILL PROVIDE LEGION MEMBERS.
"RACES THAT-- IF THEIR CITIES ARE NOT RE-ENLARGED AND PLACED IN THEIR PREDETERMINED...PREDESTINED LOCATIONS THROUGHOUT THE UNIVERSE-- WILL THROW THE FUTURE OFF TO SUCH A DEGREE THAT IT WILL UNDO TIME.
"TIME TRAVEL BETWEEN THE 21ST CENTURY AND THE 31ST WILL BE LOCKED OFF.
"AND THE LEGION OF SUPER-HEROES WILL NOT EXIST.
"AMONG THE COUNTLESS WORLDS MON-EL MUST RESEED WITH BOTTLED CITIES, THERE INCLUDES...
"...RIMBOR...
"...CARGG...
"...XANTHU...

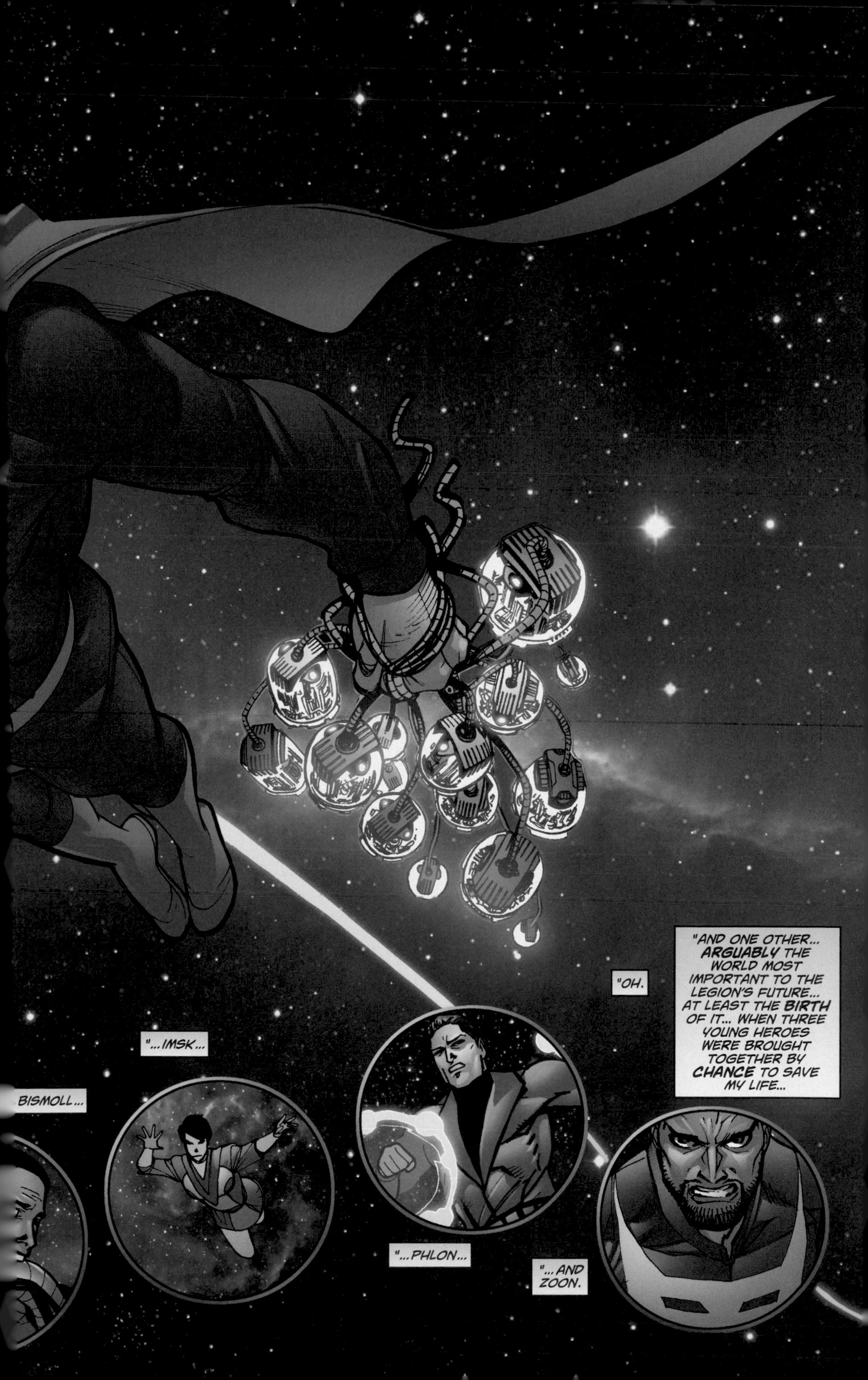
"AND ONE OTHER... ARGUABLY THE WORLD MOST IMPORTANT TO THE LEGION'S FUTURE... AT LEAST THE BIRTH OF IT... WHEN THREE YOUNG HEROES WERE BROUGHT TOGETHER BY CHANCE TO SAVE MY LIFE...
"OH.
BISMOLL...
"...IMSK...
"...PHLON...
"...AND ZOON.

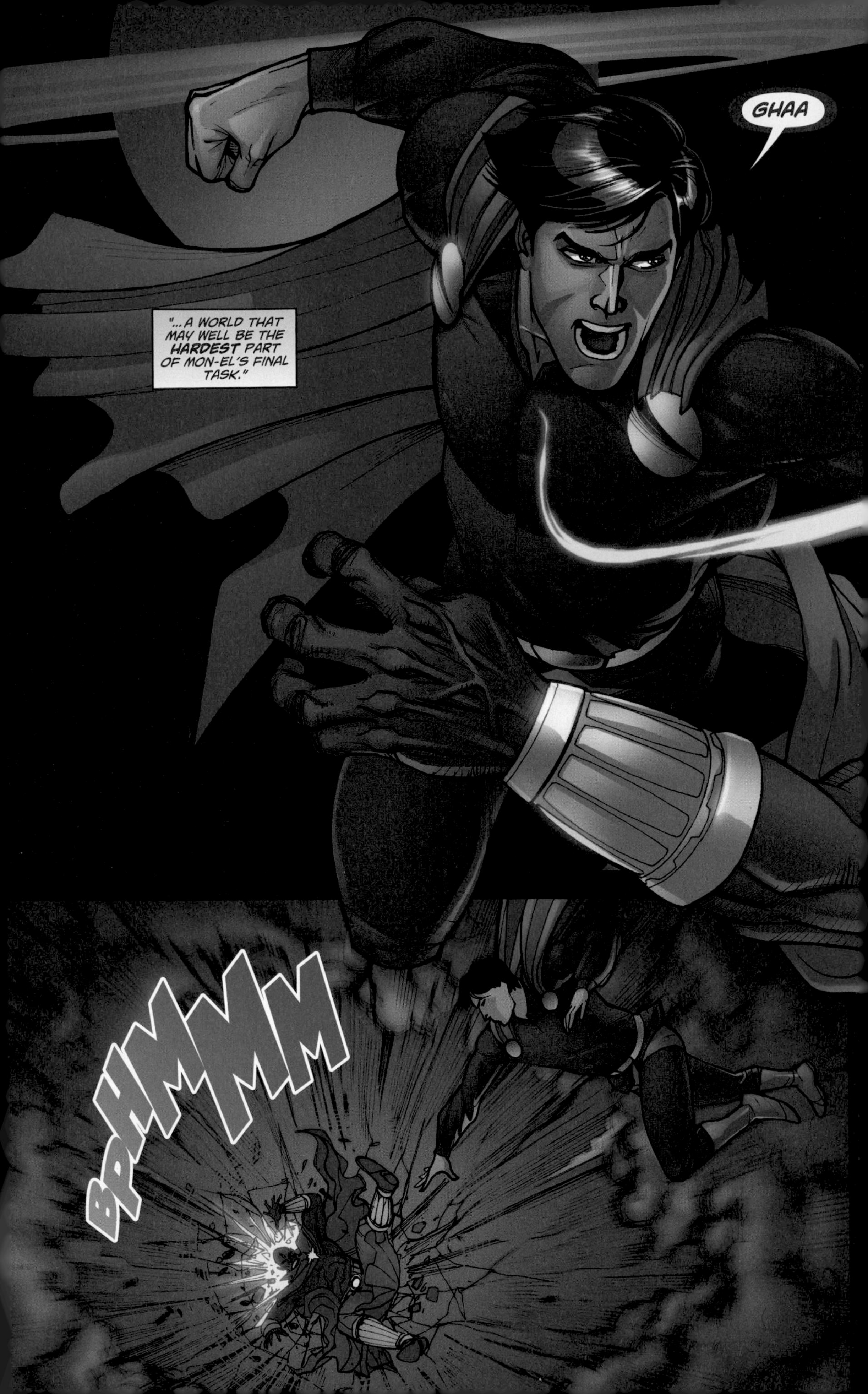
"...A WORLD THAT MAY WELL BE THE HARDEST PART OF MON-EL'S FINAL TASK."
GHAA
BPHMMM

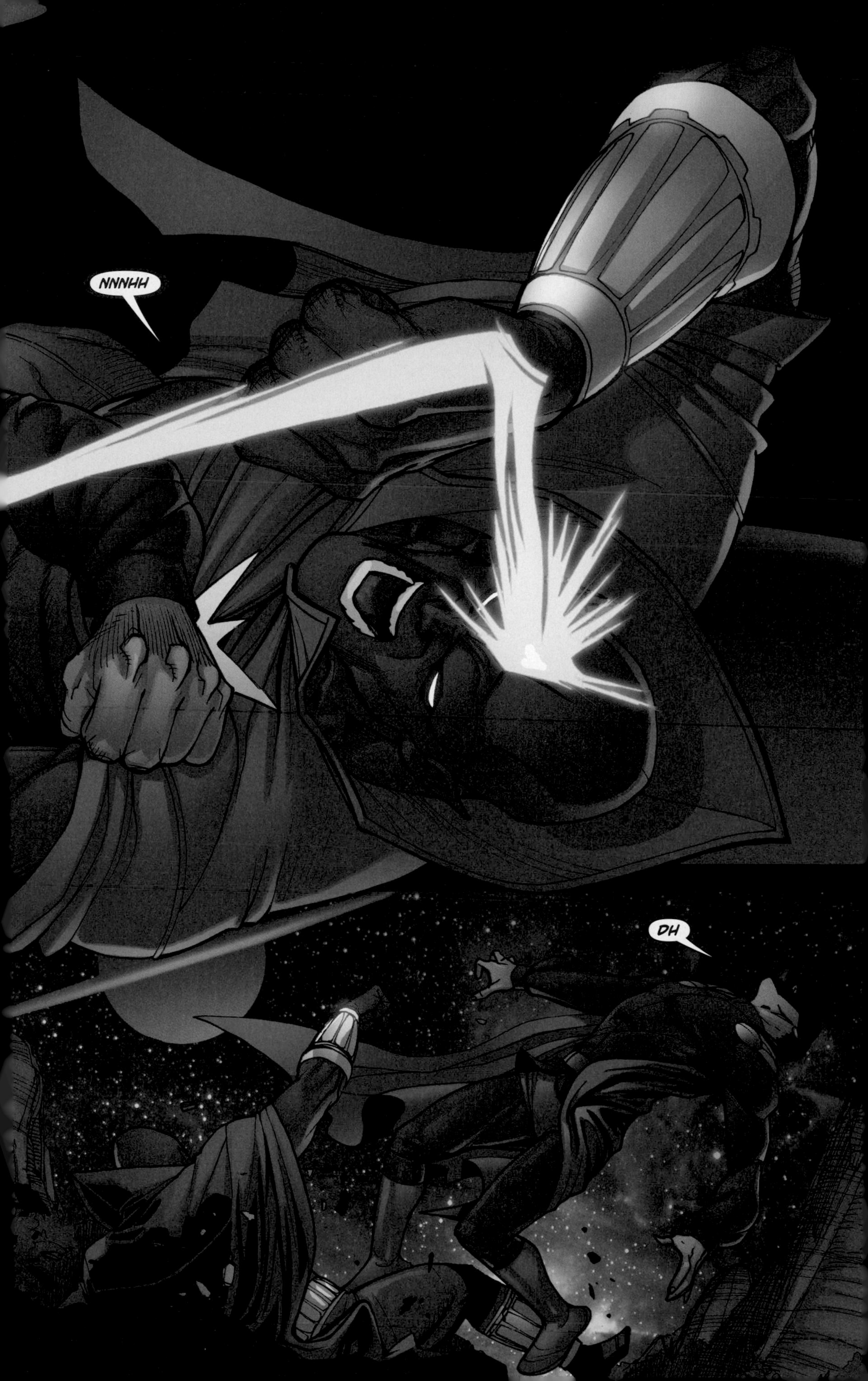
NNNHH
OH

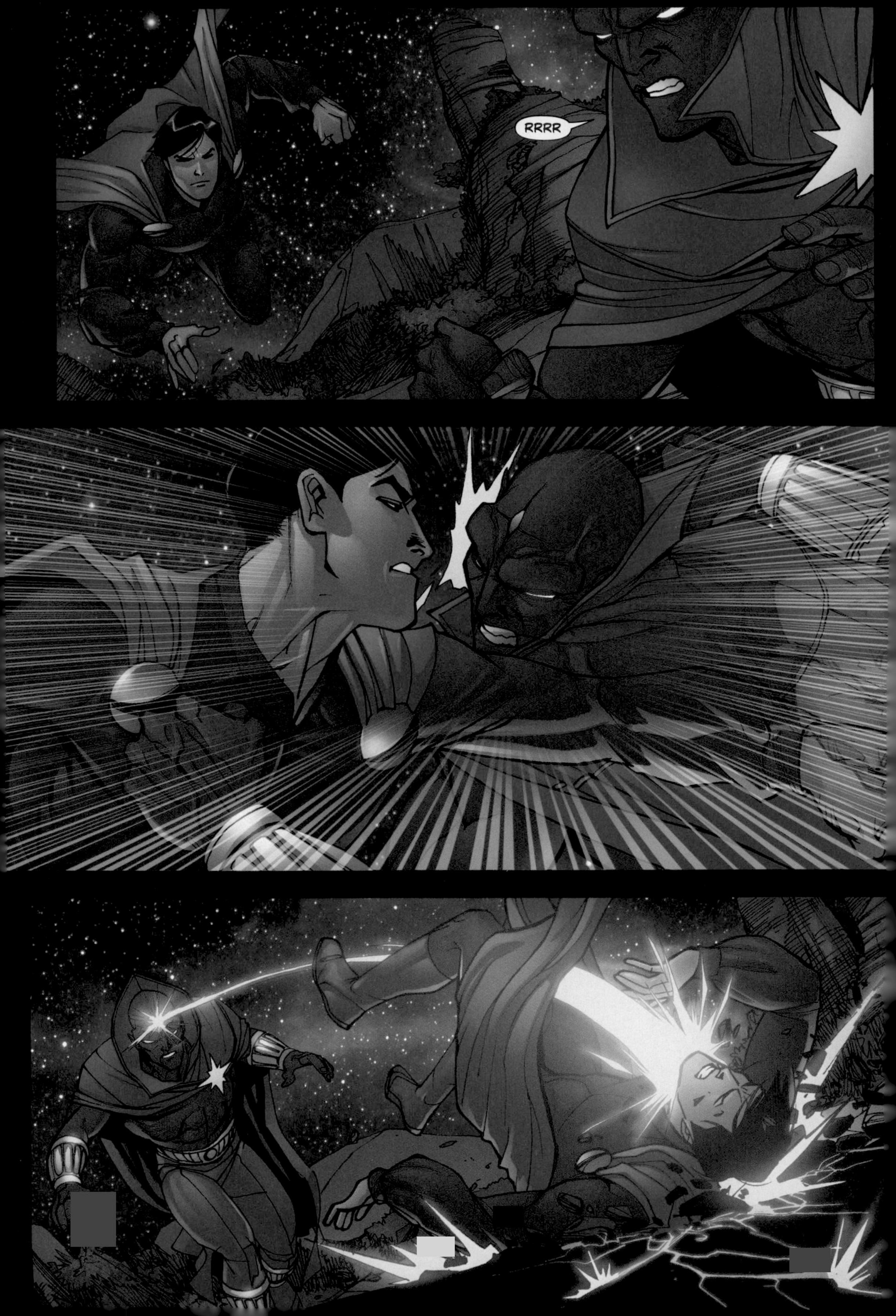
RRRR

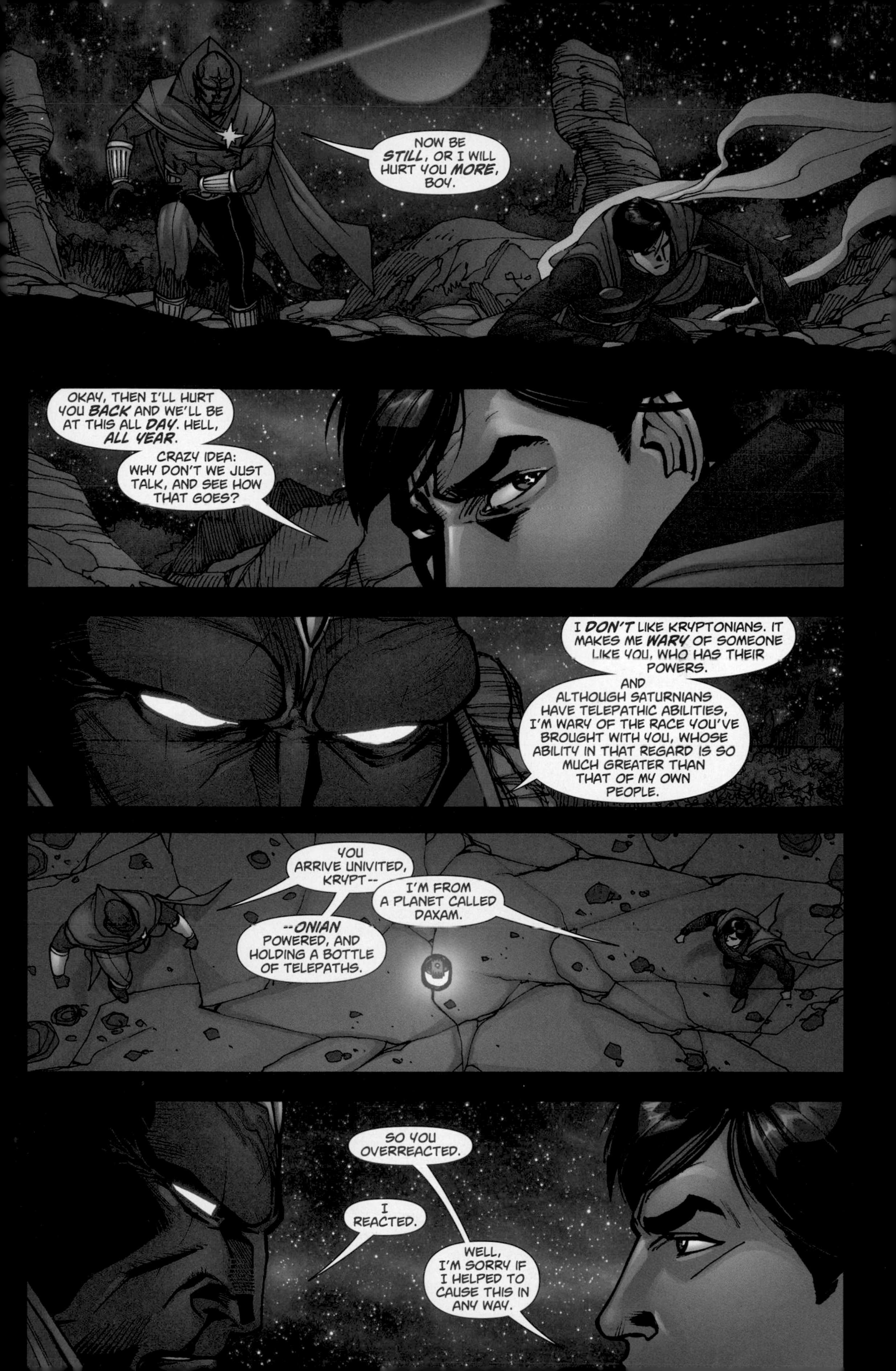
NOW BE STILL, OR I WILL HURT YOU MORE, BOY.
OKAY, THEN I'LL HURT YOU BACK AND WE'LL BE AT THIS ALL DAY. HELL, ALL YEAR.
CRAZY IDEA: WHY DON'T WE JUST TALK, AND SEE HOW THAT GOES?
I DON'T LIKE KRYPTONIANS. IT MAKES ME WARY OF SOMEONE LIKE YOU, WHO HAS THEIR POWERS.
AND ALTHOUGH SATURNIANS HAVE TELEPATHIC ABILITIES, I'M WARY OF THE RACE YOU'VE BROUGHT WITH YOU, WHOSE ABILITY IN THAT REGARD IS SO MUCH GREATER THAN THAT OF MY OWN PEOPLE.
YOU ARRIVE UNIVITED, KRYPT--
--ONIAN POWERED, AND HOLDING A BOTTLE OF TELEPATHS.
I'M FROM A PLANET CALLED DAXAM.
SO YOU OVERREACTED.
I REACTED.
WELL, I'M SORRY IF I HELPED TO CAUSE THIS IN ANY WAY.

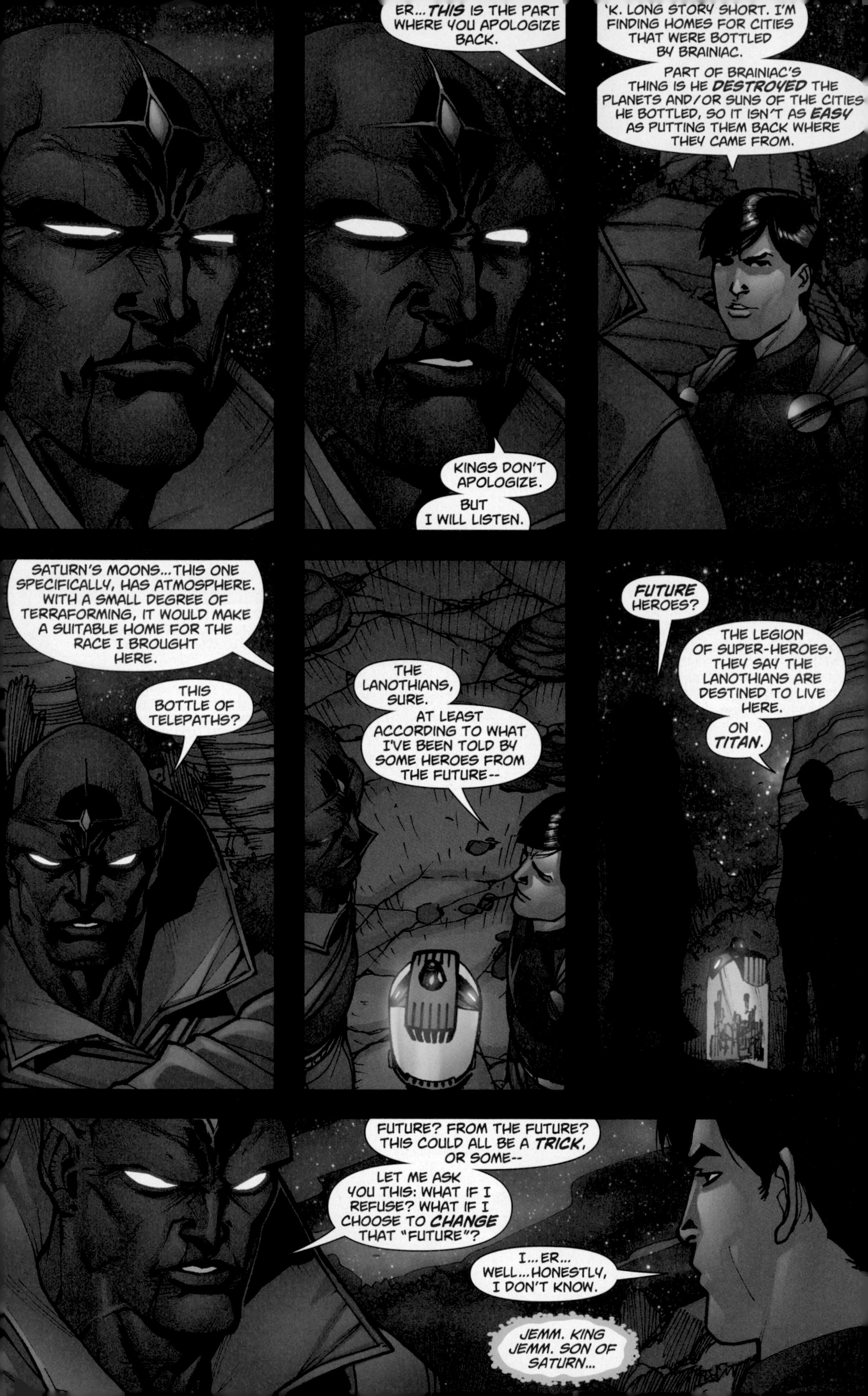
ER...THIS IS THE PART WHERE YOU APOLOGIZE BACK.
KINGS DON'T APOLOGIZE.
BUT I WILL LISTEN.
'K. LONG STORY SHORT. I'M FINDING HOMES FOR CITIES THAT WERE BOTTLED BY BRAINIAC.
PART OF BRAINIAC'S THING IS HE DESTROYED THE PLANETS AND/OR SUNS OF THE CITIES HE BOTTLED, SO IT ISN'T AS EASY AS PUTTING THEM BACK WHERE THEY CAME FROM.
SATURN'S MOONS...THIS ONE SPECIFICALLY, HAS ATMOSPHERE. WITH A SMALL DEGREE OF TERRAFORMING, IT WOULD MAKE A SUITABLE HOME FOR THE RACE I BROUGHT HERE.
THIS BOTTLE OF TELEPATHS?
THE LANOTHIANS, SURE.
AT LEAST ACCORDING TO WHAT I'VE BEEN TOLD BY SOME HEROES FROM THE FUTURE--
FUTURE HEROES?
THE LEGION OF SUPER-HEROES. THEY SAY THE LANOTHIANS ARE DESTINED TO LIVE HERE.
ON TITAN.
FUTURE? FROM THE FUTURE? THIS COULD ALL BE A TRICK, OR SOME--
LET ME ASK YOU THIS: WHAT IF I REFUSE? WHAT IF I CHOOSE TO CHANGE THAT "FUTURE"?
I...ER... WELL...HONESTLY, I DON'T KNOW.
JEMM. KING JEMM. SON OF SATURN...

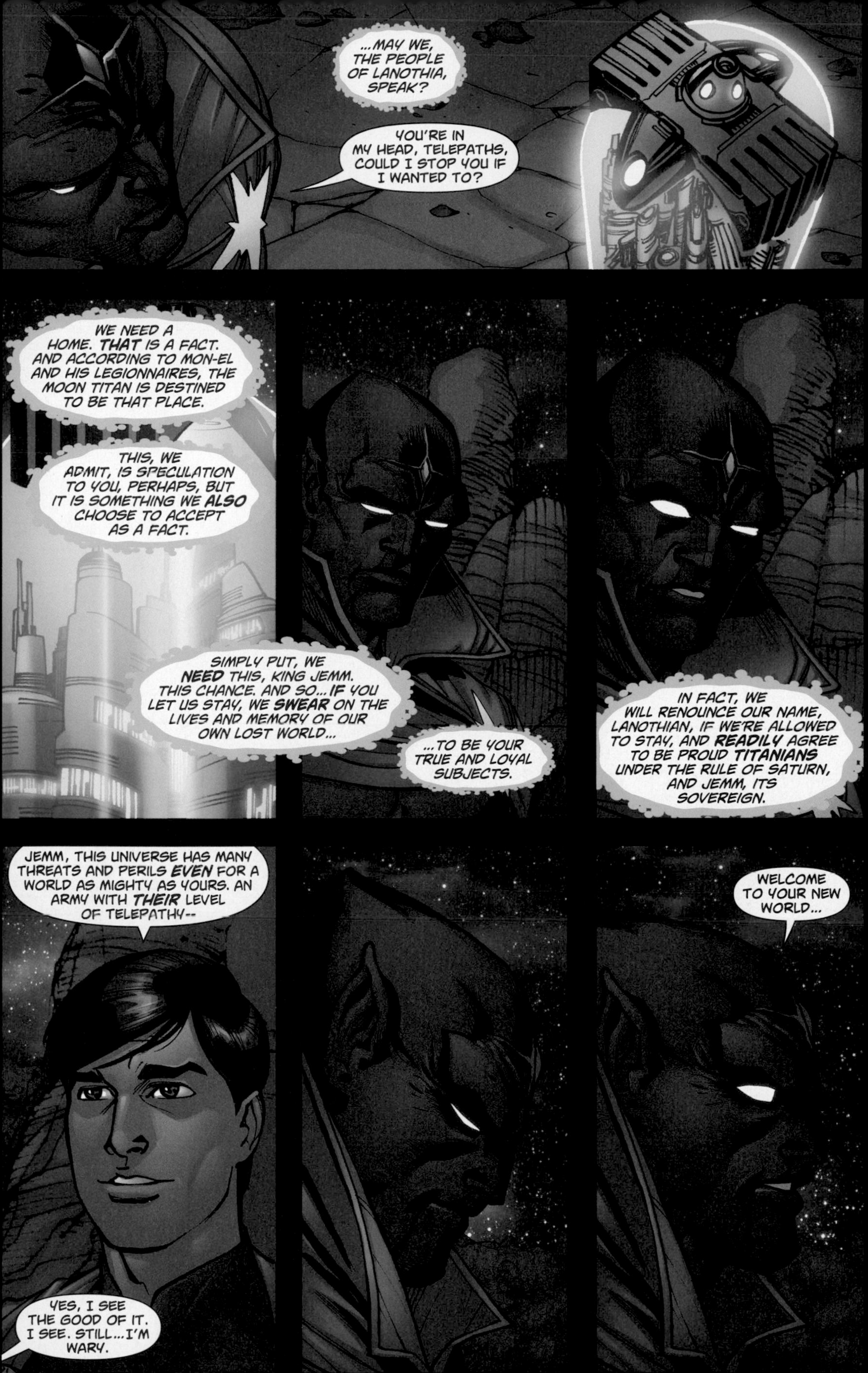
...MAY WE, THE PEOPLE OF LANOTHIA, SPEAK?
YOU'RE IN MY HEAD, TELEPATHS, COULD I STOP YOU IF I WANTED TO?
WE NEED A HOME. THAT IS A FACT. AND ACCORDING TO MON-EL AND HIS LEGIONNAIRES, THE MOON TITAN IS DESTINED TO BE THAT PLACE.
THIS, WE ADMIT, IS SPECULATION TO YOU, PERHAPS, BUT IT IS SOMETHING WE ALSO CHOOSE TO ACCEPT AS A FACT.
SIMPLY PUT, WE NEED THIS, KING JEMM. THIS CHANCE. AND SO... IF YOU LET US STAY, WE SWEAR ON THE LIVES AND MEMORY OF OUR OWN LOST WORLD...
...TO BE YOUR TRUE AND LOYAL SUBJECTS.
IN FACT, WE WILL RENOUNCE OUR NAME, LANOTHIAN, IF WE'RE ALLOWED TO STAY, AND READILY AGREE TO BE PROUD TITANIANS UNDER THE RULE OF SATURN, AND JEMM, ITS SOVEREIGN.
JEMM, THIS UNIVERSE HAS MANY THREATS AND PERILS EVEN FOR A WORLD AS MIGHTY AS YOURS. AN ARMY WITH THEIR LEVEL OF TELEPATHY--
YES, I SEE THE GOOD OF IT. I SEE. STILL... I'M WARY.
WELCOME TO YOUR NEW WORLD...

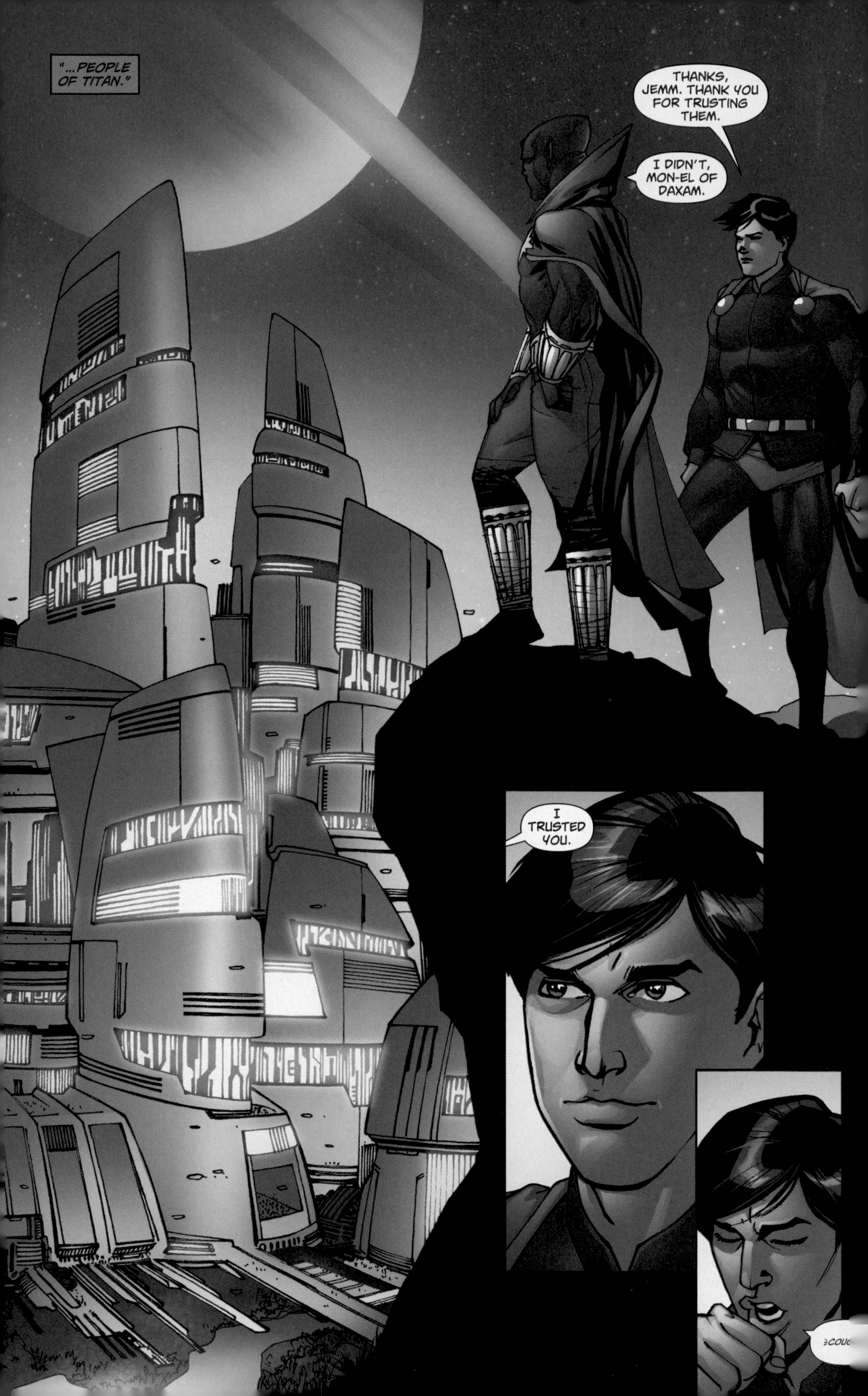
"...PEOPLE OF TITAN."
THANKS, JEMM. THANK YOU FOR TRUSTING THEM.
I DIDN'T, MON-EL OF DAXAM.
I TRUSTED YOU.

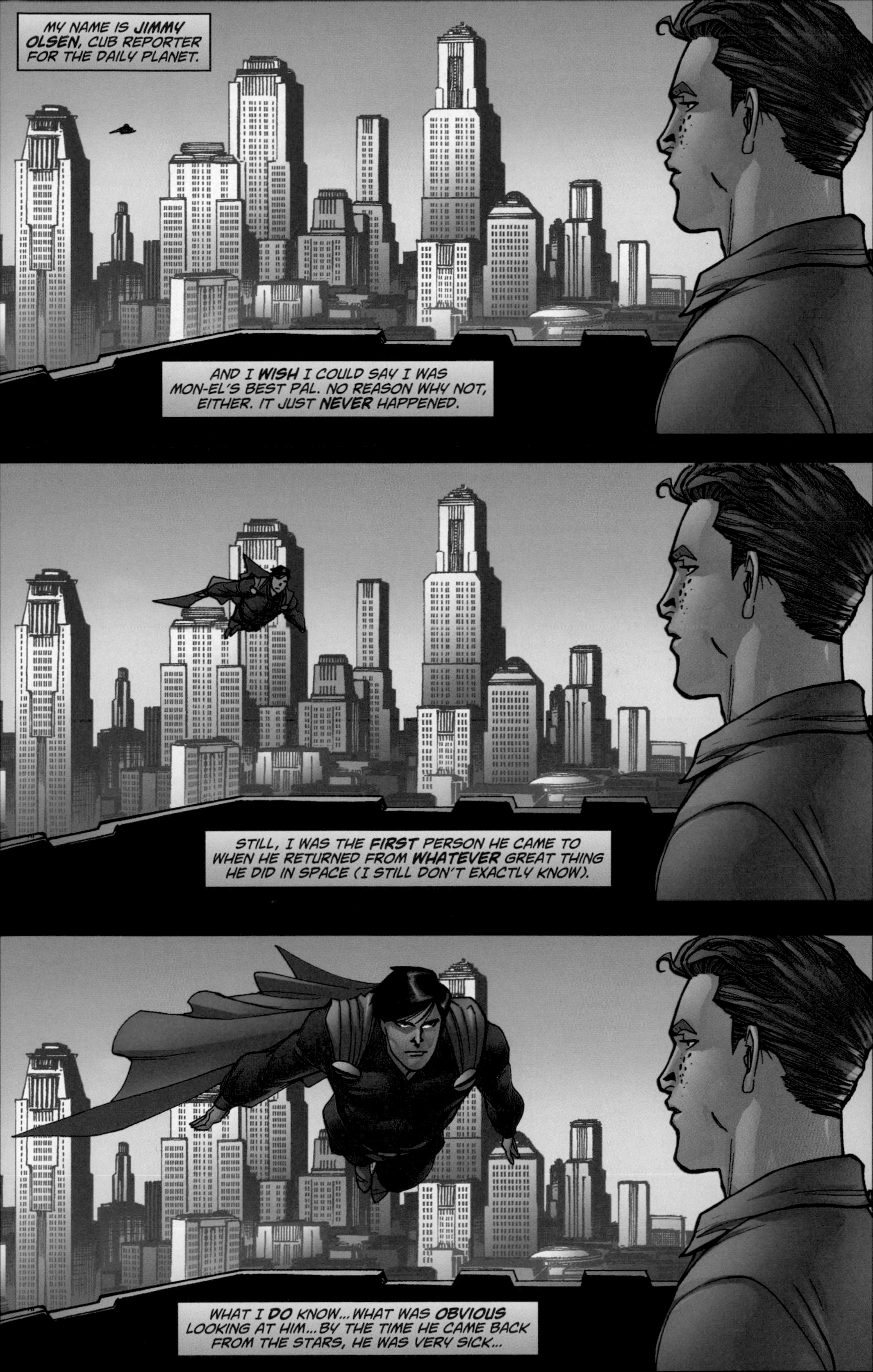

MY NAME IS JIMMY OLSEN, CUB REPORTER FOR THE DAILY PLANET.
AND I WISH I COULD SAY I WAS MON-EL'S BEST PAL. NO REASON WHY NOT, EITHER. IT JUST NEVER HAPPENED.
STILL, I WAS THE FIRST PERSON HE CAME TO WHEN HE RETURNED FROM WHATEVER GREAT THING HE DID IN SPACE (I STILL DON'T EXACTLY KNOW).
WHAT I DO KNOW... WHAT WAS OBVIOUS LOOKING AT HIM... BY THE TIME HE CAME BACK FROM THE STARS, HE WAS VERY SICK...

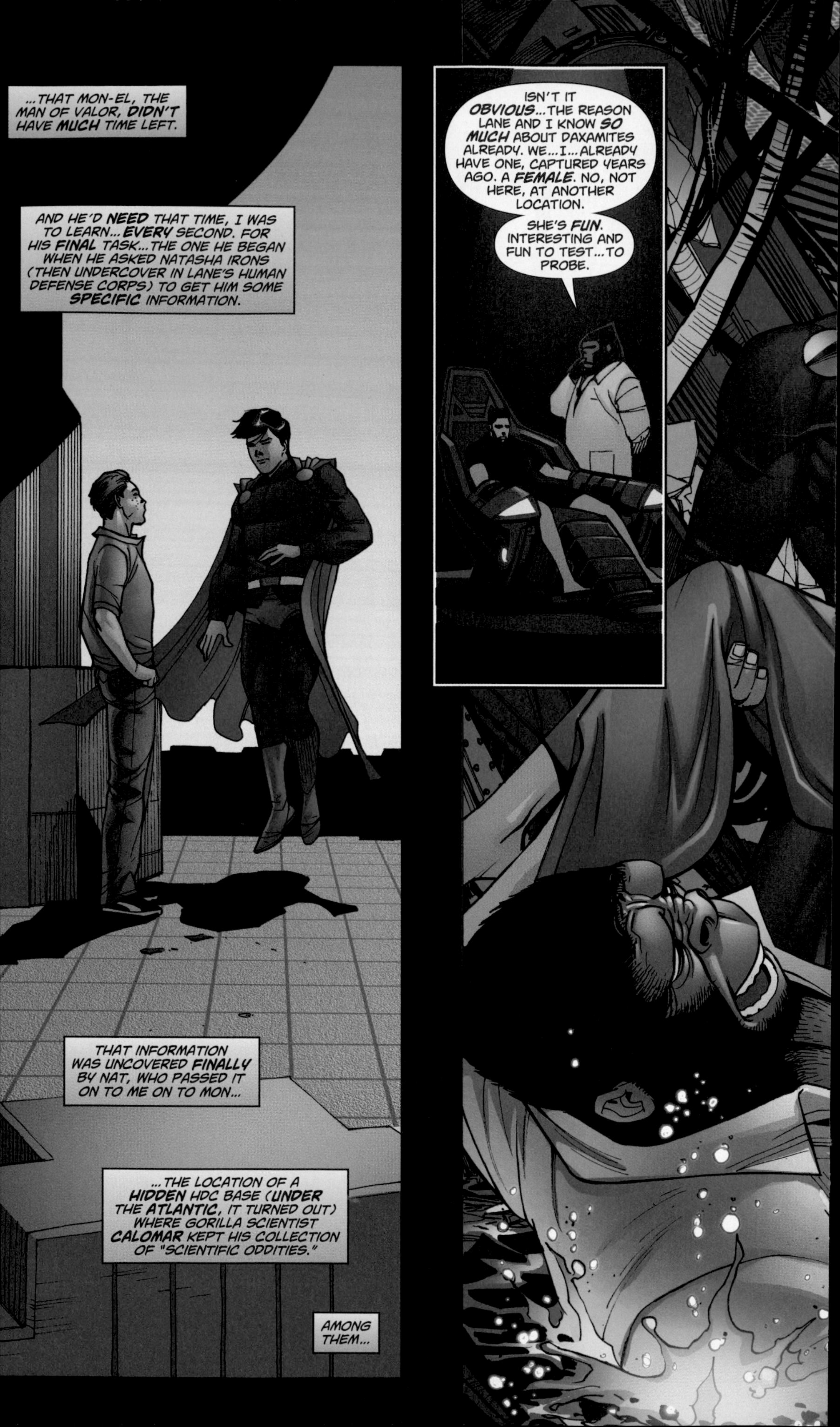
...THAT MON-EL, THE MAN OF VALOR, DIDN'T HAVE MUCH TIME LEFT.
AND HE'D NEED THAT TIME, I WAS TO LEARN... EVERY SECOND. FOR HIS FINAL TASK...THE ONE HE BEGAN WHEN HE ASKED NATASHA IRONS (THEN UNDERCOVER IN LANE'S HUMAN DEFENSE CORPS) TO GET HIM SOME SPECIFIC INFORMATION.
THAT INFORMATION WAS UNCOVERED FINALLY BY NAT, WHO PASSED IT ON TO ME ON TO MON...
...THE LOCATION OF A HIDDEN HDC BASE (UNDER THE ATLANTIC, IT TURNED OUT) WHERE GORILLA SCIENTIST CALOMAR KEPT HIS COLLECTION OF "SCIENTIFIC ODDITIES."
AMONG THEM...
ISN'T IT OBVIOUS...THE REASON LANE AND I KNOW SO MUCH ABOUT DAXAMITES ALREADY. WE...I...ALREADY HAVE ONE, CAPTURED YEARS AGO. A FEMALE. NO, NOT HERE, AT ANOTHER LOCATION.
SHE'S FUN. INTERESTING AND FUN TO TEST...TO PROBE.

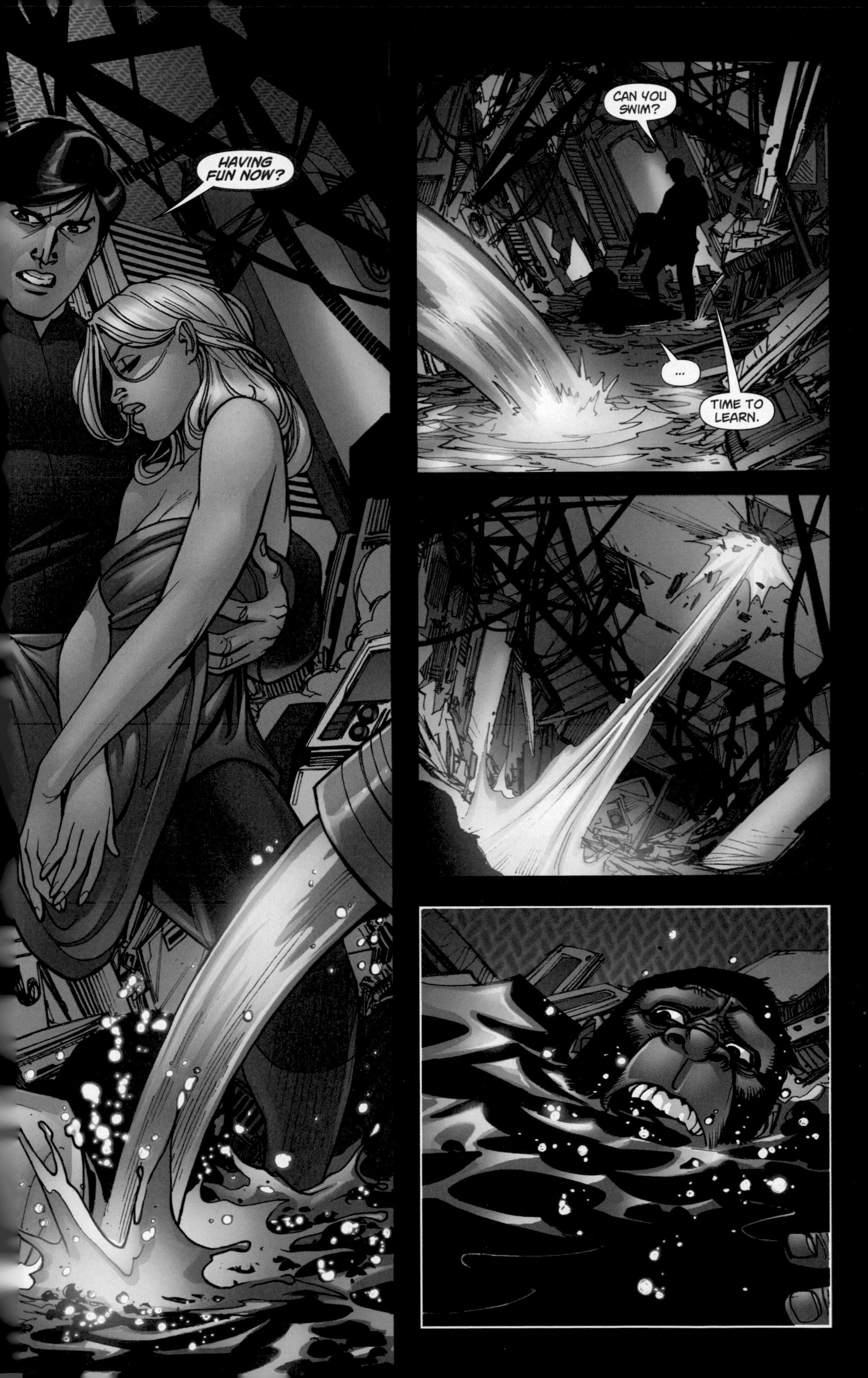
HAVING FUN NOW?
CAN YOU SWIM?
...
TIME TO LEARN.

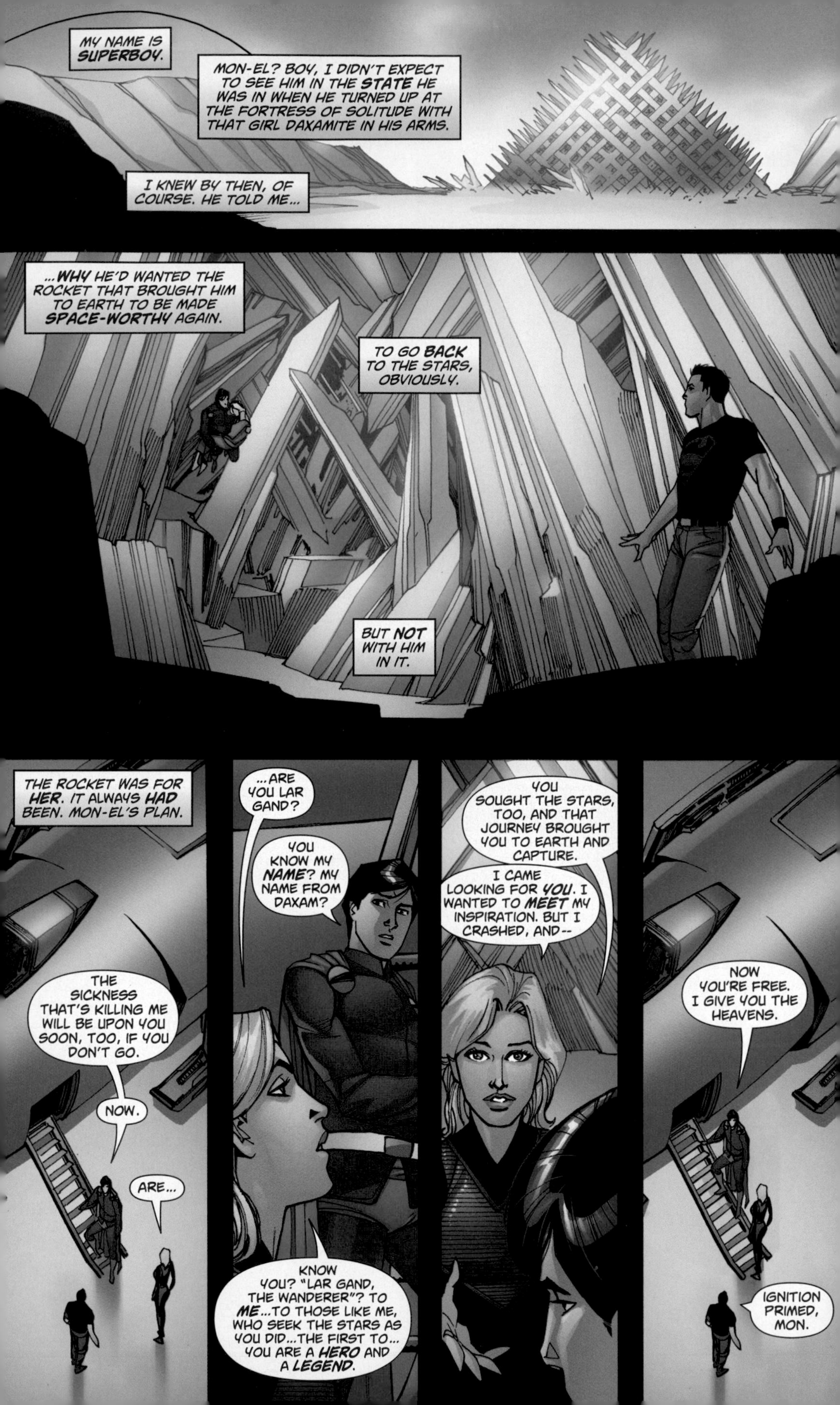

MY NAME IS SUPERBOY.
MON-EL? BOY, I DIDN'T EXPECT TO SEE HIM IN THE STATE HE WAS IN WHEN HE TURNED UP AT THE FORTRESS OF SOLITUDE WITH THAT GIRL DAXAMITE IN HIS ARMS.
I KNEW BY THEN, OF COURSE. HE TOLD ME...
...WHY HE'D WANTED THE ROCKET THAT BROUGHT HIM TO EARTH TO BE MADE SPACE-WORTHY AGAIN.
TO GO BACK TO THE STARS, OBVIOUSLY.
BUT NOT WITH HIM IN IT.
THE ROCKET WAS FOR HER. IT ALWAYS HAD BEEN. MON-EL'S PLAN.
THE SICKNESS THAT'S KILLING ME WILL BE UPON YOU SOON, TOO, IF YOU DON'T GO.
NOW.
ARE...
...ARE YOU LAR GAND?
YOU KNOW MY NAME? MY NAME FROM DAXAM?
KNOW YOU? "LAR GAND, THE WANDERER"? TO ME...TO THOSE LIKE ME, WHO SEEK THE STARS AS YOU DID...THE FIRST TO... YOU ARE A HERO AND A LEGEND.
YOU SOUGHT THE STARS, TOO, AND THAT JOURNEY BROUGHT YOU TO EARTH AND CAPTURE.
I CAME LOOKING FOR YOU. I WANTED TO MEET MY INSPIRATION. BUT I CRASHED, AND--
NOW YOU'RE FREE. I GIVE YOU THE HEAVENS.
IGNITION PRIMED, MON.

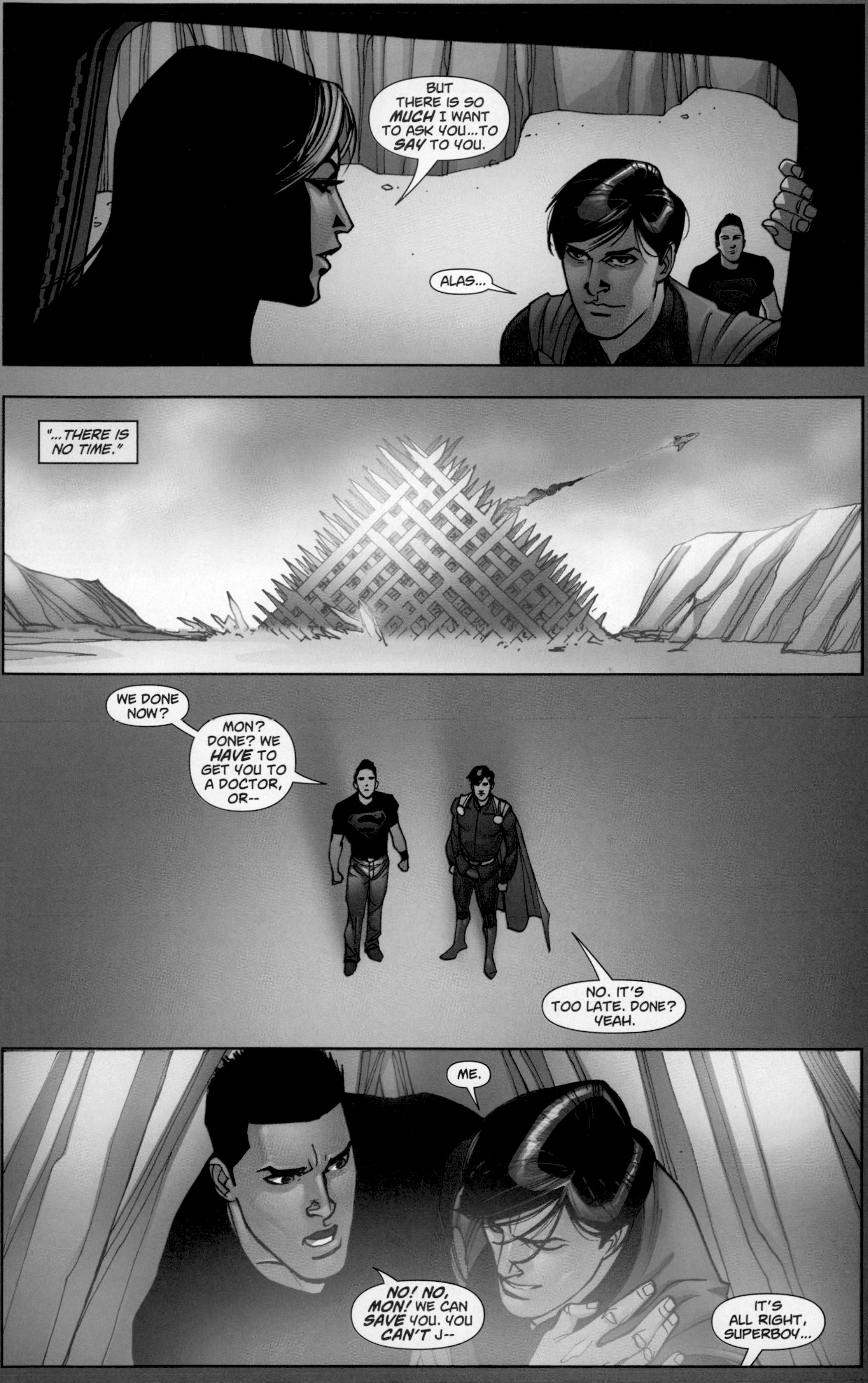
BUT THERE IS SO MUCH I WANT TO ASK YOU...TO SAY TO YOU.
ALAS...
"...THERE IS NO TIME."
WE DONE NOW?
MON? DONE? WE HAVE TO GET YOU TO A DOCTOR, OR--
NO. IT'S TOO LATE. DONE? YEAH.
ME.
NO! NO, MON! WE CAN SAVE YOU. YOU CAN'T J--
IT'S ALL RIGHT, SUPERBOY...

...EVERYTHING'S FINE.
MY NAME IS REEP DAGGLE, CHAMELEON BOY.
AND THIS IS THE LAST TASK MY FATHER, R.J. BRANDE, SET ME TO.
MON...
...THERE'S A WAY I CAN SAVE YOU.
THE POTION? YOU BROUGHT MORE FROM THE FUTURE?
NO SECOND TIMES, MON. YOUR BODY'S BUILT UP AN IMMUNITY TO IT.
THEN HOW?
THE PHANTOM ZONE. IT'S BEEN RECREATED, BUT IT'S LOCKED OFF TO THE 21ST CENTURY.
THAT'S HOW IT NEEDS TO BE. HAS TO BE.
BUT I CAN OPEN IT UP AND SEND YOU BACK IN THERE, MON. YOU'LL LIVE.
BACK TO THAT? I'D RATHER DIE. I COULDN'T BEAR IT...AFTER THIS... LIFE... EARTH.
THE LONELINESS AND ISOLATION WAS BAD BEFORE, BUT NOW? NO. I CHOOSE DEATH.
MON. YOU HAVE TO.
THERE'S MORE YOU HAVE TO DO. ONE DAY.
NO. NO. I CAN'T.

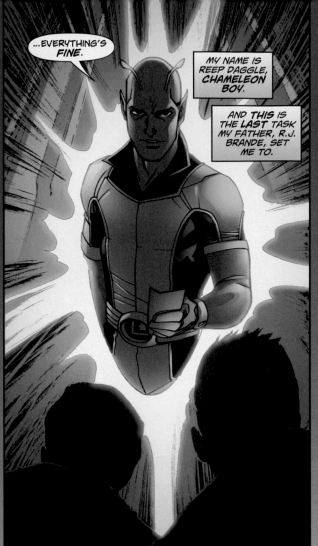

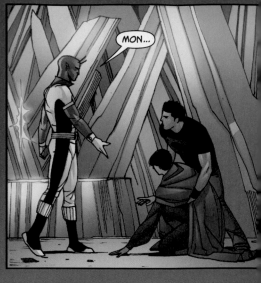

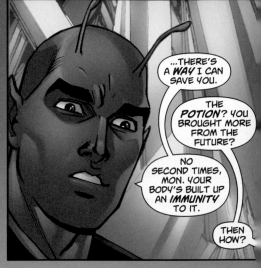

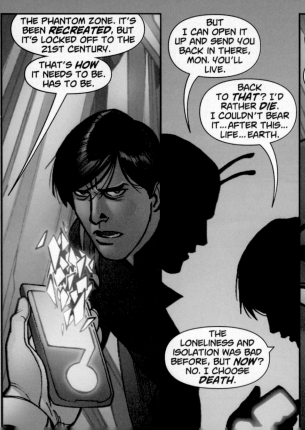

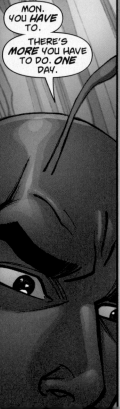

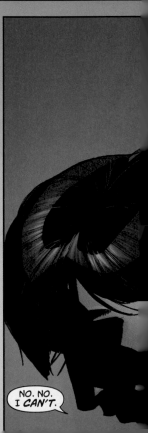

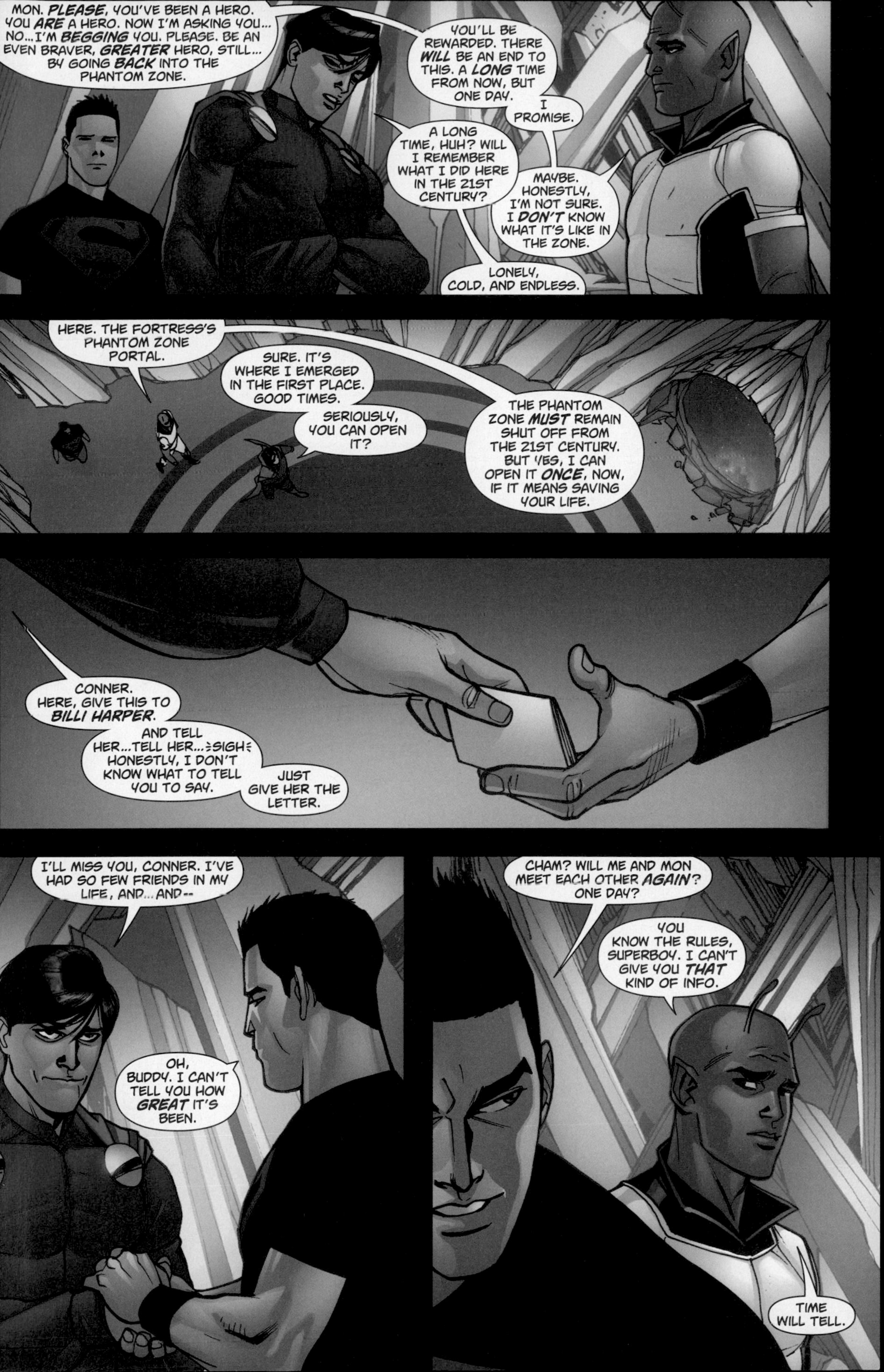
MON. PLEASE, YOU'VE BEEN A HERO. YOU ARE A HERO. NOW I'M ASKING YOU... NO...I'M BEGGING YOU. PLEASE. BE AN EVEN BRAVER, GREATER HERO, STILL... BY GOING BACK INTO THE PHANTOM ZONE.
YOU'LL BE REWARDED. THERE WILL BE AN END TO THIS. A LONG TIME FROM NOW, BUT ONE DAY.
I PROMISE.
A LONG TIME, HUH? WILL I REMEMBER WHAT I DID HERE IN THE 21ST CENTURY?
MAYBE. HONESTLY, I'M NOT SURE. I DON'T KNOW WHAT IT'S LIKE IN THE ZONE.
LONELY, COLD, AND ENDLESS.
HERE. THE FORTRESS'S PHANTOM ZONE PORTAL.
SURE. IT'S WHERE I EMERGED IN THE FIRST PLACE. GOOD TIMES.
SERIOUSLY, YOU CAN OPEN IT?
THE PHANTOM ZONE MUST REMAIN SHUT OFF FROM THE 21ST CENTURY. BUT YES, I CAN OPEN IT ONCE, NOW, IF IT MEANS SAVING YOUR LIFE.
CONNER. HERE, GIVE THIS TO BILLI HARPER.
AND TELL HER...TELL HER...SIGH HONESTLY, I DON'T KNOW WHAT TO TELL YOU TO SAY.
JUST GIVE HER THE LETTER.
I'LL MISS YOU, CONNER. I'VE HAD SO FEW FRIENDS IN MY LIFE, AND...AND--
OH, BUDDY. I CAN'T TELL YOU HOW GREAT IT'S BEEN.
CHAM? WILL ME AND MON MEET EACH OTHER AGAIN? ONE DAY?
YOU KNOW THE RULES, SUPERBOY. I CAN'T GIVE YOU THAT KIND OF INFO.
TIME WILL TELL.

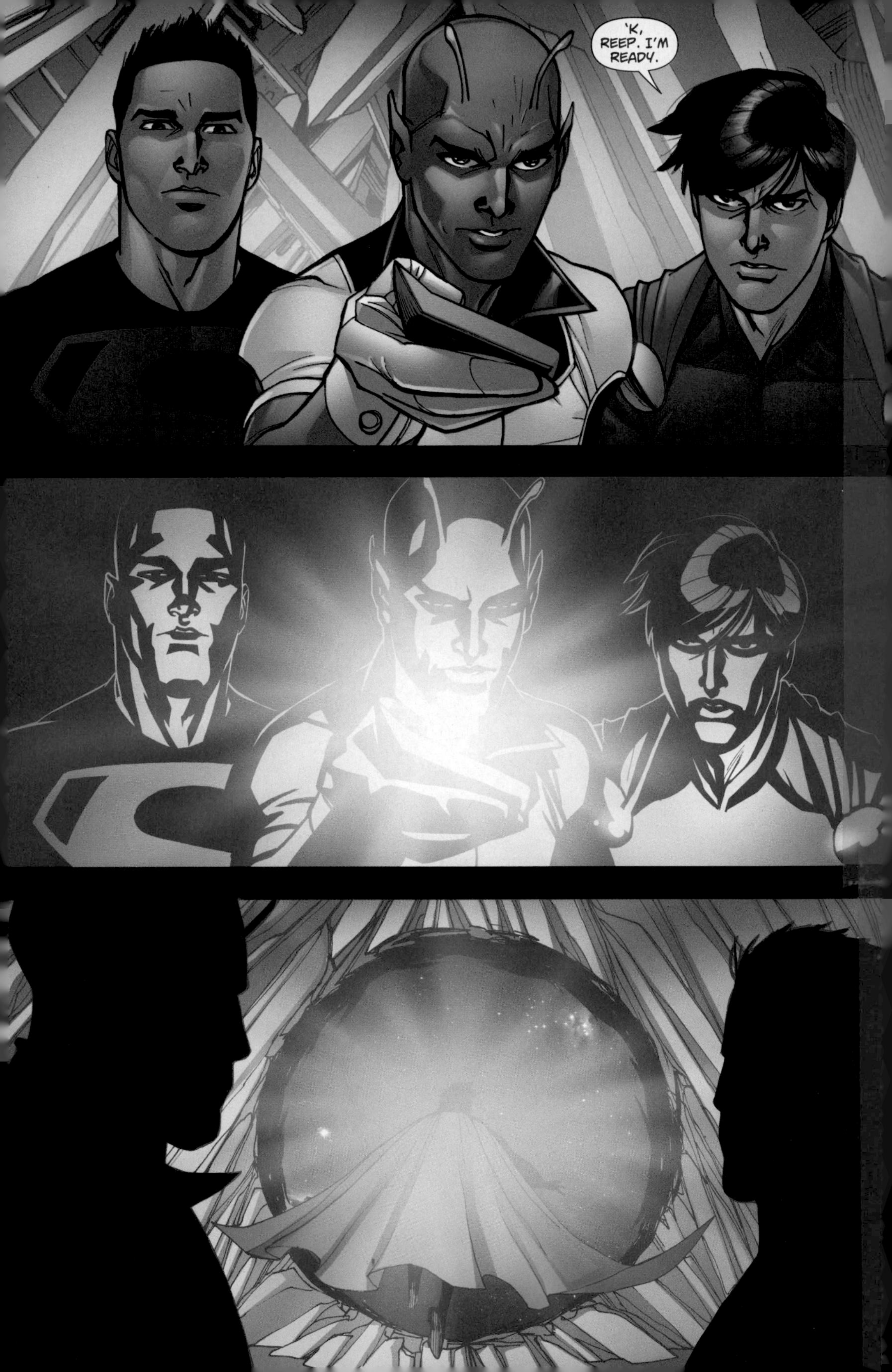
'K, REEP. I'M READY.

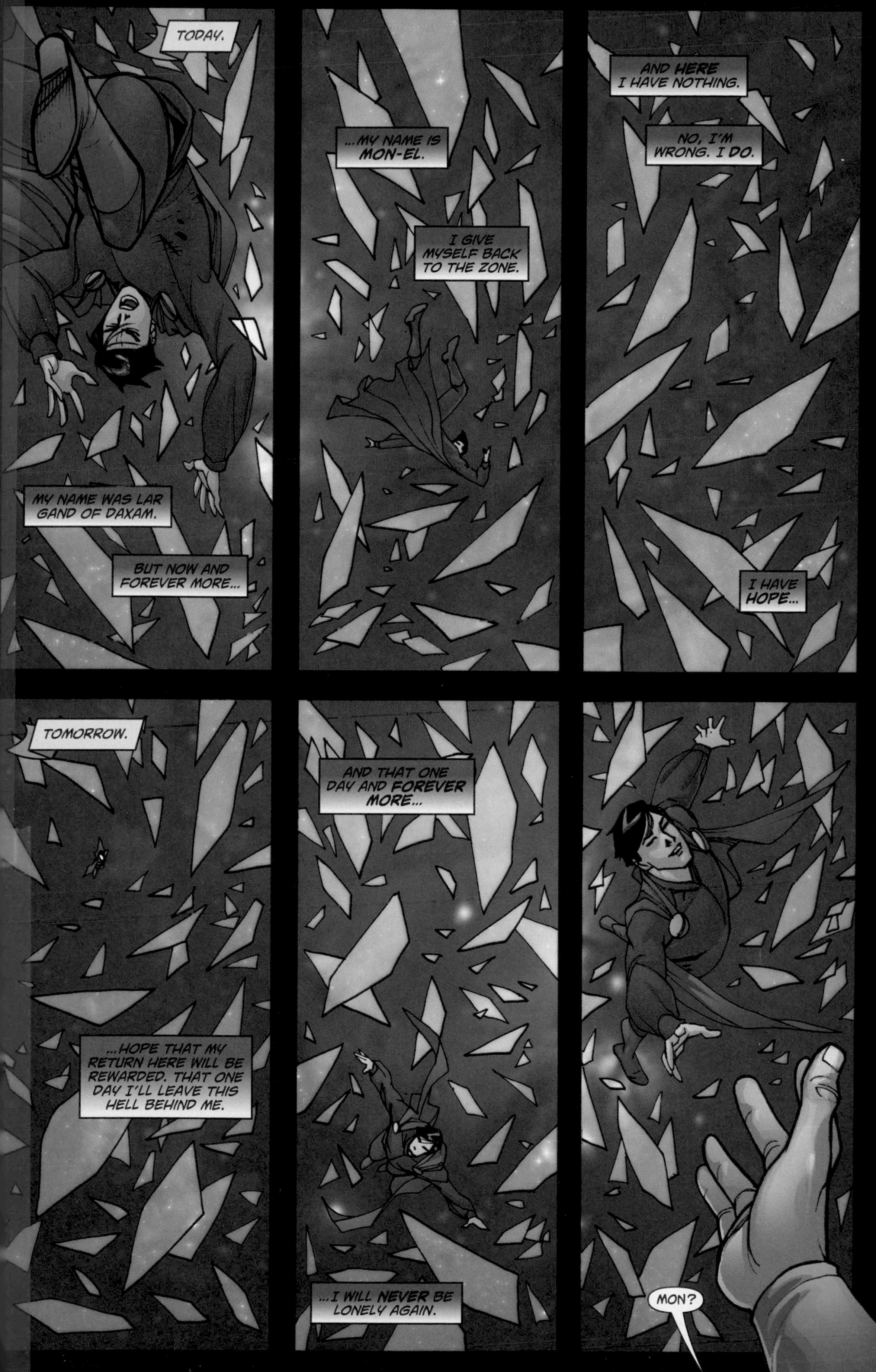
TODAY.
MY NAME WAS LAR GAND OF DAXAM.
BUT NOW AND FOREVER MORE...
...MY NAME IS MON-EL.
I GIVE MYSELF BACK TO THE ZONE.
AND HERE I HAVE NOTHING.
NO, I'M WRONG. I DO.
I HAVE HOPE...
TOMORROW.
...HOPE THAT MY RETURN HERE WILL BE REWARDED. THAT ONE DAY I'LL LEAVE THIS HELL BEHIND ME.
AND THAT ONE DAY AND FOREVER MORE...
...I WILL NEVER BE LONELY AGAIN.
MON?

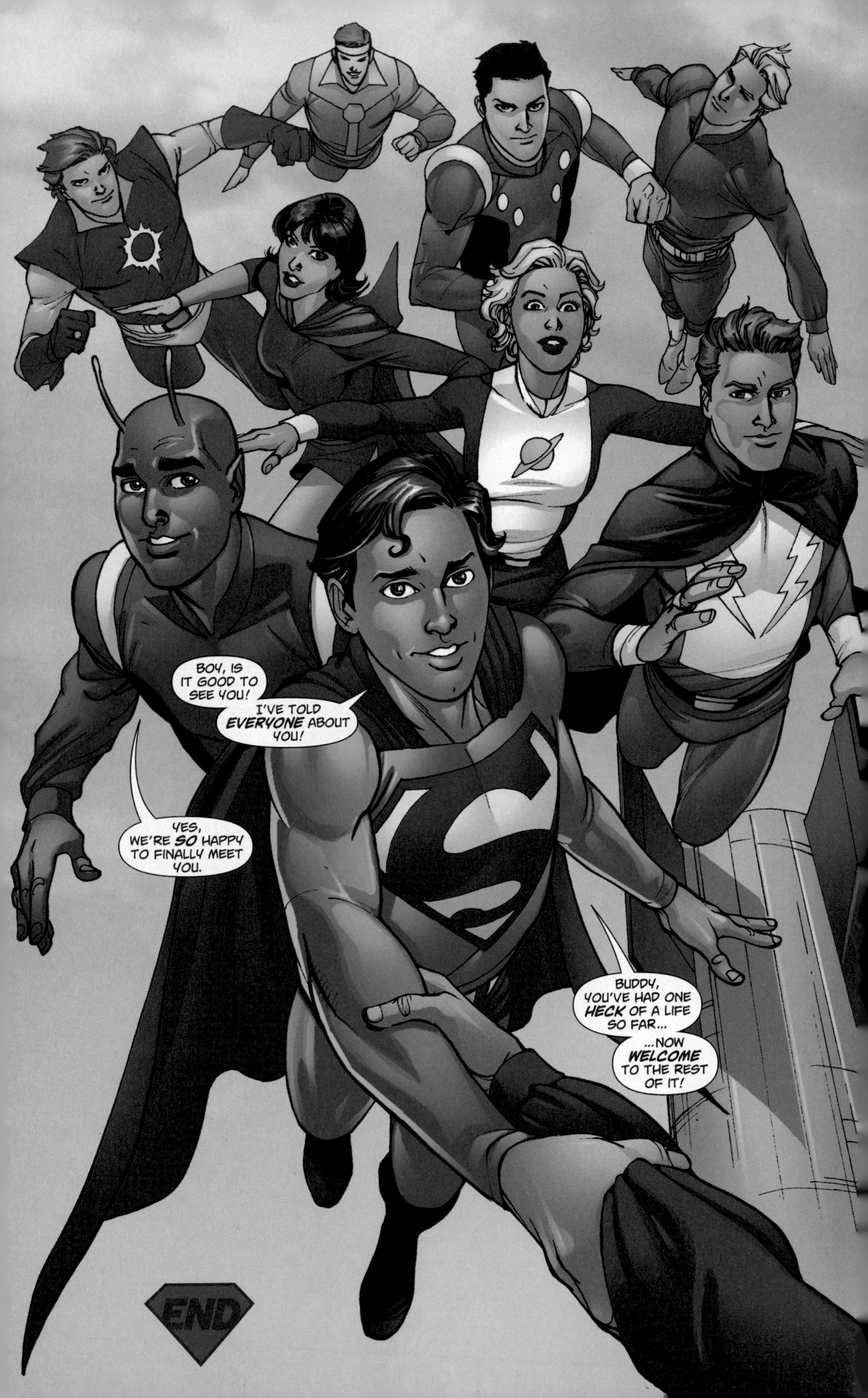
BOY, IS IT GOOD TO SEE YOU!
I'VE TOLD EVERYONE ABOUT YOU!
YES, WE'RE SO HAPPY TO FINALLY MEET YOU.
BUDDY, YOU'VE HAD ONE HECK OF A LIFE SO FAR...
...NOW WELCOME TO THE REST OF IT!
END

ADVENTURE COMICS 11 VARIANT BY **JOE QUINONES**

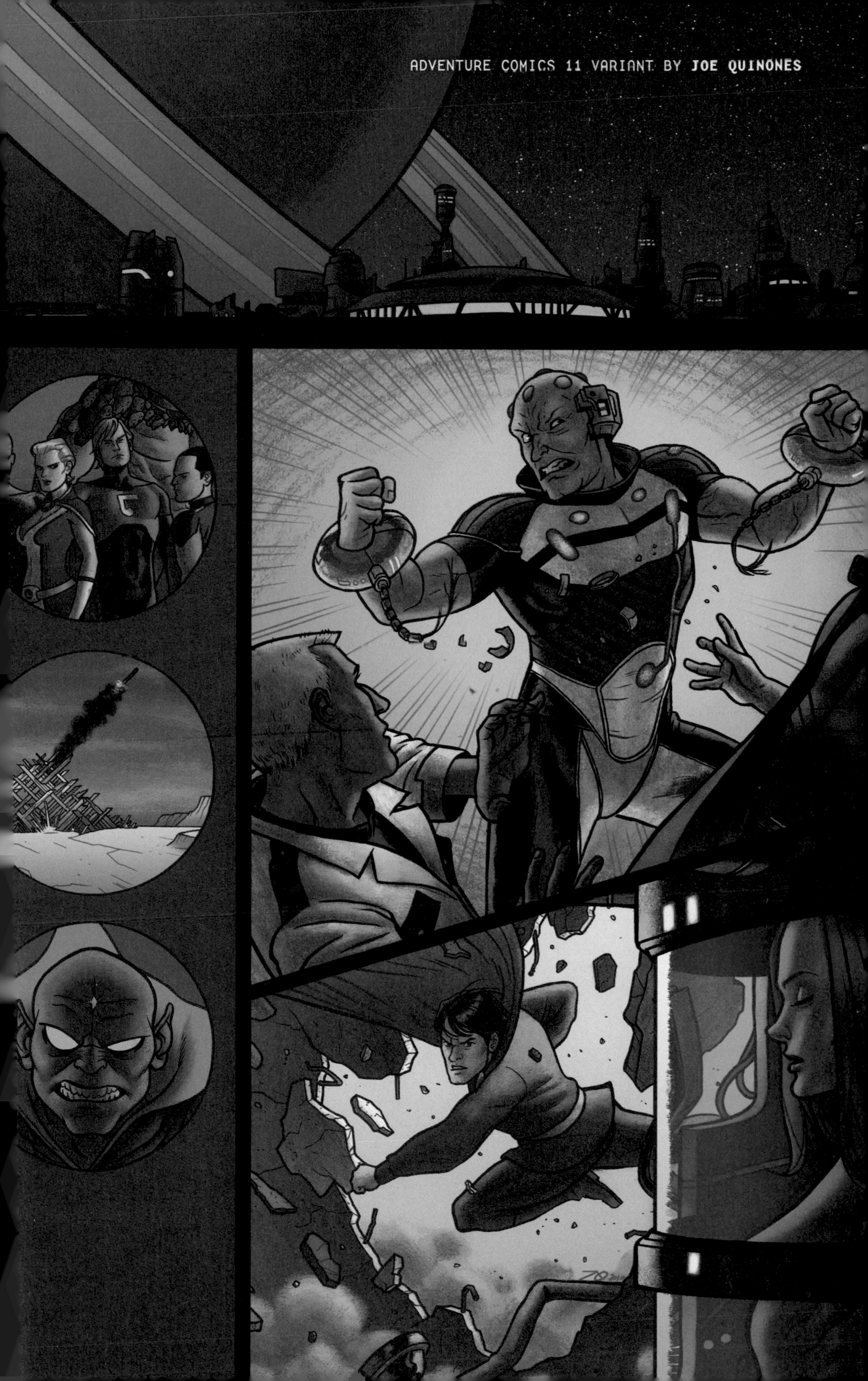

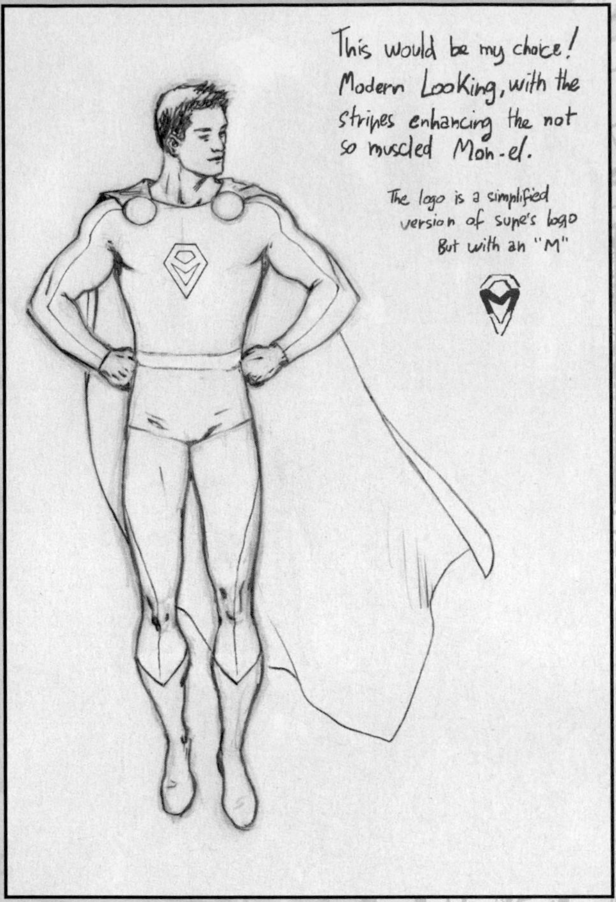
This would be my choice! Modern Looking, with the stripes enhancing the not so muscled Mon-el.
The logo is a simplified version of supe's logo But with an "M"

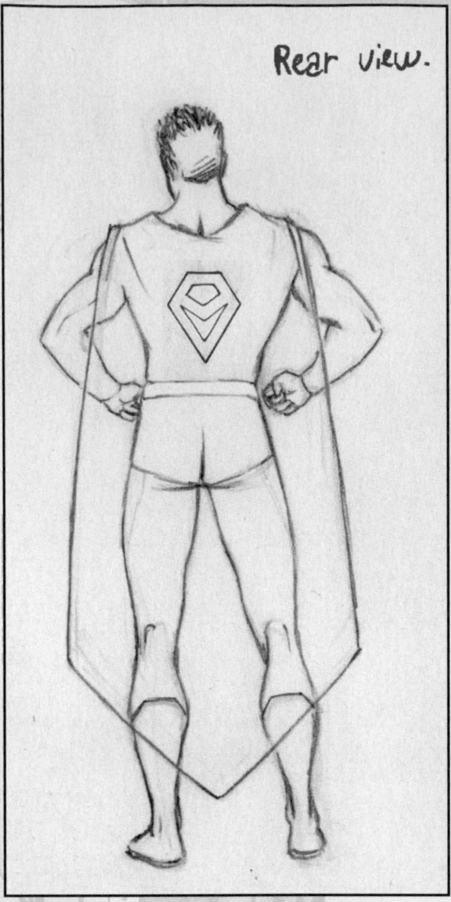
Rear view.

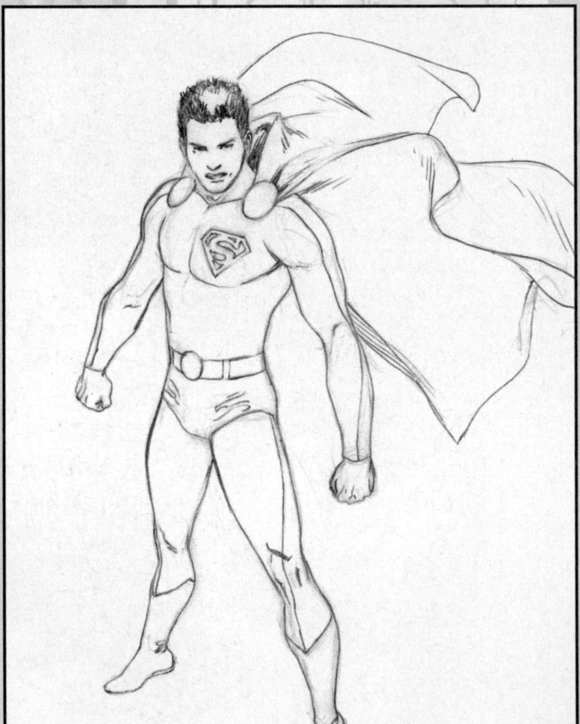

Mon-El sketches by **JAVIER PINA**

Mirabai

DIVINATION

EVOKATION

CONJURATION

NECROMANCY

TRANSMUTATION

Mirabai wears various fetishes and charms she has collected from defeated rivals. Not trophies— she only keeps what may prove useful.

She is generally in her cloak or coat. The runes on her gauntlets and cloak glow a dull red.

The tattoo styles and colors vary based on school. Illusion,curls like smoke. Dicination is a stylized eye with lines radiating away from it like roads or threads of fate. Evokation can take the form of stylized fire, water,or lightning (in Mirabai's case it is fire). Conjuration can take the shape of any variety of creature. Necromancy is a stylized skull. Tramksmutation looks something like a diagram of a molecule— Circular "Atoms" with line arcing between and conecting them representing a shared electron.

Mirabai design by
PETE WOODS

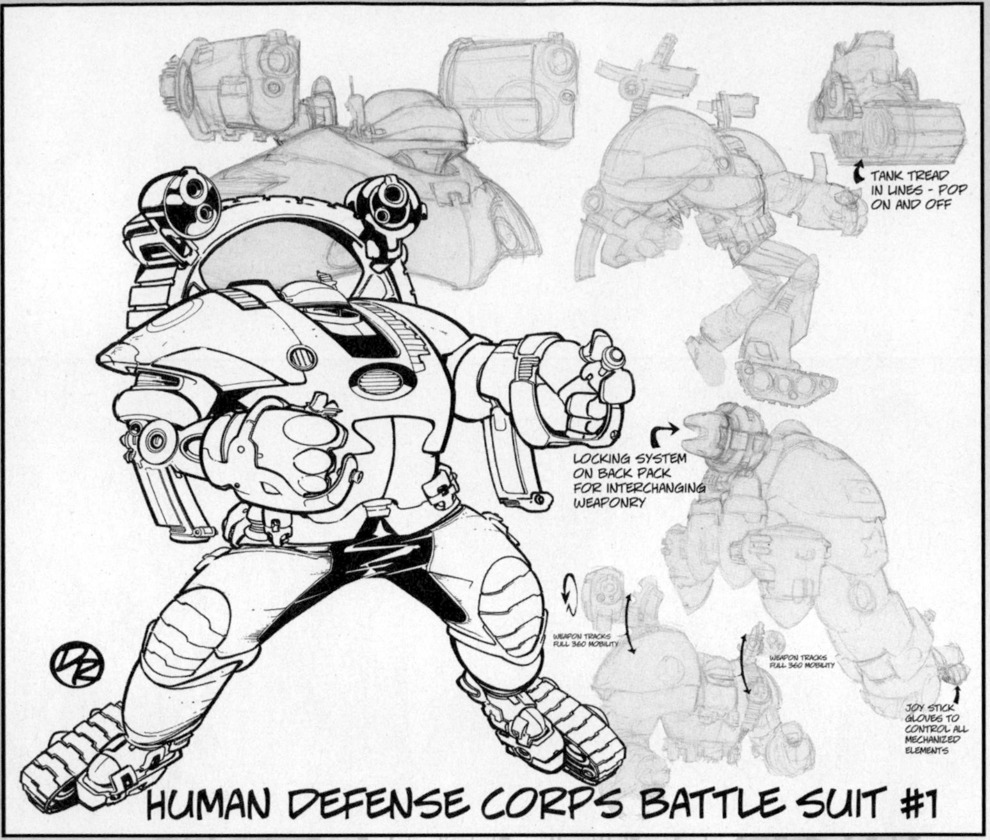
TANK TREAD IN LINES - POP ON AND OFF
LOCKING SYSTEM ON BACK PACK FOR INTERCHANGING WEAPONRY
WEAPON TRACKS FULL 360 MOBILITY
WEAPON TRACKS FULL 360 MOBILITY
JOY STICK GLOVES TO CONTROL ALL MECHANIZED ELEMENTS
HUMAN DEFENSE CORPS BATTLE SUIT #1

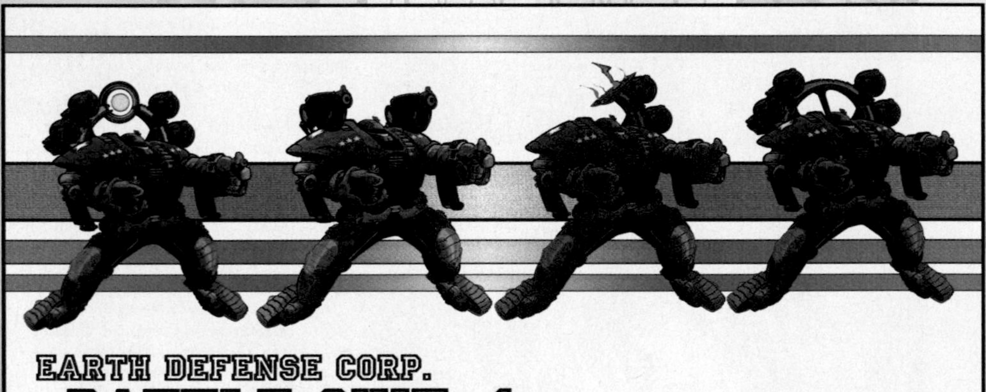
EARTH DEFENSE CORP.
BATTLE SUIT 1

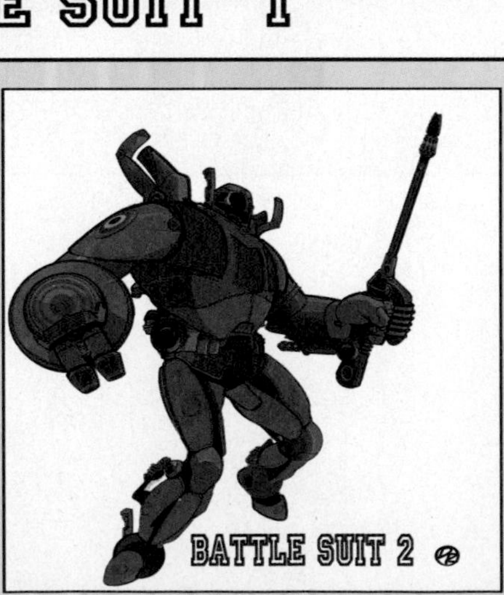
BATTLE SUIT 2

Human Defense Corps designs by **DUNCAN ROULEAU**

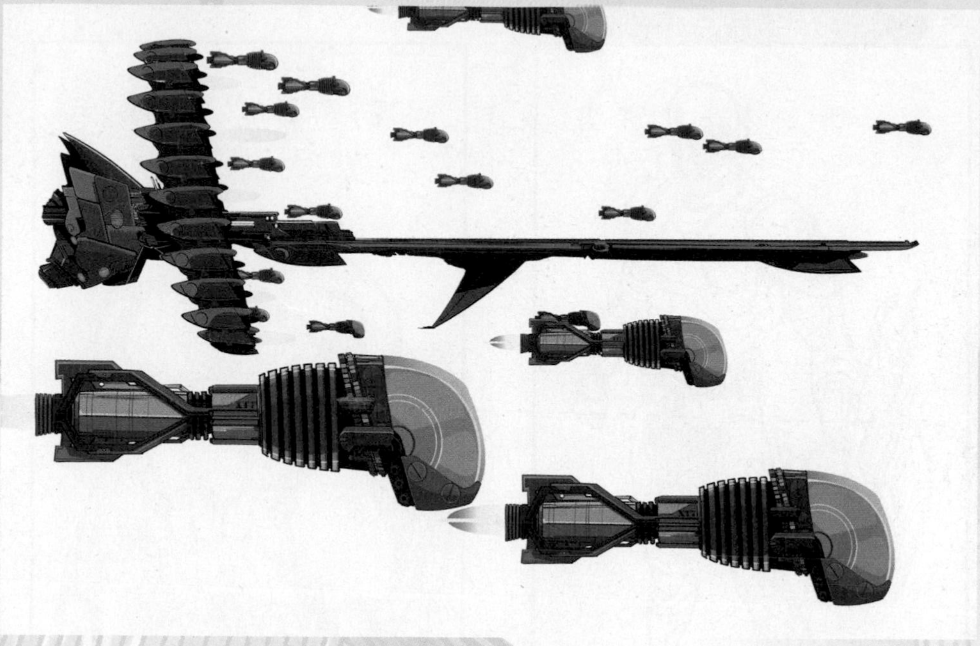

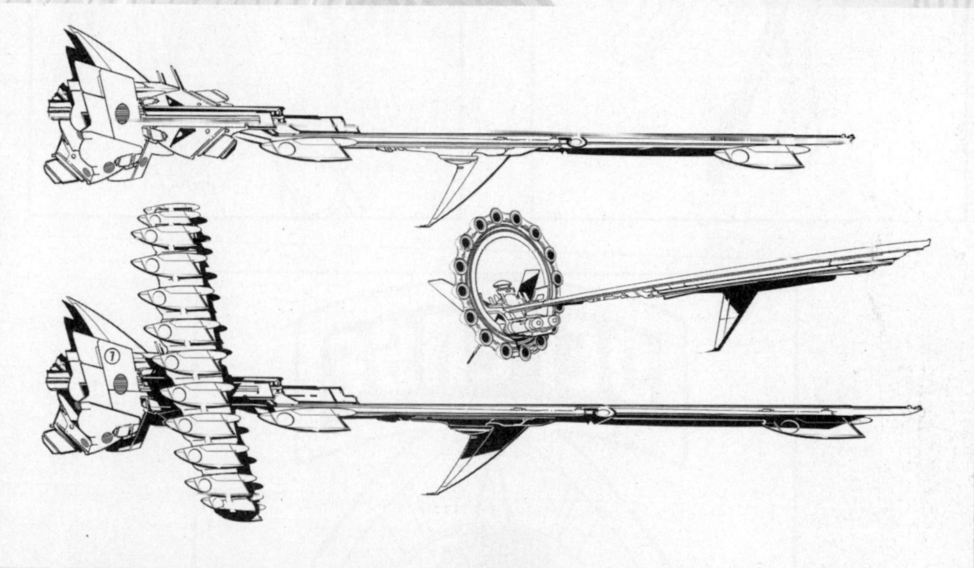

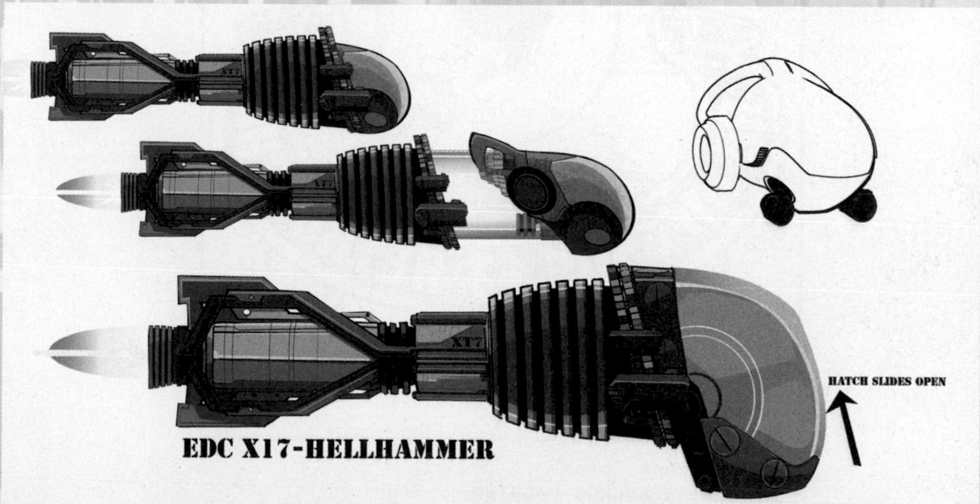
HATCH SLIDES OPEN
EDC X17-HELLHAMMER

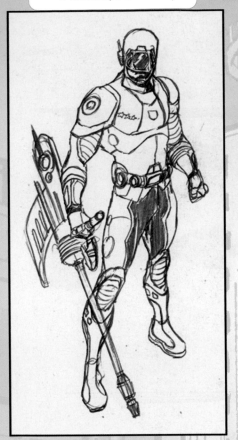

DEFENSE

AD INFEROS ET RETRORSUM

Human Defense Corps
design by **FERNANDO DAGNINO**